TAR HEEL LIGHTNIN'

BOILER
THUMPER

TAR HEEL LIGHTNIN'

How Secret Stills and Fast Cars Made North Carolina the Moonshine Capital of the World

DANIEL S. PIERCE

THE UNIVERSITY OF NORTH CAROLINA PRESS Chapel Hill

Publication of this book was supported in part by a generous gift from Vicki and Porter Durham.

Designed by Richard Hendel
Set in Miller and TheSerif
by Tseng Information Systems, Inc.
Manufactured in the United States of America

The University of North Carolina Press has been a member of the Green Press Initiative since 2003.

Jacket illustration by Derek Anderson and Joel Anderson of Anderson Design Group, Nashville, Tenn.

Library of Congress Cataloging-in-Publication Data
Names: Pierce, Daniel S., author.
Title: Tar Heel lightnin' : how secret stills and fast cars made North Carolina the moonshine capital of the world / Daniel S. Pierce.
Description: Chapel Hill : The University of North Carolina Press, [2019] | Includes bibliographical references and index.
Identifiers: LCCN 2019014008 | ISBN 9781469653556 (cloth : alk. paper) | ISBN 9781469653563 (ebook)
Subjects: LCSH: Distilling, Illicit—North Carolina—History. | Alcohol trafficking—North Carolina—History. | NASCAR (Association)—History.
Classification: LCC HJ5021 .P54 2019 | DDC 364.1/33209756—dc23
LC record available at https://lccn.loc.gov/2019014008

Portions of chapter 1 originally appeared in Daniel S. Pierce, *Corn from a Jar: Moonshining in the Great Smoky Mountains* (Gatlinburg, Tenn.: Great Smoky Mountains Association, 2013). Reprinted here with permission.
Portions of chapters 9, 10, and 13 originally appeared in Daniel S. Pierce, *Real NASCAR: White Lightning, Red Clay, and Big Bill France* (Chapel Hill: University of North Carolina Press, 2010).
Portions of chapter 15 originally appeared in Daniel S. Pierce, "Jim Tom Hedrick, Popcorn Sutton, and the Rise of the Postmodern Moonshiner," in *Modern Moonshine: The Revival of White Whiskey in the Twenty-First Century*, edited by Cameron D. Lippard and Bruce E. Stewart (Morgantown: West Virginia University Press, 2019). Reprinted here with permission.

This book is dedicated to Andy Griffith, whose appreciation of the essential goodness, creativity, and folk genius of the people of North Carolina—including its moonshiners—inspires me to this day.

IN THE NAME OF GOD
AND
HUMANITY
TEMPERANC
LEAGUE
EER
WHISKY
GIN
RU

CONTENTS

SIDEBARS

INTRODUCTION WHITE LIGHTNIN'

Well in North Carolina way back in the hills lived my old pappy
  and he had him a still
He brewed white lightnin' till the sun went down
Then he'd fill him a jug and he'd pass it around
Mighty mighty pleasin' pappy's corn squeezin' (whew white lightnin')
Well the G-men, T-men, revenuers too, searchin' for the place where he
  made his brew
They were lookin' tryin' to book him but my pappy kept on cookin'
(Whew white lightnin')

In 1958, rockabilly star J. P. Richardson (better known as the Big Bopper of "Chantilly Lace" fame) wrote the classic moonshine song "White Lightning."[1] We will never know exactly why the Texan located his "pappy's still" in North Carolina. Richardson tragically died on 3 February 1959 in the infamous "Day the Music Died" plane crash along with Buddy Holly and Ritchie Valens. Perhaps the words "North Carolina" just fit into the rhyme and rhythm of the song better than "Tennessee" or "Georgia" or the names of any of the other southern states where moonshining was common. He probably chose North Carolina, however, because by 1958 the state had a longtime, and well-deserved, reputation as one of the top producers of illegal alcohol in the United States.

Indeed, the art and craft of distilling grains and fruits into liquor runs deep in the DNA of North Carolina—and not only "way back in the hills." Whiskey making was one of the first commercial enterprises in North Carolina, and the first European settlers to the Albemarle Sound region in the 1650s brought with them the skills and equipment necessary for distilling. English settlers in Virginia had already adapted their liquor making to New World conditions, most notably through the discovery that the maize grown by the Indigenous Americans could be effectively, and tastefully, distilled. Migrations in the eighteenth century into the Piedmont of Highland Scots up the Cape Fear River and a horde of Scotch Irish, folks with long whiskey-distilling traditions, reinforced and expanded the economic and social importance of liquor production in the colony.

In the early years of North Carolina statehood, distilling became entrenched as a key component of the subsistence lifestyle practiced by most yeoman farmers. Even when the federal government attempted to tax and regulate liquor production during the Washington and Adams administrations, North Carolina's liquor production continued relatively undisturbed and unabated. Alexander Hamilton's unwise excise tax on whiskey, which led to the Whiskey Rebellion in Pennsylvania, did little but ensure that Thomas Jefferson won North Carolina's electoral votes in the 1800 election.

In antebellum North Carolina, whiskey continued to permeate virtually every facet of life. Many of the state's farmers distilled their corn and fruit into whiskey and brandy in the late fall, winter, and early spring when not preoccupied with their crops. They used the liquor as a trade item in stores and as a source of cash to pay mortgages and property taxes. Plantation owners often owned larger distilleries and used slave labor to produce liquor to supplement their income from tobacco and other cash crops. This process created a number of skilled slave distillers who added African and Caribbean distilling traditions to those brought from Europe.

Liquor also fueled the state's social life; gatherings of all types featured alcohol consumption, often in copious amounts. Politicians regularly "treated" voters to drinks at political gatherings to ensure their support. Organizers also poured generously at communal work events such as barn raisings, cornhuskings, and hog killings. Although a temperance movement began in North Carolina in the 1830s and 1840s, alcohol consumption by church members and even clergy was the rule, not the exception. Indeed, the teetotal mentality that characterized North Carolina's evangelical community during the twentieth century would not take deep root until the late nineteenth century.

With the passage of a federal excise tax on liquor during the Civil War, Reconstruction-era North Carolinians faced some hard choices. They could give up liquor production at a time when they desperately needed cash, pay the tax, which would have negated the profits for small producers, or become outlaws and make liquor illegally. For most Tar Heel distillers, the answer was pretty simple. North Carolinians generally saw the decision to make so-called blockade liquor as not just economic but political as well. They believed the hated excise tax imposed on them by federal/Yankee/Republican lawmakers violated their God-given constitutional rights. Despite their best efforts at controlling the illegal activity, federal agents faced a daunting task as huge numbers of North Carolinians chose to defy the government. Indeed, by the late nineteenth century, the blockade liquor business became cemented in the state's economic, social, and cultural life. Moonshining was one of the few things in the state that united folks across all geographic divisions, connected rural and urban communities, and transcended gender, racial, and ethnic divides. About the only folks in the state not somehow involved in the illegal business as either producers, retailers, or consumers were middle-class, town- and city-dwelling whites. They increasingly became committed to the cause of prohibition.

In one of the more amazing achievements in modern United States history, this minority of middle-class North Carolinians, many of them women, forged a highly effective social and political movement. In the late nineteenth and early twentieth centuries the state's voters severely limited legal alcohol production, distribution, and sale and then outlawed it altogether in 1908.

Prohibition, however, did not have the desired effect on North Carolina's moonshine business and, if nothing else, made it much more profitable by eliminating legal competition. To be sure, the nearly thirty years of statewide and thirteen years of national Prohibition wove this illegal activity deeper into the fabric of the state's everyday life. Even after the repeal of national and state prohibition, local-option laws kept many counties dry well into the 1960s and ensured healthy profits for moonshiners. From the late nineteenth century well into the 1960s, North Carolina had some of the most restrictive laws in the nation on alcohol production and sale and generally produced more illegal liquor than any other state. Indeed, if North Carolina has ever held the distinction of being number one nationally in anything, it is in moonshine production.

In the late 1960s, however, the business began to decline precipitously. Economic factors combined with improved law enforcement and the decline of local prohibition led the vast majority of moonshiners to put their stills away. A few held on, but they seemed a dying breed. Surprisingly, the twenty-first century has brought a resurgence in the business (both as an illegal activity and in the so-called legal moonshine business), and moonshine has experienced a kind of postmodern renaissance up to the present day.

Aside from moonshine's long history in the state, one might still wonder why it's appropriate to devote a whole book, published by a highly respected university press (at least before this book came out), to the topic. While other factors such as politics, a desire to get rich, and even the adrenaline rush of participating in an illegal activity played a role, the motivation for most of those involved in moonshine was economic. Modern-day North Carolinians often forget that the state has traditionally been one of the poorest in the nation. Making and selling moonshine often served as the poor person's hedge against desperate economic times and as a supplement to meager farm incomes even in relatively good times. Distilling, transporting, or selling illegal liquor especially helped provide some level of economic security for North Carolina's most vulnerable populations. These included single women and the African American and Native American victims of the state's oppressive Jim Crow laws. Unfortunately, we will never be able to calculate accurately moonshine's impact on the state's economy, but it was almost surely one of the largest industries in the state from the 1860s to the 1960s.

The moonshine business also demonstrates the resourcefulness, inventiveness, adaptability, and ingenuity (what historians call "agency") of North Carolinians, particularly those on the economic fringes. Indeed, over the years North Carolinians found a myriad of creative ways to make more illegal liquor quicker, distribute it more effectively, and evade the long reach of law enforcement.

Given its economic importance, it is not surprising that moonshine had an enormous impact on North Carolina culture. Moonshine and its makers captured the imagination of a variety of writers whose work is replete with vivid, though generally inaccurate, stories and depictions. In the twentieth century, movie producers made probably more moonshine-related films (both in the silent film era and in the 1950s, 1960s, and 1970s) in North Carolina than in any other state. Andy Griffith and *Dukes of Hazzard* producer Gy Waldron brought the state's moonshiners to television in the 1960s and 1970s. Musicians and songwriters, folk artists, souvenir makers, and other vendors also drew inspiration from the illegal business and produced memorable works. North Carolina moonshiners influenced the nation's sporting scene as well; the state's creative liquor runners shaped NASCAR in important ways.

A number of the state's moonshiners became famous, or infamous, nationwide and helped solidify the image of the North Carolina bootlegger in American popular culture. In the late nineteenth century, national publications featured the exploits of career moonshiners and staunch Confederate sympathizers Amos Owens, Aquilla "Quill" Rose, and Lewis Redmond. In the twentieth century, Percy Flowers and Junior Johnson found themselves featured in nationally circulated magazines. Union County moonshiner Jerry Rushing's biography formed the basis of the most important moonshine-related television show in the 1970s. Popcorn Sutton and Jim Tom Hedrick took turns creating a postmodern moonshiner image as they starred in documentaries and reality television shows in the early twenty-first century.

In exploring such a topic, it is important not to get carried away with glorifying either the product or the moonshiners themselves. Yes, there were good reasons why so many North Carolinians became involved in the business, and yes, many moonshiners became quite accomplished at making and distributing liquor. But we cannot ignore the harmful effects that resulted from the state's long and intimate relationship with an illegal product. One of the first things to understand is that while some North Carolinians have enjoyed reputations for producing high-quality whiskey, most of the product made in the moonshine era was pretty vile. Indeed, the prime mission of the moonshiner was to produce a high volume of liquor in as short a time as possible and get it out

The North Carolina Moonshine Hall of Fame (and Shame)

It has always bothered me that the state of North Carolina has chosen to highlight the accomplishments—significant as they were—of a couple of Ohio boys on its license tags. What the heck did North Carolina provide for the Wright brothers' "first flight" other than a place with miserable winter weather? And how, given the circumstances, is North Carolina "First in Flight"? It seems that state officials have some sort of inferiority complex requiring them to go outside the state and import individuals with outstanding achievements.

The strange part of this is that there are important areas that the state could highlight where North Carolinians have proven their genius on a world-class level. Would it not be more appropriate to feature North Carolina's contributions to the basketball world? How about a license plate honoring Wilmington's Michael Jordan? Or one for, in my humble opinion, the all-time greatest collegiate basketball player, Shelby's David Thompson. Or North Carolina's women's basketball pioneers Kay and Debbie Yow?

Other North Carolinians who have demonstrated world-class bona fides include bluegrass and Piedmont blues musicians, barbeque pit masters, and stock car racers. How about a license tag honoring Doc Watson or Earl Scruggs or Etta Baker or Libba Cotten or Warner Stamey or Ed Mitchell or Junior Johnson or Richard Petty or Dale Earnhardt? Fortunately, groups honor North Carolinians' accomplishments in at least basketball, barbeque, blues, and bluegrass in museums and halls of fame scattered around the state and in numerous books.

While a list of outstanding North Carolinians in these fields stacks up well against similar lists from almost any other state, or nation for that matter, there is probably no field where North Carolinians have excelled more, gained more notoriety, or demonstrated more sheer genius than moonshining. As such, I humbly offer my picks for a (strictly hypothetical) North Carolina Moonshine Hall of Fame (and Shame). I have added "and Shame" to the title because at least some inductees committed acts—including Ku-Kluxing, violent behavior, and possibly even murder—that must be acknowledged alongside their accomplishments and creativity as moonshiners.

Choosing members for this N.C. Moonshine Hall of Fame produces major challenges. First, with so many talented individuals out there, narrowing the field to a reasonable number is difficult. However, many individuals in my Hall of Fame have achieved widespread popular acclaim. They have been profiled in books distributed nationally and internationally, Hollywood movies, popular television programs, and magazines with national circulations such as the *Saturday Evening Post* and *Esquire*. Others, however, while excelling in the moonshine business, labored in obscurity. That is partly a tribute to their success in keeping a low profile and avoiding law enforcement officials' eyes and partly a product of a traditionally patriarchal and racist society that has often failed to recognize women's, African Americans', and Native Americans' accomplishments. I have tried to include some of these individuals in this list, but another challenge in creating a Hall of Fame for individuals engaged in illegal activity is obtaining information on folks in these groups, despite their importance in making North Carolina a moonshine hotbed. In some cases, I have used individuals whom we know a little about as exemplars for these important underrecognized moonshiners.

The profiles in the N.C. Moonshine Hall of Fame sidebars scattered throughout this book are presented not in any sort of hierarchy or ranking but in roughly chronological order based on the peak of each individual's career in the moonshine business. Some entries are more detailed than others, based on the amount of available information. While the list does not fully represent all groups of moonshiners, it does, I think, well represent the geographical spread of moonshining in the state. Moonshine played a key role in the Piedmont, Coastal Plain, and Tidewater and not just in the mountains, although inductees from the western part of the state do predominate. Most important, I firmly believe this group exemplifies the North Carolina moonshiners' world-class creativity, entrepreneurship, and native intelligence.

of their hands and to the market before the authorities caught up with them. In the twentieth century this led to the widespread use of refined sugar, with a little corn thrown into the mix, to make the chief product being distilled. In addition, moonshiners often adulterated the product and used cheap distilling equipment made from metals containing high concentrations of lead salts in order to get more liquor out of a run and reduce costs. The resulting product could have serious deleterious effects on consumers, most often as a result of long-term consumption but also in immediate reactions resulting in serious illness and even death.

North Carolina's normalizing of a criminal activity also created its own problems. While most moonshiners in the state were reportedly otherwise upstanding citizens, involvement in one criminal activity led some to other types of criminality including prostitution, gambling, and money laundering. The need to protect operations from law enforcement helped produce a subculture in some communities where violence and gunplay became widespread. The moonshine business also proved to be a corrupting influence on political systems; bribery of public officials became common in some areas, and the local sheriff's department was often the most reliable source for illegal liquor.

Moonshine had a disruptive impact on families and communities as well. The underground nature of the business, combined with the teetotal absolutism of many of the state's churches, led to lots of secret drinking, which tended toward bingeing, wild drunkenness, and violent behavior. Families often suffered as a result from spousal and child abuse and neglect. The business and culture of moonshine also kept moonshiners, primarily men, absent from their homes for extended periods as they tended stills in hidden places or served prison time.

All that said, understanding the history of moonshine in North Carolina is key to understanding the state's history itself. Indeed, one could argue that illegal liquor production has been as important as tobacco, textiles, or furniture, an integral part of the warp and woof of the state's economic, social, and cultural fabric. Understanding moonshine in the Tar Heel State is also key to understanding business in the south in general and fully understanding the whole region's history. The huge amount of material on moonshine in the south made a study of it in the whole region an overwhelming task, but in this case North Carolina provides a convenient microcosm for the south as a whole. The presence of moonshining in all of the state's distinct geographical regions—its mountains, Piedmont foothills, piney woods, and Tidewater swamps—reflects its spread elsewhere. In addition, the involvement of people across lines of gender, race, ethnicity, and social class was common across the south and gives us a fuller picture of these social dynamics.

Indeed, few things in North Carolina's history connect nearly all its people over the entire state over a longer period of time. As such, moonshine is worthy of serious study and, with certain caveats in place, worthy of celebration. I would not expect the state to change its license plates from "First in Flight" and "First in Freedom" to "First in Moonshine," but at least it would be historically appropriate. Perhaps the state legislature might consider changing the official state toast to one proposed by a humorist in the Raleigh *News and Observer* in 1909:

Here's to the land of the long-nosed swine
That feed upon the roots of the long-leaf pine
Where the "moon-shine's" strong and never weak—
Here's to the land that all should seek.[2]

1

WHISKEY'S "GOLDEN ERA" IN NORTH CAROLINA

The ancestors of North Carolina's early European settlers had been distilling grains and fruits into alcohol for thousands of years. The English, Germans, and Swiss who immigrated to the colony all brought distilling traditions with them to America. The large numbers of individuals who migrated to colonial North Carolina from the Celtic fringe of the British Isles, particularly from Scotland and Northern Ireland, brought an especially strong liquor culture. Indeed, the very word "whiskey" derives from the Gaelic word *usquebaugh*—generally translated as "water of life"—and the earliest records of Anglo-Saxon invaders of Scotland noted the commonality of spirit making among Celtic peoples.[1] For these people whiskey production and drinking were integral to daily life well before they crossed the Atlantic. In the words of moonshiner Lucas Doolin—the main character in *Thunder Road*, the B-movie classic filmed in Asheville in 1957—making liquor was part of the tradition of his "daddy, grandaddy, his daddy before him clear back to Ireland."[2]

As they migrated to America, Europeans adapted their cultural practices to new surroundings. As early as the 1620s, English settlers in Virginia learned to distill the common grain of Native Americans—maize, or "Indian corn"—into whiskey. Anglican missionary Capt. George Thorpe wrote to a friend back in England that he had set up a distillery on the banks of the James River and learned "to make so good a drink of Indian corn as I protest I have divers times refused to drink good strong English beer and chosen to drink that." By the time the Scotch Irish began arriving in droves in the 1720s, making corn liquor was a common practice in England's American colonies.[3] As historian W. J. Rorabaugh observed, "The success of the whiskey industry was due, in part, to the fact that many Scottish, Irish, and Scotch-Irish grain distillers had immigrated to America during the last quarter of the eighteenth century.... When these Irish and Scots settled on the American frontier, they found conditions favorable for the exercise of their talents: plentiful water, abundant grain, and ample wood to fuel their stills."[4]

While distilling corn into whiskey involves few ingredients and demands little in the way of equipment, it is a complicated process that requires experience, patience, and skill. Practically anyone can make liquor, but it takes talent to make good liquor. As Joseph Dabney, who wrote a classic work on moonshining, observed, "Making corn whiskey, as anyone in the Appalachians will tell you, is an art, not merely boiling mash and running it through a still. The secret is getting the right ingredients in those mash barrels and giving them proper timing and sequence."[5]

There are many variations on the traditional craft of making corn liquor, but the basic process is pretty standard. The first step is to locate a dependable source of water. Distillers consider "soft" water that contains few trace minerals to be best for making good whiskey. Most of the creeks and streams of North Carolina contain such water. Early settlers learned to examine the plant life along streams to determine whether the water was "soft" or "hard." The presence of yellowroot or horsemint indicates that the water is soft, while touch-me-nots are a sign of hard water.[6]

The next step is to make the mash. While recipes differ, most traditional mash contains ground corn—white corn is generally preferred—corn malt, and water. Malt produces enzymes that convert the starch in the corn into fermentable sugars. Distillers produce corn malt by taking whole kernels of corn, soaking them in water for a day, draining the water but keeping the corn damp for three to four days until two-inch sprouts emerge, drying the sprouted corn, and finally grinding it in a mill. Some makers use rye or barley malt, but the ready availability of corn made it the most common malt. The liquor maker then mixes the cornmeal with the malt and hot water in a barrel or wooden box and leaves it to sit for five to ten days to ferment. During the fermentation process the mash will bubble and produce a foamy layer on top known as the cap.[7]

When the mash stops bubbling and the cap disappears, the resulting "beer" (about 10 percent alcohol) is ready for distillation. Early whiskey producers in North Carolina commonly used a ten-to-forty-gallon copper-pot still. Traditionally, distillers have preferred copper for their stills. It is light and tough, conducts heat well and evenly, does not leach metals into the alcohol, and does not corrode. They then pour the beer into the still and start a fire in a stone furnace built around the still to contain and evenly spread the heat. Once the beer reaches the boiling point of alcohol at 173ºF, the still cap is sealed on top, usually with malt paste, and distillation begins. The alcohol vapor produced from boiling the mash rises to the still cap, where it escapes through a coiled copper tube, or worm, run through a stream or a barrel containing cold, run-

Typical still used in North Carolina in the colonial and antebellum periods. (Courtesy of North Carolina Room, Pack Memorial Library, Asheville, N.C.)

ning water. The cool water condenses the vapor back into liquid, which drips through a clean cloth, sometimes containing charcoal, to filter impurities and on into a container.[8]

For the traditional North Carolina craft whiskey maker, however, this was not the end but just the first run of low-alcohol "singlings," which contain impurities such as fusel oil. The distiller must now pour out the leftover mash residue, known as "slops," and thoroughly clean the still. Slops only run a few times can be emptied back into new mash to help speed the fermentation process, and once spent and no longer yielding sufficient alcohol, they can be fed to livestock—hogs love them.[9]

The singlings are run back through the still and filtered, and they once again trickle into a container. The distiller checks the proof of the liquor—in the United States defined as twice the percentage of alcohol by volume—by periodically running some of the product into a small bottle known as a proofing vial. Experienced makers can judge proof with a quick shake of the vial and by observing the "bead." The size of the bubbles that form—the bead—and the speed with which they dissipate, or "flash off," indicate the proof. As one liquor maker explained it, "If it's high proof—say 115 to 120—a big bead will jump up there on top when you shake it. If the proof is lower, the bead goes away faster and is smaller.... A true bead will stop half in the likker and half out on top."[10]

Another way to judge proof is to watch the stream of alcohol coming out of the worm. At 160 proof, the stream becomes twisted and spirals into the catch container. This part of the run produces what North Carolina distillers generally referred to as the "high shots." Watching the stream also lets the maker know when the run is done, when the liquor "breaks at the worm" and produces low-proof "backings." Backings are collected separately and either run with the next batch of mash or mixed with the high shots to lower the proof. Distillers pour this "doubled and twisted" whiskey into a large container called a tempering tub, where they mix the liquor from several runs and lower the proof to the desired level, usually around 100–110, by adding backings and/or water. In the eighteenth and nineteenth centuries, whiskey makers in North Carolina would then transfer the product to stoneware jugs or into charred oak barrels for aging.[11]

While distillers most commonly produced corn liquor during this period, they also produced brandy from local fruit. The process for making brandy is pretty much the same as for producing whiskey: mashed fruit—known as pomace—is placed in barrels with corn or rye malt to ferment and then double run through a still. Brandy commanded a much higher price than corn liquor, so distillers made it at every opportunity. As one producer put it, "Just anybody can't afford brandy. Mostly for judges and lawyers." Indeed, much of the sizeable apple crop in antebellum North Carolina went to making some type of alcoholic beverage, from hard cider to distilled brandy. Producers also used plums, grapes, elderberries, and even maypops. Many of the peach orchards planted in the state before the Civil War were for the primary purpose of making peach brandy.[12]

From the earliest days of European settlement, consumption of alcohol held a prominent place in the life and culture of North Carolina. Throughout much of the eighteenth and nineteenth centuries in the United States—despite the development of a national temperance movement in the 1830s, 1840s, and 1850s—there was little social or religious stigma associated with drinking hard liquor. By 1830, an average American consumed more than five gallons of liquor annually.[13]

While some North Carolina churches embraced the temperance movement of the 1830s and 1840s, most, even the Baptist and Methodist churches, only discouraged drunkenness and promoted moderation. In the antebellum period, deacons and elders in North Carolina churches commonly drank alcohol and even produced it. Indeed, the pastor of a church would not draw stares if he had a flask of whiskey on his hip. In an 1895 article, a reporter for the *Greensboro Patriot* reminisced about the antebellum period, when "the majority [of North Carolina ministers] were not averse to bracing up a little with whiskey or brandy of their own make or that of some member of their congregations." The reporter continued, "These preachers would now and then get pretty lively and seemed to enjoy the potations as much as the regenerate. In fact, it is pretty generally believed that some of them often entered the pulpit more or less tipsy

Brandy

While unaged corn liquor is the "potent potable" most commonly produced by North Carolina distillers over the years, the state also has long brandy-making traditions. Indeed, since European settlers arrived, distillers have been converting their fruit into brandy. Until well into the twentieth century, there was little market for fresh fruit, as the slow pace of transportation made it difficult to get produce to market before it spoiled. Converting fruit to brandy made planting orchards a profitable enterprise, as brandy generally yielded two to three times corn liquor's price. In fact, distillers were turning almost all fruit grown in North Carolina into brandy or hard cider well into the early twentieth century.

Brandy making does present challenges that distilling corn liquor doesn't. It is seasonal and dependent on the availability of fresh fruit, although distillers reportedly used imported dried fruit in the early twentieth century. Processing the fruit and turning it into pomace is also much more time-consuming than making corn mash, and the sweet-smelling pomace attracts lots of insects, especially yellow jackets and bees. The high prices brandy brings make it worthwhile for many producers, however, to put in the extra effort. That high price has also traditionally enticed folks to counterfeit the product. Revenue agent Garland Bunting told author Alec Wilkinson that Nash County (Bunting called it "Mash County" for its moonshine reputation) was "noted for its apple brandy." Bunting also revealed a dirty secret about Nash County's brandy reputation: producers did not actually distill apple pomace, but rather "the bootleggers simply flavor their whiskey with apple cores."

Peach brandy is also part of Junior Johnson's legend. According to sportswriter and Johnson biographer Tom Higgins, Johnson once asked Spartanburg, South Carolina, bootlegger and racing promoter Joe Littlejohn to send him some peaches. A big practical joker, Littlejohn sent Johnson a whole train car full. Johnson allegedly put some of his Wilkes County buddies to work, converted the peaches into brandy, bottled it and boxed it up, and delivered it to Littlejohn's motel in Spartanburg, stacking the cases in front of the door and blocking the entrance.

Like the moonshine business itself, brandy making has seen a renaissance in North Carolina in recent years. Dean Combs of Wilkes County got caught making apple brandy illegally in 2009. He defended himself by saying he was reviving an important historical tradition in the county: "There's not been any good apple brandy out here for years. It's better than what you buy at a store." That same year in nearby Lenoir, Keith Norden and Chris Hollifield began a successful legal business with their Carolina Distillery, producing apple brandy using heirloom apples from Perry Lowe Orchards in Moravian Falls.

and that a good drink of peach brandy ... either inspired a sermon in which hell fire primstone [*sic*] played a conspicuous part or else heaven was pictured as an elysian land of peace and plenty, according to the effect of drink on the exhorter's mind."[14]

Of course, the same was true for church members. In his autobiography, Rev. Brantley York recalled his formative days on a farm in Randolph County, where his father supplemented his income by making liquor. York defended his father to his readers, who by the 1870s had embraced teetotalism: "At this time it may be thought strange that any member of the church should follow the distillation of ardent spirits as a livelyhood [*sic*] but the views entertained by even good people at the time of which I speak, were very different; for no one supposed it was wrong either to make or drink ardent spirits moderately; drunkenness only was regarded as a sin even by ministers."[15] In an 1889 article a reporter for the *Tobacco Plant* recalled these "good old days ... when the good Methodist class-leader and Baptist deacon would sit at a still and sing, as the corn juice flowed: 'Come thou fount of every blessing,' and as the stream flowed more freely, 'streams of mercy never ceasing.'"[16]

Antebellum North Carolinians consumed corn liquor at most social events, and while most folks drank in moderation, excessive guzzling could, and did, occur. Traveler Charles Lanman commented that by the time he arrived at a barn raising in Buncombe County in 1848, "an abundance of whiskey had already been imbibed." Militia musters and court days also prompted heavy drinking. Buncombe County attorney Augustus Merrimon observed a court day in Burnsville where the crowd of Yancey Countians "tried to see how badly they could behave themselves.... At different times I noticed groups about over the Court Yard and in the center stood a large gawky fellow with a fiddle and he would saw off some silly ditty. Two or three drunken fools would dance to the same."[17]

Elections also provoked a good many North Carolina men to drink to excess. Voters generally expected those running for office to "treat" them with whiskey and provide some entertainment. Traveler Kemp Plummer Battle noted this "mountain canvassing" by a candidate for the North Carolina General Assembly in Burnsville in 1848: "The candidate, a man named Fleming, spoke from a goods-box in front of a grog-shop most animatedly and effectively, for about an hour with a tin quart-pot in his right hand. Then he went into the shop inviting the crowd to follow him to partake of whiskey. He was elected."[18] As the Murfreesboro *North Carolina Chronicle* put it in 1827, "He who treats to the most whiskey, generally has the most friends."[19] Some people condemned the practice. "A VOTER" wrote to the *Raleigh Minerva* in 1819 asserting, "I would not thank any man to vote for me whose vote could be bought with whiskey." He did concede, however, that such a policy would cost a North Carolina poli-

George Caleb Bingham, The County Election. *Although the scene depicted took place in Missouri, this would have been a typical, alcohol-fueled, election day scene in antebellum North Carolina. (Courtesy of Reynolda House Museum, Winston-Salem, N.C.)*

tician votes if he did not follow tradition: "I know there are many sots who will exclaim against a candidate who will not treat profusely."[20] Such beliefs ensured that "treating" remained a common practice in North Carolina throughout the antebellum period.

Aside from the cultural and social dimensions of alcohol consumption in North Carolina, corn liquor and brandy served as the bases for many commonly used folk remedies. Many strongly believed that alcohol was "good for what ails you," whatever that may be. Augustus Merrimon observed that farmers in western North Carolina generally assumed "that to drink [whiskey] in damp and cold weather will warm them and to drink in hot weather it will cool them."[21]

North Carolinians used whiskey in a wide variety of remedies. Most recipes for common tonics for croup, dysentery, various stomach ailments, toothache, headache, colds, and flu contained liquor. One Swain County resident told writer Horace Kephart that while people in the Smokies generally relied on herbal cures because of the distance to doctors and their "scand'lous" costs, the herbs "customarily ain't no good 'thout a leetle grain o' whiskey."[22] Even most treatments for animal ailments contained alcohol. Of course, the most legendary medicinal use for liquor was for snakebite. The Salisbury *Western Carolinian* contained a "recipe for the bite of a snake" in an 1821 edition: "As soon as possible apply the mouth of a bottle, nearly filled with distilled spirits (whiskey or brandy) to the wounds; the spirits will extract the poison and give immediate relief." Of course, this was all the more reason to have a flask of liquor with one wherever one went—just in case.[23]

In addition to its social and medicinal uses, perhaps the most significant aspect of corn liquor production in North Carolina before the Civil War was its economic importance, especially to the yeoman farmers that formed the bulk of the white population during the antebellum period. While many observers look back at these folks as living a pioneer, self-sufficient existence, recent research has revealed that market relationships tied North Carolina farmers to local towns, plantations to the east and south, growing American cities, and even international markets as far away as China. Even relatively self-sufficient farmers needed something to trade for items they could not produce themselves such as iron goods, coffee, tea, or salt. Landowning farmers also needed some cash money to pay their property taxes, as the tax man would not accept a hog or bushels of corn as in-kind payment. As Joseph Dabney observed, "What the settler needed was a cash crop to enable him to pay his taxes and thus retain his precious property—usually a few hundred acres." Even nonlandowning tenants needed some way to pay their rents and a way to accumulate some cash in order to eventually purchase their own land.[24]

Small farmers in North Carolina basically had two major products they could produce that had real cash value and would transport relatively easily: livestock and whiskey. Many used both avenues to purchase market goods and pay their taxes. Turning their corn crop into whiskey, even if they relied on a more skilled community distiller, provided the most profitable use of the farmers' time and resources. As W. J. Rorabaugh observed, "A farmer could realize handsome profits from processing his grain into spirits, since a bushel of corn worth 25 cents yielded 2½ gallons of spirits worth $1.25 or more. Even if the farmer did not do his own distilling and had to give a commercial distiller half the output in payment for his services, he could increase the value of his corn by 150 percent."[25] In a state crisscrossed by inlets, rivers, and creeks and mountains in the west, where transportation of goods was at best difficult and expensive, the portability of whiskey made it an ideal trade product. An 1836 article in the Salisbury *Carolina Watchman* argued, "Corn is not an article that will pay for hauling in wagons; the surplus Corn is generally distilled into Whiskey; this article will pay some better for hauling in wagons, the Whiskey and Brandy

All in the Family

Making liquor in North Carolina has always been a family affair. In the eighteenth century and first half of the nineteenth century, distilling was part of the work on the family farm and naturally involved all family members. In *Every Home a Distillery*, historian Sarah Meacham demonstrates the key role home distilling played in the colonial Chesapeake and the leading role often played by women. White settlers brought these distilling traditions with them into North Carolina as they migrated from the Chesapeake into the Albemarle Sound region. By the middle of the nineteenth century, family distilling practices were firmly in place across the state.

When the federal government made distilling liquor without paying the federal excise tax illegal, the family connection became even more important. Working with family made illegal "blockade" distilling more secure, as distillers were much less likely to turn in family members to authorities. If caught by law enforcement, they rarely testified against one another. Families generally divided labor in their distilling operations on the basis of gender, with men and boys doing most work around the still and delivering the product. Most of the time women and girls stayed around the homeplace and served as lookouts, calling out, sounding hunting horns, or even setting off dynamite to warn the menfolk of approaching strangers. Women also commonly sold liquor at their houses, and it was not uncommon for women to work at family stills, especially when illness, injury, or incarceration sidelined men. A "Fiddlin'" John Carson skit from the 1920s titled "Moonshine Kate" humorously illustrates the family dynamic often at work around a moonshine still. In the skit, a group of strange men approach Carson's daughter, Moonshine Kate, and promise to pay her five dollars if she takes them to the still where her daddy and momma are making illegal liquor. When the men tell Kate they will pay the promised money when they return from the still, she responds: "No sir, you give me my five dollars now. If you go over there you sure ain't coming back."

One of the most famous examples of the family connection is Wilkes County's Johnson family. The Johnsons had deep roots in the county and deep roots in the liquor-making business, long used to supplement their income from the family farm. Robert Glenn Johnson planted crops, raised livestock, ran a small sawmill, and made moonshine. His wife, Lora Belle, often helped out with the moonshine operation. With profits sky-high in the 1920s, Robert increased his moonshining. In 1935, agents raided his home and farm and seized 7,100 gallons of illegal liquor and five steam distilleries. Robert's sons—Lewis Preston (L. P.), Fred, and Robert Glenn Jr. (Junior)—followed in their father's footsteps and often pitched in to cover for their father while he served time in a federal penitentiary.

Even when Junior started a lucrative career as a star NASCAR racer, he felt an obligation to help out his family. That cost him dearly in 1956 when an arrest for moonshining sidetracked his career. Agents busted Junior when his daddy asked him to fire up his still and an obedient Junior got caught.

A number of North Carolinians with

deep family roots in liquor distilling have moved into the "legal moonshine" business in recent years. Cody Bradford's pedigree in the moonshine business goes back at least five generations in Yancey County. In 2010, he started Howling Moon Distillery near Asheville with help from his brother, a cousin, and his father. Like the Johnsons, the Call family is a leading Wilkes County moonshine family. Their family liquor business goes back well into the nineteenth century. Willie Clay Call frequently hauled liquor with Junior Johnson and was a legend on the highways. Now Call's son Brian runs Call Family Distillers in Wilkesboro. Jeremy Norris, owner of Broadslab Distillery, located on his family's farm in Johnston County, traces his roots back to early moonshiner Bill McLamb, from whom the moonshining tradition was passed down to Norris's grandfather Leonard Wood.

made in this county is generally sold in S. Carolina."[26] "A horse could carry about $2 worth of corn," Dabney noted, "but $16 worth of corn liquor."[27] Demand for corn liquor was also strong as it displaced rum as the favored spirit in the United States in the early years of the nineteenth century. Westward expansion away from the coast, the repeal of the whiskey excise tax during Thomas Jefferson's administration, and tariffs imposed on molasses and rum imported from the Caribbean made the local product more attractive.

The seasonal nature of corn whiskey production fit well with the annual cycle of farmwork. Mash ferments too quickly in the summer months and too slowly, or not at all, in temperatures below forty degrees. Ideal liquor production times were in the late winter and early spring before planting began and late fall and early winter after the harvest. Of course, demand was always high during the Christmas season for those who needed help celebrating the holidays.

Whiskey production was economically important to plantation owners as well. Planters were always looking for ways to maximize their investment in slaves and land, and distilling was a profitable way to do so. In North Carolina, evidence suggests that many plantations had distilleries. Although there is not much anecdotal evidence, one would assume that slaves provided much of the labor associated with these operations.

Historians have not conducted much research on such operations, but we do have some tantalizing recent clues about slaves and liquor production in the antebellum south. A recent archaeological dig at Mount Vernon, combined with archival research, has uncovered George Washington's extensive distilling operations. In 1797, Washington, recently retired from the presidency, hired a Scot named James Anderson as his plantation manager. Anderson soon began a whiskey distillery on the property using six slaves as his labor force and rye grown on the property. By 1799, the Mount Vernon distillery was the largest in the United States, producing 11,000 gallons per annum and generating a sizeable income for Washington. According to NPR reporter Allison Aubrey, Washington's distillery was the "single most profitable part of his plantation." Meanwhile, several of the major Kentucky bourbon distillers and brands—including Elijah Craig, Henry McKenna, and Jacob Spears—have also recently credited slaves with conducting their earliest operations.[28] Historian Sarah Meacham has observed in her study of distilling practices in the Chesapeake region of Virginia during the colonial period that slaves, generally referred to as "people" in plantation records, "performed much of the labor of producing alcohol."[29]

Perhaps the most famous slave distiller is Nearis Green of the Jack Daniel's Distillery. Tradition has it that Jack Daniel learned to distill whiskey from his adopted father, Rev. Dan Call. However, historians at Jack Daniel's now credit Call's slave Nearis Green with developing the recipe and teaching Daniel the craft. Recent research suggests that American distilling has much to thank slave distillers for, such as running the distillate through charcoal, as many brought skills and experience from west African alcohol-distilling traditions as well as from the west Indian rum industry.[30] As *New York Times* reporter Clay Risen put it, "Slavery and whiskey, far from being two separate strands of Southern history, were inextricably entwined. Enslaved men not only made the bulk of the distilling labor force, but they often played crucial roles in the whiskey-making process."[31]

Evidence of plantation and slave distilling in North Carolina primarily comes from newspaper ads selling antebellum plantation properties, which almost invariably included a gristmill and a distillery. In 1819, William Blackledge advertised the sale of his 3,000-acre plantation thirty miles up the Neuse River from New Bern, with a large commercial whiskey distillery on Chocowinity Creek "with two of the flat, patent copper stills, of about 130 gallons each, with pewter worms, and a copper boiler of about 160 gallons."[32] The great North Carolina reformer Archibald DeBow Murphey built up a 2,000-acre estate near Hillsborough in the early years of the nineteenth century that included a distillery "supported by slave labor."[33] In addition to the economic benefits plantation owners reaped from the sale of and trade in whiskey, slaves with distilling skills became valuable properties. Such slaves would also use their skills to train others to follow in their footsteps—including whites like Jack Daniel—after emancipation. One can safely assume that African Americans trained as distillers in the antebellum period formed the foundation for the thriving moonshine trade in the eastern Piedmont and Coastal Plain in the late nineteenth century and well into the twentieth.

North Carolinians, however, had a somewhat ambivalent attitude toward African Americans, both slave and free, and alcohol. Plantation owners benefitted from slave labor in their distilling operations, and alcohol distribution

My Mills & a Whiskey Distillery
ON CHOCOWINITY CREEK, AND
Two Herring Fisheries
On Blount's creek, in the county of Beaufort, with about
9000 *acres of Land*
Adjoining and near them. The improvements on this property consist of a saw-mill for two saws; a merchant grist-mill, with two pair of five feet Burr stones, and one pair of four feet Esopus stones, all of excellent quality, 2 boulting cloths, one for merchant, the other for country work, with elevators, conveyors, hopper boys, rolling screan, fan, and packing machine. A whiskey distillery, with two of the flat patent copper stills, of about 130 gallons each, with pewter worms, and a copper boiler of about 160 gallons; a pump attached to the mills, which supplies from the creek all the water wanted for every purpose in the still house and for the condensing tubs. A comfortable dwelling house, kitchen, smokehouse, and other outhouses, for the residence of the owner:

Ad for the sale of a Lenoir County plantation that included a large whiskey distillery. (Newbern Sentinel, *2 January 1819)*

was often a part of their "treating" and furnishing practices with their slaves. At the same time, they feared the disruptive and potentially dangerous impact that unsupervised consumption of alcohol could have on both slaves and free persons of color. Clandestine sales of alcohol to slaves and black freedmen especially concerned white North Carolinians. In 1825, in the hope of keeping alcohol out of the hands of African Americans, the North Carolina General Assembly passed a law that prohibited "free persons of color" from operating taverns and outlawed the sale of alcohol to slaves. Legislators followed this law up with one banning any production or sale of alcohol by freedmen and prohibiting the sale of alcohol to freedmen, although the law still allowed slaves to work in distilleries.[34] One effect of this legislation was to make free blacks and the Lumbee Indians who lived in the southeast part of the state, under law "free persons of color," the pioneers and originators of moonshining practices in North Carolina.[35]

Whiskey production provided other economic benefits to North Carolina's antebellum economy. Barrel makers, blacksmiths, metalworkers, and potters found ready markets for stills, still parts, and containers. Many distillers supplemented their income by feeding still slops to hogs, their most marketable product. Hogs love corn mash, and as the authors of the *Foxfire* series noted, whiskey producers in the mountains "were forced to put fences around their stills to keep hogs, who were kept on 'open range' then, from falling into the mash boxes and drowning."[36] Historian Wilbur Miller argued that for many small distillers, "there was actually more profit in the hogs than in the whiskey."[37] While serving in the U.S. House of Representatives, future president James Buchanan asserted that many "distillers' profits depended less upon whiskey than upon hogs fattened on distilling slop."[38]

It is difficult to judge the exact amount of corn whiskey and brandy produced in North Carolina during the antebellum period. Most small distillers operated seasonally, produced primarily for home consumption and local markets, and did not keep account books, and their small operations rarely appear in official records. But the official records we do have, primarily U.S. census reports on manufacturing, indicate that based on the distilleries that did report to the government, North Carolina was one of the leading liquor-producing states in the union. In 1840, the Census Bureau reported almost 3,000 stills producing over 1 million gallons of liquor per annum and employing almost 1,500 people in the state. The statistics indicate something of the character of liquor production during the period, as North Carolina reported double the number of distilleries of any other state. At the same time, the state's distillers produced only 20 percent or less of the volume of liquor that states like Pennsylvania, New York, and Massachusetts were producing; their average still had a much greater capacity than a Tar Heel still.[39]

While statistics show that mountain farmers may have produced a slightly disproportionate share of the liquor made in the state, distilling was common throughout North Carolina. The *Carolina Watchman* reported on a Piedmont Lincoln County small farmer—"a very exemplary industrious man, and one of our best citizens"—who produced 2,000 gallons of whiskey and 1,400 gallons of brandy in the mid-1830s. The article also noted that "in a circuit of 4 miles around this Farmer, there are 65 distilleries."[40] The *Fayetteville Weekly Observer* reported in 1839 that Davie County, also in the Piedmont, "contains 21 grist and flouring mills, 20 saw mills and 55 distilleries, several of which are in operation on an extensive scale."[41] Indeed, most of the counties with the largest reported liquor production were in the Piedmont.

Further evidence of the thriving whiskey industry in North Carolina also comes from larger store owners in the state's account books and ledgers as well as from ads for stores in local newspapers. Ledgers indicate that locally produced liquor—often referred to as "green whiskey," "old country whiskey," or "raw whiskey"—was one of the most frequently purchased store items and that patrons commonly used such liquor to purchase other store goods. Indeed, the "pint of whiskey" was one measure of currency generally valued at around three and a half grains of gold. One of the leading store owners from 1792 to 1830

NEW GOODS.

THE subscriber this day received by the Schooner Fulford, Capt. Guthrin, from Baltimore, the following articles, viz:

50 bbls. Fresh ground Howard St. Flour,
5 do. Water, Butter, & Soda Crackers,
10 do. Fresh Pilot Bread,
5 do. do. Navy do.
160 Bushels Shorts, or Wheat Bran,
500 do. Coarse Turks Island Salt,
10 Sacks Liverpool Blown do.
10 bls. Cider Brandy,
2 hhds. Baltimore Rye Whiskey,
5 bbls. Old Monongahela Whiskey, 4th proof,
2 Fresh corned Beef, put up in Baltimore market expressly for family use,
5 bbls. Loaf & Lump Sugar, from 15 to 20 cents per pound,
20 Casks Stone Lime,
50 Kegs Cut Nails assd. sizes,
25 Boxes Brown Soap,
12 do. patent mold Candles,
6 do. Poland Starch.

JOS. M. GRANADE.

Newbern, Nov. 16, 1835.

NEW STORE.

THE Subscriber respectfully informs the citizens of Newbern and its vicinity, that he has recently returned from the North, with a large and general retailing assortment of

GROCERIES, HARDWARE, CUTLERY, CROCKERY & GLASSWARE,

Liquors,	Confectionary,
Wines,	Perfumery,
Fruits,	Hats,
Nuts.	Shoes, &c. &c.

which he is now offering for sale, at the Store formerly occupied by Geo. A. Hall, Esq., and more recently by Mr. John A. Crispin, one door east of Dunn's corner. and nearly opposite the Episcopal Church.

ALSO,

At the brick store belonging to Mrs. McKinlay, New County Wharf, a large supply of such articles as are usually found in a Grocery Store, together with a good assortment of

SHIP CHANDLERY, READY MADE, CLOTHING, &c. &c.,

all of which he will sell at a moderate advance upon the cost.

JOS. M. GRANADE.

1st Nov. 1835

*Grocery ads from the North Carolina Baptist newspaper listing alcoholic beverages. (*Biblical Recorder, *9 December 1835)* in western North Carolina was John Carson of McDowell County. After reviewing Carson's account books, reporter John Parris noted in the *Asheville Citizen-Times* in 1982 that the "single item occurring with the most frequency is whiskey or some other form of distilled liquor."[42] The ledgers of William Holland Thomas, a prominent western North Carolina store owner in Jackson and Cherokee Counties from 1822 to the 1870s, also show a sizeable trade in liquor. This was despite the fact that Thomas joined his adopted father, Yonaguska, in a campaign to promote temperance among the Qualla Cherokee.[43] Stores' newspaper ads prominently featured their liquor offerings, both locally produced and imported. For a short time in the mid-1830s, even the state Baptist newspaper, the *Biblical Recorder*, regularly ran such ads.[44]

In 1878, a *New York Sun* reporter reminisced, with only slight exaggeration, about the commonality of whiskey making and whiskey drinking in the antebellum south: "Before the war every man either made his own whiskey or sent his corn to the still, and got his sweet mash in return. . . . Whiskey was as free as water. It was found in every house. Preachers, deacons, church trustees and their wives and daughters, bushwhackers and slaves drank it as Englishmen drink beer or Frenchmen red wine. No one thought of declaiming against it. With possibly a few exceptions it was rated next to hog and hominy, and could be bought at from fifteen to twenty cents a gallon."[45]

In the words of Joseph Dabney, for farmers in North Carolina, the era from earliest white settlement to the Civil War constituted a "golden era of American whiskey as a tax-free agricultural enterprise and frontier cottage industry."[46] For elites, landowning yeoman farmers, and even tenants in the state, making and drinking whiskey were tremendously important. Though he was writing on western North Carolina, historian Bruce Stewart's observations on antebellum whiskey production and consumption can be applied across the state: "Before the Civil War, no stigma had yet been attached to mountain residents who made alcohol." Antebellum distillers "were therefore not marginalized criminals but entrepreneurs responding to the marketplace. As such, they gained the appreciation of mountain people, who regarded drinking—and distilling—as a vital element of their economy and culture."[47]

FROM DISTILLER TO BLOCKADER TO MOONSHINER

The end of what Joseph Dabney called the golden era for legal whiskey distillers in North Carolina came in 1862 when the U.S. Congress enacted an excise tax on whiskey. It was this act that made most liquor production in the state illegal and turned entrepreneurs into outlaws. Contrary to most people's view, it wasn't the production of liquor that was illegal but the failure to pay the excise tax to the federal government. North Carolinians have historically made moonshine for a variety of reasons—primarily economic. However, the fact that making it was a violation of federal law, and enforcement was primarily a federal matter, shaped moonshine's early history in the state. Indeed, from the end of the Civil War to about 1890, making liquor without paying the federal tax became an overtly political act. During this period, making moonshine became increasingly tied to the Reconstruction era's contentious political environment and the successful attempt by the Conservative (later the Democratic) Party to dominate state government.

Of course, the federal excise tax had little effect on distillers in North Carolina initially. The state was part of the Confederacy and folks had other things on their mind. The Civil War did, however, have an impact on liquor production under Confederate rule. The North Carolina General Assembly passed a bill creating the state's first tax on whiskey in February 1862 and banned alcohol production altogether in December 1862. These were generally understood as war measures intended to prevent food shortages. Besides, given war conditions, both the tax and the prohibition were difficult, if not impossible, to enforce.[1]

Once the war ended, it took a while for enforcement of federal revenue laws to kick in amid the confusion of the Reconstruction era and halfhearted support from President Andrew Johnson's administration. In the aftermath of the Reconstruction Act of 1867, however, and the division of the South into twelve military districts, prosecutions picked up as the government hired more revenue collectors. For the Republican Party, the job of collector was a key patronage position, important for rewarding party loyalty and securing the party's place as a rising force in North Carolina. However, collectors faced a daunting task in trying to collect the tax and shut down distillers who refused to pay. Initially they focused on bringing large commercial distilleries into compliance before taking on smaller distillers, who continued to produce liquor on their farms in relatively open fashion.[2] Indeed, given the deep-seated nature of liquor production among farmers in North Carolina and the lack of enforcement early on, the vast majority of them kept right on making liquor.

In addition, the desperate economic conditions farmers faced in the immediate aftermath of the war gave farmers huge incentives to defy the law. Although the tax varied widely, from two dollars per gallon at war's end to as low as fifty cents in 1868, even at the low end, paying the tax took away any profit for small producers. The requirement that legally licensed distilleries be able to produce a minimum of six gallons per day also precluded most farmers from legalizing their operations, as they generally had much smaller capacity in their stills. Particularly in the state's more remote areas, simply selling corn or fruit crops was not a profitable alternative either, given the high costs of transportation and low prices farm produce generally commanded on the market. Farmers found themselves caught between the proverbial rock and the hard place, as a reporter for Charlotte's *Southern Home* observed in 1878: "This is a rather difficult question to deal with, for if the revenue law is strictly enforced against the poor and ignorant class, who carry on this trade in our mountains [and, it should be noted, in much of the rest of the state], it virtually deprives them of making the article for sale, because the license tax is so high that they cannot pay it and clear any profits. Living remote from railroads, it is impossible for them to wagon their fruit and corn to market at the present low prices of produce. The only way in which they see how to make any money is to abstract the juice, and convert their fruit and produce into a portable bulk, and this they are not allowed to do."[3] For most farmers there was little choice but to keep on making liquor as they always had. The major irony here is that most now-illegal distillers in North Carolina evaded a federal tax so that they could pay their local property taxes.

The fact that Congress passed this excise tax during a civil war fought against the federal government, in which many North Carolinians had fought and died, provided additional incentive for illegal distilling. Given the postwar political environment, many liquor makers—even those who produced enough volume to pay the tax and still make a profit—became more determined to exercise what they considered their God-given and constitutional right to "make a little likker." Conservatives who sought to restore the prewar political order in the state used the liquor tax as an important wedge issue in their battles against the Republican Party and avidly supported, at least temporarily, those defying the law. Most illegal producers did not view themselves as lawbreakers and made a clear distinction between breaking federal law and breaking state or local law. The *Charlotte Observer* reported on a "breach of peace" case in Statesville in 1894, where the accused testified that he had indeed lied under oath in an earlier illegal-distilling case in federal court: "Yes, I believe I did; but that was in one of these little Federal courts."[4]

The early names used for illegal liquor producers and their illegal product reflected this image of defiance. Producers generally became known as "blockaders," adding romance to their image based on the Confederate blockade runners of the Civil War. The product itself became known simply as "blockade" or "blockade liquor." The terms "moonshine" and "moonshiner" did not become common until the late 1870s, with "mountain dew" first used in North Carolina in the 1880s.

In the late 1860s, as so-called Radical Reconstruction began and Republicans began to solidify their hold on North Carolina politics, funding for and enforcement of federal revenue laws increased dramatically. The Bureau of Internal Revenue divided the nation into collection districts headed by an administrator, with most fieldwork—collecting revenue from legal distilleries, breaking up illegal stills, and arresting lawbreakers—conducted by deputies. In the late nineteenth century, all enforcement officials, down to deputy collector, were political appointees rewarded for their loyalty to the Republican Party. Green Raum, who became commissioner for the bureau in 1876, asserted that he "would not appoint a Democrat if I knew it; for I think the true policy of party administration is to appoint its friends so as to uphold its principles."[5] Former governor and Conservative leader Zeb Vance asserted that the "internal revenue system as it is administered in North Carolina is a political machine run at the expense of the government in the interest of the dominant [Republican] Party."[6]

Given the political nature of revenue enforcement, not surprisingly, supporters of the Conservative Party often found their stills busted and themselves arrested. One of the first major busts in the state came in the fall of 1868 when deputy collectors seized Confederate veteran and staunch Conservative Amos Owens's commercial-grade still and auctioned it off "at the Court House door in Rutherfordton" to the "highest bidder for cash."[7] Federal authorities charged Owens himself with violating federal revenue laws and set a date for a trial at the federal courthouse in Asheville. His trial points to a major challenge for revenue agents, as the jury acquitted him. Indeed, Owens even made a considerable amount of money off the deal when he had an accomplice haul forty

DEPUTY COLLECTOR'S OFFICE,
U. S. Internal Revenue,
Rutherfordton N. C, October 28, 1868.

UNITED STATES
vs
1 Still and Fixtures.

I WILL sell, to the highest bidder, for cash, on Saturday, the 14th day of November, 1868, at the Court House door, in Rutherfordton, ONE STILL AND FIXTURES, the property of Amos Owens, as forfeited to the United States for violation of the Internal Revenue laws of the same.

R. W. LOGAN, Deputy Col.
3d Div. 7th Dist. N. C.

40-td]

Ad for auction of Amos Owens's still seized by revenue agents in Rutherford County in 1868. (Rutherford Star, *7 November 1868)*

gallons of "taters" up the mountain, which he sold to the thirsty crowds gathered for court days.[8]

The Grant administration's Whiskey Ring scandal did not help increase respect for Republican revenue enforcement personnel. In the scandal, liquor producers conspired with cabinet officials to evade the federal tax. A reporter for the *Western Sentinel* pointed out the irony and injustice of arresting North Carolina's small producers in light of this corruption: "How is it . . . that if some poor devil distills a little whiskey illicitly, or blockades a little brandy or tobacco, or sells a quantity of spirits to pay taxes or get the necessaries of life, without a United States license, District Attorney Starbuck is after him with the U.S. Deputy Marshall, and wrings the poor fellow's withers till he is dry, but if a Radical office holder from Yankee land swindles the government and people out of hundreds of thousands of dollars, he is not only permitted to go free, but finds apologists among those, whose duty it is to expose and punish such crimes."[9]

Just as the cause of the blockader became tied to Democratic Party politics, it also became tied to its armed insurgency, the Ku Klux Klan. In 1871, a revenue collector in western North Carolina's Sixth Collection District wrote that the illegal liquor makers in Polk, Yancey, Jackson, Cleveland, Rutherford, Transylvania, Clay, and Ashe Counties were "under a kind of protectorship of that secret organization called 'Ku Klux Klan.'" In those and other North Carolina counties, the Klan intimidated and even attacked revenue officers and their informers. Attacks on revenue officers even convinced some Republican blockaders to switch sides and join the Klan.[10]

Amos Owens demonstrates this moonshiner-Klansman connection. In the

Amos Owens N.C. Moonshine Hall of Famer

It is fitting to begin the North Carolina Moonshine Hall of Fame (and Shame) with Amos Owens, a moonshiner who began his career as a perfectly legal distiller before the 1862 excise tax on liquor came into place. It is also fitting to start with Owens because he illustrates many contradictions, paradoxes, and complexities—equal parts "fame" and "shame"—common to almost all moonshiners. Owens was a slightly built man no more than five feet, four inches tall and weighed around 120 pounds, with rosy cheeks and a constant twinkle in his eye. He had a reputation as a cheerful person who helped neighbors, a man who publicly professed Christianity at least twenty-eight times, and a person beloved by his community.

The legendary blockader and squire of Cherry Mountain, Amos Owens. (Courtesy of the North Carolina Collection, UNC Libraries, UNC–Chapel Hill)

At the same time, Owens was a legendary backwoods, no-holds-barred brawler who never backed away from a fight; a Confederate sharpshooter who participated in some of the most brutal actions of the Civil War; a so-called chieftain in the Ku Klux Klan who brutally raided and attacked local African Americans he saw as "uppity" as well as Reconstruction-era "red-string" Republicans; a habitual criminal who served three terms in the federal penitentiary in Albany, New York; and the host of one of the most brutal bacchanalias imaginable at his Cherry Mountain estate in Rutherford County. Owens was also an astute businessman and owned a legendary and profitable cherry orchard and a productive farm. He would have been a wealthy man under any circumstances. He could have afforded to pay the federal excise tax and still make substantial profits from his liquor business. Yet he chose to defy the federal government's right to tax his liquor and made and marketed moonshine almost until the day he died at age eighty-seven.

These contradictions are apparent even in Owens's standard public dress. He generally appeared in public wearing a silk stovepipe hat, gold spectacles, and a starched high-collared white shirt befitting his economic and social status as a "squire" of Rutherford County. But he also generally sported a black sack coat, leather suspenders, homespun copperas breeches, and brogan shoes more common to a working-class farmer. In the ultimate contradiction of his life, Amos Owens became a celebrity, a public figure known widely across the state and region, a constant figure in the newspapers, and even the subject of a widely distributed biography. Yet he made his mark and public reputation in a business that required secrecy, a low profile, and the ability to escape the law enforcement's attention. Somehow, Amos Owens succeeded at both.

This notoriety makes it relatively easy to find details of Amos Owens's life, although it can be challenging to separate fact from fiction. The newspapers loved recording his exploits, and we know many details about Owens's life from a biography penned in 1901 by reporter M. L. White, who wrote entertaining local color stories for the *Morganton Herald* under the appellation "Corn Cracker." White's *A History of the Life of Amos Owens, the Noted Blockader, of Cherry Mountain, N.C.* provides numerous colorful Amos Owens stories. Additional details come from his frequent appearances on court dockets and his widely reported obituary.

Born in Rutherford County around 1822, Owens's family had deep roots in the area. His grandfather was a noted veteran of the Battle of Kings Mountain. As a young man Owens developed a local reputation, in White's words, as "a fine rider, with the woodcraft and hunting instinct of the red man of the forest . . . a noted breaker of horses," a crack shot banned from shooting matches that had anything but a trivial prize, and a bare-knuckles brawler "never known to strike his colors."

Despite this wild streak, Owens demonstrated a strong business sense and became economically successful very quickly. In the 1840s and 1850s he accumulated a sizeable estate—including farmlands, a large cherry orchard, and a slave—and built a highly profitable corn liquor business. Indeed, it was during this time that Owens's legend began to spread as a result of his distribution of Cherry Bounce, a concoction made with unaged corn liquor, sourwood honey, and cherry juice. By the early 1860s, as White noted, "his coffers bulged with filthy lucre."

The Civil War, however, disrupted Owens's wealth accumulation. When the war began he immediately volunteered and joined the Sixteenth North Carolina Regiment, C.S.A. He saw action in northern Virginia, fought at the Battle of First Manassas, and participated in the brutal slaughter of Union troops, many African American, at the Battle of the Crater. His war ended when he was captured, imprisoned (for the first time) by the federal government, and then paroled after three months.

After the war, Owens returned to Rutherford County, resumed his life as a farmer (without his slave), and despite the new federal excise tax fired up his distillery and resumed making whiskey. By 1868, Owens had attracted the attention of local collectors for the U.S. Bureau of Internal Revenue. The first public mention of Owens running afoul of the law comes in a Rutherford County newspaper in November 1868. An ad placed by deputy collector R. W. Logan advertised an auction "at the Court House Door" of "ONE STILL AND FIXTURES, the property of Amos Owens, as forfeited to the United States for violation of the Internal Revenue laws, of the same." A jury, however, acquitted him in federal court in Asheville, and he even made a profit from the experience by selling liquor to the crowd gathered for court.

In the early 1870s, Owens became famous locally and statewide not as a moonshiner but as a leader in the Ku Klux Klan. Owens, enraged by the new freedoms given to African Americans and by the actions of Republicans in aiding their cause, not to mention the federal regulation of his chosen profession, determined with other Klan leaders to take matters into their own hands. In practical application this meant a terror campaign to restore some semblance of the prewar order, return the Democratic Party to dominance, and curtail the activities of federal revenue agents. As White observed, "Many offenders were whipped, some banished, and others even slain." Owens's "energy, persistence and courage," according to White, "made him a leading spirit" in the North Carolina Klan.

Owens's "energy" also brought him a $5,000 fine and a five-year sentence at the federal penitentiary in Albany, New York, in 1871 for Ku-Kluxing. Officials charged him with attacking local Republican newspaper editor James Justice and destroying his press and for giving "a very severe castigation" to Aaron Biggerstaff, a local Republican leader. Local lawyer and Democratic Party leader Plato Durham, however, took it as his cause to have Owens's and his nine codefendants' sentences reduced, and he succeeded in having the fine canceled and getting Owens released after only eighteen months.

Once again Owens returned to Cherry Mountain and continued his illegal liquor operations unabated. Revenue agents kept after him, however, and over the next thirty-plus years they arrested and jailed him at least fourteen times and he served two more terms at the Albany penitentiary. Indeed, for Owens, attendance at federal court sessions became obligatory, even when not hauled before the bar, and court days always made for the perfect opportunity to sell blockade liquor to the crowd. He had many memorable encounters with federal judges, especially with judge Robert Dick. One story has him responding to Judge Dick, who chastised Owens for drinking and defying federal law, telling Owens he had never personally been drunk. The judge then asked the moonshiner what he had to say for himself before he sentenced him. Owens retorted: "Well, Judge, you have missed a durned lot of fun if you hain't never made, drunk nor sold no licker. As to what I have to say about being sentenced, Judge, do you know what the Governor of North Carolina said to the Governor of South Carolina? [A popular joke of the day where the response is "It's a damn long time between drinks."] Them's my sentiments."

Owens also became famous for his annual June Cherry Bounce Festival, a legendary celebration of wild excess. The affair celebrated the cherry harvest, and featured at every festival was Amos Owens Cherry Bounce. Aside from cherry picking and excessive drinking and eating, the event also featured fiddle and banjo music, wild dancing, shooting matches, bare-knuckle boxing in designated rings, and wild free-for-all melees. White reported on the carnage that the festival produced: "One man was killed outright here and others had been probed, dismembered, maimed and their faces made to resemble an animated war map." The festival was also a nightmare scenario for animal lovers because it featured cockfighting, dogfighting, and the most popular event of the weekend, gander pulling. At the gander pulling, organizers tied the feet of a goose together, greased its head and neck, and hung it upside down over a bar eight feet off the ground. Individuals on horseback, or even on the occasional ox, then rode by at full speed and tried to pull the greased goose's head off. The event made for a chaotic and gory spectacle, and White himself averred that "the scene would become revolting." The festival allegedly attracted crowds in the thousands, and many participants traveled considerable distances to witness the event and take part in its excesses.

By the turn of the twentieth century, Owens, now generally given the honorific "Colonel," became so famous he partnered with White to share his philosophy of life and politics in a journal called the *Cherry Mountain Meatax*. Despite his bent toward states' rights and white supremacy, Owens's politics were surprisingly progressive and he avidly supported good roads, public education, and even women's suffrage. Of course, he also called for "free whiskey" (the repeal of the excise tax) and opposed prohibition. Although Owens had no direct involvement, in 1902, a group of individuals used his notoriety to launch a scheme selling "Amos Owens cherry trees," blanketing North and South Carolina newspapers with ads encouraging women and girls to purchase trees for resale. Authorities later shut the scheme down when they discovered it was a scam; the company took people's money but did not deliver the trees.

Late in his life, Owens evidently made some efforts to reform. When Judge Dick chastised him once again when agents again hauled the moonshiner into his court and encouraged him to reform, Owens allegedly replied, "I'll try." He also repeatedly came forward in several area churches to repent and profess his faith in Christ. But apparently his promises to give up his craft never stuck. Indeed, his last arrest for making blockade liquor came in 1905 when he was eighty-three years old. In an article on his arrest, a *Charlotte Observer* reporter wrote, "Amos Owens is an extreme type, but he is a type."

Amos Owens's life provided an entertaining interlude for North Carolinians who eagerly followed his exploits. But he also exemplified the political component common to many early moonshiners, what White called "the deep-seated defiance of the [federal] 'Government' born of Confederate service, participation in the Ku Klux Klan, and of a firm belief that he had a God-given right to make corn liquor unimpeded."

late 1860s, he became a major Klan organizer and leader in the North Carolina foothills. Owens led raids on local African Americans who had become active in Republican Party activities, terrorized Republican officials, and intimidated revenue agents. In 1870, authorities arrested him for "going disguised, and whipping and mistreating men, women and children." In 1871, officials tried and convicted him in federal court in Raleigh for Ku-Kluxing and destroying the printing presses of James Justice, a local Republican state representative and newspaper editor. Indeed, Owens's first stint (of three) in the federal prison in Albany, New York, was not for blockading but for his Klan activities.[11]

While Klan activity subsided in North Carolina after a crackdown by state militia and federal troops in 1871, support for the blockader cause and verbal attacks on federal revenue officers remained staple issues for Democrats. Indeed, perhaps the most pivotal, and memorable, moment in the 1876 gubernatorial

Zebulon Baird Vance, North Carolina governor, U.S. senator, and chief opponent of the state's "red-legged grasshoppers," 1877. (Courtesy of North Carolina Room, Pack Memorial Library, Asheville, N.C.)

campaign came when Zeb Vance accepted the Democratic Party nomination. In his speech he told the crowd gathered in Charlotte that if they would "do their duty" the Democrats could sweep the state by a 10,000-vote majority. When that happened, he famously asserted, "Radical revenue officials, and the red-legged grasshoppers will cease to vex our people, by eating out their substance, and the places that know them now will know them no more forever." Vance was a master orator who had delivered thousands of public speeches in his career, but no phrase he coined (or borrowed) resonated more with people than his characterization of federal revenue agents as "red-legged grasshoppers." He and his Democratic Party supporters employed the line constantly during the campaign and it was a well-known "saying" in North Carolina well into the twentieth century.[12] One lawyer recalled in the *Charlotte Democrat*, "Gov. Vance was responsible for the hatred of revenue officers and for the 'idealization' of the moonshiner which has tended to make the latter more thought of as a 'good fellow' who is persecuted."[13]

While the issue of white supremacy—and Vance reminded his audience that the Democratic Party had "with a high hand and an outstretched arm brought all the white men of North Carolina out of the house of bondage"—was the key issue in returning the Democrats to power, the federal excise tax and the enforcement activities of revenue officers ran a close second. As historian Bruce Stewart has pointed out, the vote in western North Carolina, where federal revenue law enforcement was especially active, was key to Vance's victory in 1876 and the Conservatives' return to power in the state. Stewart observed: "During Reconstruction, white southerners also waged an often overlooked war against the Bureau of Internal Revenue, an agency that promoted the expansion of the federal government and its 'infernal' alcohol tax. In the end, Democrats capitalized on whites' opposition to both black political equality and federal liquor law enforcement to build support against the Republican Party."[14] With Conservative rule's restoration in North Carolina in the 1870s, the moonshiner's reputation in the state became akin to Robin Hood's: he was an outlaw, yes, but one who battled against an oppressive and corrupt regime on behalf of the people.

By the late 1870s, the Republican Party faced a real quandary in dealing with blockaders in places like North Carolina where defying the law was so common. The federal government rapidly became dependent on the revenues generated by the excise tax on liquor, but at the same time it understood that enforcing the unpopular law risked destroying the Republican Party in the south and perhaps even sparking a popular rebellion. After many years of clumsy, ineffectual, and often corrupt enforcement, a nearly ideal person emerged to at least tamp down the moonshine traffic in the south when President Grant appointed Green Raum as commissioner of internal revenue in 1876. Raum attacked the problem with a three-pronged approach: aggressively going after major producers and more defiant outlaws, offering amnesty and generous terms to turn smaller producers into legal operators, and rooting out corruption within the Bureau of Internal Revenue to make enforcement more palatable and trustworthy.[15]

In order to crack down on major liquor traffickers, Raum—who had successfully demonstrated to Congress the millions in revenue the government was losing to blockading and had his funding increased—boosted the numbers of deputy collectors and equipped them with modern repeating rifles. At the same time, he discouraged enforcement agents from using federal troops to support officers on raids, as the presence of soldiers proved an unnecessary provocation, especially to former Confederates. He also pressured his collectors in the field to step up their efforts in going after major and blatant offenders of the law. In June 1877, Raum wrote to collector J. J. Mott, head of the Sixth Collection District in western North Carolina. Mott had virtually suspended enforcement operations in his district in the lead-up to the 1876 election in an attempt to boost the chances for the local Republican Party. Raum challenged Mott's policy and demanded he take aggressive action: "It is well known that numerous persons are engaged in the illicit manufacture and sale of spirits in your district and I desire that you shall take immediate steps to suppress the same with a strong hand." In the resulting "Moonshine War" from 1878 to 1882, the numbers of stills busted and arrests of blockaders increased dramatically. In western North Carolina, the number of stills confiscated jumped from 122 in 1877 to 274 in 1879, and the number of moonshiners captured rose from 43 to 343 in the same time period.[16]

Raum's crackdown on blockaders faced a number of challenges, particularly on those perceived as Robin Hoods. Perhaps no one better fit this description during the Moonshine War than Lewis Redmond, the purported "king of the moonshiners," who headed an outlaw gang in the so-called Dark Corner of South Carolina. Redmond, who grew up making liquor with his family—both legally before the Civil War and illegally afterward—had fled Transylvania County, North Carolina, after he shot and killed deputy revenue collector Alfred Duckworth during an attempted arrest. After a number of highly publicized shootouts, spectacular escapes, and even raids on the homes of revenue collectors, the press in the Carolinas characterized Redmond as a victim of "the Yankee oppression resulting from the late war." Former Confederate general and South Carolina governor Wade Hampton became his staunchest defender. Redmond even became the subject of a highly fictionalized dime novel, which characterized him as a chivalrous, highly educated, and misunderstood outlaw forced into breaking the law by an oppressive and "unjust" federal government that had murdered his father. As Bruce Stewart observed: "Like Billy the Kid and Jesse James, he became a legendary figure, reflecting people's hopes, needs, and fears. Most mountain residents (and other Southerners) viewed him as a folk hero, an outlaw who violently fought against the Bureau of Internal Revenue and its 'infernal' revenue tax. He supposedly killed in self-defense and for a noble cause: to protect his community from an 'oppressive' federal government."[17]

Operations against high-profile illegal operators like Lewis Redmond and Amos Owens, however, began to make a difference. When the government made things too hot for him in upstate South Carolina, Redmond fled to the mountains and tried to "live a quiet and law-abiding life." Revenue agents captured the outlaw after a shootout in 1881 deep in the Great Smoky Mountains

Lewis Redmond N.C. Moonshine Hall of Famer

Any North Carolina moonshiner profiled in the *New York Times*, who serves as the subject of two dime novels which sold over 100,000 copies, and who is widely known as the "king of the moonshiners" deserves inclusion in the Hall of Fame. While it can be argued that many significant events in Lewis Redmond's moonshine career happened in the so-called Dark Corner of South Carolina, he spent his formative years in North Carolina, and the event that marked the beginning of his career as a notorious outlaw and his eventual capture both occurred in western North Carolina.

Probably born in Rabun County, Georgia, around 1854, Redmond and his family moved back to the birthplace of his father, Richard Harris Redmond, in Henderson (now Transylvania) County, North Carolina. Redmond grew up on a typical mountain farm helping his family with crops of corn, beans, and squashes, tending the family's cattle and hogs, hunting the mountains for meat and furs, and gathering medicinal herbs, berries, and nuts. He also helped his daddy make whiskey that the family consumed, sold for needed cash, or traded for store credit.

Although later fanciful accounts of Redmond's life attribute his abilities as a warrior and military strategist to experience in the Confederate army, he was too young to serve. His older brothers did join the Sixty-Ninth North Carolina Regiment, C.S.A (better known as Thomas's Legion of Cherokee Indians and Highlanders), and according to some stories Redmond frequently visited their camp and became a mascot of sorts. The young Redmond witnessed plenty of violence during his boyhood in a region wracked with internal conflict during the war, and he appears to have developed a deep affection for and commitment to the Confederate cause and a strong hatred for the federal government.

After the war, the Redmond family attempted to return to a somewhat normal existence, which included the distillation of whiskey. Families like the Redmonds, whose whiskey-making endeavors were relatively small-scale, could make no profit at all if they paid the federal tax, so they chose to take their operations underground and become moonshiners. In an 1878 interview with the Charleston *News and Courier*, Redmond told a reporter, "I worked on the farm all day and at the still at night to make a living for us. I would be so tired the next day that I have gone to sleep in the corn row between the plough handles and would wake up only when my horse stopped at the end of the furrow."

As the moonshine business became increasingly profitable, young Redmond saw an opportunity and began contracting with neighbors to transport their whiskey to market and share in the profits. His activities soon drew federal revenue agents' attention, however, and on 1 March 1876 deputy marshal Alfred Duckworth confronted Redmond and an accomplice as they hauled a moonshine-laden wagon to market. Accounts vary as to what ensued. According to a widely distributed newspaper article in 1878 recounting Redmond's exploits, Duckworth arrested the moonshiner and as they headed to jail, Redmond "drew a pistol which he had concealed in his boot, and shot the officer dead." In his interview with the *News and Courier* in the same year, Redmond said that Duckworth had been a childhood friend, but when he was hired as a deputy marshal he became "high strung" and sought to make his reputation by bringing Redmond to justice. Duckworth had talked widely in the community about his determination to do so. When the deputy marshal confronted Redmond, the moonshiner demanded he produce a warrant, which, according to Redmond, Duckworth did not have. When Duckworth threatened Redmond with a revolver, Redmond reached into the coat pocket of his accomplice, pulled out a derringer, and shot the attempted arrester in the throat, mortally wounding him.

Redmond escaped on foot into nearby Pickens County, South Carolina, where he knew friends and family members would help him hide from federal agents. While in the Dark Corner of South Carolina, Redmond was not content to lie low and instead built his legend in the late 1870s. He continued and expanded his moonshine operations, formed an outlaw gang, engaged in frequent shootouts with law enforcement officials trying to capture him, made spectacular escapes, and organized and led an expedition to free several of his gang from the Pickens County jail. Redmond and his gang even raided the homes of federal agents. His notoriety grew well past southwest North Carolina and the South Carolina upstate, and he soon became a symbol of defiance of federal authority throughout the old Confederacy and a favorite of South Carolina governor Wade Hampton. The Democratic Party press widely depicted him as a victim and a living symbol "of the Yankee oppression resulting from the late war." Even the Republican *New York Times* ran several feature stories on Redmond and his exploits, although it criticized Hampton's and other southern politicians' support for outlaws.

All the media attention created intense pressure on commissioner of internal revenue Green Raum to do something about the chaotic situation in the Dark Corner. Raum combined a generous amnesty policy for run-of-the-mill blockaders and a renewed determination to bring the most notorious violators, especially Lewis Redmond, to justice. The pressure grew so intense in South Carolina that Redmond fled to Swain County in the far western part of North Carolina.

As Redmond was on the run and trying to lie low, however, his fame spread even more widely and his legend became even more inflated and fabled. Published in Philadelphia in 1879, *The Entwined Lives of Miss Gabrielle Austin, Daughter of the Late Rev. Ellis C. Austin, and of Redmond, the Outlaw, the Leader of the North Carolina "Moonshiners,"* was an almost totally fabricated but wildly popular publication that went through at least four editions, one of those in German. *Entwined Lives* depicts Redmond as a chivalrous, misunderstood, Princeton-educated gentleman—although he had killed fifty-four federal agents—forced into the outlaw life by an oppressive and "unjust" federal government that had murdered his father. A Swain County correspondent, who claimed to interview the outlaw, wrote another popular and equally fanciful account of Redmond's life widely distributed in regional newspapers in 1880. The writer called Redmond a "fearless and daring man. . . . His favorite weapon is the pistol; and with his being a most excellent shot, he has killed three men and wounded several, always leaving the field victorious and not even singed by a ball. This monarch wears an impenetrable breast-plate of iron and such a number of pistols that he can fire one hundred and twenty times without reloading." The correspondent added that he "found him [Redmond] to be pleasant and friendly but always on the lookout and cautious."

Federal authorities finally caught up with Redmond on 7 April 1881, after a dramatic shootout near his Swain County home. Revenue agents wounded Redmond six times and finally apprehended him after running half a mile. The press reported the outlaw's arrest nationally and deputy collector Robert A. Cobb published another highly fictionalized Redmond biography entitled *The True Life of Maj. Lewis Richard Redmond, the Notorious Outlaw and Famous Moonshiner, of Western North Carolina, Who Was Born in Swain County, N.C., in the Year 1855, and Arrested April 7, 1881.* After recovering from his wounds, authorities tried Redmond in Greenville, South Carolina, for eight counts of federal revenue violations and two counts of conspiracy for leading raids against federal agents. They never charged him for Duckworth's murder. Redmond pleaded guilty and the judge sentenced him to ten years in the federal penitentiary in Albany, New York, where he probably met Amos Owens.

Although the reputation of moonshiners in the early 1880s in general began to decline in the wake of widespread violence, Redmond remained popular. Ironically, two temperance reformers led a movement in South Carolina to have the famous outlaw pardoned. In May 1884, on the recommendation of now U.S. senator Wade Hampton and U.S. attorney general Benjamin Brewster, President Chester A. Arthur unconditionally pardoned him. Crowds gathered at the Columbia railroad station for a triumphal send-off to his home near Easley. In his final communication with the press, Redmond wrote a letter to the Charleston *News and Courier* declaring, "Breathing the pure mountain air, in the enjoyment of improving health, I desire to engage in some honorable, legitimate business for a support for myself and family."

Redmond lived out his life in South Carolina's Dark Corner with his large family, quietly farming and making tax-paid, "government" liquor for distiller Dietrich Biemann. The distillery branded the whiskey he produced as Redmond's Hand Mash, and Redmond's image graced the bottles. He died of pneumonia in 1906, according to the *Raleigh Times*, "surrounded by his loved ones and a minister nearby." The paper also pointed out that Redmond had "quit the moonshining trade and he followed the simple life on the farm. . . . He became a good citizen."

The legend of Lewis Redmond far exceeded the reality of his life. As historian Bruce Stewart points out, "Redmond's career as an outlaw is unspectacular." Despite the fanciful and exaggerated newspaper and pulp fiction accounts, he only killed one man and his outlaw gang probably only numbered as high as fifteen men. For people in the post–Civil War south, however, Redmond was an important symbol of (at least temporary) successful defiance of federal authority. As such, he and other notable moonshiners like Amos Owens were useful symbols for Democratic politicians like Zeb Vance and Wade Hampton in the fight against Republican rule. His mythical exploits also provided an entertaining diversion for Gilded Age southerners and individuals across the nation. These fanciful accounts also helped create the growing national "southern mountaineer" stereotype of the violent hillbilly moonshiner.

THE CAPTURE OF REDMOND.

Woodcut illustration from The True Life of Maj. Lewis Richard Redmond, *1882. (Courtesy of North Carolina Room, Pack Memorial Library, Asheville, N.C.)*

of Swain County.[18] He pleaded guilty to ten charges for illegal liquor violations and conspiracy, and authorities sent him to the federal penitentiary in Albany, New York.[19] Owens spent two eighteen-month terms in Albany during the same time period, developing a close and cordial relationship with the warden.[20] In response to such successful arrests and prosecutions, Commissioner Raum declared that "in another year there will be no 'moonshine' operators whatever in the South."[21]

The crackdown, however, came with costs, and the level of violence between blockaders and revenue officers increased dramatically. Most encounters involved shots fired above the heads of deputy collectors, minor wounds, or horses shot out from under the officers in order to intimidate or scare them off. Deputy collector Walter M. Byrd of Montgomery County had his horse shot out from under him, and "one ball clipped the shoulder lining" of his guide's coat when he and his men busted up a still in 1879 and the owners opened fire on them from the bushes. The encounter only caused Byrd to become more determined to make these "desperadoes . . . scat" from the county. On rare occasions things became much more serious, and blockaders wounded four officers and killed one in the Sixth Collection District, much of western North Carolina, between 1876 and 1880.[22] Despite the costs, the Bureau of Internal Revenue's aggressive campaign greatly reduced the number of the largest and most flagrant violations, particularly in the western part of the state.

At the same time, Raum's amnesty plan and his cleaning up of the bureau probably had just as great an impact on the decline of moonshining during the period. In 1878, the bureau began a program that granted amnesty to any blockader who turned him or herself in, pleaded guilty in federal court, and promised to stop illegal activities. As a result, convictions for illegal distilling skyrocketed, with numbers increasing in the Sixth Collection District from 308 in 1877 to 801 in 1879. Most important for Raum and Mott, the number of licensed legal distilleries in the district increased from 42 to 198 as a result of the amnesty plan and of the lowering of the legal limit for licensed distilleries from six gallons' capacity to four. In fact, 154 of the 198 distilleries had a capacity of five gallons or less.[23] Even moonshine hotbeds such as the South Mountains of Burke County, where there were no legal distilleries in 1878, saw an uptick in legal operations. Between 1878 and 1880 several moonshiners in the county started cooperating with authorities and established legal distilleries.[24]

The clearing out of corruption, overly aggressive enforcement, and poor behavior on the part of deputy collectors and their posses also helped change the public's attitude about moonshine and moonshiners. Many North Carolinians despised collectors for being antagonistic, ignoring the civil rights of citizens, and displaying arrogant and rude behavior. As the *Asheville Citizen* noted, "they have trampled upon justice with a lordly air is a notorious fact."[25] The public also criticized agents for corrupt, hypocritical, and even illegal behavior. One of the major accusations following collectors was that of drunkenness, especially when they were on duty. The *Chatham Record* reported in 1880 on two revenue officers who confiscated a wagon loaded with kegs of illegal liquor and arrested the driver. On their way to town to incarcerate their prisoner and proudly display their trophies of war on the courthouse square, the officers decided to confirm that the substance in the kegs was indeed "blockade whiskey" and began to taste the contents. As the *Record* reporter noted, "They soon became HORS DU COMBAT, and unable to return in triumph, or indeed to return at all that night." One officer spent the night in a ditch on the side of the road and the other, "being unable to travel was kindly cared for in the house of a negro." Their prisoner dutifully went on to town and attempted, unsuccessfully, to turn himself in. In resignation, he drove his team back home and "left a message for his former captors where they could find him whenever they recovered from the effects of the night's adventure."[26]

In western North Carolina, Collector Mott teamed up with federal district judge Robert Dick to improve the efficiency and reputation of the bureau. Dick instructed federal revenue officers that arrests "must be made in accordance with law, and only upon warrants duly issued" and threatened violators with expulsion. In turn, Mott pledged to hire only "men of character and honesty," tightened the qualifications for employment, and required each applicant to submit an "endorsement from the citizens and well-known people of the neighborhood" as to his character.[27]

Despite the arrests of high-profile blockaders and the reforms instituted by Raum, Dick, and Mott, law enforcement still faced a daunting task in stemming the flow of illegal liquor from hidden distilleries to thirsty customers. Federal revenue agents were pretty much on their own in enforcing the law, as local and state officials felt little urgency in enforcing a law many still believed unjust, unconstitutional, and downright un-American. Local sheriffs were also loath to antagonize voters or, as was often the case, family members involved in the moonshine business.

For the most part, the raids launched by federal collectors were much more mundane than the campaign to bring Lewis Redmond to justice. They generally resulted only in overturned barrels of mash and the capture of a still. Officers perforated the stills with an axe or a modified hatchet with a pointed pick on one end, known as a "devil." An article in the *Tobacco Plant* described an 1889 raid in Stokes County where "the officers destroyed the stills by cutting small holes in them, sometimes cutting their initials, as a forcible reminder of their presence."[28] Indeed, the common parlance in the moonshine business referred to destruction of a still by officers as "having your still cut down."

The blockaders generally got away, often with their still cap and worm, which were harder to replace, and their liquor. Critics asserted that too often reports on still raids contained the words "no arrests were made." G. M. Garren of Buena Vista wrote a letter to the *Asheville Daily Gazette* in 1899 complaining: "There have been more than half a dozen moonshine distilleries destroyed here by officers of the law, and each time the same tale is heard, 'No arrests were made.' Why is this?" Earlier in the year a *Gazette* article sarcastically remarked that "something new has happened here in the revenue service" when officers arrested some moonshiners. "It is a new experience for revenue officers to catch anybody. The guilty ones generally get word in time to vanish, so that a few gallons of beer and a still to hack is all that rewards the raiders."[29]

By the 1880s, blockading had become less associated with Reconstruction-era politics, and blockaders began to lose their heroic status as modern-day Robin Hoods. As historian Wilbur Miller noted, "Unlike white supremacy, moonshining itself was becoming increasingly disreputable, and many people did not accept the violence employed to defend it."[30] The election of Democrat Grover Cleveland as president in 1884 stripped the partisan connotations from the moonshine issue, as Democrats seemed just as eager as Republicans to use revenue collector appointments as rewards for party loyalty. Indeed, under Cleveland's two administrations (1885–89 and 1893–97), enforcement of federal revenue laws in North Carolina continued unabated. Zeb Vance and other Democratic

A still "cut down" by revenue agents. (Courtesy of State Archives of North Carolina, Raleigh, N.C.)

Party leaders even stopped referring to revenue agents as "red-legged grass-hoppers," at least until Republicans came back into power. A Republican editorialist for the *Union Republican* condemned the hypocrisy of Democrats like Vance: "I have lived to see a time that I never expected to come, that is to see the country flooded with Democratic revenue officers. I did think that when they were speaking all over the country and telling the people that they would repeal the revenue law that they would do it. That they would turn the rogues out of office and stop their hunting every branch and smelling for the still houses like a coon dog hunts a coon. Have they redeemed their pledges? If so they did it by cutting up stills and destroying property.... The revenue dogs are doing more damage in one year than the Republicans did in two in this county."[31]

As the nineteenth century neared its end, sympathetic public notions of the "poor man trying to feed his family" or the "heroic defender of the traditional right to make a little 'likker'" gradually changed as well. Increasingly, particularly among middle-class North Carolinians in towns and cities, press reports characterized blockaders as ignorant, violent, sexually menacing beasts or, as *Harper's Weekly* called them in an 1879 article, "big-boned semi-barbarian people." National press coverage of the Moonshine War and the increasing number of "local color" magazine articles that blatantly stereotyped North Carolina's mountain residents contributed to this image. However, the local North Carolina press in small towns and cities became the chief disseminator of negative stereotypes of moonshiners.[32] By the 1890s, these newspapers increasingly characterized their blockader neighbors as "bloodthirsty desperadoes," "tobacco-spittle squirters," and even "human hyenas." Accounts especially emphasized their violent nature. On seeing John Davis, a purported "king of the moonshiners" from Moore County, in court, a *Raleigh News* reporter commented, "It doesn't take much stretch of the imagination to see them [his beady eyes] peering along a cool steel barrel at you. But it isn't pleasant for they say they have done so many a time and more than one revenue officer is today wearing a memorial of the occasion."[33] Dr. Charles Hall, rector of Holy Trinity Church in Brooklyn, loved to tell the (probably fictional) story of a conversation he had with a mountain guide in the 1890s that reflected the moonshiner's "inbred hatred of the revenue officer":

> "Man killed over there last week," said the guide.
> "What had he done?" asked Dr. Hall.
> "Revenue officer," replied the guide.
> "But," persisted Dr. Hall, "what crime had the officer committed?"
> "He was a revenue officer," again said the guide.[34]

The papers often warned people going into so-called moonshine districts that they needed to be careful lest a blockader shoot them down in cold blood. Rev.

J. C. Jackson wrote in his account of a visit to western North Carolina in 1895 in the *Pittsburgh Christian Advocate* that "you need to satisfy these moonshiners you are not a government spy, or you might catch a bullet in the head from the long rifles they carry."[35] The *Bakersville Republican* derided the behavior of a moonshiner on the Toe River who supposedly accosted a Reverend Connolly, a Baptist preacher from Asheville who was on his way to Watauga County. Suspecting he was a revenue officer, the moonshiner brandished a pistol and told Connolly "he could go no further." The *Republican* lamented: "When a peaceable citizen cannot travel the public road without being stopped by a desperado with pistol in hand the law should be enforced with utmost vigor."[36]

Of course, the blockaders themselves benefitted from this fear and promoted the stereotype to keep people from nosing around their stills. A Washington County resident who happened upon a still in the Chocowinity District in 1890 was left a poetic warning attached to a turpentine box reading:

You have seen our still
And if you don't keep still
We will keep you still.[37]

In reality, violence against people stumbling on stills was rare. As Wilbur Ziegler and Ben Grosscup observed in *The Heart of the Alleghanies*, their 1883 account of their hunting and sightseeing trips into the wilds of western North Carolina, the widely circulated stories that "an unobtrusive stranger stands in danger of being shot down by a blockader on suspicion of any kind" is a "bug bear ... almost too absurd for consideration."[38]

The physical descriptions of illegal distillers contained in North Carolina newspapers also implied their menace and reflected genetic deficiencies that might help explain their behavior. John Davis's appearance in court prompted this description from the *Raleigh News* in 1897: "He is a man of forty-odd years, his face almost covered with a wild growth of beard and his hair standing out in wild tufts like dead sedge in an old field. His eyes are small, penetrating black beads that snap at you in a vicious fashion."[39] A *North Carolinian* report on the court case of Bill-Punch Edwards described him as "white-skinned and frizzle-whiskered, with eyes shifty, close together, and Police Gazetly [*sic*] looking."[40] Reporters even claimed moonshiners had a distinctly foul odor. The Raleigh *Morning Post* commented on this as it covered federal court days in 1899: "The presence of the irrepressible moonshiner sufficiently advertises the fact—even to a blind man—for it is not necessary to get a view of one of those gentry to ascertain his presence, if your olfactory organs are in good order.... The aroma of moonshine 'cawn licker' pervaded the government building and the floors of Uncle Sam's edifice were dyed with the juice of illicit tobacco yesterday again, and these facts announced as plainly as trumpet blasts of ye olden time herald could have done that a term of the United States District Court had begun."[41]

Harper's Weekly *illustration showing a "typical" mountain moonshiner, 1877. (Library of Congress)*

Reporters also depicted moonshiners as morally depraved and sexually promiscuous. The *North Carolinian* pointed out that Bill-Punch Edwards had "several more children than jobs."[42] Press accounts accused John Davis of having "Mormonistic tendencies" and having four wives and thirty-six children.[43] The *Raleigh News* reported he had denied this and averred that he only had three wives and twenty-six children.[44]

A bizarre incident in Bakersville in 1893 demonstrated that people both outside the region and in towns in the region would believe almost anything negative about North Carolina's blockaders and their communities.[45] On 3 January 1893 the Johnson City, Tennessee, *Comet* reported that a mob of 500 had descended on the Mitchell County courthouse in Bakersville to lynch three men involved in moonshine-related killings. When Sheriff Moomaw and the twenty-five men he had deputized to protect the jail from the mob refused to turn the men over, a gun battle ensued that resulted in more than fifty deaths—including Sheriff Moomaw's. The *Comet* also reported dozens more wounded and the lynching of the three prisoners. The news quickly spread across the country and across the Atlantic, and an article even appeared in the London *Times*. The *New York Times*, in an article entitled "Bloody Lynching Fight," informed its readers, "Bakersville is the county seat of Baker County [it's actually the county seat of Mitchell County], one of the wildest districts in all this country. It is here that the illicit distiller of mountain dew has plied his profession for years."[46] News service reports run all over the country quoted Bureau of Internal Revenue commissioner John W. Mason reinforcing this image of the area: "The whole section is in almost deadly opposition to authority in any form."[47]

However, on 6 January, press accounts revealed that the *Comet*'s sensational story was a hoax perpetrated by an "obscure newspaper man" by the name of J. W. Hyams, a Bakersville native. Hyams even invented the names of the victims, including Sheriff Moomaw. While the national and international press condemned Hyams for the fraud, it should have looked inward to its own willingness to accept such an outlandish story about North Carolina moonshiners. Such introspection, however, never took place, and even as newspapers decried the hoax, they continued to spread stereotypical images of moonshine and moonshining in the state.[48]

Indeed, seven years later, news agencies ran a story about Mitchell County headlined "FAMED FOR MURDERS, WICKEDEST COUNTY IN UNITED STATES

IS IN NORTH CAROLINA WHERE SHOOTINGS ARE THE RECREATION OF ITS DESPERATE INHABITANTS." The article went on to explain the reasons: "No other county in any state or territory of the union has been the scene of more murders and homicides than Mitchell County. . . . Most of the men served in the union army, and there have been many combats between them and the ex-confederates. The county is also full of moonshiners, and they fight anybody and anything that interfere with their distillation of blockade whiskey." The incidents described in the vague story told of the exploits of sheriff George Pritchard, who had killed two men in self-defense in the past three years, and alleged a rash of murders in the county without giving much in the way of specifics.[49] But it was apparent that the image of lawlessness and outlaw behavior by moonshiners had made an almost permanent imprint on the nation's psyche.

An 1895 article in the *Charlotte Observer* commented on the changing attitude toward the moonshiner in North Carolina: "For it has not been a great while since the moonshiner was, unluckily, too, made a sort of hero in North Carolina, while the revenue officers were considered a set of persecutors. The passage of time has taught the people, save the most densely ignorant or the debased, that the moonshiner lacks all qualities of a hero and is a public enemy."[50]

On occasion, newspapers depicted blockaders in a more favorable light. In 1898 the *Charlotte Observer* reported on a "notorious moonshiner" in Alleghany County by the name of Ben Heisling, "a veritable hermit, who had one room in his log cabin and three rooms in the cave adjoining." Surprisingly, the old man was a "bookworm" who spent the proceeds of his illegal activity on old books, "some of which were worth fortunes because of their rarity."[51] Chatham County moonshiner Jap Johnson, whom the Raleigh *North Carolinian* characterized as a "moonshiner of long experience, with all that word implies," and a "terror" to his community, launched a campaign to convince the public that the press had unfairly maligned him. D. T. Johnson wrote a letter to the editor of the *News and Observer* responding to an article in that paper that had described Jap's arrest for making illegal alcohol; D. T. asserted the article was "calculated to make your readers believe him to be a real desperado." D. T. argued that, to the contrary, Jap came "from one of the best families of Chatham," had married the daughter of one of the county's "best citizens," had two brothers who died in defense of the Confederacy, and was a "brave, kind and good hearted man."[52] Jap shocked the *News and Observer* editors when he subsequently showed up at the newspaper's offices. The blockader told the editors he had "called at the office" to let them "see if he looked the hardened and bad man he was represented to be." An editor responded in an article the next day: "It must be confessed that he looks anything else but a blockade desperado, and seems a pleasant sort of man."[53] In 1895, a reporter for the *News and Observer* gave a poetic defense of the moonshiner: "Long live the corn licker man, he who with a stroke bring not fountains of water from a rock, but a gush of sunshine from a still; who starts the dance-music in the banquet halls of the heart, and fills the brain with all-night breakdowns where partners swing till morning. Can he be spared?"[54] Even with these few favorable reports, however, negative popular images of the blockader became the norm by 1890.

Despite the illegal distiller's increasingly negative image among "respectable" sorts, by the 1890s the North Carolina moonshiner had survived the Moonshine War and federal efforts to eliminate illegal liquor, and he was not only "spared" but thrived in the state. Reconstruction-era political issues, and the purported defense of natural and constitutional rights, provided less motivation, but the economic problems in the state continued to provide powerful incentives for continued defiance of the federal excise tax. Reflective of this change in motivation, the term "blockader" became less commonly used and most folks began referring to illegal distillers as "moonshiners." The moonshiners also survived the national and statewide campaigns that took them from the status of Robin Hoods to that of violent and ignorant hillbillies. Indeed, while outsiders and the forces of "decency" in the state might consider moonshining "deviant" and "exotic" behavior, for most rural North Carolinians it was simply normal.

NORMALIZING THE MOONSHINER

By the 1890s, despite numerous claims that the blockade liquor business was on its last legs in North Carolina, the state consistently ranked at or near the top of Bureau of Internal Revenue statistics for stills busted, gallons of untaxed liquor seized, and arrests made for illicit distillation, sale, or transportation. The blockade business was on the increase as the growing prohibition movement led to a decline in legal distilleries and saloons and the demand for the illegal product skyrocketed. As an 1895 article in the *Charlotte Observer* noted, making moonshine had become something deep-seated in the psyches of some North Carolinians: "The moonshiner is a man of sorrows. His still is small—so as to be easily portable—and if he could not do much more than make buckle and tongue meet owing to his capacity being so limited ... why doesn't he quit the business? Why don't you quit batting your eyes? He can't. He is a victim of a hereditary infirmity, confirmed by habit ... a moonshiner is built to do a moonshine business. Put him in jail, but it isn't worthwhile to quarrel with him. When he gets out he will go at it again and will keep at it until he finally turns his moccasins to the sun."[1]

Indeed, during the latter part of the nineteenth century, moonshine became inextricably linked to the image of North Carolina and North Carolinians for better or worse. In 1885, the Raleigh *Chronicle* shared a joke about how New Yorkers "distinguished a North Carolinian—by the odor of fried rabbit and blockade whiskey."[2] A native of the state wrote a letter from his new home in Texas in 1898 referring to North Carolina as the Old Moonshine State.[3] Even when North Carolina dipped to number two in stills seized in 1896, the *Charlotte Observer* did not attribute this fact to a reformed and more law-abiding populace but mused that "the boys are hiding them more successfully, or it represents the number of moonlighters who have died or gone to the pen. None of them have reformed—that is certain."[4] In a long 1901 article on North Carolina moonshine, an investigative reporter for the Charleston *News and Courier* asserted, "In spite of the vigilance of Uncle Sam's revenue officers the blockaders [in North Carolina] are increasing in number every year.... The old North State is putting lots of contraband 'booze' on the market and will continue to do so as long as the world stands."[5]

Given the intensification of federal enforcement, and as it became apparent that the excise tax and federal revenue enforcement were in North Carolina to stay, distillers turned outlaw blockaders had to change their behavior in significant ways. Producers now had to go to great lengths to conceal their operations. Proximity to good water was still crucial to the whiskey-making process, but now the illegal distillers generally had to locate their stills far up in mountain hollows, swamps, or other backwoods areas. Blockaders prized locations both difficult for revenue agents to access and with ready escape routes. Horace Kephart vividly described the typical illegal-still location in the mountains of western North Carolina and the lengths moonshiners went to so as not to leave any sign of their activities: "Some little side-branch is chosen that runs through a gully choked with laurel and briers and rhododendron as to be quite impassable, save by such worming and crawling as must make a great noise. Doubtless a faint cattle-trail follows the backbone of the ridge above it, and this is the workers' ordinary highway in going to and fro; but the descent from ridge to gully is seldom made twice over the same course, lest a trail be printed direct to the still-house."[6] A site with a good, bold spring where the water later flowed back underground was an ideal, and prized, spot.

To screen their operations from revenue agents, informers, or innocent wayfarers, blockaders often felled a large tree, particularly an evergreen, on the downhill side of their still. The branches of the tree would also help disperse the smoke from the fire to help avoid detection. They also might move operations to the base of a cliff, or even into a cave, to secure at least one side. Many moonshiners built a small shed, or stillhouse, over their operations to help conceal them and protect them from the elements.[7]

Moonshiners also had to be much choosier about the type of fuel they used to stoke their furnaces. Hardwoods had always been favored, as they produced hotter and steadier fires. Now illegal distillers became concerned about which woods produced the least smoke to make sure the stills did not attract the attention of revenue agents. When they could get it, moonshiners preferred either locust or green ash. One moonshiner told Joseph Dabney he preferred green ash because it "just lays there and fries, and don't make no racket or no smoke." Of course, locust and green ash were not always readily available, so the moonshiners had to use the hardest wood they could find.[8]

The excise tax and the rise of moonshining also led to the end, for most whis-

What's in a Name?

Although "moonshine" is the most common term used for illegal liquor in North Carolina, folks have employed many names for it over the years. The term most commonly used when federal excise tax enforcement began in the state in the late 1860s was "blockade," "blockade whiskey," or "blockade liquor." The term reflected the widespread belief that illegal liquor producers were akin to Civil War–era blockade runners, heroic individuals defying an oppressive government. The term was most commonly used during Reconstruction and continued in common usage until the late nineteenth century, although folks still used "blockade" well into the twentieth century.

"Moonshine" was a term appropriated from the British Isles, which was used to describe a product made in the moonlight in defiance of various British excise taxes in the seventeenth and eighteenth centuries. It came into common usage in North Carolina in the 1890s. The words "popskull" and "busthead" originated before the 1860s as descriptors for poor-quality liquor and became commonly used in the prohibition era when such liquor became more widespread. "Mountain dew" was another import from the British Isles, probably Scotland, used in North Carolina for better-quality legal liquor before the Civil War. In the federal excise tax era, people used the term both for the legal variety and high-quality illegal stuff, particularly that made in western North Carolina's mountains. An 1880 article in the *Kinston Journal* praised the mountain region, its people, and its products: "It is a famous country for raising kind hearted, hospitable people; for producing illustrious lawyers and Statesmen . . . and it is further noted for its fine 'mountain dew' both under sunlight and moonshine auspices."

The 1880s and 1890s brought a proliferation of new terms, some uniquely used in North Carolina. "Bug juice" was one such term that came into common usage in the 1880s, as did "tulu" (sometimes spelled "toulu" or "toolu"), a word credited by some to a reporter from the Statesville *Landmark*. "White lightning" also came into common usage in the 1890s. According to Gavin Smith in *The A to Z of Whiskey*, folks used the term "lightning" in the late eighteenth century as a slang term for gin. It soon became a common term for high-proof, low-grade liquor. It was almost inevitable then that the clear, or "white," liquor illegally produced would become known as white lightning.

Probably the most uniquely North Carolina term for illegal liquor was "sowpaw," employed across the state from the early 1890s into the 1920s. According to a 1904 article in the *Charlotte Observer*, "sowpaw" was "a Western North Carolina colloquialism." The term came from a concoction purported to cure "anything from corns to consumption" bottled by a quack doctor in the region named Davis, who came up with the name "sowpaw" for his product. The key ingredient in Davis's sowpaw was unaged corn liquor. As the *Observer* reporter put it, the product's "basis was white corn whiskey and it was nearly all basis." After Sowpaw Davis, as he came to be called, "retired from business . . . through the operation of unfeeling laws," the name became "the generic name of all liquids which enjoyed the stimulative properties that belong to sowpaw."

As sugar and molasses became more commonly used to make illegal liquor in the prohibition era, names reflecting the change in ingredients entered North Carolinians' vocabulary. By the 1920s, "sugar liquor," "sugarhead," and "sugar drip" became common. In eastern North Carolina illegal liquor made with molasses became known as monkey rum. The *News and Observer* credited the term to a New Bern illegal distiller named Arthur Ipock, whom authorities busted in 1909. Although the reasons Ipock chose this name are obscure, it appears likely that it has racist connotations given the fact that illegal distillers primarily marketed the product to African American communities. Confirmation of that possibility comes in a sidebar reference to Ipock's arrest in the Raleigh *Caucasian* that reads, "It is said that 'squirrel brand' whiskey will make them climb trees and we suppose that 'monkey rum' will make them do stunts on the top of a telegraph pole." While the article does not specify who "them" refers to, given the paper's masthead it is probably safe to assume the racism inherent in the term.

Less commonly used terms often cropped up in newspaper accounts, probably invented by reporters or in reference to local concoctions. "Funeral juice," "splo" (short for "explosion"), and "black dynamite" reflected the high proof and powerful effect of much illegal liquor. Terms like "laurel root juice," "skat," and "tobacco licorice" are local inventions. "Rabbit whiskey" was based on an often-used humorous North Carolina adage that referred to illegal liquor so strong it would "make a rabbit spit in a bulldog's face." The most recent term, which first appears in print in the 1950s, is "peartnin' juice." This name most commonly appears in columns written by *Asheville Citizen-Times* reporter John Parris who was from Jackson County, and it appears to be a term used most commonly in the far reaches of western North Carolina.

key makers, of aging their product. Moonshiners had to be mobile and ready to take their still and run if they sensed the presence of revenue agents. As Horace Kephart observed, "He has enough to conceal, or run away with, a mere copper still, to say nothing of barrels of whiskey." In addition, most blockaders were relatively poor and needed their money quickly, even if it was only to purchase more stills or materials for making whiskey. As a practical matter, illegal distillers got their whiskey out quickly to market. Kephart shared a common story in *Our Southern Highlanders* on legendary Smokies moonshiner Aquilla "Quill" Rose's views on the merits of aging whiskey: "A slick-faced dude from Knoxville told me once that all good red-liquor was aged, and that if I'd age my blockade it would bring a fancy price. I kept some for three months—and, by godlings, it ain't so."[9]

Making moonshine was a strenuous business, and the stereotype of the "lazy moonshiner" is a long way from the reality of the actual work involved. As still sites generally lay far off the beaten path, blockaders had to carry stills, haul in

Illustration showing blockaders distilling in the moonlight. Illegal distillers had to find creative ways to conceal their activities. (Courtesy of North Carolina Room, Pack Memorial Library, Asheville, N.C.)

sacks of cornmeal and malt, and then haul the product out, all through heavy brush, up and down steep mountainsides, or through swamps. Arthur Young, who made illegal liquor in the shadow of Clingman's Dome as a young man, recalled the work: "I've heard said back in them days, 'That man ought to be out workin' instead of makin' likker, He ain't doin' nothing, just taking it easy.' The fact was, the moonshiners were the ones who were really working. We carried meal on our backs.... A bushel of meal would weigh 62 pounds.... I was stout. At 18, I didn't know how stout I was. We brought liquor out in five and ten-gallon kegs." This hauling in and out came on top of the normal heavy labor and intensity inherent in making whiskey. All the while, blockaders had to be on high alert for spies or revenue agents, never knowing when they would have to make a run for it through the woods or swamps to maintain their freedom. As one moonshiner put it, "Blockadin' is the hardest work a man ever done. And hit's wearin' on a feller's narves."[10]

The vast majority of North Carolinians in the blockade business were small producers, working with other family members as they did on the farm. Family members not only provided cheaper labor but also were much less likely to inform on a moonshiner to authorities. Making liquor was part of their sub-

Horace Kephart, author of Our Southern Highlanders, *a primary source of information on early moonshining in the North Carolina mountains. (Courtesy of Great Smoky Mountains National Park Archives, National Park Service Collections Preservation Center, Townsend, Tenn.)*

sistence and not only provided cash for taxes and other necessities for which they could not barter but fit nicely into the farm cycle. In fact, moonshining farmers were often excellent recyclers, who continued the antebellum practice of using spent mash to fatten their hogs. In 1894, while Deputy Collector Gibson was cutting down Sol Hayworth's still in Montgomery County, "a monstrous squealing was heard about twenty feet away from the still in the bushes." When the officer investigated he discovered "25 large specimens of swine that had reached a splendid state of perfection from a steady diet of that nourishing article, 'moonshine' beer."[11] Most North Carolina farmers continued in the tradition of making blockade liquor as a seasonal activity used to supplement their farm income, not as a full-time career. For the most part, making moonshine was the small farmers' hedge against hard times, and by keeping their operations small, sporadic, and well hidden, they could generally escape the attention of federal revenue agents.

Not only did blockaders have to modify the way they made their liquor, they also had to develop new ways to transport, market, and sell their product. Transporting was a seriously risky endeavor for blockaders, so they had to use care in concealing their cargo. Farmers often hid their product under loads of

FRANK LESLIE'S ILLUSTRATED NEWSPAPER

Entered according to Act of Congress, in the year 1883, by Mrs. Frank Leslie, in the Office of the Librarian of Congress at Washington.—Entered at the Post Office, New York, N.Y., as Second-class Matter.

No. 1,458.—Vol. LVII. NEW YORK—FOR THE WEEK ENDING SEPTEMBER 1, 1883. [Price, 10 Cents. $4.00 Yearly. 13 Weeks, $1.00

NORTH CAROLINA.—AN ILLICIT WHISKY-STILL IN THE MOUNTAINS SURPRISED BY REVENUE OFFICERS.

From a Sketch by J. S. Hodgson.—See Page 21.

Cover of Frank Leslie's Illustrated Newspaper *showing a moonshiner and the ever-present hog. (University of North Carolina Asheville Special Collections)* apples, hay, "taters," or other produce. As the Raleigh *Morning Post* noted, "Of course, all the hay wagons which come to Raleigh cannot be watched." Agents also reported cases where blockaders shipped barrels of flour, and "in the center of each was secreted a keg of blockade whiskey."[12] Illegal producers also reused barrels procured from legal alcohol retailers that had tax stamps on them. A reporter for the *Wilmington Messenger* noted, "A favorite scheme of the blockaders is to procure barrels and packages which contained liquors and tobaccos on which tax has been paid, and refill them. These they boldly put out on the market for a second time absolutely 'Scott free' from tax."[13] Peter Sellars was "perhaps the most prosperous distiller in Alamance County" in the late nineteenth century but skirted the law to sell illegal liquor in his legal saloons and maximize his profits. He had a legal license to distill and dutifully paid his tax "on what the agent could find." According to local legend, Sellars "kept about half the liquor he made hid and sold it in his saloon tax free."[14]

While some blockade liquor was sold in this way through "legal" outlets, much was sold through "blind exchange." In a blind exchange, the customer places the money for his or her liquor purchase in a secret place, leaves, and then comes back hours later to collect his or her gallon, pint, or single drink. The *Asheville Daily Gazette* described one local variation on the process: "A hollow tree or cave adjacent to the nearest village is designated by common consent of the moonshiner and some of his friends one of whom acts as agent between seller and buyer. When a resident of the village wishes some whiskey, he hands the necessary money, together with a jug or bottle, to the agent who deposits both in the secret place and goes his way. After a lapse of several hours, usually 12 or more, the agent returns and finds the money gone and the receptacle full of the desired liquor, which he delivers to the customer. The latter seldom knows who actually made and sold him the stuff."[15]

Some retailers operated what some observers called "traveling groceries," wagons loaded with liquor that rode around the countryside dispensing their illegal products. Revenue officers captured one such "portable saloon" operated by three men in the Asheville area in 1898. As the *Asheville Citizen* reported, "A horse and wagon, double barrel shot gun and several whiskey kegs, some empty and some filled, were among the trophies of the capture."[16]

Despite the popular perception that moonshining was predominantly a western North Carolina problem, by the 1890s it had become common in all parts of the state. In 1901 the *Biblical Recorder*, the official organ of the North Carolina Baptist Convention, praised the growing "temperance sentiment" in western North Carolina but claimed there were "as many moonshine distilleries in Central Carolina as there are in the West and more drunkenness." The *Recorder* went on to argue that moonshining was not "the peculiar curse of the mountains" but a problem "rather more peculiar to the balance of the State."[17]

While the production of blockade liquor was common throughout the state, by the late nineteenth century some counties and communities had earned reputations as moonshine "hotspots," where the business permeated the local culture and economy. Joseph Dabney asserted that many of "these areas had a lot in common—a longtime liquor-making tradition, a lack of economic opportunity, and a location relatively near metropolitan centers where booze could be marketed easily and profitably." He added that most also had a "wild and wooly terrain, and isolation that afforded maximum security from prying federal eyes." This, of course, described much of North Carolina in the late nineteenth century. But locations with close proximity to the growing Piedmont mill towns or near timber camps in the east and west with large populations of young men became especially prominent in the illegal business in the late nineteenth century.[18]

Many of these "moonshine counties" were in the western part of the state and received significant attention from the national media during the Moonshine War and from the local-color literary movement, which depicted moonshining as an essential component of mountain people's "peculiar" culture. From an early date, the press prominently featured Wilkes County in discussions of North Carolina moonshine. A *Charlotte Observer* reporter commented in 1880 that "the [federal revenue] officers say they have more difficulty with Wilkes than any other county. The whiskey business is a very large interest in that region, and the opportunities for concealment in the fastnesses of the mountains are better than in almost any other county where the business of distilling is carried on to any great extent."[19] At least as early as 1893, newspapers commonly referred to the county as the "State of Wilkes" due to its reputation for defiance of federal revenue laws, a name that still crops up on occasion.[20]

The South Mountains of Burke County probably ran a close second to Wilkes in terms of moonshining reputation. Well-known characters such as Jake Mull kept the area in the news. The Morganton *Blue Ridge Blade* commented in an 1880 article, "The Mulls of the South Mountains are the most notorious blockaders in all the West. It is said they are quite wealthy, and a story is told that some time ago, just after Jake had served a term of eighteen months in the Albany penitentiary, he returned home and telling his brother that he wanted some money, they went to a hiding place near the house and tearing up an old plank, drew out $4000 in cash."[21] The *Lenoir Topic* described a White House reception given by President Rutherford B. Hayes where "diamonds were as plentiful as blockade whiskey in the South Mountains."[22]

While Wilkes and Burke consistently held the top positions in the west, almost every other county in the region had its claim to moonshine fame. In 1894, the *Marion Record* asserted that "Mitchell and Cherokee counties seem to be striving for the championship in the 'moonshine' or blockade business."[23] During the 1890s Henderson, Transylvania, Rutherford (home of Amos Owens),

Polk, and Jackson Counties and the Shakerag and Shelton Laurel sections of Madison County drew significant attention from both the press and law enforcement.[24]

While the mountains of North Carolina often drew the appellation of the "moonshine district," the Piedmont did not lag far behind. Lincoln County had a long tradition in the production of legal liquor and became a leading Piedmont producer of moonshine in the late nineteenth century. In 1883, the *Charlotte Observer* commented on the passing of Rufus Hovis, one of the county's leading citizens: "Hovis was in some respects a remarkable man. He could outwit the Revenue men better and dispose of more blockade whiskey, without punishment, than any other man that ever sucked a syphon. He had a genial, jovial disposition and had many friends."[25] In the 1880s neighboring Gaston County had a reputation as a place "where the blockade whiskey industry is carried on and seems to flourish in spite of the vigilance of the officers."[26] The moonshine business seems to have declined there in the ensuing decade, however, as more and more cotton mills came to the area. The 1890s saw a surge in moonshining in Chatham and Moore Counties. In 1895, the Raleigh *News and Observer* referred to these counties as a "regular moonshine nest."[27] The *Wilmington Morning Star* commented in the same year, "The farmers of Chatham raised so much corn last year they were compelled to turn it into whiskey to get clear of it. But Moore county is not far behind her neighbor in the moonshine business. We hear of stills being cut up in some part of the county nearly every week."[28] The Raleigh *Morning Post* referred to the "Hunt's Old Field" section of Durham County as a "locality which has much enlarged the docket of the United States court in recent years."[29]

Near the end of the century Stokes County probably became the most notorious moonshine haven in the Piedmont region, the home of legendary moonshiners Jim Taylor and Bill Smith. Taylor became notorious for a shootout with revenue officers at a church meeting in 1897. Smith was a leader of a community known as "Smith country," where his family members operated a moonshine empire. The *Tobacco Plant* asserted in 1889 that "perhaps no county in the State has as many illicit distilleries as Stokes. This is one of the chief industries and many good citizens are in sympathy with them."[30] In 1891 a "war" broke out in Stokes and nearby Surry County when the Smiths were implicated in the murder of revenue agents R. J. Boswell and S. G. Brim in a shootout near Mount Airy. As the *Greensboro Telegram* observed, "The Smith country ranks along with Shelton Laurel in Madison County as being the most fertile moonshine territory in the State. There are many stills there. They mock the olfactories of the raider on every breeze. And there is menace and danger in their breath."[31]

By the 1890s, the Coastal Plain and Tidewater regions also had a significant share of illegal liquor hotspots. In 1896, the *Wilmington Messenger* quoted a

Revenue Collector Simmons as averring, "There is more illicit distillation in the eastern section than heretofore." Simmons attributed this growth to the migration of tobacco farmers from the Piedmont who "have carried with them the knowledge of making moonshine whiskey." There is plenty of evidence, however, that easterners, particularly among former African American slaves who had learned distilling on plantations and the Lumbee who distilled as part of their subsistence activities, had long liquor-making traditions of their own.[32] The *New Berne Weekly* pointed to Richmond and Rockingham Counties as moonshining hotbeds in 1895: "Since January 1st no less than ninety-four illicit distilleries have been seized in this district.... It is a record breaking array of seizures within so short a period."[33] The *Wilmington Messenger* noted the large number of boats seized on the Roanoke River "loaded with moonshine brandy" in 1891.[34] During the same period authorities cited Dare and Pender Counties for large-scale illegal liquor operations.[35] The press also prominently mentioned Cumberland County as a moonshine hotbed. The *Fayetteville Observer* named the Scuffletown section of the county, the very heart of Lumbee territory, as "a place of moonshine stills and desperate characters."[36]

As moonshining became more and more common across the state, the business transcended racial and gender lines. As the *Charlotte Observer* noted in 1895, "There are black and white moonshiners and some female ones."[37] To be sure, since moonshining served as the poor person's hedge in times of economic uncertainty, it is not surprising that poor people across the racial spectrum turned to distilling illegal liquor in the late nineteenth century. The *Observer* could also have added Native Americans to the list, particularly the Lumbee and Tuscarora of southeast North Carolina. All of these groups tapped into long traditions of liquor making to help them survive at a time when life on the farm became increasingly difficult.

In the late nineteenth century, while many middle-class women in North Carolina flocked to the causes of temperance and prohibition, poor women in larger numbers had at least some involvement in the blockade liquor business. Some observers depicted women involved in the moonshine business in a similarly negative light as male moonshiners. In 1895 the *Charlotte Observer* claimed, "The latter are gaudy as to dress, and they incline to bright greens in dresses, with big poke bonnets, which enshroud their homely and weather-beaten faces, while the inevitable snuff-brush is another mark."[38] But for the most part, women moonshiners appeared as either sympathetic figures or intriguing exotics.

During this period, it became common in many areas for women to operate illegal liquor houses serving liquor by the shot, generally out of their home. In rural areas and in poor urban neighborhoods in North Carolina, it was generally acceptable for widows and women abandoned by their husbands to run

Women and girls often helped out at family stills or acted as lookouts and warned blockaders of approaching strangers. (Courtesy of Great Smoky Mountains National Park Archives, National Park Service Collections Preservation Center, Townsend, Tenn.)

such establishments. Women liquor house proprietors also took advantage of a patriarchal legal system and a jail and prison system that had few facilities for women, where judges and juries often either acquitted them or suspended their sentences, especially if they had small children. Liquor houses, in many ways, operated as a social safety mechanism in these communities, providing for the needs of women without male providers and at the same time providing a "service" to the community.

One of the most notable cases of such behavior occurred in Robeson County in 1897, when federal agents arrested Rhoda Lowry for "retailing liquor without a license." Lowry was the widow of Lumbee Indian freedom fighter and outlaw Henry Berry Lowry, who disappeared, and reportedly died, in 1872. Left with three small children, Lowry evidently supplemented her farm income by retailing illegal liquor, much of it probably made by her late husband's associates, the Swamp Angels, who distilled blockade liquor in the swamps of southeast North Carolina. Like many women, Lowry drew sympathy from the court due to a purported illness and was "stricken out" of the local jail before she completed her thirty-day sentence.[39]

Newspapers frequently reported on women arrested for "retailing without a license" in the late nineteenth century. Authorities arrested Rosa Hopson of House Creek Township in Wake County, a divorcee, in 1899. She defended herself to a federal judge by challenging the character of her accusers, whom the judge had referred to as "respectable citizens": "Respectable! If one respectable man will swear he's bought liquor from me I'll submit." She continued that she

The Moonshiner's Daughter, *1901. On occasion, young women took up arms in defense of male moonshining kin or in defense of their own stills. (Library of Congress)*

Rhoda Strong Lowry N.C. Moonshine Hall of Famer

Rhoda Lowry appears very briefly in the historical record, but she symbolizes and represents a number of important themes crucial to understanding moonshine's significance in North Carolina history. Lowry lived in Robeson County and was a legendary Lumbee beauty who married the infamous outlaw and famous freedom fighter Henry Berry Lowry in 1865. When Henry disappeared in 1872 (most accounts say he accidentally shot himself, but some reports have him living in the shadows for years afterward), Lowry was left to provide for herself and three small children. She eked out an existence on the family farm, but recent evidence uncovered by historian Malinda Maynor Lowery and her students reveals that in November 1897, authorities arrested Lowry for "retailing liquor without a license." Convicted in federal court, the judge fined her $100 and sentenced her to thirty days in jail. Less than a month later, the *Wilmington Morning Star* reported that the judgment against her was "stricken out," as the judge deemed her "very sick and her condition is such that she ought not to be confined to prison." Lowry, however, survived the experience and lived another ten years.

Despite this somewhat limited biography, Lowry's story tells us a great deal about moonshine in the eastern North Carolina Coastal Plain, moonshine among the Lumbee Indians, and most important, the significant role that illegal liquor played in the lives of many North Carolina women. While most books on moonshine focus on western North Carolina, blockade liquor was as common in the Piedmont, the Coastal Plain, and the Tidewater as it was in the mountains. In particular, Robeson County possessed many of the same qualities that made moonshining in the western part of the state so prevalent. Its people were relatively poor and desperately needed to find ways to supplement their income. The isolated nature of the county with its swamps and backwoods also provided plenty of spaces to hide stills from authorities. Indeed, Robeson County has long been known as one of North Carolina's moonshine capitals. In 1934, a reporter for the *Statesville Daily Record* commented that Robeson County sheriff Pat Kornegay had busted 607 stills in the county in only three and a half years. The reporter further asserted that while Wilkes County "has maintained the reputation of outstanding leadership [in the moonshine business]," the title of moonshine capital "now apparently has been shifted to the east [to Robeson County]."

Since before the passage of the federal excise tax in 1862, whiskey making had been important among the Lumbee Indians. Given their relative poverty and the fact that civil authorities actively discriminated against them, the Lumbee had much need to supplement their income and little incentive, or inclination, to obey the law, whether it be federal, state, or local. The *Raleigh Signal* reported in 1889 that remnants of Henry Berry Lowry's outlaw gang, known as the Swamp Angels, "have since [the death or disappearance of their leader] given the revenue officials a world of trouble over moonshine whiskey." Whether Rhoda Lowry was working in cooperation with some of the Swamp Angels in her moonshine-retailing business is not known, but it does not take a stretch of the imagination to think that she probably was.

Moonshining remained common among the Lumbee well into the 1960s and 1970s, and Robeson County had a reputation as one of North Carolina's leading illegal liquor hotbeds throughout much of the twentieth century.

Perhaps most importantly, Rhoda Lowry represents thousands of North Carolina women who participated actively in the illegal liquor business. She exemplifies one of the prime reasons women made and sold moonshine: the lack of a male provider. Lowry made and sold liquor because she needed to piece together a way to support herself and her children in the absence of any sort of public assistance. In many poorer communities, making and selling liquor was a perfectly acceptable way for widows, and abandoned or abused women, to make a living. The historical record contains many examples where Lumbee women used their homes as so-called liquor houses, selling illegal alcohol by the shot.

Lowry's example also provides insight into the benefits for women working in this illegal business. As women were the so-called weaker sex, judges and juries often treated them more leniently, especially if they had small children or became ill. In fact, since towns, counties, states, and even the federal government generally lacked appropriate facilities for incarcerating women in the late nineteenth and early twentieth centuries, they often let them go with a promise to stop making or selling liquor. Whether Lowry stopped selling liquor after her conviction is hard to say, but she gives us an early example of the important, and growing, role of women in the moonshine business.

sold "commodities" to people and that she "always gave her customers a drink when they wanted it," but she did not sell it. The judge did not buy her story, however, and sent her to jail to await trial.[40] Frances Green Dillon of Granville County came off better when agents hauled her before a judge in 1897 for retailing. While the judge found her guilty, he suspended her sentence and sent her home with a simple reprimand "to return to her husband and lead a better life."[41]

Women often played other important roles in the moonshine business in the late nineteenth century as well. Wives and daughters served as lookouts and sounded alerts when revenue officers approached an operating still. The *Raleigh Observer* reported an incident on the McDowell-Rutherford county line in 1878 when a group of officers went out on a raid. As they passed a house, a woman appeared on the porch "and began a most vigorous blowing of a dinner horn." She refused their orders to "desist," and by the time they arrived at a distillery "in full blast," the moonshiner was long gone.[42]

Other women became even more active in trying to prevent their husbands', fathers', or brothers' arrests. A Mrs. Sudderth of Caldwell County, described by the *Morganton Herald* as a "broad shouldered, powerful woman," followed along as her husband, Kelly, and his captors headed to the local jail. When

Kelly escaped and bolted for a rhododendron thicket, Mrs. Sudderth "sprang at [Deputy Collector] Deal like a tigress, and hurled him to the ground." Kelly escaped and responded to a command to "halt" from the thicket by inviting Deal "to visit a country where the moonshiners suppose that all good revenue officers go." Mrs. Sudderth calmly "bade the officers farewell" and headed back home.[43] A seventeen-year-old Wake County woman took even more drastic action when she took a gun and "drew a bead in the head of a deputy" who attempted to serve a warrant for illegal distilling on her brother-in-law. Fortunately for the deputy, the brother-in-law disarmed her. Asked later if she would have actually fired, she responded, "Would I have shot him?" The reporter covering the story for the Raleigh *Morning Post* interpreted her "demure" response by asserting that "the very tone of her voice explained more eloquently than words could have done, how very certain she would have been to do it."[44]

While rarer than accounts of retailing, warning, or defending, cases of women actually making blockade liquor were not uncommon during the period as well. Revenue officers arrested a young woman in Stokes County in 1890 who admitted her crime but, like many men, claimed it was a matter of economic emergency and that "she intended to make a run in order to pay a debt."[45] Distilling illegal liquor was not just an enterprise for young women, however. Officers in Clay County arrested an "old woman making moonshine whiskey" in 1898. "The skirted 'chemist' insisted she was doing no harm," although she did admit to violating her religious principles by "breaking the Sabbath" and making liquor on Sunday.[46]

On occasion, women fought it out with revenue agents when caught in the act of making blockade liquor. In 1895, a group of federal marshals staked out a still and "laid in wait for the moonshiners." The appearance of a woman, Lalalla Thomas, coming to fire up the still early in the morning shocked the agents. Thomas did not initially resist arrest, but she "looked so sad and forlorn and wept so bitterly that the officer who held her, released his hold." Thomas then "sprang into the breach with a wonderful display of temper and determination," grabbed an axe, swung it at the deputy, and as he stood there "dazed," grabbed the still cap and "dived into a marshy marsh." Officers eventually tracked her down and hauled her off to the Sanford jail while she loudly complained, "I don't see what you bothered us for when there's a still so much more convenient to the railroad."[47]

As the case of Rhoda Lowry illustrates, Native Americans in North Carolina actively participated in the moonshine business. The Lumbee and Tuscarora of southeastern North Carolina, primarily in Robeson County, had a longtime tradition of making liquor. Indeed, whiskey making had deep roots in this region, brought by the Highland Scots who emigrated to the area in the 1740s and 1750s. In addition, moonshine making had evolved as part of resistance to

*Newspaper ad for Moonshine Tobacco. (*News and Observer*, 31 December 1915)*

discriminatory practices instituted by white authorities. Indeed, the Lumbee and Tuscarora had even longer traditions of making liquor illegally than white moonshiners, as the North Carolina General Assembly had banned "free people of color" from making and selling liquor in 1825 and again in 1840. Sponsors of the bills argued that alcohol only exacerbated the freedmen's "generally indolent, roguish, improvident, and dissipated" state. In the late nineteenth century, moonshining became linked to the outlaw activities and resistance to local white authority associated with Henry Berry Lowry and the so-called Lowry Gang. Aside from the political and cultural overtones among the Native population of southeast North Carolina, moonshining filled an important economic niche in an area, and era, where many farmers struggled to subsist and in a social environment rife with racial discrimination. As historian Malinda Maynor Lowery observed, "Lumbees lived within an economy largely controlled by outsiders' interests, and throughout the South, race limited economic opportunities. . . . Farming and education generated both self-sufficiency and inequality; Indians often tried to mitigate this irony by participating in the black-market economy, which offered more economic independence but entailed its own dangers." Of course, the most common "black market" activity in the region was making moonshine.[48]

As moonshining became more common in eastern North Carolina, African Americans also became more involved in the illegal business. There is little information on liquor-making traditions among the state's African Americans, but the commonality of distilleries employing slave labor on plantations indicates that there were probably many former slaves who had both experience and knowledge in making corn liquor. Most accounts of African American involvement in moonshining indicate that blacks involved in the business generally operated stills owned by whites, apparently in a sharecropper sort of arrangement, where the still hands received a share of the profits.

As the moonshine business became normalized, spread to all sections of North Carolina, and became common across demographic lines, it also became an important part of the cultural image of the state and of many counties, cities, and towns. One of the most popular brands of chewing tobacco in the state was Moonshine Tobacco, one of whose ads read, "You can tell better yarns if you have a chew of Moonshine Tobacco in the south corner of your mouth."[49] Ashevillians especially embraced moonshine as part of the city's branding. When city leaders formed a professional baseball team in 1894, the owners named them the Asheville Moonshiners, a moniker that stuck through the 1890s and that the current Asheville team, the Tourists, has recently reintroduced in the guise of its mascot, Mr. Moon.[50]

Even as the illegal liquor business thrived, however, homegrown prohibition forces began to step in where the federal government had failed, to stem the flood of moonshine inundating the state. In an amazingly short period of time, a movement largely begun in North Carolina's evangelical churches transformed the state politically, socially, and culturally. The goal of the prohibitionists was to eliminate alcoholic beverages in the state altogether and in the process consign the North Carolina moonshiner to the extinction faced in the same era by the passenger pigeon, the gray wolf, the panther, and the Carolina parakeet.

A "DRY" STATE

Ironically, much of the credit for the moonshine business becoming such an established part of North Carolina life in the twentieth century can be attributed to the attempts to curtail, and even totally eliminate, liquor production, both legal and illegal, and consumption. The religious, political, and social movement to prohibit the production, distribution, and sale of alcohol is one of the most amazing in American history. That movement transformed a nation once characterized as the "alcoholic republic" in the not-too-distant past into one that passed a constitutional amendment prohibiting the production and sale of alcohol, and North Carolina led the way.[1]

While several factors gave rise to prohibition, and in recent years historians have pointed to numerous causes as significant, there is no doubt that religious organizations led the way in North Carolina. In 1872, temperance leader Dr. J. F. Foard expressed his view on the dangers of alcohol: "What is to be the future condition of a people, who exhaust their talents, energies, lands and strength in producing an article to make drunkards of their sons, widows of their daughters, orphans of posterity, to fill jails with culprits, penitentiaries with paupers, hospitals with patients, society with wrecks, the church with hypocrites, the world with misery, the grave-yard with the slain, and hell with immortal souls for whom Christ died."[2] Foard's view that alcohol was the root of most of society's problems and a sure ticket to hell was a decidedly minority one in 1872. However, by the turn of the century the largest organized Protestant denominations in the state endorsed the cause, and a majority of churchgoers embraced it as well, at least on the surface. This dramatic revolution in religious viewpoint provided unprecedented, and almost unstoppable, momentum in turning North Carolina into a dry state.

This transformation was all the more dramatic given the deeply engrained status of both alcohol production (including the illegal variety) and consumption, even among the staunchest church members. As late as the 1890s, most church people in North Carolina agreed with the former moonshiner who was asked by a *Charlotte Observer* reporter if he thought it was wrong to make moonshine. The man responded by pointing to his Bible lying nearby and asserted, "Well, I have read that good book, and I never found anything in it against making moonshine whiskey."[3] Indeed, church leaders struggled throughout the period to combat this viewpoint and turn their churches and denominations into havens of teetotalism, often with limited success, especially in the state's more rural sections.

While many pastors preached temperance to their congregations during the period, they also understood alcohol's deep-seated position in North Carolina culture and the important economic role making liquor, legally or illegally, played in the lives of their parishioners. Indeed, churches often had unexpected connections to the liquor business. The *Charlotte Observer* noted the testimony of a federal revenue officer who told the story of a raid in a community that had four reported illegal distilleries. When officers came upon the first still and proceeded to cut it up, the owner ran to a nearby church and "began to ring the bell with all his might." He kept on ringing it until he heard pistol shots from the three other stills indicating their owners had gotten away with the most valuable parts of their liquor-making apparatus. Officers arrived to find only smoldering fires and empty furnaces. As the *Observer* reported, "This was one time the church bell was made an instrument of the devil."[4]

Involvement in even the illegal side of the liquor business did not disqualify one from being a member in good standing in many rural churches. An oft-recorded, and probably apocryphal, story in the *Asheville Citizen*, as told by a Tryon revenue officer, tells of a man going to a known liquor house to make a purchase. When he heard voices inside the house he decided the "signs were not right for his purchase" and left empty-handed. The next day the man ran into the moonshiner, who asked him why he had left. When the man told him, he responded, "Oh, we were only holding prayer, and I couldn't stop praying to sell you whiskey."[5]

For many churches, the tithes and offerings of their liquor-making congregants were crucial to keeping buildings in repair and in operation. Rev. Tom Jimison, who had a four-point circuit in the Mount Airy area, told the Lexington *Dispatch* a story about a painter who had borrowed some money from a local bank to purchase paint to spruce up the church. When the church was not able to come up with the money, Jimison went with the painter to ask for an extension on the payment. Jimison explained the situation to the banker: "Tell you how it is, you see the blamed revenue officers went up there and tore up a moonshine still within about 100 yards of the church, and since then these folks haven't paid [their tithes and offerings] worth a cent. It is about time for them to have another one fixed up, so they'll come across with the pay pretty soon."[6] The banker, knowing the area well, did not hesitate to allow the extension. Popcorn Sutton told the story that his grandfather "Little" Mitch Sutton used money he received from a run of liquor to purchase materials to construct the first Baptist church in the Hemphill area of Haywood County.[7]

The *News and Observer* reported in 1897 one of the most notorious incidents involving moonshine in the late nineteenth century. The episode revolved around a Baptist associational meeting in Stokes County and noted moonshiner Jim Taylor. When the Treasury Department appointed George Preddy deputy marshal in the county, he publicly announced that he had five warrants for Taylor's arrest and intended to bring the outlaw, who "openly ran a moonshine corn juicer," to justice. Preddy got word that Taylor planned to attend the annual meeting of the Pilot Mountain Baptist Association, dragooned two other revenue agents to accompany him, and headed for the meeting at the Oak Ridge Baptist Church. Near the end of the service, Taylor somehow got wind of Preddy's plan to arrest him, grabbed his wife, headed out the back door of the church, and jumped in his buggy. At about that time, the deputy marshal arrived and commanded Taylor to halt and submit to arrest. Taylor jumped from his buggy, pistol in hand, but Preddy got the drop on him and shot him through his gun hand, grazing Taylor's wife in the process.[8]

Taylor reportedly fought with the officers for ten minutes before officers finally subdued and hog-tied him for transport to the Danbury jail. At one point in the midst of the melee, Preddy reportedly pulled his pistol and yelled out, "Jim Taylor damn you, you have done enough to justify me killing you and I'm going to do it. Stand back!" Fortunately for Taylor someone grabbed Preddy's arm before he could follow through with his threat. Of course, by this point the church had emptied and "the tumult of the crowd present made a scene of great excitement lasting over an hour." The Reverend John E. White, secretary of the Baptist Home Mission Board, who preached at the meeting, told reporters that he saw four guns pulled in the crowd. "I do not know for whom they were drawn, though the sympathy of the crowd was decidedly in Taylor's favor, except among the very best people." White later quipped that in his long experience as a preacher, "I have often had my meetings close with shouting but never with a shooting."[9]

While White made it clear that his sentiments were not with the moonshiner, such was not always the case with preachers who both defended illegal distilling and participated in it themselves. In 1908, even as a prohibition referendum was about to pass in the state, Rev. S. M. McCall of Caldwell County publicly announced his opposition to the measure and argued that Jesus was a distiller who turned water into wine. He predicted dire consequences for Christians not following the dictates of the Bible: "If those interested in the effort to establish

Prohibition prove to the satisfaction of the American people that Christ committed a sin, and that Christ set a bad example to future generations then we fear they will have succeeded in destroying the very foundation of the Christian faith."[10]

Newspapers were replete with accounts of the arrests of pastors and church leaders for making moonshine. In 1895, a *New York Sun* article reported Rev. Baylus Hamrick's capture. The *Sun* noted that the pastor from Burke County's South Mountains, a notorious moonshiner's haven, "is sixty years of age, and stands high in his church and with the mountaineers generally." Commenting on his arrest, Hamrick averred, "I escaped the revenue officers for a long time, though didn't I?" He claimed he only got caught because revenue officer Tom Vanderford was "breaking the Sabbath day by shooting at ducks on the creek at the back of my house." The "huskings" of Hamrick's still slops floating in the creek tipped Vanderford off to the location of the preacher's illegal distillery.[11] Johnston County authorities caught the Reverend John Wells, a Free Will Baptist preacher whom officers called "the busiest stiller you ever saw," in 1899.[12] Revenue collectors also captured the superintendent of a local Presbyterian Sunday school with "an illicit distillery and a large quantity of 'blockade whiskey'" that same year.[13]

In 1899, Primitive Baptist church leader Joseph H. Creeh drew the ire of a Raleigh *Morning Post* reporter when authorities caught him distilling "liquid damnation." The *Post* reporter took the church clerk to task for his hypocrisy, calling him the "greatest 'professional Christian' in the county—the clerk of the church in which he has long passed as the goody-goody 'amen brother' not second even to the pastor in his outward show of the pious life which he really did not live."[14]

The deep-seated pro-liquor position among many of their congregants didn't deter church leaders, however, and as early as the 1870s they began demanding action from their legislators to at least curb production and consumption, especially in public saloons. In 1874, the General Assembly responded to this pressure and established the first local-option laws in the state. The law allowed a township to call a referendum on prohibiting the sale and production of alcohol within its corporate limits if one-quarter of its voters signed a petition. Holding altar calls to encourage and pressure congregants to sign such petitions soon became a staple of church meetings in many North Carolina churches, especially among Methodists and Baptists.[15] In 1879, the town of Dallas in Gaston County, a county with fifty-five legal distilleries and countless moonshine stills, drew praise from the *Raleigh News* for its approval of a local-option bill: "But notwithstanding the fact that the whiskey business is just now the chief source of revenue to the country, the pretty little village of Dallas is protected by the vote of two-thirds of its people against the sale of intoxicating drink—a rather

Baptists and Booze

As the son of a Southern Baptist minister and a Baptist myself for most of my life (I have very recently strayed over to the Presbyterians), I have often pondered the rather complicated relationship between Baptists and alcohol. On the surface, and in most people's view, Baptists are teetotalers, totally opposed to alcohol consumption in any shape, form, or fashion. Indeed, historically Baptists led the way in North Carolina in the temperance movement, then the movement for statewide prohibition, and after the end of prohibition, the maintenance of dry counties. But as both a longtime observer of Baptist life and a historian, I know both doctrine and practice among Baptists are much more diverse and complicated than that.

First, there are Baptists and there are Baptists. As most folks who can read a church sign, and who have driven around North Carolina, realize, there are a number of Baptist denominations. Southern Baptists are the largest, but the state contains countless congregations of Independent Pre-Millennial Baptists, Missionary Baptists, Free Will Baptists, Regular Baptists, Separate Baptists, Two-Seed in the Spirit Predestinarian Baptists, and Primitive Baptists, just to name a few. Some of those groups take a more, shall we say, biblical approach to alcohol, particularly the Primitives, who have always taken communion with real wine. Charles Thompson's fine book *The Spirits of Just Men* does an excellent job exploring Primitive Baptists' more tolerant views on alcohol.

There is also a real divide between rural and urban Baptist churches. In the late nineteenth and early twentieth centuries, urban and town Baptists, especially Southern Baptists, led the way in first taking their churches into teetotalism and then leading their communities and the state into prohibition. The state's influential Southern Baptist newspaper, the *Biblical Recorder*, has long been a leading voice for prohibition. It's pretty amazing to note the passionate rhetoric of many Baptists who see alcohol as the proverbial "root of all evil" and a "sure ticket to hell and damnation." This despite the fact that people in the Bible, including Jesus himself, drank lots of wine. Somehow, many Baptists convinced themselves that the Bible condemned all alcohol. My father wanted to believe this, but he learned enough Greek in seminary to not push the issue that far, although his sons, and his church, understood that he firmly believed teetotalism was the only way to go.

While Baptists have historically rejected creeds—"We have no creed but Christ"—many Baptist churches in North Carolina adopted something called the Church Covenant. The covenant is a set of principles and behaviors expected of church members, written by New England minister J. Newton Brown in 1853 and often read responsively at Communion. The covenant includes a pledge to "abstain from the sale and use of intoxicating drinks as a beverage." While North Carolina Baptists were reluctant to give up their liquor in the antebellum period, the covenant became common in many Baptist churches in connection with the temperance and prohibition movements around the turn of the twentieth century.

Rural Baptist pastors, however, realized that many of the people in their congregations were dependent on the income moonshine brought them to keep body and soul together. Indeed, in these areas of North Carolina, many a church was built, pastor paid, building maintained, and hymnbooks purchased with the proceeds from illegal liquor. Popcorn Sutton's grandfather purchased materials to build the first Baptist church in the Hemphill area of Haywood County. Percy Flowers generously supported the White Oak Baptist Church in rural Johnston County. Pastors of such churches knew that if they harped too much on the "evils of drink," many in the congregation would think the pastor had moved from preaching to "meddling" in an area where he had no business. Founder of the Crossnore School and antiliquor activist Mary Sloop argued that such alcohol-tolerant religion was "all wrong." "It is the sort of religion that allows a man to make moonshine whiskey and drink all week and then go to church on Sunday and lead in prayer."

In addition, the moonshiners knew that their pastors could be counted on to testify to their fine character if authorities hauled them into court. Percy Flowers's pastor, Rev. A. D. Parrish, testified on the moonshine kingpin's behalf on several occasions. An editorial in the *Robesonian* in 1968 criticized a pair of local pastors for writing letters to the court testifying to the good character of an alleged bootlegger in 1968. The editorial pointed out the hypocrisy of the ministers, arguing that if a local option vote came up in the county these same ministers "would scream out against legal alcohol."

There was still another divide among North Carolina Baptists, between members who stuck to their covenant pledge and those with a tendency to secretly backslide. This divide has prompted a number of jokes over the years:

> Why do you always take two Baptists with you when you go fishing?
> If you only take one, they will drink all your beer.

Folks also referred to a condition called "Baptist blindness," which befell Baptists when they encountered, and totally ignored, a fellow church member at a bootlegging joint or liquor store. When the group of boys I grew up with came to realize the existence of this divide, we would glance around the sanctuary during the reading of the Church Covenant to see who was either mouthing the words or omitting them altogether.

Even after the end of national Prohibition, Baptists led the way in trying to keep liquor out of their communities. Indeed, whenever a local-option referendum came up on allowing Alcohol Beverage Control liquor stores in their county or municipality, local town Baptists and local moonshiners could be counted on to make sure they stayed legally "dry." While things have changed somewhat in recent years and many Baptists have become more tolerant of alcohol, teetotalism is still the default position for many more conservative North Carolina Baptists. Indeed, the legacy of the temperance and prohibition movements in the state retains a significant influence among Baptists.

1874 temperance poster highlighting the role of women in the campaign against liquor. (Library of Congress)

singular circumstance it would seem, and yet greatly to the credit of the citizens."[16] In 1881, the General Assembly expanded the power to call local-option referenda and allowed whole counties the same privilege as townships.[17]

Heartened by the success of local option, church leaders began to push for statewide prohibition. Most dramatically, the two most important religious organizations in the state called on the General Assembly to pass such a law. In 1879, the General Conference of the Methodist Episcopal Church, South, led the way with a resolution calling on the newly elected legislature to "take into consideration the propriety of enacting a general prohibitory liquor law." In 1880, the North Carolina Baptist State Convention passed a similar resolution, instructing its board of missions "to memorialize the next Legislature of North Carolina to pass a law to prohibit the making and selling of spirituous or malt liquors within the bounds of the State of North Carolina." In an additional resolution in 1880, the Methodists called liquor an "incubus" and argued that the sale of liquor "is not, in any sense, necessary to the well-being of society, but on the contrary, productive of a great deal of moral and social evil; educating the youth of our land down to drunkenness and other vices; producing poverty and crime throughout the country and such moral obliquity as greatly retards the cause of Christ."[18]

In January 1881, denominational leaders demonstrated rare unity when over 300 delegates gathered in Raleigh for a prohibition convention to pressure the legislature. Statewide leaders from the most influential Methodist, Baptist, Presbyterian, and even Episcopal organizations and politicians, including judge and Republican leader Augustus Merrimon, gathered to demand action from the legislature. The *Farmer and Mechanic* praised the "cordial coaction of discordant denominational elements" who came together to publicly roll "the popular wheel towards the State House door!"[19]

Although both political parties feared the divisive nature of the liquor issue, the flood of petitions and the pressure from religious leaders forced them to act in 1881. Most politicians of the era probably agreed with Democratic Party leader Zeb Vance's sentiments. Senator Vance reportedly quipped to a woman who accosted him and begged him to support prohibition, "My dear madam, my heart is with you, but my stomach is against you."[20] Loath to cast a vote directly on the liquor question, the legislature decided to call a statewide referendum on 4 August. While the forces for prohibition had a lot of momentum at the time, they faced an uphill challenge, especially as legal liquor producers and sellers fervently defended their industry. In June, representatives of North Carolina's legal alcohol industry met in Raleigh and raised considerable funds for a statewide anti-prohibition campaign, arguing that prohibition would "destroy one of the great industries of the state." In particularly ironic wording, the convention passed a resolution asserting that prohibition "was destructive to the moral, social, and material progress of the people."[21]

On election day, it soon became apparent that the forces for prohibition had much work to do, as voters soundly defeated the resolution 166,325–48,370. Breathing a sigh of relief, both political parties came to rare agreement and called for "letting the people decide." Both parties threw their active support behind local option as a way to blunt the growing calls for the creation of a Prohibition Party. As the *Wilson Advance* reported in 1888, "The old political parties ... have a chance to take the wind out of the sails of the third-party movement by voting for local option. This they can do without interfering with their old party relations."[22]

While the North Carolina Baptist Convention avidly supported the statewide prohibition referendum in 1881, after its decisive defeat the denomination struggled to find consensus on the issue. Speaking on this period, the historian of the South Fork Baptist Association asserted, "The temperance question has caused more heated or intemperate speaking and more divisions and animosities than any other question that has come before the Association." As historian Daniel Whitener observed, "From 1882 to 1900 no official action was taken by the Baptist State Convention on the subject of temperance; committee reports and recommendations which formerly had caused bitter discussions were now omitted."[23]

In 1894, the Brushy Mountain Baptist Association, which included Wilkes County, passed a resolution at its annual meeting calling on congregations to file a report to the group naming church members who either manufactured, sold, or consumed alcohol. The resolution required churches to dismiss such individuals from their congregations or risk being expelled from the association. However, association leaders had run far in front of their members, and most churches either ignored the resolution or put up active resistance. At its 1895 meeting the association voted just to "recommend ... Bible temperance."[24]

While much of the religious agitation died down in the 1880s and 1890s, legislators still could not ignore calls for more control of alcohol. In 1893, legislators passed a bill allowing for local-option laws outlawing liquor production near schools, churches, and businesses. In 1895, the legislature passed a bill allowing Haywood County to adopt a new local alcohol policy pioneered in South Carolina and championed by its governor, "Pitchfork" Ben Tillman: the dispensary. Dispensaries were government-chartered liquor stores that allowed no drinking on-site and were closed on Sunday. The idea appealed to some of the more moderate temperance advocates by eliminating saloons and public drinking while maintaining lucrative tax revenues that came from the legal manufacture and sale of alcohol.[25]

While local-option and dispensary laws did lead to a decline in legal liquor

Josiah W. Bailey, editor of the Biblical Recorder, *leader of the Anti-Saloon League, and later, a U.S. senator. He pushed for temperance but opposed prohibition. (Courtesy of State Archives of North Carolina, Raleigh, N.C.)*

production in the state, by the late 1890s church leaders saw these as half measures and began to push once again for outright prohibition. In 1896, Josiah W. Bailey, editor of the *Biblical Recorder*, the paper of the Baptist State Convention, boldly asserted that "no Christian can afford to vote for any man who drinks liquor, or who is not firmly opposed to the liquor traffic." Bailey became an important leader as the first head of the Anti-Saloon League in the state. The Methodists continued to take a hard public stand on the issue even after the referendum defeat in 1881, and their Committee on Temperance declared in 1890, "We are emphatically a prohibition church."[26] In 1900 the General Conference of the North Carolina Methodist Episcopal Church, South, the church's "highest legislative body," adopted a platform that forbade its members, on penalty of expulsion, from engaging "in the manufacture or sale of liquors" and called for church "punishment for drunkenness."[27]

Several other factors further emboldened the prohibitionists around the turn of the century, most notably the influx of national prohibition groups who brought a new level of organization, expertise, and political savvy to the effort. While the Women's Christian Temperance Union (WCTU) organized its first "unions" in the state in 1883, it experienced tremendous growth in the late 1890s and early 1900s. By 1903, the WCTU had enlisted over 3,000 women in its crusade for prohibition and had sixty-eight unions statewide. In 1907, legendary WCTU firebrand Carrie Nation came to Salisbury, which she consid-

Carrie Nation in North Carolina

Charlotte News cartoon welcoming Carrie Nation to Charlotte in 1907. (Charlotte News, *3 July 1907)*

In 1907—in the midst of intense debate over the future of legal alcohol production, saloons, local option, and statewide prohibition in North Carolina—noted Kansas prohibitionist and colorful, hatchet-wielding saloon smasher Carrie Nation visited Salisbury. She came to this town because of its reputation as a "hell hole" that contained numerous saloons and welcomed alcohol manufacturers. According to the *Charlotte News*, Nation's visit came as the result of a chance meeting with Salisbury alderman W. L. Heilig as she passed through North Carolina on a train in May 1907. The two struck up a conversation, and the feisty Nation, also an antitobacco activist, made "a vigorous attempt to knock a cigar from the alderman's mouth" even as she told Heilig she would come to his town.

Nation made good on her promise to visit Salisbury and arrived with much fanfare in late June 1907. When she arrived, she took a walking tour of the town, followed by a horde of newspaper reporters and townspeople, visiting four different saloons, although she evidently left her trademark hatchet at home. She made a typically brusque assessment of the town to the crowd: "It's a hell hole and I can see you have plenty of poverty, degradation and suffering in your midst." For Nation, the reason for that suffering was clear: "You have plenty of saloons and every one is a ticket office to hell." She even accosted a boy smoking a cigarette on the street and used the opportunity to rail against the evils of tobacco: "O, look at that boy smoking a cigarette. Ain't you ashamed of yourself? What makes you want to ruin your body and soul that way. Every time I see a tobacco leaf growing, I call upon God to blast it. I think it is worse than whisky and I think tobacco users will steal, lie and murder if they use it enough."

Nation stayed in the area for more than a week and gave several public talks, including one in nearby Charlotte, "in lurid castigation of makers, sellers, and consumers and sympathizers with whisky, tobacco and kindred narcotics and soporifics." In a speech in Salisbury on 29 June, before a large crowd, she condemned those who would make any accommodation with liquor, including those who only supported local option or dispensaries. She backed her position by creatively using the Bible: "God is a prohibitionist and there is nowhere in His word any dogma to support the whisky man's contention that his business must be regulated. We don't have laws to regulate crime, we prohibit them. The command 'Thou Shalt Not' came down from Sinai. And I am not a temperance worker as I am often represented. I am a prohibitionist and I believe the way to stamp out this curse is to wipe it out root and branch. Cut it off at the head. You don't kill a snake by lopping it off little by little, you smash its head at once."

While it is impossible to gauge the impact of Nation's visit in the state, increasingly North Carolina's antiliquor forces moved toward a strict prohibition position. They plunged ahead with a push for a statewide referendum, even when their radicalism alienated important allies who took the more moderate temperance position. Indeed, Josiah W. Bailey resigned as head of the state chapter of the Anti-Saloon League when his moderate views put him at odds with the new mainstream of antiliquor thought. Of course, the prohibition forces won a huge victory with an overwhelming majority in the May 1908 referendum, and North Carolina became legally dry for twenty-four years. Perhaps most important, the teetotal views of Carrie Nation came to dominate the thinking of many North Carolinians for generations to come, kept liquor illegal in much of the state well into the 1960s, and created a thriving market for moonshine.

ered a "hell hole" because of its many saloons, to rally her followers to call for outright prohibition of alcohol.

The most important national organization to come to the state, however, was the Anti-Saloon League. According to historian Daniel Whitener, the "impetus" for bringing the league to North Carolina "came from the Baptist State Convention in 1901." Further cementing the Baptist relationship to the organization, Josiah W. Bailey became the group's first executive secretary. While the initial push to bring the league to North Carolina originated with the Baptists, its organizational meetings featured strong Methodist input and also had representatives from the leading Presbyterian, Christian, and Friends church organizations. The league proved especially adept at understanding and negotiating North Carolina's political waters and used that skill in effectively promoting the prohibition cause.[28]

Economic, social, and political changes shaping North Carolina during this period also brought new and influential allies to the prohibition cause. By the turn of the century, the Piedmont of North Carolina rapidly transformed from an overwhelmingly rural and agricultural area to one dominated by cotton mills, furniture factories, and tobacco-manufacturing facilities. Mill and factory owners wanted sober, reliable, and industrious employees and welcomed the prohibition movement as they sought to keep liquor out of their production facilities and mill villages. S. B. Tanner recalled his frustrations with alcohol in the early days of building mills in Rutherford County: "When we built our mill villages, this vicinity was noted for its blockade distillers, and we had no end of trouble among our operatives, which interfered seriously with the running of our mills, and it was difficult for us to retain decent and respectable people at our mills, on account of rowdyism, midnight brawls, etc."[29] The *News and Observer* noted in 1908 that, with very few exceptions, "the successful manufacturers [in North Carolina] are strong advocates of temperance legislation." Indeed, counties crowded with cotton mills like Gaston and municipalities dominated by manufacturing like High Point were early local-option and dispensary adopters and employed every legal means to keep alcohol away from local workers.[30]

Increasingly, however, manufacturers looked to statewide prohibition as the answer to their problems. Johnston County mill owner Moses Winston testified before a state house committee looking into the prohibition issue in 1908. He challenged the legislators by passionately asserting, "Gentlemen, there is a liquor shop, a dispensary, two miles from Selma, and you must shut up that place or I must shut up my cotton mill. It is for you to say which you will encourage in North Carolina, liquor mills or cotton mills—the two cannot go together."[31]

Perhaps the most important change in making prohibition almost inevitable in North Carolina was the state's effective transformation into a one-party state dominated by the Democrats. Like the Democrats themselves, the prohibition cause gained a boost as it related to settling the so-called Negro question. Indeed, Democrats had often used the bugaboo of the dangers of the "drunken Negro" in their successful campaign to deny African Americans their political rights and maintain, and even expand, white supremacy. In 1907, the New York *Telegraph* asserted, "The states which have been his [the moonshiner's] stronghold are one after another going dry. They are discovering that the liquor question, in the rural districts at least is inextricably tangled with the negro problem. The country people are afraid of the drunken negro. The outrages which have aroused the entire South and resulted in lynchings innumerable have been traced to the mountain still. For it is there that the low negro dives get their supplies, and it is 'moonshine' that drives the vicious, loafing negro of the country districts mad."[32] Daniel Whitener claimed that many North Carolinians who "would have regarded prohibitory legislation as invading the field of their private rights" changed their minds and "lent hearty cooperation for prohibition to keep liquor away from the Negro."[33]

Prohibitionists became natural allies in the Democrats' disfranchisement campaign, as most believed that the African American vote provided the greatest impediment to ending the scourge of liquor. Indeed, the popular view among antiliquor forces was that the sound defeat of the 1881 referendum was due to the African American vote. In an 1881 article, the *Charlotte Observer* tied together the "drunken (and dangerous) negro" meme and the voting behavior of African Americans in an account of a Wadesboro anti-prohibition rally: "Yesterday a great multitude of negroes assembled at Wadesboro to hear their champions on anti-prohibition. . . . The surging masses of negroes were thoroughly around and further excited with whiskey. Just then some drunken negro had to be arrested by town officers. He resisted and was knocked down, whereupon the already maddened negroes set upon the officers crying 'Kill them! Kill them!' The officers fled for safety, followed by about 500 enraged negroes throwing stones, flourishing sticks and pistols, and making fearful threats."[34]

Prohibitionists hailed the passage of a state constitutional amendment in 1901, which effectively prevented almost all African Americans from voting in the state. In 1902, the *Biblical Recorder* asserted, "As was long hoped, the first fruits of disfranchisement of the negroes bids fair to be progress in legislation prohibiting saloons." Disfranchisement also provided prohibitionists with a great deal of political leverage. The threat that they would launch a Prohibition Party challenged the Democrats, who had just eliminated threats from both African Americans and Republicans to their one-party rule. Such a test of Democratic Party dominance came in 1902 when the Prohibition Party put up a statewide ticket and called on all supporters of prohibition to rally to its cause.[35]

Not surprisingly, the principal architects of the white supremacy campaign and one-party rule in the state—U.S. senator Furnifold Simmons, Governor Charles B. Aycock, and *News and Observer* owner and publisher Josephus Daniels—realized that the party could no longer be neutral on the liquor issue. In order to head off any serious threat from the Prohibition Party, or from a Republican Party that might beat them to the punch and endorse prohibition, they moved to place the Democratic Party firmly in the antiliquor camp. As Daniel Whitener observed, "Just having experienced a decade [the 1890s] of revolt, third partyism, and fusionism, these leaders of the Democratic party had no stomach to face a similar decade."[36]

With the weight of the Democratic Party machine now firmly in its camp, the state moved rapidly toward total prohibition. In 1903, Simmons and Aycock pushed through the so-called Watts Law, which forbade the sale or distillation of liquor outside of an incorporated town, dramatically reducing the number of saloons and distilleries in the state. The bill also led to a rise in the number of incorporated towns in the state that used local option to ban the sale, manufacture, or distribution of liquor. Indeed, by 1908, only twenty-eight of the state's counties had either a saloon or a distillery.[37]

Prohibition rally on a bridge over the French Broad River at Riverside Park. Men pour liquor into the river while a crowd, complete with ice-cream vendor, watches. (Courtesy of North Carolina Room, Pack Memorial Library, Asheville, N.C.)

Some Democratic Party leaders decried their party's position as a move toward tyranny. In 1907, state legislator Capt. Swift Galloway of Greene County stood on the house floor and declared that the liquor laws were the product of "an era of fanaticism upon this country that came with the epizootic, the grippe and hog cholera." Galloway blamed the Puritans and, confusing them with the Pilgrims, asserted that he wished "that instead of their landing on Plymouth Rock, Plymouth Rock had landed on them." He concluded his remarks lambasting enforcement of the new laws and the resultant loss of individual freedom: "I do not hesitate to say that if I lived in a community of free men who would submit to such tyranny, I should want to get an occasional furlough and get relief from outraged feelings by brief visits to hell."[38]

However, despite such eloquent and passionate opposition, by 1908, the Democratic Party, the Anti-Saloon League, and most Protestant denominations in the state saw the opportunity to deliver a death blow to legal liquor in the state. Momentum was so strong that even the Episcopal Diocese of North Carolina passed a resolution in support of statewide prohibition. In response to the popular outcry, the legislature approved a bill calling for a statewide referendum "to prohibit the manufacture and sale of intoxicating liquors in North Carolina" to be held on 26 May 1908. If the vote passed, North Carolina would become a dry state on 1 January 1909. Governor Robert Glenn led the way in the campaign and traveled the state delivering over fifty speeches in support of the dry cause. Women took an especially active role in the campaign and organized marches and rallies, often featuring groups of schoolchildren. Rallies sported banners with slogans such as "Vote for Prohibition and Protect Us" and "You Protect Your Horses and Dogs By Law, Why Not Protect Us?"[39]

When officials counted the votes, the prohibition cause won overwhelmingly, 113,612–69,416. Celebration ensued across the state and the Beaufort *Washington Progress* equated the prohibition victory with the bravery of North Carolina's Confederate troops in the Civil War: "North Carolina first at Bethel, farthest at Appomattox, and the first State in the Union to banish the liquor traffic by popular vote."[40] As 1 January 1909 approached, the *News and Observer* ran the headline "BIG EXPLOSION" and claimed, "The Old Adage 'Friday is an Unlucky Day,' Will Be Shattered Next Thursday Night at Twelve O'Clock—Instead of Being Unlucky, Mothers, Wives and Sisters Will, in the Future, Not Have to 'Trust to Luck,' for the Comforts of This Life—With the Dawning of Next Friday Morning an Era of Happiness and Prosperity Will be Inaugurated."[41]

While prohibition supporters had no illusions that the act would totally end liquor consumption and distilling in the state, they saw this as the beginning of the end of the moonshine business. Not long after the law went into effect, the *Concord Daily Tribune* reported on the former "moonshine district" of western North Carolina: "With the march of prohibition, the education and uplift of the people, the 'moonshine' distilling has gone into innocuous desuetude in the region beyond Asheville.... Nobody claims that the law is not evaded in Western North Carolina, but the truth is that the law is generally respected. Public sentiment frowns upon the blockading and illicit sale of whiskey, and the great bulk of the people will not tolerate that running spring of evil that long held in chains a people capable of the highest development. Schools and churches have taken the place of stills in the mountain coves, temperance is steadily gaining ground, and prohibition prohibits."[42]

While it is true that the prohibition laws took alcohol consumption and sale out of public view, they turned the business into a widely practiced underground activity. Indeed, prohibition, and its long persistence in the state, proved to be one of the key factors that entrenched the moonshiner so firmly in the economic, social, and cultural fabric of North Carolina. While the overwhelming dry vote in 1908 seemed to indicate that most male North Carolinians sup-

Billy Borne cartoon on the day after North Carolinians voted in statewide prohibition in 1908. (Asheville Citizen-Times, 27 May 1908)

ported prohibition, demand for alcohol remained high. Many middle-class and elite North Carolinians cast their votes for the social control of African Americans and white mill workers knowing full well that their ability to procure alcohol, given loopholes in the law and lack of enforcement, would not be appreciably limited. The vote also did not take into account the numbers of disfranchised men who opposed prohibition who were going to continue to drink. In addition, many of the men who succumbed to pressure from pastors and wives to cast a prohibition vote planned to continue to drink on the sly. To be sure, with the legal avenues for access to alcohol now "dried up," demand for the illegal product skyrocketed.

At the same time, the economic problems that already made making moonshine an attractive prospect had not improved and, if anything, had worsened. While the state legislature and the Democratic Party focused on wiping out the Republican Party, disenfranchising African Americans, and enacting prohibition legislation, they did little or nothing to address the state's underlying economic problems.

In the aftermath of the passage of statewide prohibition, ongoing demand, continued economic distress in rural North Carolina, and the skyrocketing prices moonshine now commanded made the temptation to make illegal liquor too strong for many to resist. As the *Statesville Sentinel* observed in 1910, "Before the prohibition law was passed in North Carolina the price of moonshine whiskey became so low that few of the mountaineers found it profitable to make it. However, things have changed and the moonshiner has come into his own again. In the past few years the price has risen from $1.00 a gallon to as high as $6.00 a gallon and now the stills are running harder than ever."[43]

5

MODERN MOONSHINE

In response to the massive demand for illegal liquor that prohibition created, the years between 1900 and 1920 marked some of the most momentous years in the history of moonshine in North Carolina. Instead of following the Carolina parakeet into extinction, the moonshine business and the moonshiner thrived. Indeed, the attempts at eradicating alcohol by prohibitionists in North Carolina did not consign moonshine and moonshining to the mists of history as a vestige of the state's more primitive, premodern past. Indeed, prohibition engrained them even more into North Carolina's economic, social, and cultural life. In the process, the illegal liquor business more and more took on the trappings of a modern industrial enterprise as a number of innovations in both production and distribution transformed the industry. Increased demand, high prices, lax enforcement, and the seemingly endless creativity and energy of the state's moonshiners produced unprecedented change to the ways illegal distillers manufactured, marketed, and transported their liquor.

One of the first major measures taken by moonshiners as demand for illegal liquor increased was to boost the capacity of their stills. Traditionally, North Carolina moonshiners used copper stills with a forty-to-sixty-gallon capacity. That changed rapidly across the state well before statewide prohibition was passed. The press began regularly reporting busts of stills with capacities over 100 gallons as early as 1901. With the passage of the Watts Law, stills of 150-gallon capacity became common, and by 1906 the press reported stills with over 250-gallon capacity. In 1906, the *Roanoke News* recounted the capture of a 300-gallon still near Grifton.[1] Of course, such large stills required lots of mash barrels and beer to distill, and agents reported pouring out thousands of gallons at a time. Durham County agents busted a 233-gallon still and poured out 7,000 gallons of beer in 1906.[2] The Kinston *Daily Free Press* reported on this phenomenon and its connection to prohibition laws in 1904 when deputy collector A. F. Surles reported destroying a large still. "The size of the still was probably fixed by the extent of the drouth it was intended to moisten. All of Harnett County is 'prohibition,' there being neither still, barroom nor dispensary licensed to do business in the county."[3] While most moonshiners did their distilling employing the old smaller stills, as the twentieth century progressed, stills with 200-gallon capacity or more became increasingly common. In 1919 a bust near Kinston netted a 430-gallon still.[4]

At least some of these larger stills were the direct result of the prohibition of legal distilleries. Naturally, some of the formerly legal distillers hid their stills and started operating illegally. Others sold their stills to illegal operators who set them up in swamps, hidden hollers, and outbuildings on their farms. The Winston-Salem *Twin-City Daily Sentinel* reported in 1910 on a 500-gallon-plus distillery captured near Hoffman: "In that case a distillery had gone out of business and several unassuming gentlemen bought the alcohol-making apparatus as junk. A few months later the government officers discovered that the 'junk' had been set up in a swamp and was producing contraband liquor in vast quantities."[5]

Making such large stills out of copper was a very expensive enterprise, and many distillers looked for other materials. When the automobile arrived on the scene, the large containers commonly used to transport gasoline at the time became prized for use in large-capacity stills. The *Asheville Citizen-Times* reported in 1916 that "the Standard Oil Company is an innocent contributor to the industry of making whiskey that does not pay the government tax. The moonshiners have gotten into the habit of buying, borrowing or stealing galvanized iron gasoline barrels and using them in their business. While the product is not quite so good as that made from a copper still, in a pinch it will do."[6] The Greensboro *Daily News* commented on the decline in the "supply of copper plants" and reported that the "'stills' captured" in 1915 "have been of every class of material imaginable. Sheet iron, galvanized iron, tin, or almost anything that can be soldered and can hold water has been pressed into service."[7] While much cheaper, making liquor using such materials had a severe downside, as poisonous materials leached into the liquor. As the *Charlotte Observer* commented, "Liquor made in this way is often dangerous and deserving of the name it carries as 'mean liquor.'"[8]

One of the common uses in North Carolina for gasoline and oil barrels was a revolutionary type of still reportedly developed in Wilkes County known as a steamer still (also known as a Wilkes-type still). It is difficult to know exactly when the first steamer still came on the scene, but the *News and Observer* mentioned their use in Wilkes County as early as 1904.[9] Using knowledge and experience gained from the steam engine's common usage in the railroad and

Wilkes-type steamer still and large moonshine operation. (Courtesy of the North Carolina Collection, UNC Libraries, UNC–Chapel Hill)

logging industries, illegal distillers adapted this technology to produce a highly efficient moonshine still. Instead of using a heat source to "cook" the mash into distillate, the steamer still used a steam boiler to force steam through the mash, distilling it in the process. Using steam technology created numerous advantages for moonshiners, as it eliminated the problem of scorching the mash and ruining the liquor run, and it eliminated time-consuming cooker cleanups. The steam process also proved quicker than traditional distilling and made it easier to use large-capacity stills. The primary downside to the steamer still was the danger inherent in using steam equipment. Because the steam was under such intense pressure, pipes that were not securely attached could come loose, spraying steam on unlucky moonshiners. Exploding steam boilers created another hazard for distillers.

In addition to learning about modern-day steam technology, some North Carolina moonshiners discovered the virtues of using coke to fire up their stills. Coke is a form of refined coal baked to burn off impurities and concentrate the carbonaceous material. The great advantage for the moonshiner is that it burns at a consistent temperature and is virtually smokeless, a great benefit when one desires to avoid the revenue agents' notice or that of nosy neighbors. In 1916, the *Asheville Citizen-Times* noted that one moonshiner arrested by authorities "was a modern blockader who believed in abating the smoke nuisance, for the revenue men found a nice little stock of coke which was being used to boil the mash."[10] While it was not common in the early years of the twentieth century, its use, particularly with steamer stills, became increasingly popular.

As illegal liquor makers sought to make more liquor more cheaply, they also looked for ways to speed up the distillation process. One of the great innovations that came out of the moonshine business was the "doubling keg," "doubler," "single footer," or "thump keg." Traditionally, distillers had to run liquor through a still twice to get rid of fusel oil and other impurities and make a drinkable product. Distillers placed the thump keg, usually a small wooden barrel, between the cooker/still and the condenser. They then partially filled this barrel with the low-alcohol "backings" from earlier runs, and a pipe ran the distillate from the cooker into the bottom of the doubler. The steam distillate passed through the backings, which both removed some of the impurities and boosted the alcohol content, all the while making a distinctive thumping sound. This important innovation reduced the time required to produce a run of liquor and, as the Greensboro *Daily News* observed in 1915, "is of considerable advantage from the operator's standpoint as it enables him to cut the time in two, and thus lessen the risk of interruption by half."[11] Doubling kegs appeared in both eastern and western North Carolina in the late 1890s, but it was not until the 1910s that they came into common usage.[12]

Perhaps the biggest change that came to the moonshine business in the early years of the twentieth century was the use of refined sugar in the basic liquor recipe. Indeed, as the twentieth century progressed, the product that came out of North Carolina's illegal distilleries increasingly became distilled sugar, with a little cornmeal thrown in to maintain some vestige of the taste of traditional moonshine. Mash made with sugar ferments quicker and when distilled yields a higher alcohol content than the old all-corn product. Refined sugar also became much cheaper due to the industrial revolution and improvements in transportation. Distilling sugar definitely changed the taste of moonshine—and not for the better. As historian Charles Thompson observed, "When people started buying sugar by the hundred-pound sack to make sugar whiskey in order to increase output and work quicker, the taste did change dramatically. The old-timers knew instantly they didn't want to drink the new rotgut, but in the cities,

Small still with doubler, or thump keg, in the middle. This device cut the time in half needed to distill liquor. (Courtesy of Great Smoky Mountains National Park Archives, National Park Service Collections Preservation Center, Townsend, Tenn.)

especially in the speakeasies, it didn't seem to matter.... Prohibition was not making the liquor business go away, it was just making it bad."[13]

Notwithstanding the changed taste of the product, the economic appeal of using sugar was too attractive to resist. The *Charlotte Observer* noted in 1909 that "six bushels of cornmeal and 200 pounds of sugar made 30 gallons of whiskey, which sells faster than hotcakes at $4 a gallon. A small still can turn out 30 gallons a day easily, giving the enterprising 'shiner a profit of $100 for a day's work. And the risk doesn't bother him much. Ability to convert about $16 of raw material into $120 worth of liquor has made him more fearless than ever."[14] Hundred-pound sacks of sugar soon appeared on the shelves of country stores all over the state and wholesalers did a land-office business. Although this did attract the attention of law enforcement, they could do little about the sugar traffic. When asked why he carried so much sugar, one store owner allegedly replied that he didn't "rightly know" why his customers demanded so much sugar. He mused that they must be making lots of "preserves."

A related development in North Carolina's Coastal Plain and Tidewater regions was the use of molasses, which cost even less than sugar. The *Wilmington Morning Star* reported early in the twentieth century on this phenomenon: "Officers say those distilleries generally take cheap molasses and from it make rum. Few of them use meal and malt. This rum they make is generally vile stuff, but it makes drunk come, and finds ready sale."[15] Moonshiners in eastern North Carolina generally called this product "monkey rum." The roots of the name are

Liquor Lingo

In addition to the many names for illegal liquor that folks have used over the years, a whole vocabulary also developed surrounding the illegal liquor business. Most commonly people called distilleries simply "stills," but they also used terms such as "plant," "laboratory," or "mill." More imaginative folks, particularly reporters, called stills "corn juiceries," "wildcat distilleries," or in one obscure case, "a delightful." In addition to the most common names of "blockader" and "moonshiner," North Carolinians called illegal distillers "wildcats," "chemists," "coppers," and "knights of the moonshine still." They named those who sold illegal liquor "bootleggers" but in the late nineteenth and early twentieth centuries called them "blind tigers." Early on, "blockaders" or those "running the block" were the common terms for people who took the product to market. Later, folks called them "liquor haulers" or, once the automobile came on the scene, "trippers" or "whiskey trippers."

Moonshine vocabulary also extended into the area of the cat-and-mouse game played between law enforcement and illegal distillers. People have most commonly used the term "revenuers," or "revenooers," for federal agents, from the earliest days of the federal excise tax to the present day. Of course, North Carolina governor and U.S. senator Zebulon Vance popularized the term "red-legged grasshopper," common in the state into the early years of the twentieth century. When agents destroyed a still, it was "cut down," often with a combination axe and pick known as a "devil." Even later when they generally destroyed stills with dynamite, revenuers "cut down" a still. Moonshiners running from law enforcement took "leg bail" or "foot bond," and if caught and convicted went off to jail or a federal penitentiary to "build time."

One of the most colorful stories related to the special language of moonshine comes from Bascom Lamar Lunsford's memoir *It Used to Be*. Lunsford talks about the half-pint bottle containing moonshine called a "shorty" that men around western North Carolina commonly carried in their hip pocket. Lunsford recalled church meetings he attended where "a friend would step up in the crowd talking and joking, and some fellow would ask if he had seen Shorty. He'd say, 'No, I have not seen Shorty yet.' So they would carry him around back of an old buggy, or a little patch of pines close to the meeting house and let him have a little taste of 'shorty.'"

lost in the mists of history, but it perhaps has racist origins, as both the producers and the consumers of the product were generally African American. Monkey rum, like sugar liquor, also had a reputation for producing violent behavior and painful headaches, and as a result, folks often referred to it as "busthead," "stingo," or "rotgut."

As prohibition progressed, the primary goal for North Carolina moonshiners became producing a product with high alcohol content that would get folks drunk in a hurry. This lack of concern for taste and quality, and the lack of any government oversight, led to the use of a variety of adulterants added to the liquor to make it appear high proof. At the same time, adulterating allowed the producer to actually cut the proof to make his liquor go further and boost profits. North Carolina moonshiners most commonly used lye, or potash, for this purpose even before prohibition came around. Using lye gave the liquor the proper sting factor, which made it appear stronger than it was. It also caused the liquor to "bead" like high-proof liquor when placed in a small bottle—ones used for laudanum were especially popular—and shaken. Horace Kephart commented on this practice among mountain moonshiners in *Our Southern Highlanders*:

> Every blockader knows how to adulterate, and when one of them does stoop to such tricks he will stop at no halfway measures. Some add washing lye, both to increase yield and to give the liquor an artificial bead, then prime this abominable fluid with pepper, ginger, tobacco, or anything else that will make it sting. Even buckeyes, which are poisonous themselves, are sometimes used to give the drink a soapy bead. Such decoctions are known in the mountains by the expressive terms "pop-skull," "bust head," "bumblings" ("they make a bumbly noise in a feller's head"). Some of them are so toxic that their continued use might be fatal to the drinker. A few drams may turn a normally good-hearted fellow into a raging fiend who will shoot or stab without provocation.[16]

The *Hickory Record* reported that moonshiners in Catawba County even added "a little barnyard fertilizer, preferably that from chicken coops, to the spirits in order to get the 'bead.'"[17]

The increasing distances between producers and their markets and the number of intermediaries, often operating some sort of blind exchange, involved in the illegal liquor business as prohibition progressed increased the incentives to adulterate. As the *Foxfire* books' authors asserted, "It is apparently not that difficult to get away with making bad whiskey, because most of it is sold through bootleggers who themselves don't know where it came from. In addition, much of it is shipped to the poorer districts of some of the bigger cities, and the people who buy it have no means of finding out who made it. Thus the operator of the still is reasonably safe, rarely having to pay for his sloppiness."[18] The *Charlotte Observer* put this new relationship between the moonshiner and the product succinctly in 1917: "The North Carolina moonshiner is too respectable a gentleman to drink the stuff he makes. The doctor may take his own physic, but the moonshiner places a higher value than that on his own life. He makes his pizen to sell."[19]

The late 1910s also saw an innovation that would later become a signature facet of moonshining in North Carolina: the use of automobiles to transport illegal liquor. The use of the automobile was not yet common and, not surprising given the cost of early automobiles, generally involved individuals with considerable means. Indeed, one of the first arrests for hauling liquor in an automobile in North Carolina occurred in Henderson County. Sheriff Allard Case pulled over a car containing "four well known business and society men of Asheville" in an automobile piloted by a "negro chauffeur" a few miles outside of Hendersonville in 1917. When he searched the car, Allard found a ten-gallon keg and a one-gallon demijohn containing moonshine.[20] *Everything* reported the increased commonality of automobile hauling in the Greensboro area that same year: "And there are a great many citizens engaged in nothing else but retailing corn likker fresh from the still. They use automobiles and it is hard to locate these bar rooms on wheels."[21]

In 1919 revenue agent Tom Vanderford explained the advantages of transporting liquor in automobiles: "The automobile ... has proved a valuable agency to the 'moonshiner' in disposing of his goods and also proved one of the most difficult conveyances to locate. A farmer, snugly hidden in the mountains of North Carolina, can make liquor to his heart's content one day and have it on sale near the cities and cantonments the next. Within two hours after he puts it in a car, it is many miles away from him, and the chances of detection are reduced considerably. Even when automobiles laden with whiskey are seized ... it is difficult to trace the crime back to the mountaineer. By reason of his large profits, he is enabled to pay the carrier a large amount to take his jail sentence and keep silent."[22] Moonshine runners also began to quickly adapt their cars to hide the liquor so that if law enforcement stopped them they could evade arrest. In 1919, the *Gastonia Daily Gazette* reported on the capture of Arthur Leonard and Wellean Sparks, caught hauling twenty-six gallons of moonshine in their Ford from the South Mountains to Gastonia. When officers searched the car they discovered a "false bottom" in the floorboard. Inside the hidden compartment they found eleven hot-water bottles, fruit jars, and nine "oblong, flat Polarine oil cans," all containing illegal liquor.[23]

Of course, not long after moonshiners began regularly hauling liquor in automobiles, the legendary "thunder road" car chases on the state's highways and byways became more and more common. In 1919, the *Charlotte News* reported, "The moonshine industry in western North Carolina is running wild.... The city police has the greatest trouble these days with 'whiskey runners' a class of criminals, usually made up of young rough necks of the city, who know how to drive automobiles 'like hell.'"[24] As would generally be the case, the liquor runners had the advantage over law enforcement in both horsepower and motivation and regularly outran pursuing law enforcement agents. The *Asheville Citizen-Times* reported on one dramatic chase where the haulers got rid of the evidence of their crime and lightened their load so they could outrun police:

"While the driver put the highly geared machine into a gait that seemed to give the vehicle wings, his companions began to discard their holdings. The engine used for unlawful transportation was a better racer than that which purred in turning the legal machinery and the detectives [who had staked out the route] were outdistanced. But they drove as best they could in a fine mist of moonshine corn and occasional hail of glass."[25]

Law enforcement did, however, have occasional successes, although they often involved considerable danger. Greensboro citizens witnessed a particularly dramatic and dangerous capture on their downtown streets in 1919. Officers staked out an alley off Bain Street where J. W. Hubbard, a "well-dressed young white man" from Stuart, Virginia, planned to deliver a load of liquor. When Hubbard pulled his Dodge into the alley, two officers drew their pistols and jumped on the car's running boards. The officer on the passenger side fell off but succeeded in shooting out a tire. Captain Glenn held on and grabbed a gun from the driver and steered the car into a telephone pole, ending the chase.[26]

The use of the automobile is another case where the moonshiners benefitted from and adapted to the modern world. They also profited from the automobile's adjuncts in North Carolina, the rise of the Good Roads Movement and the dramatic expansion of state-maintained highways. As Horace Kephart observed, "I used to think that good roads would help to check moonshining, by making it easier for mountain farmers to market their corn in bulk at a fair profit.... But I never dreamed, in those days, that distilled corn juice would be retailing at ten to twenty dollars a gallon. As things are, our new highways will make the distant marketing of blockade liquor a veritable line of trade. 'Mountain dew' will be collected by fly-by-night cars and carried to a far extended market."[27]

The increased demand for moonshine and resultant increase in its profitability also further spread its manufacture into regions of the state where illegal liquor had been relatively uncommon and into every ethnic and social demographic in the state. While whiskey making had been occurring across the state since the colonial era, most observers associated the trade with the mountainous western part of the state. As prohibition took root, however, many commentators noted moonshining's rapid spread into other regions of the state. In his annual report in 1918, Revenue Agent Mutt considered 54 of North Carolina's 100 counties to be "good moonshine territory." He cited expected counties in the mountains and foothills, such as Henderson, Polk, Transylvania, Wilkes, Alexander, Yadkin, McDowell, and Burke, but also listed Orange, Johnston, and Wake Counties on the "conditions are bad" list.[28] Indeed, stories of the decline of moonshining in the west and the increase in illegal production in the east filled North Carolina newspapers in the early years of the twentieth century.

Model T liquor hauler with cases of moonshine captured by police in 1922. (Library of Congress)

As early as 1901 the *Asheville Citizen-Times* declared, "The day of the western moonshiner has almost gone by. The traffic has moved east to the pine woods section of the state."[29]

While Agent Mutt had ignored this section of the state in his comments, most observers saw the pine forests of the Coastal Plain and the swamps of the Tidewater as the new hotbeds of moonshining in the state. In 1911, IRS commissioner Roy E. Cabell claimed that "eastern North Carolina is making more liquor than at any previous time."[30] The Reidsville *Webster's Weekly* cited the Cape Fear River region around Dunn as a hotbed of moonshining in 1913 and asserted that deputy marshal A. F. Surles cut up an average of "200 stills a year" in that district.[31] The *Concord Daily Tribune* quoted a "revenue raider" in 1911 as stating that moonshiners in Johnston County (on the edge of the Coastal Plain) produced so much illegal alcohol "it was impossible to keep the stills cut up."[32] Most observers agreed that the biggest growth in the business had come in the swamps of the Tidewater area. They often cited Brunswick, Hyde, and Dare Counties for dramatic increases in blockading. As the *New Berne Weekly Journal* commented in 1915, "Certain parts of these counties is [*sic*] uninhabited and is in fact a vast wilderness which furnishes an excellent rendezvous for the maker of illicit whiskey."[33]

Although counties in the Piedmont with large numbers of cotton mills and furniture factories liked to tout the fact that the mills had driven out the stills in their counties, more rural counties along their borders saw dramatic increases in moonshining activity. In 1903 the *Gaston Gazette* crowed, "Ten years ago Gaston county probably led the State in the production of moonshine whiskey. To-day Gaston leads in cotton factories, is striving for leadership in good roads and is at the tail of the class in the matter of moonshine."[34] However, if the *Gazette* were honest, it would have noted Gaston was at the "tail" of moonshine production because cotton mill towns, despite herculean efforts from mill management, provided some of the best markets for moonshiners. One revenue agent told the *Concord Daily Tribune* in 1920 that Cabarrus County, which adjoins the mill hotbed of Mecklenburg County and is not far from Gaston, "is known as the worst moonshine county in the United States."[35] The Raleigh *Morning Post* in 1905 called Iredell County, also on the edge of mill country, "the most prolific of blockaders" in western North Carolina. The paper even went so far as to claim that Iredell had surpassed Wilkes as the "'banner' moonshine county" in the region.[36]

With prohibition making liquor production a violation of local and state law, as well as a federal offense, more and more illegal operations moved their plants near state lines. Doing this enabled them to transport themselves and their operations easily out of local and state officials' jurisdictions. In 1919, the *Watauga Democrat* averred, "The Sheriff says the blockaders are plying their trade along the State line, and will be hard to capture by county officers on either side."[37] The *Asheville Citizen* in 1908 reported on a "shanty" containing a moonshine still located "partly in Transylvania county, N.C., and partly in Oconee county, S.C." The paper concluded the "site was an ideal one for such a plant not only on account of accessibility, but because the nearness to the state line would allow the operators to skip across the line to evade the officers."[38]

By the early years of the twentieth century, moonshiners had also developed creative tactics to outsmart their pursuers and keep folks away from their stills. They had a keen interest in keeping hunters, hikers, and curious folk from wandering in the woods and stumbling on their stills and possibly reporting them to authorities. The popular stereotype of violent, sadistic, and murderous moonshiners attacking or shooting anyone who came near their still was one that the moonshiners themselves approved and helped spread themselves. As Horace Kephart noted, such stories were generally fanciful and far from the reality of the illegal liquor business. Kephart asked a neighbor what would happen to him if he was out hunting and stumbled upon an operating still. The neighbor responded that the moonshiners would probably make him stir the mash and taste some of the liquor as that "would make you one o' them in the eyes of the law." When asked if the blockaders would then mistreat him, the neighbor replied in surprise, "Shucks! Why, man, whut could they gain by hurtin' you? At the wust, s'posin' they was convicted by your evidence, they'd only git a month or two in the pen. So why should they murder you and get hung for it? Hit's all 'tarnal foolishness, the notions some folks has!" Of course, Kephart did not advocate folks going out and looking for stills; rural North Carolinians did not take kindly to people sticking their noses into other people's business. But he did inject some reality into a situation that had taken on mythical proportions.[39]

Moonshiners were also adept at spreading rumors about ghosts, evil swamp creatures, Sasquatch-type figures, Boojums, Wampus cats, savage bears, mountain lions, and wolves that roamed the swamps, forests, hills, and mountains terrorizing the countryside. Indeed, most such stories in North Carolina originated with moonshiners trying to keep people away from their stills. The Greensboro *Daily Industrial News* reported on such an incident near Statesville in 1907:

> It has been related here that there is some varmint in north Iredell killing and eating dogs and hogs.
>
> The informant further says that several people who have got glimpses of the varmint declare it is six feet long and has large tusks.
>
> The animal roams in the land of the moonshiner and while some think it is really an animal, others say it is a man in disguise trying to scare Deputy Marshal Wright, of Statesville, who has been so fearless in the arrest of blockaders.[40]

Still another tactic used to avoid detection and capture was to keep distilling operations mobile. This tactic actually worked against the tendency to build larger and larger stills, but many moonshiners discovered they could more successfully use small stills that could be easily picked up, moved, and concealed somewhere else. Some blockaders kept an old still already perforated by law enforcement to put in place while they made off with their good one. As the *Concord Times* reported in 1909, "When the alarm of danger is sounded the operator quickly removes the new still and substitutes the old one, which bears the scars of many revenue raids and it is this worthless affair that the officers cut instead of the one that does the work. When the officers depart the new still goes back into the furnace and the business promptly resumed."[41]

North Carolina moonshiners also adapted well to new conditions when World War I, arguably the first "modern" war, came to the state. While the war helped propel the nation down the path toward the Eighteenth Amendment and national Prohibition, it mainly proved to be an added boon for the already booming illegal liquor business in the state. The construction of military camps and the mobilization of troops from all over the country to populate those camps helped concentrate the target demographic of most moonshiners and increased demand tremendously. In 1917, the *Asheville Citizen* noted, "The great number of workmen who have been engaged in the construction of buildings and the presence of the vanguard of the soldiers has given rise to an illicit trade in moonshine whiskey."[42] In 1918, the *Salisbury Evening Post* noted, "The military camps [are] where most of the moonshine liquor is sold, despite the precautions by military and civil authorities."[43]

Of course, increased demand meant that the price of moonshine increased as well. In 1918 the *Charlotte Observer* asserted that "blockade whiskey was selling as high as $10 a gallon. There is great profit in making whiskey at these prices as three or four gallons of whiskey can be made from one bushel of corn and men will go to the limit in taking risks where an investment of $1.50 on a small amount of labor will bring in returns of $50 to $60."[44] At other times during the war, the press reported prices as high as eighteen to twenty-four dollars a gallon, especially near military camps.[45] Demand and prices went even higher in the fall of 1918 when the Spanish flu epidemic hit North Carolina. Rumors spread throughout the state that "physicians have said that whiskey was the best medicine to treat the malady and the best preventative to ward it off."[46]

In addition to the high demand and high prices illegal liquor commanded during the war, the risks were low and moonshiners could operate relatively unmolested as illegal liquor enforcement dropped well down the list of governmental priorities. Indeed, government funding for enforcement decreased at the federal, state, and local levels, and the prime candidates for enforcement positions were also prime candidates for the military draft. In 1917 Josiah W. Bailey, North Carolina's collector of internal revenue at the time, complained to the press about the quandary of an understaffed force and the perennial problem of lack of support from local law enforcement: "I have reason to believe that illicit distilling has rapidly increased throughout my district in six months. If I had the men I could make 300 successful raids in six weeks within 50 miles of Raleigh; it is not a question of finding distilleries, the question is how to cope with the situation in 56 counties with only nine deputies. But with only nine deputies we are making ten raids to one by the 56 sheriffs and their deputies and constables—say 500 of them."[47] By late in the war, moonshiners even became better armed as military weapons filtered into the civilian population. In 1919, the Greensboro *Daily News* reported that in raids on the notorious Jim Rose gang in Cherokee and Graham Counties, officers recovered eight high-powered U.S. Army Springfield rifles.[48]

Authorities became especially concerned about the moonshine business as the war progressed, because the illegal liquor business often went hand in hand with draft dodging and desertion. In 1917, the *News and Observer* reported that the Lebanon Township of northern Durham County—"long haunt of the moonshine blockader"—had become a haven for draft evaders. The "forests and devious streams [of the area provide] a cloke [*sic*] of protection around

Billy Borne cartoon depicting the dangers of "blockade liquor." (Asheville Citizen-Times, *21 July 1921)*

the evaders. They are wanted for failure to register under the conscription act and are branded as defiant slackers."[49] When internal revenue commissioner Daniel Roper sent out a "flying squadron" of fourteen agents in 1918 to clean out "nests of moonshiners who had been operating without serious difficulty for years," the officers rounded up "more than a score of deserters from the army [who] were discovered participating in moonshine manufacture." Officers subsequently killed two of the deserter-moonshiners.[50] In a 1918 shootout, three deserter-moonshiners exchanged hostile fire with revenue officers that resulted in the serious wounding of two of the blockaders.[51]

Authorities tried to use war conditions to their advantage to crack down on the moonshine traffic. The U.S. Food Administration, responsible for maintaining a reliable source of food for both the military and civilian populations, even chipped in to cut off supplies to the blockaders. In 1918, Food Administration authorities in Lenoir County used their authority to limit the supply of molasses to the county's "monkey rum" producers. Stores could only sell one barrel to their customers and, as the *News and Observer* reported, "persons buying more than a barrel of molasses will immediately be called upon to explain."[52] The *Charlotte Observer* reported that the state's food commissioner had "issued a clear-cut warning to millers and dealers [in corn] to have a care as to whom they have dealings with."[53]

Wartime propaganda campaigns criticized the waste of valuable food supplies, as well as the overall corrupting nature of moonshine, and characterized the moonshiners as unpatriotic or even "treasonous." In 1918, judge Frank

Carter, editor of the *Albemarle Enterprise,* launched a diatribe against "the most despicable traitors at large in North Carolina" for "using grain, sugar and molasses to make blockade liquor." Using such commodities to make liquor took these crucial products from the food supply "as if sunk in the sea by a German submarine." Carter continued by declaiming against the "evil" produced by moonshine: "The vile product is debauching our soldiers, weakening our civilian man power, corrupting the very springs of national life, and is doing it far more effectively than Germany is able to do through dissemination of the moral poisons of her germ cultures. The blockader is therefore doing the double work of the German poisoner of wells and of thought. The overwhelming shame of it for us of North Carolina is that our State is officially rated at Washington as standing at the very head of this monstrously treasonable traffic."[54]

The war did bring one new and important law enforcement tactic that bore fruit later in the battle against North Carolina's moonshiners. In 1919, Commissioner Roper asked the War Department to loan the Alcohol Tax Unit several planes to use for "spying upon hidden liquor makers from the sky." While the army did not comply, Roper's request signaled the coming of a new era in liquor law enforcement once airplanes became more common.[55]

To be sure, the coming of statewide prohibition demonstrated the overall intelligence and creativity of North Carolina moonshiners as they adapted to the new laws by making their business ever more productive and efficient. New types of stills, improved production methods, new recipes, and new methods of distribution revolutionized moonshining and helped entrench it even more firmly in the state's economic, social, and cultural life. In addition, the increased profits brought new individuals into the business and made it more reflective of the state's demographic diversity.

6

NORTH CAROLINIANS "HARD AT WORK MAKING THAT STUFF THAT SPLITS THE HEADS OF MANY"

While most moonshiners at this point came from the same social and ethnic backgrounds as moonshiners at the passage of the excise tax, the new era of local and statewide prohibition also brought almost every demographic group in the state into the business. Increased profits from moonshining attracted individuals from all races and ethnic groups in the state, including considerable numbers of Native Americans and African Americans. Women as well as men became more involved, and wealthier and more socially respectable middle-class individuals succumbed to the temptation to make, transport, or sell illegal liquor. Indeed, participation in the moonshine business united almost all North Carolinians during this period, particularly among the state's poor and working-class individuals.

Most of the people involved in moonshine, or at least the ones that appear in police reports, were white, male, and relatively young and owned, or lived on, family farms. They made, transported, or sold moonshine to supplement their family income, pay their taxes, hold on to their farms, and avoid mill work. As historian Charles Thompson observed, "It was illegal money—that much is true—but it was money made from sweat. That sweat money made liquor bosses rich, but it also bought and preserved small farms, keeping people out of mills and mines and on their own land for a generation or two longer, leaving people some independence to determine their own direction and to change their families' futures ultimately."[1]

For most moonshiners, making illegal liquor was a part-time and seasonal enterprise that fit in nicely with the rhythms on the farm and the chemistry and realities of moonshining. A reporter from the *Asheville Citizen-Times* explained the business's seasonal aspect in 1916:

Bayard Wooten photograph of a still hidden in rhododendrons in western North Carolina. The photo, like many similar ones, was probably staged. (Courtesy of the North Carolina Collection, UNC Libraries, UNC–Chapel Hill)

> Comes fall when the corn has been laid by, as the saying goes, and those who believe the government has no right to say what a man shall do with his own corn or rye begin to think of some sequestered cove, modestly shielded from inquisitive revenue men, where the harvests may be turned into moonshine liquor.
>
> The industry of making blockade booze lags during the summer, and there are several good reasons for this. First, the beer is not so good during the warm months, and then again the moonshiner is too busy in his fields cultivating his crops to devote the necessary time to his still. When the corn has been laid by, which means after the fields have been given their last cultivation, he begins to look around for a quiet spot, close by a running stream, of course, and there he proceeds to erect his furnace. The still is gotten in on some dark night, while the neighbors are asleep, for your blockader is a quiet and unobtrusive man who courts no unnecessary publicity. Finally the frosts come, the grain is ready and close at hand, and on some fair day he starts the fires and soon the process of making the whiskey never destined to see a government stamp is in full swing.[2]

The Christmas season was a prime time for liquor making, as it was a slow season for the farmer and moonshine was in high demand for holiday celebrations. In addition, revenue agents were, as the Greensboro *Daily News* observed, "off their beats" and tied up attending and testifying in district court.[3]

But white men were not the only poor farmers in North Carolina. The poor rural economic conditions, combined with prohibition's high profits and the limited opportunities afforded African Americans due to the Jim Crow system and overt racial discrimination, brought more minority North Carolinians into the business in the early twentieth century. Newspapers noted an especial increase in moonshine activity among the state's Native Americans. The Cherokee of far western North Carolina had a strong tradition of temperance going back to 1819, when Chief Yonaguska (Drowning Bear) of the Quallatown Cherokee had a vision that caused him to lead a campaign to end liquor consumption among his people. He drew up a pledge, which most tribal members signed, where the signatories agreed to "abandon the use of spirituous liquors." The strong Baptist faith of most eastern Cherokee helped to maintain this tradition into the twentieth century.[4] In 1901, an *Asheville Citizen* reporter commented about "the Eastern Band of the Cherokees, which is composed of Indians as law abiding as any white people of the mountains—more so, indeed, for the Indians never distil the unlawful 'moonshine,' they only drink it—when they can get it."[5] By the 1910s, however, that had changed, as it appears that many Cherokee, one of the more impoverished groups in the state, had succumbed to the temptations of moonshine. In 1919, the Greensboro *Daily News* noted, "Despite the diligent work of the large force, which operates here in the west, the business of making moonshine liquor seems to be increasing and reaching sections, notably the Indian reservation in Swain and Cherokee counties, which heretofore have been free from the violations, or at least for a long time."[6] Moonshining on the reservation grew so much during the period that the Bureau of Indian Affairs sent in a special undercover investigator to root out the problem.

Prohibition, combined with widespread poverty and few viable options for gaining income otherwise, also strengthened the long-term liquor- and moonshine-making traditions among the Lumbee and Tuscarora in eastern North Carolina. Malinda Maynor Lowery noted that, during this period, "Indian farmers and laborers often turned to making whisky and homemade wine to supplement their incomes and compensate for their losses." She quotes one federal agent who asserted, "We could go to the Lumber River and chop up ten to twelve stills on any afternoon.... They were lined up beside the road. I had never seen moonshining in western North Carolina carried out to that extent."[7] In 1948, University of North Carolina sociologist Guy Johnson traveled to Robeson County to do field research on the Lumbee. In an interview, a local auto dealer, identified as Mr. Singleton in Johnson's field notes, asserted that the Lumbee not only actively participated in the illegal liquor business during prohibition but also showed a real talent for the enterprise: "There is probably more liquor made or sold in this section than in any ABC [Alcohol Beverage Control] store in the state. During Prohibition, the Indians made a lot of money on whiskey. People would come in here from far away to buy it from certain Indians who had a reputation for making really good liquor. Some of the wealthiest Indians got their start that way. A lot of them still make it too."[8]

Lumbee and Tuscarora culture put its own stamp on the moonshining business during the Prohibition era. As Lowery observed, tapping into communal traditions, "Indian moonshiners formed a network and pooled their whisky in cooperative fashion, splitting the proceeds from sales in large quantities." It also appears as if Native American women, in response to matriarchal traditions, participated more actively in the illegal liquor business than white women. Following in the footsteps of her kinswoman Rhoda Lowry, Lizzie Lowry developed quite a reputation as a bootlegger during the prohibition era. She operated a gas station/country store as a front for her wholesale liquor operation, as well as several liquor houses. Although authorities arrested her on at least three occasions, like many women, she generally received a suspended sentence "provided she relocated and that she be 'of good behavior.'" Malinda Maynor Lowery noted, "For all her arrests and convictions over ten years, Lizzie Lowry spent less than five months in jail."[9]

Prohibition also increased the number of African Americans involved in the illegal liquor business. In 1906, the *Charlotte Observer* noted, "There are a good many negro moonshiners, but these are employed by the whites who really own the plants."[10] Jim Crow culture and the racial hierarchy made African Americans nearly ideal employees in such an illegal business. Informing on their bosses produced consequences generally too dire to even consider. An *Asheville Citizen-Times* reporter noted this exploitative arrangement and quoted an attorney asserting that "men with money . . . are taking advantage of ignorant negroes [*sic*] desire to earn large sums with little work by using them as transporters. . . . The negroes, feeling they must protect the men higher up, take their punishment in silence while those who held out big rewards for them in the event of success let them suffer alone in failure."[11]

African Americans and poor whites often worked together at stills, a fact decried by many observers. After law enforcement arrested four African Americans and three white men in an illegal distilling operation near the Creedmoor community in 1905, the Oxford *Public Ledger* responded in high dudgeon: "It is to be deplored that any white man would stoop so low as to enter with a gang of negroes and still and sell liquor by moonshine as some have done here, and try to do all they can to uphold this damnable business, the worst curse that was ever put on any community."[12] In some cases, the racial status quo and a patriarchal system provided some benefits and protection to African Americans in the moonshine business. After agents killed two men and arrested a number of others in a raid in 1913, the *Winston-Salem Journal* reported on a mixed-race community in Yadkin County known as a moonshine haven:

> In that small section of Yadkin county usually known as the "Green Pond Section," "The Little Nation" or "The Big Woods" . . . they are a "Nation" to themselves. . . . A great many negroes along with the white people, although not thickly settled, compose the population for several miles around, and whatever is of use to one is of interest to all the people of this section, with few exceptions.
>
> The one thing persistent in this neighborhood, and which it seems impossible to stop entirely, is the manufacture of whiskey contrary to the laws of the land. . . . The negroes are used as "stools" and are always taken care of by the white folks behind them and these negroes have belonged to the clan [so] long they have become much worse than they would have been otherwise and are very impudent.[13]

While rare, it appears some African Americans owned moonshine operations and even achieved a significant level of success. The Kinston *Daily Free Press* reported on the arrest of John Stancill, a "well-to-do negro planter," near Greenville in 1916 on a charge of "illicit distilling." The paper noted that "Stancill owns an automobile, has a fine crop of tobacco and a nicely furnished home."[14] In

1913, Wilson County officials arrested Henry Barnes, "a big burley, black blockader," and destroyed six stills he owned.[15]

African Americans who transported illegal alcohol to, and marketed the product in, the African American sections of North Carolina's towns and growing number of cities were often the ones who benefitted the most from the illegal trade. The *Asheville Citizen-Times* noted the story of George Switzer, "the slickest bootlegger and criminal Hendersonville has ever produced," in 1921. The paper noted that Switzer operated at a high level and succeeded "in evading the hand of the law for many years." The affable bootlegger, however, was "captured red-handed" while accepting two gallons of the "jog-givin fluid known as moonshine" from illegal distillers. Switzer not only forfeited his freedom but had his seven-passenger Cole automobile confiscated as well.[16]

While the general stereotype of North Carolina women, particularly white women, in the early twentieth century shows them firmly in the prohibition camp, and often leading the way, the period saw an increase in women making the newspapers for their involvement in the illegal alcohol trade. Of course, women were subject to the same economic conditions as men—as well as the same temptations when moonshine yielded such high profits under Prohibition. Many women who came into the illegal liquor business had circumstances unique to their gender that made their situations even more desperate and led them to violate the law. Indeed, working in the moonshine business had long been a form of acceptable social welfare for widows and divorced women, like Rhoda Lowry, especially those with small children. In addition, judges often gave them a light sentence or suspended their sentence altogether and simply warned them not to make or sell liquor again.

Indeed, early twentieth-century newspapers contained numerous such hard-luck woman-moonshiner stories. The *Winston-Salem Journal* reported in 1907 on a Wilkes County woman convicted for "blockading" who was sent home and "given the chance to reform ... as she was a widow with five girl children, the oldest being only 11 years of age."[17] In 1921, Davidson County sheriff Sink took some flak for not arresting a Mrs. Jones Wilson of Emmons Township despite the fact that authorities caught her red-handed making illegal liquor. Sink explained to the Lexington *Dispatch* that the woman had seven children and was pregnant, and although she had a husband, he was "blind and a burden on the family." The sheriff declared that "the most distressing poverty imaginable existed in the home" and referred the woman to the Red Cross. He also asserted that arresting the woman would serve no purpose and that "it would be a clear violation of the dictates of humanity to take her away from the children."[18] A reporter for the North Carolina Baptist publication *Charity and Children*, however, was not so sympathetic but did seem to understand the woman's motivation: "The Davidson county woman who engaged in the selling of moonshine liquor in order to support her children, failed to arouse any sympathy. There are a great many things a healthy woman can do to support her family besides selling monkey rum; but nothing else is quite so profitable. A day put in over a wash tub, for instance, will bring good returns at present prices, but it is harder work than handing out a pint of liquor."[19] Of course, the reporter did not note that it was prohibition, so avidly supported by *Charity and Children*, that made "handing out a pint of liquor" so profitable.

Most women, like most men, participated in the business as a seasonal enterprise and for only a short period when they were under economic distress. Some, however, who might have initially become involved for traditional reasons, became quite skilled at the business, quite successful, and in some cases, quite notorious. The *Asheville Daily Gazette* reported on the arrest of Nancy Smith, "a professional unlicensed manufacturer of mountain dew" whom authorities caught "hard at work making that stuff that splits the heads of many."[20] In 1903, agents caught Huldah Nines of the notorious Dark Corner of northwest Wake County running a sophisticated still on the banks of the Neuse River, which she had operated for ten years. She cleverly concealed the still under a mill dam, and a "ventilation pipe ran up through a cane break, smoke came out the mill house chimney, water [came from] the dam, and slops [were] disposed into the river."[21] Authorities busted widow Mary Jones in 1909 with "the most skillfully concealed moonshine still" McDowell County revenue officials had ever seen. She hid her ninety-gallon still in a loft in her home.[22] In a 1912 interview with the *Lenoir Topic*, Burke County sheriff F. C. Berry called Mary Williams of the South Mountains moonshine haven "the most skilled moonshiner" he had ever seen. The paper asserted she was "cunning enough to baffle the officers for years."[23]

Columnist John Parris interviewed an eighty-six-year-old mountain woman in the 1950s who had been involved in the moonshine business for most of her life. She started out of economic necessity at age sixteen when her widower moonshiner father "came down with the miseries and had to take to his bed. With him sickly, it was either me to do the makin' or else starve." Her father evidently had quite the reputation for making quality liquor and his daughter learned the craft well. She commented that the liquor she and her father made "was spoke for quick" and "kept us in meat and coffee and sugar and flour. And a store bought dress now and then for me." She and her father made liquor the old-fashioned way, without using a thump keg, or as the woman termed it, "double-footin'" it. "Pa always said a feller that wouldn't take the time to double-foot ought to have to drink every drop of his own makin's and he'd get religion mighty quick." Like many women moonshiners, and many successful men in the business, the woman declared, "These lips of mine ain't never tasted whiskey."[24]

One of the most successful women moonshiners in the state in the early twentieth century, and definitely the most notorious, was Betty Sims of Polk County. A divorcee with four small children, Sims became a statewide sensation and a newspaper reporter favorite in 1906. Over more than six months, she fascinated reporters and the state when authorities arrested her for attempting to make a sizeable sale of liquor on the South Carolina state line. She became especially notorious as newspaper reports recounted her flouncing into court dipping snuff and wearing fancy dresses and hats, allegedly (although she denied it) setting fire to the Polk County jail, and then attacking a jailer with a knife when she tried to escape. The *Charlotte Observer* referred to her as a "daring Amazonian woman who goes armed and is notorious as a blockader" and as "the Queen of the Moonshiners."[25]

Women also became involved in the distribution of illegal alcohol. Police arrested Emma Walker, an African American woman from Asheville, in 1918 in a plainclothes operation for being a "whiskey jobber," essentially a wholesaler who acted as an intermediary between moonshiners and retailers. Given Asheville's status as a tourist town, Walker had a good business "supplying bell boys at some of the local hotels." Lt. Fred Jones of the Asheville police hailed her arrest: "She has given us more trouble than any other one dealer in whiskey here and her offenses have been flagrant."[26]

Women, especially in Native American and African American communities, often used their homes to dispense illegal liquor as a hedge against poverty. Generally called "blind tigers" in the early twentieth century, these informal saloons provided an important link in the chain between producers and consumers. The historical record is replete with examples of Lumbee and Tuscarora women using their homes to sell illegal alcohol by the shot. In 1904, the *News and Observer* called women liquor vendors "blind tigerines" when it noted that the Raleigh police were "having it out" with them and arrested one white woman and two African American women for retailing illegal liquor.[27]

Of course, women were also active on the other side of the liquor issue and even went beyond the normal organizing and lobbying of the Women's Christian Temperance Union and other prohibition organizations. Some actively engaged with law enforcement to fight the "scourge of alcohol." Women, even in active moonshine areas, often served as government informers. Deputy collector W. G. Pool asserted, "Strange as it may seem, the best informers the government has are women. The men in the community become debauched by the operation of the still or by liberally patronizing it, and as a result some woman gives the officers a tip to put an end to the demoralizing influence."[28] On some occasions, women took the law into their own hands and sought out and busted up stills on their own, not waiting for law enforcement to take action. In 1919, fifteen women from the Alliance section of Pamlico County, "incensed over the

Elizabeth "Betty" Sims N.C. Moonshine Hall of Famer

Perhaps the best-known woman moonshiner in North Carolina history—dubbed the "Queen of the Moonshiners" by the *Charlotte Observer*—was Elizabeth "Betty" Sims of Polk County. While she only appears in the historical record for a short period of time, she made a huge splash in 1906 when three federal revenue agents interrupted her in an attempt to sell illegal liquor in south Rutherford County near the South Carolina line. Like Lewis Redmond, Rhoda Lowry and the Lumbee, and Quill Rose, she was well aware of the advantages of operating near a state boundary. When the agents appeared from hiding, Sims ran across the border, but the agents caught her about 100 yards beyond the state line. Sims called for help and five heavily armed "confederates" confronted the agents. Outnumbered and outgunned, after a brief parley where Sims's defenders put up a twenty-five-dollar cash bond to ensure she appeared in court, the three law enforcement officials "gracefully retired unwilling to risk battle with the moonshiners."

In May, Sims became a statewide sensation when the press started to cover her trial in the Polk County courthouse in Columbus to answer to three state charges for trafficking in moonshine. The *Charlotte Observer* set the tone for subsequent accounts of Sims's court appearances when it described her colorful exploits and flamboyant attire as the twenty-two-year-old beauty (some accounts say she was twenty-six) strode into the courtroom: "She wore a Skyuka blue silk gown with a long flowing train, a nobby hat trimmed in sky blue and her mouth was decorated with a wood tooth-brush and snuff." Evidently Sims's career as a bootlegger had been very successful, as she appeared in another eye-catching outfit the next day. This time she marched into the courtroom with a checked shirtwaist, brown skirt, and wide-brimmed hat "trimmed with pink roses," with a wad of chewing gum in her mouth instead of snuff. On the court's third day in session, she sported still another new dress, and the *Observer* reported that "the men smiled as her rosy cheeks and new dress passed by." The judge, however, was not impressed by Sims's dresses or her defense that it was "accordin to natur for men to drink," and he declared that "such women" were a "menace to society and must be punished for the good of Polk."

When Sims did not appear on the fourth day of court, the judge had her rearrested and sentenced her to four months in the Columbus jail. This is where the case became even stranger. According to news accounts, Sims set fire to a trapdoor leading to a third-story cell, which held a man sentenced to a year in jail for manslaughter. The man escaped, but jailer Walker Newman grabbed Sims as she tried to get away. As she later reported, "We had it out right there," with Sims cutting Newman four times with a knife and the jailer retaliating "when he felled her by one blow to the floor" and put her back in her cell. Sims later told a *Charlotte Observer* reporter, "I didn't set fire to the jail. No, I didn't. The old man [her fellow prisoner] fired it. I didn't see that I was in there to fight fires and so I let it burn. When it began to get hot I pushed down the door and walked into the hall," where Newman confronted her. This incident led to a legend that Sims was "as strong as ten men and as fierce as a tiger when mad."

Although Sims was unique in her flamboyant appearance and sometimes outrageous behavior, reporters eventually delved into the details of her life, which make her an exemplar of the reasons many women entered the illegal liquor business. She reportedly came from a stable family background, "of good and honest parentage," although her brothers "also knew something about moonshine." She married Taylor Sims in her late teens, an alleged moonshiner as well, and soon thereafter bore four children. Taylor was abusive and probably an alcoholic, and Betty took the children and left him. As the Lexington *Dispatch* reported, she "was a good woman until finally driven to lawlessness to make a living, as she could not live with her brute of a husband. She took to selling whiskey because there was money in it."

Like Rhoda Lowry and countless other women, Sims took advantage of what was available and at hand to help her young family survive. In fact, she became so successful for the two years or so she was in the illegal liquor business that she not only supported her family but brought in enough money for luxuries like fancy dresses. Like many moonshiners before and after her, Sims was also evidently highly intelligent and creative, reportedly "one of the shrewdest blockaders in the business." She impressed a *Charlotte Observer* reporter not only with her fancy dresses but with her intelligence as well: "Her eyes are bright as sparks of fire. . . . She speaks well and talks with great animation." Indeed, while necessity brought Sims into the business, she, like many others, became attracted by the economic benefits a successful moonshine business could bring. For a bright woman, moonshining brought other opportunities rare in a patriarchal society. She seemed to thrive on the intellectual challenge of operating her own business, the adrenaline rush of evading law enforcement, and the unique freedom and opportunity the moonshine business gave a single woman.

After 1906, Betty Sims disappeared from the historical record. We do not know if she continued moonshining or if she remarried and settled down in a more normal life. But her extraordinary two-year career in the moonshine business tells us much about the possibilities and provision that illegal liquor provided for women, particularly in the rural south.

operation of a moonshine still in the vicinity," conducted their own raid on a reportedly "mammoth" operation. The women "divided the worm into 15 parts" and triumphantly "carried it out of the woods."[29] Women in Madison County's Bull Creek section in 1920 "banded together and searching out the still, found it, destroyed the outfit and threw the pieces into the main highway, leading near the place, as warning to others."[30]

In order to root out moonshining in her Avery County community, Crossnore School founder and superintendent Mary Sloop had herself deputized. She asserted "that education and liquor just didn't go along together" and determined to fight "liquor with every means I could devise."[31] She once found a still operat-

Mary Sloop, founder of Crossnore School in Avery County. The local sheriff deputized her and she fought a long campaign against moonshine in the county. (Courtesy of Crossnore School and Children's Home, Crossnore, N.C.)

ing near the school, busted it up, "carted it away in a wheelbarrow," and arrested the men operating it and hauled them to jail. Her work did not stop there, as she felt the need to help rehabilitate the men. Each Sunday, "she went to preach and pray for them." According to the Asheboro *Courier*, "The prisoners became so impressed that on the day of their trial they pled guilty and asked that a sentence of imprisonment be pronounced upon them that they might suffer for their sin."[32]

Some women also saw it as their civic and Christian duty to try to help out and rehabilitate women caught up in the moonshine business. When authorities incarcerated a Chatham County mother of two small children in the Wake County jail for moonshining with her husband, some "good ladies of Raleigh" went to the revenue commissioner's office and "indignantly denounced the imprisonment" of the young mother. When they did not receive acceptable answers there, they approached the governor's wife, "a very noble-hearted and sympathetic woman." She then accompanied them to Governor William Walton Kitchin's office. Governor Kitchin sent his lawyer and his personal secretary to the revenue commissioner's office, where they ended up posting bail for the woman. These charitably minded women then proceeded to provide the woman moonshiner with "some comfortable clothing to replenish her depleted and much soiled jail apparel." Later, they purchased a train ticket so she could return to Chatham County to be reunited with her children. The story did not end as the good women of Raleigh might have hoped, however, as the husband, upon hearing the news, "made his escape from the road gang, stole a cart and horse," picked his wife and children up, "and simply faded out of sight; none of them ever having been heard of since."[33]

While most moonshiners were individuals trying to find some way to help alleviate their poverty, the high prices for Prohibition-era illegal liquor also attracted financially stable and even wealthy individuals to the business. The *Raleigh Times* reported in 1906 on several "substantial well-to-do appearing citizens" who showed up in court in Wilkes County. According to the paper, these men "carried on the business with a high hand, using steam boilers and modern equipment, having fine horses and wagons."[34] In 1912, law enforcement arrested Alfred Cox from the Grassy Creek section of Ashe County for operating a large and elaborate illegal liquor operation in the wood house on his farm. The Greensboro *Daily News* reported, "Mr. Cox is a very wealthy farmer and owns two farms that are estimated to be worth $15,000 beside having a large amount of personal property. He lives in the richest and best section of Ashe county and is said to be a very prominent citizen."[35] In 1915, Grover Lamm and Wyatt Eatman, "prominent young merchants of Wilson," received sentences of sixty days on the county road crew for "violation of the prohibition law."[36]

The high profits from moonshine during the Prohibition era also led to new forms of business organization among moonshiners. Wealthier North Carolinians got involved in the business and financed and supplied materials to poorer still operators. Acting as suppliers separated these individuals from actual production and distribution and gave them "plausible deniability" that they were unaware moonshiners used those supplies for illegal activities. In 1906, agents arrested the "King Bee" of the Durham County moonshine business, D. T. Turner. Authorities alleged that Turner, who owned a farm worth $20,000, provided meal "and other supplies for a great number of distilleries in that section" and brought supplies in by the railroad car. He provided the moonshiners with sugar and other liquor-making materials in exchange for "part of the output of the stills" and probably had others doing the actual exchange and delivery of the product.[37] Store owners W. F. Clayton and J. R. Reagan of the Limestone Township in Duplin County faced charges for using moonshine as legal tender in their stores in 1917.[38]

Creative Wake County blockaders organized a "communistic, profit-sharing, socialistic defiance of iniquitous taxes" in 1905. The group sold stock in the enterprise throughout the Cedar Fork Township, and the group's still reportedly

Two moonshiners with an old-style still, taken by Japanese photographer George Masa. Masa staged the shot to use for a postcard. The "moonshiner" on the left is folklorist Bascom Lamar Lunsford. (Courtesy of North Carolina Room, Pack Memorial Library, Asheville, N.C.)

had twelve to fourteen owners, all "prosperous and self-respecting citizens." The operation was not only a "community still" but also a "movable neighborhood convenience." For a moonshine share, investors hauled the still to someone's property, "like a threshing machine," where "two negroes" employed to run the still turned a farmer's corn crop into liquor. The *Gaston Gazette* reported that on at least one occasion, "its stand was at a Sunday School."[39]

Given Al Capone's and other notorious organized crime figures' escapades during the Prohibition years, and movie and pulp fiction depictions from the era, folks have often assumed crime syndicates ran much of the North Carolina moonshine business. However, there is surprisingly little evidence of this, although some tantalizing clues do appear on occasion. In 1918, the *News and Observer* reported on suspicions of a "crime trust" in Asheville. The paper claimed local police "are working on the theory that the bootleggers of the city, of whom there appear to be myriads, are working under the leadership of some powerful individual 'higher up,' who is putting up for the whiskey and receiving the lion's share of the profits." As evidence for this bootlegger organization, police cited the fact that no matter how poor or friendless an arrested bootlegger may have appeared, he or she always appealed convictions and the accused "seldom remains in jail for any length of time, the necessary bond being quickly forthcoming." Although they never tracked a kingpin down, the police firmly believed "there is every evidence of some powerful head of the organization taking care of its members."[40]

If statewide alcohol prohibition had any real effect in North Carolina, it was to unite almost all of those who opposed the law in a vast criminal conspiracy and ensure that alcohol remained widely available. Although this sometimes meant illegally importing legally produced liquor from outside the state, it most often meant some involvement in illegal production and distribution. Indeed, for much of the twentieth century the moonshine business was one of the few enterprises that connected North Carolinians of all stripes, rural and urban, black and white, male and female, rich and poor. This widespread illegal behavior produced tremendous challenges to federal, state, and local law enforcement as they tried to enforce such unpopular, and widely violated, laws.

7

CHASING THE MOON

North Carolina's prohibition laws, and the illegal activity they supposedly banned, meant that law enforcement had to step up its game to try to stem the growing tide of illegal alcohol. Federal agents, still charged with enforcing the federal excise tax, especially hoped that now that local and state laws outlawed the sale and distribution of alcohol, they would receive more help cracking down on the illegal liquor business from local and state law enforcement agencies. While some sheriffs and state officials did become more active, that was generally not the case, and federal agents and prohibition supporters constantly complained about the lack of support from local and state police forces. The interactions between law enforcement and moonshiners did, however, provide excellent fodder to fuel the general public's ongoing fascination with the illegal liquor business and spawned numerous expressions in early twentieth-century popular culture dramatizing and sensationalizing this cat-and-mouse game.

Despite the new local and state laws enacted in the earliest years of the twentieth century in North Carolina, most local law enforcement officials remained reluctant to antagonize voters and alienate friends and family members by actively enforcing the laws. In addition, the traditional fiscal conservatism of the state kept those agencies underfunded and made the task of even the most zealous sheriff difficult. The *Chatham Record* complained in 1907 that in the aftermath of the Watts Law "there is little or no effort made by county officers to capture 'moonshine' stills. In a very few counties of the State is an illicit distillery ever captured by a sheriff or his deputy."[1] Several years after voters instituted statewide prohibition, complaints continued about the lack of enthusiasm from sheriffs in enforcing the law. In 1915, the North Carolina Anti-Saloon League superintendent, the Reverend R. L. Davis, sent a letter to all of the state's sheriffs challenging them to do their duty and making an indirect threat to their future electoral prospects if they did not: "Although some of our sheriffs are complimented for their active work in breaking up blockade stills, many complaints have come to me that other sheriffs are not doing their duty in this respect, and some are even accused of being friendly to the moonshine still. I, therefore, desire to call your attention to this law, and to emphasize the fact that it requires all sheriffs and police officers to search for and seize blockade stills. My opinion is that the majority of people will not be satisfied unless their sheriff measures up to his duty."[2] Even after some counties offered bounties for capturing stills, sheriffs and deputies generally remained less than enthusiastic about enforcement. As the *Randolph Bulletin* commented, "There's a lot of talk about the blockaders getting scarce, etc., but evidently there's nothing to it but talk for a deputy sheriff can usually scare up one any old day in this county if he happens to be in need of the twenty dollars that the county pays for a moonshine outfit."[3] Even where federal and local agents did attempt to enforce the law, critics complained that while they often captured stills, they rarely made actual arrests. The *Asheville Citizen-Times* referred to the capture of three men by federal agents in Graham County in a still raid in 1904 as an "unusual occurrence."[4]

Corruption among law enforcement, even among federal agents, also made capturing and convicting moonshiners difficult in North Carolina. In 1905, a statewide scandal hit Wilkes County when newspaper editor R. A. Deal exposed evidence of "collusion between revenue officers and blockaders." The corruption even included the man in charge of federal enforcement in the county, local deputy collector L. E. Davis. While authorities indicted Davis "for running a steam distillery," they had not yet tried, much less convicted, him. He even continued in his office and still collected his salary. As the *News and Observer* noted, "It was notorious that he was the proprietor of the still and that he was doing a prosperous business uninterrupted, naturally by his brothers in the revenue service, over whom as boss of the district, he exerted almost perfect control." Authorities only arrested Davis after two of his accomplices, and fellow deputy collectors, attacked Deal. The *News and Observer* closed its article on the Davis case with the claim, "There are plenty of cases where the owners of illicit distilleries have . . . procured protection by the payment of money to United States officers. Some of them pay as much as $150 per month; others smaller sums and still others pay different amounts to secure immunity from arrest while hauling whiskey over the roads."[5]

Wilkes County had no monopoly on such corruption in North Carolina. In 1906, the *Raleigh Times* accused Republican U.S. representative Spencer Blackburn of "having given his promise to protect certain blockaders in the mountains if they would give him money for his campaign and furnish liquor for the election."[6] After arresting three men for moonshining in Burke County in 1910, the *Statesville Sentinel* noted that "two out of the three men were officers of the law," a magistrate and a deputy sheriff. The third man was a deputy's son.[7] In 1915, in Transylvania County, authorities discovered an impromptu barroom in the county courthouse in Brevard: "The saloon was running in full blast while court was in session. In fact, 'court week' seemed to have been selected as a time when business would be brisk. The 'counter' was located in an alcove just off the court room, while the 'dispensary' was hidden in the belfry. There a barrel of liquor was found. A certain sign given in the alcove would be answered by a lowering of a string through the hole in the trap door when a bottle and the proper amount of coin could be sent up, the bottle returned in a few moments filled with whiskey."[8]

On those relatively rare occasions where raids resulted in the actual arrest of moonshiners, penalties were relatively light and the accused had many advantages in the courts. The more successful moonshiners hired the best lawyers to defend them. In 1919, the *Asheville Citizen-Times* asserted, "The whiskey makers have plenty of money with which to conduct their defense." The paper quoted a lawyer in an adjoining county who allowed as how he and other lawyers generally charged the accused blockaders "a much higher scale for professional services than applies to other alleged misdemeanents; and the money is always readily forthcoming without complaint."[9] Even those caught in the act at stills were difficult to prosecute. As the *Charlotte Observer* noted in 1908, "In the trial of moonshine cases in the past persons found at the blockade still when the raid was made have testified 'that they were just passing by and stopped a minute'; and thus escaped."[10] Even though some judges cracked down on such excuses and claimed that presence at a still was "prima facie evidence," such excuses still worked. A defendant in Cherokee County in 1915 successfully used the excuse that he was on his way to a revival meeting when he happened on a still and that he "had never heard that there was an illicit still on that creek."[11] In addition, it often proved nigh on impossible to convict someone unless law enforcement caught him or her red-handed at the illegal distillery. When Nash County officers accosted three men driving a wagon loaded with a still and 200 gallons of beer ready to distill, the men escaped into the night. The next day a Mr. Lancaster boldly came to town and filed a claim to retrieve his wagon and horses seized by the officers. Lancaster claimed that the moonshiners had stolen his horses and wagon from his barn. Since the officers could not identify the men hauling the illegal goods, the man successfully reclaimed his property, sans beer and still.[12]

Prosecutors also had difficulty getting witnesses to testify against friends and neighbors in illegal alcohol cases. The fact that informing could often have dire consequences made many individuals eager to avoid making a public accusation. In 1909, the *Asheville Citizen-Times* reported that a deputy marshal had to

Carl Schenck, chief forester on the Biltmore Estate and head of the first forestry school in the United States, the Biltmore Forest School. He tried to keep moonshiners off the vast estate but avoided testifying against them in court. (North Carolina State Special Collections Research Center)

physically chase Biltmore Estate forester Dr. Carl Schenck to serve a subpoena for him to testify against T. C. Whitaker, arrested for making moonshine on the vast property. The deputy successfully served the subpoena but not before "running a Marathon race in which he won the blue-ribbon over the learned doctor of the Kaiser-like appearance." While he lived most of his life in Germany, Schenck's eleven years in western North Carolina managing George Vanderbilt's estate and founding and operating the nation's first forestry school (the Biltmore Forest School) taught him that he needed good relations in the community. Testifying against moonshiners was a good way to encourage retaliation against the estate and its forests; arson served as a favored tactic for revenge in the south.[13]

Even if convicted, those involved in the illegal liquor business often got off with relatively light sentences. Those convicted with state crimes who could afford to pay often got off with just a fine. In 1911 in Mecklenburg County, a judge sentenced J. M. Hunnicutt to twelve months on the county chain gang or a $250 fine and C. J. Tucker to three months or a fifty-dollar fine. Both paid the fine and walked free.[14] Although federal penalties were stiffer, first offenders generally got off with a sentence of a "year and a day," most often for North Carolinians in the federal penitentiary in Atlanta. In most cases they served less than a year "on good behavior." Repeat offenders usually received from eighteen months to two years plus a $100 fine as their sentence. The *Mount Airy News* reported on a special railcar traveling through town in 1911 with several repeat offenders "on their doleful journey to Atlanta. Some of them will not catch sight

On the "Man's" Land

Finding locations for their secret stills has always challenged North Carolina moonshiners. While they have long favored hidden coves, swamps, deep woods, caves, and underground bunkers as still sites, placing an operation on one's own property was risky. Given that risk, many moonshiners preferred to site their stills on someone else's land, especially on large tracts owned by wealthy individuals, corporations, or federal or state government.

Although relatively common, locating a still on government land, particularly federal property, increased the possible penalties illegal distillers could face if they got caught. But given the vastness and remote nature of these lands, the temptation was strong. Jim Tom Hedrick got his start helping a man make moonshine at a still hidden in the Great Smoky Mountains National Park. National Park Service and U.S. Forest Service rangers have long battled moonshiners, and later marijuana growers, to keep them from setting up their illegal operations on public lands. Rangers, however, walked a fine line with local moonshiners and understood that if they were too zealous they risked retaliation, generally in the form of arson. Audley Whaley, who patrolled a section of the Great Smoky Mountains National Park in North Carolina well known for its moonshine, asserted, "Most of the time if I found a still I'd leave a note on it and tell them to get it out by a certain date or we'd take care of it." The one thing Whaley would not do, however, was turn people in to revenue agents. Whaley once told an Alcohol Tax Unit agent who asked him if he'd seen any "suspicious activity," "I'll do my job without your help and you do yours without mine."

North Carolina moonshiners also placed their stills on large tracts of private land. Timber companies always faced this challenge and generally used the same "warn but don't turn in" approach as Forest Service and Park Service rangers. On many occasions, "respectable" citizens expressed shock when agents discovered stills on their property. In 1915, the *Albemarle Enterprise* reported on a "brand new copper still" found on the property line of two of Stanly County's most prominent and respected citizens: county judge O. J. Sikes, "a leading member of the Baptist church," and register of deeds John M. Boyett, "a steward in the Methodist church." Big-time operators took advantage of this common practice by purchasing large tracts of land and hiring people to make moonshine on their property. If authorities discovered these illegal operations, they acted shocked that anyone could be making liquor on their property and argued that authorities could not expect them to know what happened in such a large area. The fact that such individuals never went near an actual still made it difficult for officers to charge them with a crime.

One of the more interesting private tracts that had moonshiner problems in the late nineteenth and early twentieth century was the Biltmore Estate. At its peak, George Vanderbilt owned 125,000 acres that stretched from the south side of Asheville to the Pink Beds area of Transylvania County. Forest managers, first Gifford Pinchot and later Carl Schenck, tried to rehabilitate the cutover lands and make them profitable as a forest preserve. Given the size of the estate and the economic conditions at the time, they frequently ran across stills. They generally employed the tactics used by rangers on public lands, but occasionally revenue agents beat them to the punch and arrested moonshiners on Vanderbilt land. In 1902, officers captured four men and a sixty-gallon still near Vanderbilt's hunting lodge on Mount Pisgah. The estate even had problems after Edith Vanderbilt sold 87,000 acres to the U.S. Forest Service in 1914. A year later, newspapers across the state reported, "Doubtless believing that raiders would never suspect that whiskey was made illegally within a short distance of the Biltmore mansion . . . moonshiners have done big business in a secluded spot within sight of the most elaborate residence in America."

of their native hills for two years; others will be away from their beloved crags and peaks and dark ravines for periods ranging from 15 to 20 months. It will be a sad crowd."[15]

While the press, and prohibition forces, tended to sensationalize any violence associated with the moonshine business, by and large relations remained fairly amicable between moonshiners and law enforcement during statewide prohibition. As the *Citizen-Times* reported in 1909, "As a rule, he [the moonshiner] does not go armed to kill . . . and he relies on his heels rather than the accuracy of his fire when the revenue men put in their appearance."[16] Apparently little had changed by 1916, as the *Charlotte Observer* noted: "A mistaken idea has gone out that the moonshiner is an extremely dangerous man or willing to risk death rather than be captured, but generally speaking they are far from the outlaw class as some think and when caught submit quietly and make sure to avoid injury to the officers or attempt to kill them but rather their scheme is to be too sly for the officers and outwit them and when brought to a show-down take it quietly and as a part of the business."[17]

Horace Kephart wrote extensively on moonshiner–law enforcement relations in *Our Southern Highlanders*. He interviewed revenue agent Charlie Beck on the subject and asked him about the moonshiners he encountered. Beck responded, "Nicest kind of people; they make good liquor." Beck continued to tell a story about catching an old moonshiner in the act: "I told the old man that I wouldn't arrest him at all if he'd give me his word to appear before the United States Commissioner at two o'clock the next Wednesday." The man agreed and Kephart asked, "Did he show up?" "Sure, he showed up," Beck replied, "punctual to the minute, and he made bond. Then he invited me to come and stay with him any time I'm down there. We're the best of friends." Such cordial relations extended to judges as well, who often took into consideration special circumstances in handing down sentences. As Kephart observed, "When a man, otherwise of good repute, was hailed before a court in spring or summer, for illicit distilling, and it was found that he had no one left at home to look after the farm, it was customary for the judge to parole him until the following winter, so that he could go back and make his crop. This being done, and his family provided for, the man would return without escort, give himself up, and serve his term."[18]

When violence did break out, it was most often in the form of retaliation against revenue agents. This often came when moonshiners doubled back on revenue agents and damaged their means of transportation. In 1916, moonshiners in Onslow County untied, shot, and drove off deputy collector J. P. Kennedy's horse while the officer tried to track them down. They then fired a few shots in his general direction to warn him away.[19] A group of officers successfully captured "a well-equipped moonshine outfit" near the Brown Mountain area of Burke County in 1912. However, when they returned to their automobile they "found the machine almost demolished. All the tires had been cut to pieces and two emergency tires carried off. All the lights had been shot out the wind shield shot to pieces and the indicators and other fixtures destroyed."[20]

While violence, particularly with guns, remained relatively rare, the capital investment, increased pressure from anti-alcohol forces to arrest people, and large incentives that came with prohibition did increase the intensity of some encounters between moonshiners and law enforcement. The Raleigh *Morning Post* noted in 1904, in the aftermath of the passage of the Watts Law, "For the past six or twelve months the officers say they have noticed that the maker of 'moonshine' whiskey is becoming more bold and has been developing a spirit of resentment when his property is attacked. Several times they have sulked around in plain view of the officers, with guns in their hands. Now they are seemingly more bold and fire occasionally."[21] In 1905, a group of seven or eight "blind tiger men ... white and black," terrorized the community of Columbia in Tyrell County when they fired random shots at the hotel room of Solicitor Ward and into the home of Mayor Woodley. The *News and Observer* reported, "Several window panes were broken ... but no one was hurt."[22]

In 1919, when war conditions caused the price of moonshine to skyrocket, Kephart wrote an article in the magazine *All Outdoors* and claimed, "Some five years ago when whiskey was still generally obtainable and the price lower, the 'moonshiner' was not apt to put up a fight to defend his still, and information could readily be secured by the officers." But now that the price of illegal liquor had risen to ten, or even twenty, dollars a gallon, "the prospects of big profits has provided an incentive to the 'blockaders' to defend his plant from raiders, and therefore ... fights with officers have become more common and the number of those killed has increased, both officers and law breakers."[23]

Shootouts between moonshiners with individuals killed or wounded did

Revenue agents, like moonshiners, liked to project a menacing image and loved posing next to "capturd" stills with drawn pistols. (Courtesy of Great Smoky Mountains National Park Archives, National Park Service Collections Preservation Center, Townsend, Tenn.)

occur, and the press, naturally, covered these rare cases widely. Stokes County's Smithtown area was one place with a reputation for the "extreme boldness and pugnacity" of its blockaders.[24] Angered by a successful June 1907 undercover operation and raid by twenty-one officers that netted thirteen stills and thirty-five blockaders, Oscar Sisk, "one of the most desperate characters of the notorious Smithtown section," ambushed, shot, and killed revenue officer J. W. Hendricks. Hendricks was cutting up one of Sisk's stills when Sisk attacked.[25] In 1911, a "pistol duel at close range" occurred "in the wilds of Wilkes County" when deputy marshals tried to arrest two moonshiners. Their relatives allegedly attacked the marshals as they searched the house, and the gunfight ensued. The authorities wounded three attackers, one seriously.[26] Such violence begat more violence and only two months later, moonshiners shot a revenue agent in the head in the same area of Wilkes County. The deputy collector recovered with only the loss of an eye.[27]

The early twentieth century did produce a number of noted North Carolina "desperadoes" and "outlaws" who did not share many of the redeeming qualities often attributed to early moonshiners. Most of these individuals had long criminal records for crimes other than moonshining, openly defied law enforcement, and regularly carried multiple weapons in public. In 1905, the newspapers along the North Carolina coast ran numerous stories about Nick Rogers, a convicted counterfeiter who had served time in a federal penitentiary. When released, he set up a still in Newport in Beaufort County, where he openly defied the prohibition laws. Agents arrested him numerous times, but he either bailed out or escaped. The *New Berne Weekly Journal* called Rogers "a desperate character ... [who] has debauched every neighborhood in which he has carried on his illicit business."[28] Oscar Sisk of Stokes County developed a similar outlaw reputation, especially after he shot and killed Hendricks.[29]

Hiram Wilson of the Cane Creek section of Yancey County became one of North Carolina's most notorious outlaws during this period. Between 1902 and 1907, Wilson was allegedly the "master of Yancey County in sundry evil ways." A career moonshiner, Wilson was accused of terrorizing the county, destroying ballot boxes, intimidating voters and shooting over their heads, shooting up communities, and tearing up churches all to make sure "county affairs have gone according to his will." The charismatic Wilson also allegedly corrupted "hundreds of youngsters caught under his hypnotic eye" and brought them into the moonshine business.[30] He first became known statewide in December 1902, when he shot and killed his brother, state senator Zeb Wilson, in a dispute over a horse. A jury acquitted him on the basis of self-defense, but news reports asserted that Hiram had earlier murdered a man named Hunnicutt in cold blood.[31] In 1904, officials arrested him, seized his four handguns, handcuffed and shackled him, and later convicted him of violation of the newly passed Watts Law and sentenced him to four years in the state penitentiary.[32] Strangely, and probably as a result of Wilson's political connections to the state Democratic Party, Governor Charles B. Aycock pardoned him on the dubious grounds that "he was led to violate the law by people who advised him that the [Watts] law was unconstitutional and would not be enforced."[33]

Aycock's pardon seemed to inspire Wilson, and he returned to Yancey County, where he became even bolder in his criminal actions. In 1906, the statewide press reported his death in a shootout, but that turned out to be a false rumor. When the *Statesville Record and Landmark* reported that Wilson had not really been killed, the reporter asserted that was "a pity, for from all accounts Wilson's death would be a happy riddance."[34] That year, however, county officials had finally had enough and organized a posse to hunt down Wilson, now "the leader of a gang no less desperate than himself," and bring him to justice. Authorities did have difficulty in organizing a party to go after him, as Wilson had the reputation of being "amazingly quick in the use of a gun. There's no Yanceyite who can claim to be his equal.... With one stroke of the hand he loads his empty revolver, and with what seems a single finger pull he empties it again." Wilson also took advantage of the geography of Yancey County, running his moonshine empire from across the nearby state line, in Tennessee.[35] In 1908, Wilson left

North Carolina and headed for greener pastures in Colorado, where authorities arrested him for killing a man in a shootout. In April 1908, the press once again reported Wilson's demise when a prison guard allegedly shot him when he tried to escape.[36] However, later accounts assert that he escaped the Colorado prison and reappeared years later in North Carolina, where authorities charged him on numerous occasions for various moonshine- and weapons-related crimes over the years. He ultimately died of natural causes at the age of eighty-six.[37]

Andy Orr was another North Carolina moonshiner and outlaw whose life and escapades took on legendary status. In 1916, the Greensboro *Daily News* reported that the Graham County blockader's "record reads like a fiction story, and many are the stories the revenue officers who have been located here for the past few years tell of him. He has been hunted, surrounded, shot at and almost captured numerous times, but always he has eluded the officers." In true outlaw fashion, Orr "boasted that he would never be taken alive, and that he would never serve time for making 'moonshine' liquor."[38] Between 1909 and 1916, authorities accused Orr of several murders in the area, although he either got off in court or hid out in the mountains. Orr developed quite the moonshining empire in far western North Carolina by taking advantage of a fruitful new market for his product as industrial logging operations brought thousands of thirsty young men to his doorstep. Orr reportedly had a gang "of desperate characters" and made a handsome living visiting "the lumber camps of that region on pay days to distribute 'fire water' to the employees."[39] Like Wilson, Orr went west when things grew too hot for him in western North Carolina when the lumber companies teamed up with law enforcement to try to bring him to justice. In 1917, however, he was "taken alive" by authorities in Cherokee County, Oklahoma, on a fugitive warrant for allegedly murdering Pleasant Birchfield in the fall of 1916 near Robbinsville. In April 1917, a jury convicted Orr, and the judge sentenced him to twenty-five years in the state penitentiary for second-degree murder.[40] These "notorious outlaws" were relatively rare, but they did play an important role by helping the prohibitionists and legal authorities demonize the moonshiner as a violent criminal.

While shootouts between law enforcement and moonshiners probably did increase in the first twenty years of the twentieth century, most violence related to the illegal liquor business came, as it did in the late nineteenth century, as retaliation against informants. Most of that revenge came primarily in the form of damage to property. As the *Charlotte Observer* noted in 1908, "If they [the moonshiners] find out [who the informer was] then there is trouble for that person, varying all the way from burning the informant's barn to cutting his harness to pieces, or in some way injuring his horses or cattle, or perhaps in the way of petty annoyances, all done very secretly and in a most underhanded fashion."[41] A man near Greenville in 1901, who allegedly "piloted" revenue officers to a local still, found his "buggy cut to kindling wood and his harness into scraps." *King's Weekly* noted, "The moonshiners are supposed to have had their revenge."[42] John Massey of Durham County had over 4,000 hills of his tobacco crop "cut down with a mowing blade" or "pulled up by the roots" by moonshiners bent on revenge in 1904.[43] The Oxford *Public Ledger* reported that the blockaders had erred, as Massey was a tenant on a farm belonging to John Hopkins, their intended target.[44] Barn burning served as an especially traditional form of revenge in North Carolina, and John Phillips of Yadkin County had his feed barn burned to the ground in 1919. The *Winston-Salem Journal* reported, "The supposition is that the fire grew out of the officers raid on the [local] moonshine plants."[45]

At times, revenge-minded moonshiners threatened physical violence or death to suspected informants. In 1903, blockaders in the Owlsboro area of Durham County placed a coffin at Sandy Hopkins's front door with a note attached: "You had better never report another still."[46] Moonshiners in the New Hope section of Iredell County in 1915 sent W. M. Mathahey a note "accusing him of warning officers of the whereabouts" of a still "and threatening personal injury if he warned officers again." As a point of further emphasis, the note's author also sketched a coffin at the bottom of the note with "DEATH" written across it.[47]

Moonshiners did on occasion resort to direct physical violence or shooting at informants. Four men horsewhipped J. L. Howard for informing in 1903.[48] Evidently the note to Mathahey had not been enough to ensure his silence, as a "gang of moonshiners" fired shots at his "aged mother," Mrs. Eliason Clementine.[49] On extremely rare occasions, retaliation took the form of outright assassination. In 1902, "prosperous young farmer" John Clayton was "sitting by his fireside reading to his mother," when someone shot through the window, hitting him in the neck and killing him.[50] Most often deaths occurred when random shots fired into a house, a common revenge tactic, accidentally hit someone. The Greensboro *Daily News* reported on the trial of five men for Riley Easter's murder in Surry County in 1919. The men killed Easter and wounded his six-year-old granddaughter when they "came to the little frame house and proceeded to shoot it up" in retaliation after Easter's father provided information on their distilling operations to the sheriff. Since the shots were random, the men thought they would go free, but the jury convicted three of them and sentenced them to death for capital murder.[51]

Despite the moonshine business's seamier side and the efforts of prohibition forces and law enforcement in the state to emphasize its negative aspects, many North Carolinians embraced the state's status as one of the leading moonshine states in the nation. Indeed, in the early years of the twentieth century, moonshine became a key component of the state's popular culture. Asheville especially embraced moonshine imagery as part of its tourism promotion. In 1901, the Battery Park Hotel, the city's premier resort hotel at the time, "had a moonshine still on display" in its lobby. Hotel manager E. P. McKissick even dispensed souvenir bottles to convention goers of a substance reputed to be "a liquid sometimes known as 'mountain dew' and sometimes 'moonshine,' in which latter form it has been known to get men in trouble in Judge Boyd's court."[52] In 1902, in a speech to attendees at a Knights of Pythias convention in town, Alfred S. Barnard waxed eloquent in extolling Asheville's virtues and beauties. Included in those virtues was "mountain moonshine warm from the secluded still, redolent with the fragrance of the native nubbin, gurgling from the worm with somnolent melody."[53] When the Grove Park Inn supplanted the Battery Park as the top resort hotel in town in 1913, hotel manager Fred Sealy also had a still placed in the hotel's lobby.[54] When Asheville Rotarians attended a convention in Atlanta in 1917 to promote Asheville and its "pure" water supply, they planned "to take along the typical clothing of the mountaineer and at some secluded spot in a hotel lobby in Atlanta are going to set up and apparently operate a regular moonshine still. Revenue officers also from the city will raid the still and when it is opened it will be found to contain a run of regulation pure Asheville water."[55]

North Carolinians coined a number of humorous colorful phrases for illegal liquor and told jokes poking fun at the business during the period. William McCall referred to moonshine as "that powerful rank pizen what cheers the heart of even a man with a nagging wife."[56] In an article in *Mountain Life and Work*, Cratis Williams shared moonshine metaphors he had heard in the Watauga County area. Bad liquor was referred to as "white mule" or stuff that makes "a rabbit twist a rattlesnake's tail" or "a tomcat spit in a bulldog's eye." Williams also shared some jewels on the virtues of good liquor, which would make "a preacher lay down his Bible," "a man wink at his mother-in-law," or "the lion and the lamb lay down together."[57] North Carolina native and University of Virginia president E. A. Alderman coined perhaps the most famous and popular of these moonshine metaphors during the period. He often quipped that only one drink of his home state's moonshine would "make a jackrabbit walk up and spit in a bulldog's face."[58] In 1903, the Southern Pines *Free Press* poked fun at North Carolina's reputation as the nation's number one moonshine state: "North Carolina has issued a pamphlet on the 'Hidden Resources of the State,' but it throws not light on the moonshine stills."[59] During the Philippine conflict, the *Charlotte Observer* jokingly reported, "The Filippino [*sic*] general who tanked his soldiers up on wine and then ordered them to attack the American lines at San Fernando is a genius, but he could doubtless get better results if he had a supply of North Carolina moonshine sow-paw on hand, as that compound is said to be the greatest fight producer yet discovered."[60]

Better-known moonshiners in some places in the state even took on celebrity status. In 1905, officials announced plans for a big picnic at the Old Scotch Fairgrounds in Ellerbe in Richmond County. The main attractions at the picnic included traditional treats such as "lemonade stands, photograph tents, talking machines and baskets of fried chicken and pies." The Ellerbe event, however, included the novel attraction of the "probable appearance of the Cagle boys, a pair of local desperadoes, who make moonshine whiskey in the hills of Mountain creek, and on gala occasions come forth to mingle with the civilized folks, wearing long hair, long pistols and big hats."[61] Amos Owens and Quill Rose were other celebrity moonshiners whose exploits became widely known and publicized during the early twentieth century. They also gained popular recognition for their highly entertaining exchanges with judges.

By the early 1910s, North Carolina had become a popular site for turning many of the moonshine stereotypes and colorful metaphors into popular movies, which often featured law enforcement efforts to crack down on the illegal activity. One of the first films made in North Carolina was more in the vein of a "reality" production, featuring an actual raid on a still in Burke County's South Mountains. The film, produced in 1913 by the Ray Film Company of Asheville, began with the payoff of an informant and the organization of a raiding party in Morganton—led by Daniel Kanipe, the purported only survivor of Custer's Last Stand. The climax of the film came with "the charge down the mountain side on the still in full blast, the fight, flight and final capture of the operators." Of course, the real "operators" of the still had long since fled, given all the commotion, but producer C. F. Ray solicited the services of some local men who supposedly had some expertise in moonshining. As the Morganton *News-Herald* reported, "In this way the real operations were secured. ... There will be more reality in these pictures than any ever shown here." The film screened locally at the New Theater, with the captured still prominently displayed in front of the theater.[62]

While this early film has not survived, it did begin an era of moonshine-themed movies filmed in the mountains—most in the Bat Cave and Chimney Rock area—that lasted through the decade. The movies generally portray moonshiners as villains. The first of these was *Moonshine Maid and the Man*, filmed by silent-movie giant Vitagraph and featuring Ned Finley, who produced and starred in numerous films in the area. *Moonshine Maid* tells the story of Dave (Finley), who tries to earn the affection of Nancy by securing a $1,000 reward for informing on local moonshine kingpin Job. Unbeknownst to Dave, Nancy is Job's daughter and is at the still dressed as a man to help her sick father, when a raid ensues. When the obligatory shootout breaks out, the moonshiners wound Dave mortally. He dramatically apologizes to Nancy as he dies, uttering the words "I didn't know, Nance, that you and your dad ran it."[63]

Celebrity moonshiner Aquilla "Quill" Rose of Eagle Creek in Swain County. The colorful, and highly quotable, Rose was featured in several books in the late nineteenth and early twentieth centuries. (Courtesy of Great Smoky Mountains National Park Archives, National Park Service Collections Preservation Center, Townsend, Tenn.)

Aquilla "Quill" Rose N.C. Moonshine Hall of Famer

No individual in North Carolina history, except for maybe Popcorn Sutton, better fit the popular stereotype of a moonshiner than Aquilla "Quill" Rose. Rose spent most of his life on Eagle Creek in the far reaches of western Swain County, an area referred to by author Horace Kephart as the "back of beyond." An *Asheville Gazette-News* article in 1911, after federal authorities arrested Rose for the first time, characterized him as "the type of mountaineer that you read about but seldom see." He definitely looked the part and reporters and writers described him on many occasions as an impressive physical specimen, six feet two with broad shoulders and a long black beard, sporting a black felt hat and suspenders, and invariably puffing on a pipe. His lifestyle also fit the classic moonshiner stereotype. He was a legendary deer and bear hunter, played a mean fiddle, served in the Confederate army, was known far and wide as a storyteller, and was famous for his hospitality to friends and visitors. But he also had a penchant for violence and killed at least one man (and according to some legends, many more).

Born just over the state line from Eagle Creek in Cades Cove, Tennessee, in 1841, Rose probably moved to North Carolina in the 1850s. He made legal whiskey as part of his subsistence before the Civil War. During the war he, along with Lewis Redmond's brothers, joined Gen. William Holland Thomas's legendary Legion of Cherokee and Highlanders as a private. We know little about his service record, although like Amos Owens's, his stint in the Confederate army probably compounded and solidified any feelings he had about federal authority, or even authority in general.

Several accounts, including John Preston Arthur's *Western North Carolina: A History*, claim that Rose's first major brush with the law came when he got into a brawl soon after the war near Bryson City with a man named Rhodes. According to Arthur, Rhodes shot Rose, wounding him severely, but Rose killed his adversary with a knife. Although it was a clear case of self-defense, Rose fled to Texas for a short time, probably in fear of retaliation from Rhodes's family and friends. In 1871, the *Raleigh Sentinel* reported on a "fatal affray" at Deep Creek near Bryson City, where Rose and Harry Burns, "under the influence of liquor which both had been freely indulging," shot it out, with Burns being "immediately killed" and Rose "dangerously if not mortally wounded." Given the times and lack of reporting and sketchy records, this might have been the same incident, although many accounts credit Rose with having several "notches on his gun."

Rose next appears in the historical record in Wilbur Ziegler and Ben Grosscup's 1883 account of their adventures as tourists and hunters in western North Carolina, *The Heart of the Alleghanies*. This book first introduced Rose to a national audience. The authors and two of their friends made the long ride into Eagle Creek to hire Rose and his brother Jake to lead them on a deer hunt with dogs. By this point, both apparently were legendary as hunters, moonshiners, and fiercely independent mountaineers: "The Rose brothers are known to be men good-natured, but of desperate character when aroused. They have been blockaders. Living outside of school districts, and seemingly all State protections, they refuse to pay any taxes. . . . Thus recognizing no authority, they live in a pure state of natural liberty, depending on its continuance upon their own strength and daring, the fears of county officers, the seclusion of their home, and their proximity to the Tennessee line." Zeigler and Grosscup emphasized the "good-natured" aspect of the brothers' temperament and emphatically declared that the widely circulated stories that moonshiners were prone to attack and kill anyone straying near their stills were ridiculous.

Most of Ziegler and Grosscup's story of their encounter with Quill Rose involves their deer hunt, but there is an interesting little sidebar concerning Rose's drinking habits. As Rose woke the men up early in the morning for their hunt, he reached under one of the beds and produced a gallon jug of moonshine. "I reckon we'll have a dram before breakfast," the authors reported Rose asserting, "with a jolly twinkle in his eye," as he passed around a "glass of liquor as clear as crystal." Rose himself "drained off a four-fingered drink."

As the late nineteenth and early twentieth century came to the Great Smoky Mountains bringing thousands of loggers and miners, Rose, in the words of Horace Kephart, "an original genius," adapted to the times. Indeed, while he was of a relatively advanced age for this time in the mountains, he did some of his most prolific business during this period with a market of thirsty young male loggers virtually at his doorstep. Rose developed an ambivalent relationship with local mine and timber owners who tried to keep liquor out of their towns and mining camps and who, at the same time, loved to hunt with him, hear his colorful stories, and drink his liquor. Trying to keep Rose out of their towns and camps proved a losing battle as, in the words of Haywood County historian Clark Medford, the moonshiner was "such a sly and smooth operator." In addition, his winning personality made local elites some of Rose's greatest defenders when he, as he often did, got into trouble with the law. Rose had an especially close relationship with Bryson City timberman and land speculator Jack Coburn, and Rose even gave Coburn his well-used revolver late in the moonshiner's life.

Rose's most notable, and best-documented, encounter with the justice system came in 1911 when, at the age of seventy, he was caught by federal agents at his still dipping out slops to feed his hogs. Amazingly, it was the first time in his almost fifty years as an illegal distiller that federal revenue agents had caught him. Rose had well lived up to his alleged personal motto of "Don't get ketched," but his age and perhaps his overconfidence betrayed him on this occasion. His trial in Asheville before judge James E. Boyd became a media sensation and was covered statewide. While the *Raleigh Times* reported that Rose "was not 'exactly' engaged in moonshining" when the officers accosted him, he was "'so near' the scene of operation" that the jury convicted him. However, Rose's age and the influence of "big lumbermen" who intervened "on behalf of the old man" helped him "escape Atlanta," the federal penitentiary where he would have been sent, and the judge sentenced him to a fine and probation on his promise that he would not moonshine again.

Rose received perhaps his greatest, and longest-lasting, fame and notoriety when, in 1913, Horace Kephart prominently featured the moonshiner in his classic work on southern Appalachian culture, *Our*

Southern Highlanders. Kephart's account of Rose's exchange with a judge over aging his liquor falls into the popular "moonshiner humorously responds to the judge" genre. Similar stories attributed to moonshiners like Amos Owens and Quill Rose became a firm part of the moonshiner stereotype, constantly retold and embellished in the popular press by the early years of the twentieth century.

Accounts of Rose's exploits in the works of John Preston Arthur, Horace Kephart, and many other western North Carolina writers made him the archetypal moonshiner in the region. Poet Rebecca Cushman even memorialized Rose in a long poem, evidently based on an interview with Jack Coburn, that begins,

> Back in the early part of the century
> Quill Rose was the most picturesque
> blockader
> In the Smokies, and it is safe to guess
> The Revenue agents regarded him much
> as a baffled cat
> Regards the bird that is just out of reach;
> For few there were who dared the trip to
> Eagle Creek.
> Quill's aim was quick and deadly as is
> lightning,
> And he knew no fear of devil or of man.

Perhaps the best known of the silent-era moonshine films is *Heart of the Blue Ridge*, based on a novel by Elkin writer Waldron Bailey. Filmed at the Esmeralda Inn in Bat Cave, the movie tells the harrowing story of Plutina; her true love, Zeke; and jealous moonshiner suitor Dan. When Dan kills Plutina's pet bear after she spurns his advances, Zeke retaliates and destroys Dan's still. In revenge, Dan kidnaps Plutina and takes her to the mountains, where Zeke tracks him down and fights it out with the villain on the edge of a cliff. Dan "plunges on to the rocks below and Zeke saves Plutina from an awful death."[64]

Another silent film shot at the Esmeralda Inn, *The Midnight Raid*, was a dramatic reenactment of a raid on a still by "twenty khaki-clad troopers" who "charged the embattled blockaders ... as the deadly rifle fire shrieked through the air." Again, the forces of law and order win out and the menacing hillbillies bear the brunt of the dying. The film featured forty extras from the Asheville area hired to play both troopers and moonshiners. Director Fred Balshoffer complimented the extras on their enthusiasm and realism. "Those mountaineers certainly enter into the spirit of the thing, for I never saw men die more naturally in all my life."[65] Bat Cave and the Esmeralda Inn's heyday as "the motion picture studio capital of the Southeast" ended with the 1918 production of another Ned Finley vehicle, *The Raiders of Sunset Gap*, another shoot-'em-up with the moonshiners once again getting the short end of the stick.[66] A few more similar films were shot in the 1920s, but by that time the moonshine movie genre had run its course and the silent-movie era in North Carolina came

MOVING PICTURES OF THE

Capture of a Moonshine Distillery

WILL BE SHOWN

Princess Theatre

MONDAY, SEPT. 29th

Only moving picture ever made of a genuine "moonshine still," showing moonshiners at work, surprise and capture by local revenue officers.

Mack Reed, former chairman of county commissioners of Buncombe shown making his first raid.

D. A. Kanipe, only surviver of Custer's band who escaped massacre in charge of raiders.

T. F. Roland, Deputy Marshal of Asheville, one of the Revenue officers making the capture.

Made by Ray Film Co., of Asheville.

The captured still is on display in front of Princess theatre.

*Ad for one of the first silent movies filmed in North Carolina, a "reality" picture showing a raid on a moonshine still led by the alleged only survivor of Custer's Last Stand, Burke County revenue agent Daniel Kanipe. (*Asheville Gazette-News*, 26 September 1913)*

Cabin at the Esmeralda Inn in Bat Cave, North Carolina's silent-movie capital. A number of "moonshine and feud" movies used this cabin in their filming. (Courtesy of North Carolina Room, Pack Memorial Library, Asheville, N.C.)

Carl Schenck's Biltmore Forest School boys in the early 1900s. The boys often wrote funny songs for Schenk's "sangerfests," including the school's unofficial theme song, "The Little Still." (Courtesy of North Carolina Room, Pack Memorial Library, Asheville, N.C.)

to a close. Hollywood did not show much interest again in North Carolina and its moonshine until the 1950s.

Moonshine was also a popular theme in music composed in North Carolina during the early twentieth century. Vaudeville acts performed in the state's cities included such tunes as "My Moonshine Girl down in North Carolina" and "I'm Wild about Moonshine."[67] Perhaps the most memorable moonshine song composed in the state was one popularized by students at the Biltmore Forest School, America's first school of forestry. The school was operated in the Pink Beds section of rural Transylvania County on property owned by George Vanderbilt. Prussian Carl Schenck founded and headed the school and liked to promote camaraderie, often fueled by alcohol and group singing, among his students. In 1903, one of Schenck's students, Douglas Rodman, wrote a song with "an almost irresistible lilt" entitled "The Little Still," which had the lyrics:

Down under the hill there is a little still
And the smoke's all curling to the sky.
You can easily tell, by the sniffle and the smell,
There's good liquor in the air close by.
Oh, it fills the air, with a perfume rare,
And it's only known to a few,

So turn up your lip, and take a little sip,
Of the good old mountain dew.[68]

The fact that Schenck and his students often encountered stills as they went about their work in the forest, and that they were known to enjoy the local product at their regular "sangerfests," led them to adopt the song as the school's unofficial theme song. There is no record of whether George Vanderbilt approved or not. Rodman tragically died young after a short but distinguished career as a pioneering forester in New Mexico and Oregon in 1916.[69]

By 1920, the moonshine business had experienced a tremendous boom and, like much of North Carolina, been transformed by the modern industrial world. Statewide prohibition had done little, if anything, to stop the flow of liquor in the state, and if anything, it helped turn huge numbers of its citizens into criminals or, at the least, accomplices to criminal behavior. Unfortunately, the nation at large learned little from North Carolina's example and followed the state in enacting a sweeping ban on the manufacture and sale of alcohol.

NATIONAL PROHIBITION IN NORTH CAROLINA

For North Carolina's moonshiners, national Prohibition ushered in the most profitable era in the history of the state's illegal liquor business. The state's moonshiners now had a national market for their product. They also had a competitive advantage, with existing infrastructure, long expertise in the business, and a reputation as one of the top moonshine states in the nation. Indeed, like statewide prohibition, national Prohibition only further solidified the North Carolina moonshiner's prominent position in both popular culture and reality.

By far the biggest effect of World War I on the North Carolina moonshine business was the war's impact on bringing about national Prohibition. While the prohibition movement already had tremendous momentum before the outbreak of war, and twenty-six states had already become dry, the war gave the issue new urgency. Propaganda campaigns by pro-prohibition groups characterized alcohol and drinking as unpatriotic and pro-German. Near the war's beginning in September 1917, Woodrow Wilson used his war powers to ban the manufacture of liquor. That same year, Congress passed the Eighteenth Amendment to the Constitution and sent it to the states for ratification. In November 1918, Congress passed a temporary Wartime Prohibition Act stopping the legal sale of alcoholic beverages with more than 1.28 percent alcohol for the duration of the war. States approved the Eighteenth Amendment in near-record time, in only eleven months, with the final required state ratifying it on 29 January 1919. National Prohibition went into effect one year later.

As many critics of prohibition pointed out, the passage of the Eighteenth Amendment did not appreciably dampen the nation's thirst for alcohol and fueled a huge boom in its illegal manufacturing in North Carolina. The *Charlotte Observer* issued a cry of alarm not long after national Prohibition went into effect in

Iconic postcard produced by the Asheville Postcard Company using a George Masa photograph. (From the author's personal collection)

1920: "Reports coming to the treasury department from the south indicated a heavy increase in illicit liquor making and selling. Conditions in some sections of North Carolina are alarming. Moonshiners of a very bold and prominent type are gaining a foothold in communities heretofore described as 'good.'"[1] As the Greensboro *Daily News* reported in early 1920, high profits fueled this moonshine-making frenzy in North Carolina: "The moonshine industry is running wild, both county and federal officers agree. . . . Witnesses in police court tell of paying as high as $8 to $10 a pint for blockade liquor, which a few years ago could be purchased for $2 per gallon of a vastly superior quality."[2] Horace Kephart observed in 1922 a similar phenomenon in the far western part of the state: "The immediate effect of prohibition was to put an enormous premium on illicit distilling. Formerly the profit on moonshine whiskey had been only seventy-five cents to a dollar a gallon, at the stillhouse; today it is three to six dollars. A man working a still so small he can pick it up bodily and run away with it, at the first alarm, can make a thousand dollars in profit with it in a few weeks."[3]

Further boosting incentives to produce illegal liquor, national Prohibition came along at a time of extreme economic hardship in North Carolina, particularly for farmers. As Charles Thompson observed, "We have to remember that all of this was happening when farm prices were already plunging in the aftermath of World War I. In the rural South, particularly in the deepest sharecropping regions and in the Appalachian Mountains, the 1920s were anything but

Popular postcard created by the Asheville Postcard Company. Such postcards helped fill the huge demand for moonshine-related souvenirs by tourists to western North Carolina. (Courtesy of North Carolina Room, Pack Memorial Library, Asheville, N.C.)

roaring. With people desperate for money, they were ready to take risks."[4] The *Twin-City Daily Sentinel* eloquently connected low farm prices and moonshining in North Carolina in 1921: "The farmers are dispirited because tobacco does not sell for higher figures and in their desperation to make value and tongue meet they resorted to the manufacture of moonshine liquor."[5] Of course, poor economic conditions only increased incentives to make, transport, or sell moonshine in the late 1920s and 1930s when the Great Depression hit the state.

With these incentives in place, people all over the country jumped into the illegal alcohol business making "bathtub gin" and other concoctions. But North Carolina producers had a competitive advantage in the business due to the state's long-standing reputation as a haven for moonshiners and for the reputed quality of its liquor. The *Charlotte News* reported, "The statistics reveal that the moonshine industry flourishes in North Carolina as in no other state." The paper then repeated a ditty popular in the state equating the state's moonshine reputation with its reputation for fighting prowess in the Civil War: "First at Bethel, farthest at Gettysburg, last at Appomattox and longest at the still."[6] The state continued to uphold its national reputation throughout the period, as the Burlington *Daily Times-News* noted in 1934: "The North Carolina brand of corn likker is famous the nation over. It is a known fact that many New Yorkers stock up on native North Carolina corn juice instead of more expensive legal stuff manufactured in plants."[7] Although the story is probably apocryphal, the

Twin-City Daily Sentinel reported in 1921 that illegal liquor seized in western North Carolina sported labels reading:

> PURE MOUNTAIN
> KORN LIKKER
> Bottled in Bond
> Made in the backwoods of the mountains of western
> North Carolina by an old-time honest-to-god blockader that
> don't give a d——n for laws and prohibition.
> Retailed on the Asheville market by all high class
> bootleggers for five bones a pint and worth every cent of it.
> Guaranteed to be strong enough to make you drunk as the
> devil in ten minutes and mean enough to make a she-baby
> bulldog spit in a whale's face.
> Shake well and get ready to have a fit before drinking.[8]

The same year, the *Charlotte Observer* quipped that the organizers of the Made in the Carolinas Exposition should display a beautifully constructed copper still seized by law enforcement in the Mallard Creek area of Mecklenburg County. The still, the paper observed, "would afford ample demonstration of the fact that the coppersmith has a place in the ranks of native genius."[9]

Observers frequently noted the fact that North Carolina's reputation as one of the nation's top moonshining states was particularly ironic given its equally strong reputation as an antiliquor state. In 1921, the *Winston-Salem Journal* noted, "North Carolina, one of the first to taboo the saloon, has about the most trouble giving John Barleycorn a real knock-out blow. Moonshine plants fairly blossom in this State."[10] The Burlington *Daily Times-News* noted in 1933, "It is a peculiar irony of the fact that a state noted for its moonshine liquor should go overwhelmingly into the dry column, but this she did and therefore, we are officially as dry as the Sahara."[11]

The moonshine business did not experience many major changes during national Prohibition. Innovations toward industrial and businesslike operation that had begun in the early twentieth century did, however, accelerate. Manufacturing using sugar and molasses, adulteration, thump kegs, steamer stills, and stills made of cheaper materials became more common. Earlier changes made to transportation and distribution, such as hauling liquor to market in automobiles and trucks and so-called big-time bootleggers handling more and more of the transportation and sales, became the norm as well. The use of steamer stills particularly expanded due to their ability to make liquor faster and in higher volume. In addition, the increased availability of metal drums used to store gasoline and oil, which came from the dramatically increased availability of automobiles, made such stills more cost effective. The *Winston-Salem Jour-*

Huge steamer-still moonshine operation. Such large plants became more common as national prohibition caused moonshine prices, and profits, to soar. (Courtesy of the North Carolina Collection, UNC Libraries, UNC–Chapel Hill)

nal noted in 1920 that "the manufacturers of steel gasoline drums have unconsciously conferred a boon upon enterprising members of the A.M.M.A. [the fictitious Associated Moonshine Manufacturers Association], according to local prohibition officers, who have discovered that excellent steamers, capable of producing from ten to twelve gallons of whiskey per day are now being operated by blockaders who make use of the gasoline drums with but few minor changes needed to put them to illicit operation."[12]

One innovation that did make its way into North Carolina from elsewhere, probably from Virginia, was the use of huge submarine, or groundhog, stills. These distilleries combined the mash barrels and the still itself so that moonshiners did not have to transfer beer into the still. All the operator had to do was put the sugar, cornmeal, malt or yeast, and any other "secret ingredients" into the long tank, allow them to ferment, and then light a fire—increasingly using some sort of propane or natural gas system—and distill the liquor. Most of the time, illegal distillers dug these stills into a hill or dirt bank, with about a two-foot space left around the tank. They then placed the heat source at the front of the still, with a chimney or some sort of exhaust hole in the dirt at the back. This caused the flames to spread on either side of the tank, heating up the cavity in the bank and distilling the beer.[13] Many of these stills easily held over 1,000 gallons and greatly speeded up the liquor-making process. In addition, some distillers developed ways to construct submarine stills at least partially using wood and cheaper metals, greatly decreasing costs. These stills began to crop up more commonly in the late 1930s and early 1940s, mainly in the Piedmont and eastern North Carolina. In 1940, the *Daily Times-News* reported that authorities near High Point had seized a "submarine-shaped still that measured three and one-half feet tall, four feet wide and eight feet long and [held] between 1,000 and 1,500 gallons of mash."[14]

Other practices that speeded up the process of fermentation and distillation and made the liquor appear to be higher proof than it actually was became much more common under national Prohibition as demand soared. Indeed, quality and taste became less of a concern as supply lines stretched into the urban south, the Northeast, and the upper Midwest. Distillers had less and less contact with their actual customers, who were separated by several layers of middlemen (and women). The market was for liquor that would get folks drunk quickly, so high proof—or at least the appearance thereof—became the primary consideration for most moonshiners. Practically all of the moonshine that came out of North Carolina stills was now primarily distilled with sugar or molasses. The *Statesville Record and Landmark* wrote that Alcohol Tax Unit (ATU) chemists had reported that North Carolina moonshiners had "abandoned the painstaking distilling process of their forefathers for haphazard practices that result in quick 'runs' and terrible liquor. . . . The chemists call it 'sugarhead.' It's described as a general mixture of water from the most convenient brook, sugar, molasses, just enough grain mash to assure fermentation, and whatever insects or mice chance to fall into the open vats." The *Record and Landmark* quoted one agent as claiming, "Frequently we find snakes. And once a dead hog had fallen into a vat and drowned."[15]

Even as early as 1920, the *Charlotte Observer* reported that the increase in moonshining in western North Carolina "is largely responsible for the sugar and molasses shortage in the country."[16] The increased use of sugar and molasses did give law enforcement a new weapon to use for tracking down moonshiners, however. As the *Observer* also reported, "Revenue agents are busy chasing consignments of sugar on their way to the back country districts where the booze factories are flourishing as never before."[17]

Adulteration to make the liquor appear higher proof also became more and more common. One relatively benign substance used to adulterate moonshine was so-called beading oil, or glycerin. Commonly available in North Carolina due to its use in the textile industry, beading oil took advantage of the traditional method of proofing liquor by pouring some into a small bottle or vial,

Unique Stills

One thing you learn about North Carolina moonshiners the more you study them is that they are endlessly creative in finding ways to make their product. From the late 1800s to the present day, illegal producers in the state have come up with all kinds of imaginative ways to make a still, often using whatever materials they may have had at hand.

One of the earliest reports of a unique still came from Moore County in 1892. Bill Jordan of the Long Leaf community got busted for the possession of a tiny four-gallon still "made of a powder can set in a mud furnace, having as a top or cap a large coffee pot. The 'worm' is made of tin." Jordan claimed that the still made "fine and strong" liquor and that "one gallon of it had made twenty men drunk."

Agents ran across any number of such very small stills, which were easily concealed and carried away, in the late nineteenth century. In 1894, revenue agent Samuel Kirkpatrick reported on a still he had confiscated made from an "ordinary dinner pot of iron" and capped with a "big wooden spigot inserted into a wooden lid." The worm for the still was made of hollowed-out alderwood branches pieced together and run through a water-filled hog trough to keep the branches from burning up. Kirkpatrick reported, "It was a small affair and easily carried under one's arm." This was not the only worm to be made of wood; Yadkin County deputy collector E. E. Hunt found a still made from "one-half of a fish barrel" with a worm made from a "sourwood sapling." A Dunn agent discovered a still made from a five-gallon lard can with an oyster can for a cap. Rutherford County authorities caught a still whose "diminutiveness takes the cake," whose "daily capacity is estimated to be from 10 to 20 drunks." The still was "scarcely larger than a tea kettle," and the agent who captured it was "too bighearted to cut up the baby" and decided to preserve it "among the curios of the department."

In 1909, sheriff N. A. Watson of Cumberland County, reportedly "North Carolina's champion moonshine still destroyer," preserved another still, not for its unique design or materials but for its historical significance. The still had supposedly been captured and cut down by legendary Scottish poet Robert Burns, who worked as a liquor-tax collector, or exciseman, near Dumfries, Scotland. According to the story, someone repaired the still and somehow it ended up in Cumberland County, whose original European settlers came from Scotland. According to the *Fayetteville Index*, Watson donated the "Bobby Burns Still" to the Hall of History in Raleigh, where it "now occupies a conspicuous place."

With more manufactured metal products available in the early twentieth century, reports often surfaced of everyday products being made into stills. Moonshiners made large steamer stills, prized in areas where moonshining was common, using fifty-gallon oil barrels. A report from Lenoir County described a still made of two galvanized-steel thirty-gallon washtubs soldered together. Authorities in the Blowing Rock area in 1915 found "one five-gallon and two 10-gallon milk containers" stamped with the logo of the Catawba Creamery Company, "rigged up as a blockade still." In 1919, the *Asheville Citizen-Times* reported on a still that used a "washing machine as a thumper."

After World War II, stills got larger and larger, more sophisticated, and more mechanized. Many operations had stills with capacities of over 1,000 gallons, electric or gasoline-powered pumps, conveyor belts, secret electric doors, and ventilation systems for indoor operations. One Alcohol Beverage Control official argued, "Some of these guys could be rocket scientists." One such creative "rocket scientist" converted his home heating system into a still. Iredell County moonshiner Julius Rogers got caught in 1965 with a "unit made by boring holes in the regular [heating] stove of the home." The heating unit had a removable top that Rogers had replaced with a thirty-five-gallon mash boiler he stored in his attic. He also connected his creative still with the home's water system. One big advantage of the system was that it did not produce the "tell-tale smoke which usually leads to detection of stills." Rogers told the deputies who arrested him that his creative apparatus "took considerable time" to fabricate and that he had operated it for three years. The officers reported that Rogers "'seemed kinda proud' of his ingenious contraption."

shaking it up, and judging the proof by looking at the size of the bubbles and the speed with which they "flashed off." As author Alec Wilkinson observed, "Bootleggers ... know something about beading oil.... Added to a quantity of fifty or sixty proof liquor, a few drops of beading oil will sit the bead properly," meaning they will show that the liquor is more than 100 proof, the preferred level for "genuine" moonshine.[18] Another relatively benign adulteration method came when people tried to make moonshine appear as if it were an aged, commercial product. In 1934, agents arrested the manager of the Isaac Shelby Hotel in Statesville for possessing "gallons of Carolina moonshine, colored with caramel, and hundreds of fake bottled-in-bond labels, distillers' stamps, and other equipment for the production and distribution of corn liquor masquerading as Canadian rye."[19]

Other substances added to liquor, primarily intended to give the moonshine the sting of high proof and mask the actual low proof of the liquor, were not so benign. Stanly County officials busted up a still site in 1921, according to the *Stanly News-Herald*, that contained a seventy-five-gallon "outfit" plus "a quantity of Red Devil lye, Brown Mule chewing tobacco, and saw dust."[20] The *Salisbury Evening Post* reported moonshiners in the area adding hog manure to their mash: "There was a batch of manure from a hog pen by the side of the distillery and the operators were using it in the beer. The odor given off from the condenser was nauseating, smelling worse than a pig pen in hot weather. I understand the blockaders use this for the purpose of adding the kick and causing the whiskey to bead high."[21] Wilkinson noted reports of especially dangerous adulterants sometimes used by moonshiners that contained wood alcohol. Moonshine adulterated with wood alcohol, according to Wilkinson, gives the product a "fiery taste, and result[s] in a long drunk, followed by an extended or belligerent hangover." He also reported the use of embalming fluid, formaldehyde, and when "the liquor runs cloudy from the still for no apparent reason," Clorox.[22]

Other practices that became increasingly common during the period made moonshine even more dangerous to consumers. As Wilkinson observed, "The most pervasive pollutant in moonshine is lead." Still builders often used lead solder to piece together still parts, so even in the finest copper stills, some lead leached into the liquor. As automobiles became more common, the temptation was high for moonshiners willing to take shortcuts to find ways to avoid using increasingly expensive copper. The best way to do this was to use a car or truck radiator, which contained even more lead solder to seal the many seams, to condense the alcohol steam back into a liquid. Steam from the distillation process passing through these radiators incrementally dissolved the lead and leached lead acetate, also known as lead salts, into the product. The head of an ATU lab in Atlanta, Clarence Paul, told Wilkinson that "one part lead per million" is considered toxic. He noted, "Eighty to eighty-five percent of the white liquor we got for testing contained some level of lead salts, and twenty-five percent of that had more than one part per million. We would get moonshine that ran from that sometimes up to several hundred parts per million, and sometimes right off the scale of our instruments." The presence of lead salts was especially problematic for longtime moonshine drinkers, as lead accumulates over time in the body's fatty tissues. After years of drinking lead salt–contaminated moonshine, consumers, according to Wilkinson, could experience anything from "failing appetite, constipation, and colic to total blindness, paralysis, convulsions, and death." Indeed, most communities in North Carolina had firsthand experience with individuals with obvious lead poisoning.[23]

In 1921, the chairman of the Burke County Commissioners asked J. S. Rogers, a chemist at Burke Tannery, to analyze an unnamed liquid, which was in actuality confiscated moonshine. While it would be impossible to properly judge the validity of Rogers's tests, he issued a report to the chairman, which the Morganton *News-Herald* printed:

> As to my opinion as to the nature of this compound, you failed to inform me the use for which it was intended.... The Caustic Alkali [lead salts] present would attack any mucous membrane subjected to its influence, and its corrosive qualities would forbid its use in a gasoline engine, although

it does have some elements of fuel value, although its ammonia content and the presence of chlorides indicate the possible presence of a manurial nature sometimes used in fertilizer manufacture. It is undoubtedly a germicide and disinfectant. It could be used in cleaning poultry housing of lice and other vermin, and from the animal nature of this solid content I suspect this sample might have been used for this purpose. In any event it should be kept from all careless and irresponsible persons as if swallowed by mistake, and Methyl alcohol is present, it might cause blindness or other serious mental and physical troubles. It has a considerable fire hazard and should never be exposed to open flame.[24]

There are a number of potential problems with this report, and it could be simply a propaganda piece crafted by prohibitionists or law enforcement and intended to try to scare moonshine consumers. If that was the case, this wouldn't have been the first time, or the last, that authorities used exaggerated reports in this fashion. At the same time, the Rogers report does point to some legitimate problems with moonshine that arose during Prohibition and that remain to the present day.

R. A. Kohloss, the federal government's director of the Bureau of Prohibition in North and South Carolina in the early 1920s, used the "vileness of the stuff" in much of his antiliquor campaign. As the *Charlotte Observer* noted, "He wants to kill it [moonshine] by weaning away its customers by descriptive propaganda in which denatured alcohol, dead bugs, hair tonics and other things unpleasant to contemplate figure. Kohloss wants to make the public believe that the product of the average moonshine still is not 'fitten.'" The *Observer* did, however, point out the limitations and relative ineffectiveness of this approach, as most drinkers remained unconvinced short of seeing the actual dead bodies of those poisoned by moonshine: "But until the coroner has a few more cases which may be directly traceable to the deadly stuff described by the revenue man, the moonshiner will yet have a little business left. Some of them will not be inclined to admit that Kohloss is telling the truth until they are dead of moonshine 'pizen.'"[25] And again, national Prohibition increased the possibilities of such "bad liquor," as the distance from producer to consumer, and the number of people involved in the distribution chain, increased. Moonshiners knew that the likelihood of being confronted by a customer or tracked down by law enforcement for making bad, or even poisonous, liquor was small.

As a result of national Prohibition, liquor law enforcement changed. The Treasury Department's ATU now morphed into the Bureau of Prohibition and expanded dramatically to attempt to enforce the new laws. While stretched thin because of the widening scope of federal enforcement, the bureau remained the primary agency dealing with illegal liquor in North Carolina. State efforts under the Alcohol Beverage Control Commission also continued, and cooperation increased between federal and state agencies. Perhaps the most important change in the state, however, came with increased involvement from local law enforcement, although questions often remained as to local officials' commitment to eliminating illegal alcohol in their communities.

During national Prohibition, local and state authorities, at least in some counties, finally began to take enforcing the prohibition laws more seriously. In 1922, the state prohibition director reported over 1,000 convictions in federal court in North Carolina, over 300 individuals sentenced to jail by state courts, over 1 million gallons of illegal liquor seized, over $100,000 paid in fines, and 132 automobiles confiscated.[26] Indeed, some sheriffs developed quite the reputation during the period for busting up stills. One such well-known still-busting sheriff was the colorful, and colorfully named, Jesse James Bailey of Madison County. Madison County's dry forces elected Bailey in 1920 to clean up the notorious mountain county, often referred to as Bloody Madison, and drive out its many moonshiners. As Bailey recalled later in life in an interview with *Citizen-Times* reporter Bob Terrell, "They expected me to dry up the county overnight and, of course, I couldn't do that; but I raised the price on liquor from fifteen dollars a gallon to seventy-five. I made it scarce." Bailey, like most successful sheriffs, did, however, understand something about diplomacy and dealing with voters. He told the county's moonshiners, "Now boys, I won't be too hard on you unless you put your stills out here in the road where I can stump my toe on 'em." However, when Bailey was on the hunt for a still, he was aggressive and tough: "In my day, you went up to a man and knocked him down and when he got up you said, 'I've got a warrant for your arrest.' You couldn't mollycoddle them fellers if you wanted to stay sheriff long." Even on the day he left office in 1922 to take a better-paying job as a railroad detective, Bailey was out capturing a still on the state line near Hot Springs. As he put it, "I went in a-running 'em and came out a-running 'em."[27]

Despite the efforts of Bailey and others to bring local law enforcement into the picture, many among the dry forces suspected that some sheriffs, like Bailey's predecessors, were "light on the liquor laws" and less than eager to take on the moonshiners. Even when they made arrests or, as was most commonly the case, seized stills and illegal liquor, people suspected them of being complicit with moonshiners. Indeed, prohibition supporters commonly complained that sheriffs and deputies seemed to break up stills and seize some liquor but made few actual arrests. They accused sheriffs of staging raids to appease dry voters and tearing up already dilapidated stills that moonshiners could no longer use. In addition, they voiced concerns about what actually happened to the liquor seized in raids. A common adage in North Carolina was that the best place to buy liquor was at the back door of the courthouse. Cab driver Talven Thompson

Madison County sheriff Jesse James Bailey next to a mountain of busted stills. (Courtesy of the North Carolina Collection, UNC Libraries, UNC–Chapel Hill)

recalled a situation in Buncombe County, where sheriff Laurence Brown held sway from 1930 to 1962 and headed up the county's Democratic Party machine: "If you needed liquor he would supply you. You could get it any time you wanted it from local law enforcement."[28]

In order to avoid such accusations, and to also put on a show for the voters, sheriffs often triumphantly transported stills and still parts into town to put them on display. In addition, officers made a public display of destroying the illegal liquor they had seized to blunt claims that they were just recycling the liquor back into the market out the back door of the courthouse. In 1921, the Greensboro *Daily News* reported on such a display in Dunn. Prohibition enforcement officers A. B. Adams and A. A. Jackson brought twenty-two gallons of moonshine to an intersection at the center of town. After advertising the event, officers burst a "dozen jugs of the stuff" and "let the ardent stuff trickle into a sewer." Officials even invited local minister and prohibition leader John L. Thompson to ceremoniously take a hammer, bust the first jug, and "christen" Dunn's sewers.[29] Authorities put on an even more dramatic display in Jacksonville in 1922 when the sheriff dumped several gallons of moonshine into the town square and set it on fire.[30]

In order to curry favor with locally influential dry forces, particularly teetotal churches, local law enforcement often recruited civilians to accompany them on raids and actively participate in busting up stills. In 1921, the *Fayetteville Observer* reported that dry forces, fed up with moonshining in their community, had formed the Upper Gray's Creek Township League. League members pledged to "rake over the woods, the swamps, the bottoms and the hillsides of the territory" so thoroughly that "no booze plant, however remotely it may be located, will escape their thorough searching." The paper reported that several league members went on raids with law enforcement, with forty accompanying the sheriff "on a booze search in this section."[31]

Pastors and church leaders also participated in such raids. Local authorities deputized evangelist Bexter F. McClendon, "with his broad-brimmed hat, bulky black mustache and unfailing curiosity," in Jones County in 1919. He "brought good luck to a posse of Federal and county officers" when he accompanied them "into the devil's own territory," a notorious moonshine district on the border of Jones and Lenoir Counties. The posse came back to town and proudly "exhibited" the fruit of its efforts: "a handsome copper still, a burnished shiny affair."[32] The Reverend N. H. Shepherd of Halifax County took matters into his own hands and single-handedly put "the sword of Gideon into play against the moonshine" when he seized a twenty-five-gallon still in the Hollister section and told officers the name of the operator. Ironically, the operator was a "negro youth," allegedly the son of Rev. Elisha Evans.[33] In 1920, Col. Tom Vanderford, the head state prohibition enforcement agent, announced his intention to recruit "an honest to god preacher as a member of my force." Vanderford wanted a diplomat, a skilled convincer, not a pastor who wielded the "sword of Gideon" but someone who would lead an effort to convince moonshiners of the error of their ways. Indeed, he asserted that he didn't want an individual in the position who believed "every man who takes a drink and enjoys it, is going straight to the place where snow balls last but a few moments." To show the seriousness of this effort, Vanderford announced that the position would pay a hefty salary of $3,000 a year.[34] On occasion, these still-busting preachers found themselves in dangerous situations. In 1920, the Reverend Tom Cauble was on a raid with Yadkin County sheriff Van Zachary, when moonshiner Rodey Baity opened fire and killed the sheriff.[35]

While having preachers and civilians participate in raids was little more than a publicity stunt to keep sheriffs in the good graces of dry forces, a more effective tactic at actually making a dent in illegal liquor traffic was the use of undercover officers. One reason undercover officers became more commonly employed during this period was that informers proved problematic on many counts. The general public almost universally hated informers, even the drys. In many cases informers were moonshiners themselves or had other criminal offenses, and juries perceived them as unreliable witnesses. Undercover operatives came from the ranks of professional law enforcement agents, and juries saw them as much more trustworthy and convincing. Indeed, even for those who favored the moonshiners, these folks were "just doing their jobs." As ATU agent Garland Bunting put it, "Far as I'm concerned, undercover is the best way in the world to catch a man. It's the most sure way. If I walk up to a man and he puts that liquor in my hand and I put money in his, there ain't no doubt about whether he's been set up.... But if I go raid his house, somebody could have gone and put it in his house. But if he transfers it from his hand to mine, I know damn well he's guilty."[36]

Undercover operations proved highly successful, especially in high-profile cases. In Virginia's Franklin County, just over the North Carolina line, a federal undercover operation in 1934 successfully revealed a countywide conspiracy to protect and extort moonshiners, which resulted in the conviction of thirty men. The commonwealth's attorney, Charles Carter Lee, did, however, escape conviction, despite overwhelming evidence of his guilt, primarily on the grounds that no grandnephew of Robert E. Lee could do such a thing.[37] As early as 1922, the Winston-Salem *Twin-City Daily Sentinel* reported that federal revenue agents often conducted undercover operations in rural areas, posing as "bums," hotel guests, and "honest-looking men wanting work and needing it badly."[38]

Perhaps the most famous undercover operation in North Carolina during the period was one conducted in the Bryson City area and memorialized in Horace Kephart's 1922 edition of *Our Southern Highlanders*. Kephart recounts the arrival of a mystery man he calls Mr. Quick at the boardinghouse where he lived in 1919. The man was ostensibly in the area "taking a vacation" and wanted to "ramble about over the mountains." Kephart soon discovered the man was not a typical visitor when he saw him reading books in Spanish. As they struck up a conversation, Kephart learned that the man also had extensive knowledge of Native American culture and shared his fascination with the American West. Mr. Quick soon displayed other talents he shared with Kephart, as a "gun crank" and crack shot. He was also an excellent photographer and fascinated many locals with his skill as a wood-carver, particularly of walking sticks decorated with creative depictions of snakes. In fact, most locals took to referring to him as the Snake-Stick Man. After staying in town for a few weeks, Mr. Quick appeared ill and told people he had periodic cases of "nervous dyspepsia" and needed whiskey to treat his illness. Not suspecting anything, locals referred him to folks who could supply his need, especially on the nearby reservation of the Eastern Band of Cherokee Indians. The real identity of the Snake-Stick Man came to light when local federal courts handed down a number of indictments and arrested several Cherokee moonshiners for illegal liquor activities on the reservation. As it turned out, and as Kephart revealed in his book, Mr.

Quick "was a secret agent of the Indian Bureau [Bureau of Indian Affairs] who had been picked for the job of finding out who was making or vending liquor in the Indian Reservation, and to make their paths straight to the chain gang."[39]

Officers also began using airplanes late in the period to spot stills, although the expense limited such surveillance. Jesse James Bailey became a pioneer in this practice when he was elected sheriff of Buncombe County in the late 1920s. In a 1930 flight from Asheville to Salisbury, Bailey spotted nine different stills from the air. He took note of the stills' locations and when he arrived at Salisbury, he "dispatched telegrams to various points along the way," giving local law enforcement the locations of the stills. The *Burlington Daily Times* quipped, "Some moonshiners are still wondering what happened."[40] ATU agents in Wilkes County used a plane in a major three-day search-and-destroy mission in 1938. On the first day, the pilot and a spotter, who "knew the lay of the land," flew over the county and made notes on likely still locations. The next two days, after a briefing from the spotter, ATU agents went out on foot after the stills, guided by the spotter in the plane, "who directed them toward the copper stills by waving a white flag." In the operation, authorities seized or destroyed sixty-one stills and confiscated 250 gallons of illegal liquor.[41] Sheriff John W. Moore was a pioneering aviator in Iredell County and had his own airplane. In 1940, the *Statesville Daily Record* noted that the Flying Sheriff "has been instrumental in removing a great many stills by this method."[42]

Despite increased enforcement, most observers claimed that relationships between moonshiners and law enforcement still remained relatively cordial. J. A. Farrell, a deputy sheriff in Chatham County during this period, described a typical raid where agents caught moonshiners in the act: "Normally what would happen is, they'd run like the devil. If you caught them, you'd have no problems. They were real nice. You'd just cite them, they'd pay their fine—not much, just $100 to $300. And then they'd be back there doing again that night." Undercover Alcohol Beverage Control agent Russell Poole, also of Chatham County, recalled the often amicable relations between moonshiners and enforcement agents: "I know one man we raided, he had a still and, I don't know, 30–40 gallons of liquor there. Well in the evening, me and him went out 'coon hunting together.... He weren't mad at me. He'd say, 'Heck, that's your job, and I'm just trying to make money.'"[43]

The relatively light penalties courts meted out to convicted moonshiners also generally made resistance and violence against agents unlikely. First offenders could often get off with a fine if arrested by local or state authorities. If they worked for some kingpin, the fine would often be paid for them. Even subsequent state convictions rarely resulted in lengthy jail or prison sentences. Convictions in federal court resulted in stiffer penalties, generally a year and a day for a first offense, but for many moonshiners the price was not too steep to pay.

In an interview about his long career as a Chatham County moonshiner, John Vestal commented on his six-month incarceration in the Atlanta Federal Penitentiary in 1930: "Now that sounds terrible, doesn't it. But in 1930, you'd find a lot of good folks down there, a lot of liquor folks. So it weren't bad at all."[44] In addition, in many of the rural communities where moonshiners lived, "building time" in a local jail, state prison, or federal penitentiary was not a social disability but an almost expected rite of passage.

As the stakes rose during the period, however, others observed a rise in criminal behavior among moonshiners (other than making illegal liquor), even murder. This is a common phenomenon in such an environment as criminal behavior becomes more profitable and the stakes become much higher. Theft of stills and still-making materials, especially oil barrels, was one crime that definitely increased. The Greensboro *Daily News* reported in 1920, "Small merchants in the county report that as fast as iron or galvanized tanks are bought by them, to be used for storing oil and gasoline, the moonshiners steal them, using the tanks for the still."[45] In 1922, the *Charlotte News* reported on "war" between moonshiners over the theft of stills in Lenoir County. The war began when one group of moonshiners stole the stills of another group, thinking that "the losers would infer that raiding posses had taken away the stills." Unfortunately for the thieves, the "losers" found out that the thieves were their competitors and began sending anonymous messages to authorities offering "accurate descriptions of stills." The notes resulted in the capture of "four 'modern and handsome' plants with capacities aggregating 320 gallons." One note angrily asserted, "D——d if any man can steal my property like that and get away with it!"[46]

Moonshiners also began to offer more physical resistance to officers. In 1935, Percy Flowers and his brothers Dick and Jimmie caught federal revenue agent A. E. Bennett and Wake County constable Garland Jones raiding one of their stills. The brothers held the officers at gunpoint and beat Bennett, whose injuries required hospitalization. The brothers surrendered to authorities when they learned a judge had issued federal warrants for their arrest and posted a $30,000 bond, indicative of the profitability of their operations.[47] The judge sentenced the Flowers brothers to three years in a federal penitentiary, but surprisingly, the men received relief from their sentence after they paid a $5,000 fine.[48]

Of course, the most serious criminal behavior also saw an increase in gun violence in the illegal liquor business. In 1921, the *Gaston Gazette* observed this change: "The killing of a policeman in Greensboro Wednesday by a whiskey trafficker shows to what length this class of lawbreakers will go to carry out their ends. Time was not so long ago when we looked on the moonshine liquor dealer as a comparatively harmless fellow who took to the tall timbers when molested. Latter day events tend to show that he is becoming a character that must be reckoned with in our scheme of things."[49] Horace Kephart noted a similar rise in violence in the western part of the state in his 1922 revision of his classic work *Our Southern Highlanders*: "The greater the reward in sight, the greater the risks will be run for it. The blockaders are getting ugly. Arrests have rapidly increased, since [national] prohibition, and so have mortal combats between officers and outlaws. Spies are everywhere, and a hated gendarmerie patrols the country. The war between enforcement agents and blockaders is more widespread and deadly than ever before in our history. We who live in the mountains are fairly within gun-crack of it."[50]

The bigger the operation and the more money on the line often meant that those involved were more likely to resort to gunplay. In Warren County in 1921, eight federal revenue officers came upon a huge operation with three stills, 25,000 gallons of mash ready to distill, and 150 gallons of already-distilled liquor, owned by African American illegal liquor kingpins Joe and Hayes Baldwin. Agents estimated the value of the distillery and its products at $25,000, with at least fifteen men involved in the operation. When the officers neared the still, three guards opened fire. In the resulting shootout, agents killed all three guards. The twelve others, including the Baldwin brothers, escaped.[51]

Such shooting by moonshiners at deputies and revenue agents almost ensured that officers became more likely to shoot back or even fire the first shots, despite regulations prohibiting this. The need for greater numbers of officers on the federal, state, and local levels, combined with the old adage "It takes a thief to catch a thief," meant that authorities were not extremely careful in weeding out unsavory characters from the job pool, especially if they proved successful at the work. As Horace Kephart observed, "Among them were some desperadoes, men already stained with blood and reckless or ruthless about shedding more." Perhaps the most famous such officer in North Carolina was Hol Rose, whom Kephart memorialized in *Our Southern Highlanders*. The nephew of famous Swain County moonshiner Quill Rose, Hol had experience in the illegal liquor business himself. Attracted by the regular paycheck, he went over to the other side and zealously enforced North Carolina's prohibition laws. As Kephart noted, "Rose displayed more than usual activity in running down offenders. Man-hunting, for him, was a sport: he thoroughly enjoyed it." Rose's zealousness, however, led to his demise, as moonshiner Babe Burnett killed him in a shootout in 1920.[52]

With this uptick in violent confrontations between law enforcement and moonshiners, violence against informers increased as well. Property crimes against informers were still the most common type of retaliation during the period. In Union County in 1921, blockaders "drained the fish pond and cut the wire fencing in about five hundred places" at the farm of L. S. Williams in the Fairfield community, believing—erroneously, according to Williams—that

Swain County prohibition agent Hol Rose (right) poses with a captured still. (Courtesy of Hunter Library Special Collections, Western Carolina University, Cullowhee, N.C.)

he had informed on them.[53] In the same year in Wake County, "night riders," in retaliation for a major raid by both federal and county law enforcement, set fires in the New Light Township that destroyed two schools, two homes, and a church. The Winston-Salem *Twin-City Daily Sentinel* offered an explanation for this extreme action: "Having been frustrated by the federal agents on the one hand and defeated financially by the tobacco market, the theory is that farmers have been driven to desperation."[54]

On occasion, retaliation against informers reached the extreme of outright murder. In 1926, someone murdered Eagle Rose of the Yellow Creek community of Graham County, another nephew of Quill Rose, with a "shotgun blast at close range to the back of the head." The assassin hid the body in Yellow Creek, where authorities finally recovered it forty days later. *Asheville Citizen-Times* columnist John Parris reported in 1983 that the killer allegedly confessed on his deathbed that he had shot Rose "mistakenly," assuming that Rose had informed on him to authorities.[55]

Despite increased enforcement, profits during national Prohibition proved to be too high and economic conditions too poor to make much of a dent in the illegal liquor trade. If anything, those high profits attracted more individuals to the business, attracted more finance capital, and led to greater use of modern business organizational techniques. As North Carolina had already demonstrated during statewide prohibition, prohibiting liquor only increased the number of moonshiners, made them more efficient, and made the moonshine itself viler and more dangerous to consumers' health.

MOONSHINE KINGPINS AND MOONSHINE CAPITALS

During national Prohibition, perhaps the greatest change to North Carolina's moonshine business was the consolidation of its huge profits into fewer and fewer hands. The so-called kingpins, who controlled an increasing proportion of the manufacturing and distribution of moonshine in North Carolina, came from the ranks of both working-class moonshiners, whose luck, creativity, and intelligence allowed them to reap huge profits and use them to create an empire, and wealthier individuals looking for a profitable business investment. The rise of kingpins also meant that the production of moonshine became concentrated in particular areas of the state. While moonshiners produced illegal liquor throughout the state during the period, this consolidation concentrated moonshining into several counties, which took on the status of "moonshine capitals" and developed reputations to that effect across the country.

The combination of high profits and poor economic conditions evidently tempted many of the more "respectable types" to risk fines, incarceration, or a loss of reputation in their community. As early as 1920, the Internal Revenue Service reported, "A 'higher type of citizen' is making 'booze' now because of the great demand, and the enormous profit to be had." The IRS noted that those profits drew respectable merchants into the business to supply needed materials, especially the quite considerable amount of sugar required for large operations. "In some towns wealthy merchants and moonshiners of the 'better' class cooperate. The merchants get the sugar and the moonshiner buys it at an advance in price while smaller customers are told that sugar cannot be had."[1]

As a general rule, kingpins stayed as far away from the stills and the liquor itself as they could, primarily providing supplies, financing, management expertise, and bail money and lawyers to keep their operatives from implicating them. In 1921, the Greensboro *Daily News* quoted North Carolina's director of the IRS, R. A. Kohloss, describing information the department had received about such syndicate-type operations: "We have information in two cases where there is a wholesale syndicate formed of men who are making moonshine whiskey. The distillers of these syndicates are men who stand high in their community and in a business way, and while not personally engaged in the illegal making of whiskey, they furnish supplies and money to little fellows who are doing the work, and we find that while we often catch these little fellows, from the magnitude and size of the operations I am convinced that the fellows we capture are not the real brains of the proposition."[2] As journalist Vance Packard observed, "Frankly, the chances that the owner will get caught and jailed are pretty slim. Instead, he hires (or goes 50–50) with young mountain lads who do the work, and they are the ones who usually get caught."[3] John Vestal of Chatham County was a kingpin who ran a relatively small wholesale operation in the 1930s and 1940s, primarily supplying dealers in nearby Greensboro with moonshine. Vestal did participate in the risky business of hauling the liquor, racing "down the winding dirt roads at around 100 miles per hour," but spent "as little time as possible at the still sites," and "he never got caught in the act of making whiskey."[4]

The distillers, still hands, and transporters who did the real labor experienced the most risk. Vestal hired young men without criminal records to make the liquor so that if they were "pulled in" by local law enforcement, "he would pay a fine ... and his workers would be allowed to return home ... or back to the stills."[5] Percy Flowers and other eastern North Carolina kingpins generally employed African Americans. When authorities arrested their workers for moonshining they posted bail, provided them with lawyers, paid the fines, and if their workers went to prison, even supported families to ensure their silence. The marginalized status of these individuals in the Jim Crow south and the severe consequences that would come to them and their families for testifying against a wealthy white man provided another layer of protection for men like Flowers.[6]

During Prohibition many "men that stand high in their community," even at the highest levels of society, had some involvement in the moonshine business, if only as buyers and consumers. Country clubs and other elite private clubs in the state reportedly kept higher-quality North Carolina moonshine on hand and had local well-known makers supply them with corn liquor and brandy. The *Wilmington Morning Star* reported in 1921 that North Carolina moonshine was readily available in the halls of the U.S. Congress: "It is a notorious fact that good North Carolina corn 'hooch' can be had in either one of these buildings [on Capitol Hill] any day of the week for $7 a quart. Bootleggers offer real corn for sale.... North Carolina moonshine is circulating in high official circles of the national capitol."[7]

Howard Creech N.C. Moonshine Hall of Famer

One of North Carolina moonshine's "invisible men," Howard Creech, who did much of the physical labor in the illegal liquor business in the eastern part of the state. (Courtesy of Perry Sullivan and the Johnston County Heritage Center, Smithfield, N.C.)

Ralph Ellison referred to his most famous literary character as the "invisible man," as many African Americans lived and labored in obscurity due to racism and discrimination. Such African American "invisible men" brought their skills, creativity, sweat, and blood to moonshine operations in North Carolina, particularly in the eastern Piedmont, Coastal Plain, and Tidewater regions. We know few names, as none have had books written about them, the *Saturday Evening Post* or *Esquire* did not profile them, and their stories and biographical details did not make their way into local-color columns in the state's newspapers. They generally only appear in brief mentions in police records, court dockets, and newspaper articles that mention "John Doe - colored" in arrest, indictment, or conviction reports for federal revenue or state or local prohibition law violations.

Be that as it may, these "invisible" individuals played a key role in the moonshine business at every level from being basic still hands and skilled metalworkers who produced stills to being master distillers, delivery men, and distributors. Most such individuals labored for white men who financed and directed their operations, bailed them out when they got caught, and either intimidated them or used their paternalistic power to ensure their silence and complicity. We do have some tantalizing clues indicating that there were African Americans who operated independently, had their own big-time operations, and lived lavish lifestyles, carrying around big rolls of cash and driving brand-new, high-dollar Cadillacs and other luxury automobiles. Few solid details, however, exist as to these individuals' identities and life stories. Like much of what life had to offer African American men in North Carolina from 1865 to the 1980s, these "invisible men" labored hard—at the direction of others who often had little regard for them—took lots of risks with their lives and liberty, and reaped few rewards.

We do know at least some life details on Johnston County native David Howard Creech. Creech made a significant impact on the North Carolina moonshine business in his own right and serves as an exemplar in many ways of his fellow African American moonshiners. For much of his life, Creech labored as a "whiskey man" for Percy Flowers and served as one of the illegal liquor baron's closest associates, most skilled liquor makers, and most trusted confidantes. Like many African American men with patrons such as Flowers, he also did a variety of odd jobs around Flowers's store and home, forming close relationships with Flowers's wife, Delma, and his four children, Percy Jr., Rebecca, Perry, and Tammy. Rebecca has even posted a loving tribute to Creech, entitled "The Man behind the Legend," on the website of her Flowers Plantation real estate enterprise. The tribute concludes rather awkwardly, but lovingly, with the words "The family regards Mr. and Mrs. Flowers as characters who will long be remembered for each one's special gifts of knowledge and life's lessons. However, David Howard Creech, is their greatest legend as well as the man behind the Flowers legend!" *Lost Flowers*, a book by Flowers's son Perry Sullivan, is also as much a tribute to Creech (whom Sullivan called "Reno") as it is to Percy Flowers. Sullivan called Creech his "best friend" growing up and "the seed of truth and fairness." These two individual accounts provide much of the little we know about Creech, but they also give us important insights into his life and the lives of so many African American men involved in the moonshine business.

Howard Creech was born 10 July 1917 in Johnston County near the Flowers homeplace. His mother died when he was four, and an automobile accident killed his father when he was sixteen. His grandmother Mamie raised him. Creech began hanging out at the Flowers Tavern as a young teen doing odd jobs, anything to earn a few dollars to help his grandmother. He soon drew Flowers's attention for his hard work, honesty, and drive to succeed under difficult circumstances, something Flowers appreciated given his own background. From the early 1930s to his death in 2013, Creech worked for the Flowers family in one capacity or another. For much of that time, that work included making and selling moonshine liquor for his patron. Indeed, he quickly developed the distilling expertise that made him invaluable to Percy Flowers's burgeoning moonshine empire.

In Creech's prime years he honed his craft and became expert in setting up multiple still sites and making liquor using the huge Wilkes-type steamer stills that Flowers began employing when he "imported" a couple of expert still builders from Wilkes County. As an unobtrusive black man, Creech was an ideal person for such work, as he, like many other African American men of his generation, had a knack for "invisibility," or blending into the background. As far as I can determine, he was only indicted once for his activities as a "co-conspirator" of Flowers's, in a 1965 case where federal authorities tried Flowers in Wilmington for "conspiracy to violate federal liquor laws" after they busted two huge stills in Martin and Brunswick Counties. It appears as if government prosecutors dropped the case against Creech when a jury reported that Flowers's case was "hopelessly deadlocked" and the kingpin, once again, walked free.

By the 1970s, Creech's, and Flowers's, moonshine activities declined, and both men spent much of their time at the Percy Flowers Store. Creech handled much of the retail illegal liquor activity that continued to take place at the store's back door. Customers "in the know" parked their cars in a special spot. As Perry Sullivan observed, "That was where people who wanted more than groceries parked." Creech kept an eye on the spot and when customers pulled in, he took their orders and discreetly brought them pints or half-gallon jugs wrapped in brown paper. Creech got back into the making business in the late 1970s when seventeen-year-old Perry bugged his father to teach him to make moonshine so much that Flowers instructed Creech to dig an old still out of the weeds, get it refurbished, set it up near a hidden spring, and teach his son the "family business."

Howard Creech was also an important link in Percy Flowers's liquor empire between the white moonshiner and the area's African American liquor houses. He often supplied liquor to these houses, and when he and Perry made their first illegal liquor run, he took the boy to sell to local liquor house proprietor Sutie Hooper.

Fortunately, we have this bit of information on Howard Creech that gives us insight into the life experienced by so many African American men who labored invisibly in North Carolina's moonshine industry. Unfortunately, we have little specific information on others, making African American men woefully underrepresented in this Hall of Fame given their level of involvement in the business.

One of the problems that such large-scale bootleggers encountered was what to do with the cash that accumulated from their business. Stories of bootleggers burying money in their backyards were common, and legends still circulate of moonshiner treasure buried around the state. Of course, this did happen, especially with small-time moonshiners. When agents busted moonshiner Frank Lethco on his farm near High Point in 1923, he calmly retrieved a shovel "to dig up $500 in his yard with which to make his appearance bond."[8] Burying the money in the backyard was not a practical solution for big-time bootleggers, so they looked for other solutions. Banking laws prevented them from depositing large amounts of cash without generating lots of questions and investigation from the IRS. The preferred solution for most such operators was investing in real estate, livestock, or legitimate businesses. Cash transactions for such sales were still common at the time, especially in rural areas, so moonshiners could move money undetected by authorities. Those selling to the moonshiners would have the evidence of a deed transfer or bill of sale that they could use to then deposit the money in a bank. In the late 1930s, Percy Flowers began buying up Johnston County farmland, eventually adding up to over 4,000 acres, and contracted with tenants to grow large crops of tobacco, cotton, corn, and soybeans and to distill moonshine. Purchasing real estate, particularly farmland, had an additional benefit, as the wooded parts of the land provided plenty of places for still sites. In Flowers's case, the vastness of his holdings always left him with a handy alibi if agents found a still on his property: that he had no knowledge, and indeed was shocked to learn, that someone had set up a still on one of his farms.[9]

Investing in a business had the additional attraction of providing opportunities to launder the cash earned from moonshine through the legitimate business and into a bank. Flowers built a country store across the highway from his home at a rural crossroads in the late 1930s that not only was a central shopping and gathering place for the community but served as a front for his operations and a convenient conduit to move cash from moonshining into banks. In addition, owning a store let him make large purchases of sugar, yeast, canning jars, and metal goods needed for his illegal operations without attracting attention.[10] We will never know to what extent such money-laundering activities occurred across the state, but as profits skyrocketed, the temptations for store owners, businessmen of all types, and even bankers to become involved, or at least pretend not to notice, became extremely high. Vance Packard observed this phenomenon in Wilkes County in the early 1950s. He noted that Tater Johnson, a rural Wilkes County storekeeper, kept a huge pile of coke, a relatively smokeless fuel for moonshine stills, next to his store. Packard wrote, "Who buys the coke? Probably Tater wouldn't rightly know. He does know that there isn't any law that says you can't sell coke to anybody who wants it." Packard continued, observing that in Wilkes County, "most of the county's hardware stores, garages, tinsmiths, sugar dealers, and other merchants prosper directly or indirectly from this secret wealth-producing industry."[11]

By the 1930s, the production of illegal alcohol permeated the economy and life of many North Carolina counties. Indeed, the state was home to at least two places known as the moonshine capital of the world. Not surprisingly, one of those was Wilkes County, whose reputation went back to the earliest days of moonshine production. As NASCAR and moonshining legend Junior Johnson observed of his home county, "If they wadn't making it, they's selling the stuff to make it with, or they's hauling it. In some kind of way about every family [in Wilkes County] was involved in the moonshine business."[12] In 1935, the "largest inland seizure" of illegal liquor to date occurred in the Ingle Hollow section of

Wilkes County. Alcohol Tax Unit agents seized "7100 gallons of whiskey, 9150 pounds of sugar, four copper condensers, five complete distilling plants having a combined capacity for the manufacture of 2000 gallons of liquor each week." All this equipment and product belonged to Robert Glen Johnson, Junior's father. Junior, a child during this time, remembered when "it was stacked up in our bedrooms in cases so high we had to climb over 'em to get into bed."[13] An apocryphal story that circulated widely at the time and to the present day told of a young man who came to North Wilkesboro and asked an elderly local fellow where he might buy some liquor. The old man pointed up the street to the U.S. post office and replied, "That's the only place you can't get it."[14]

Wilkes County's geographic position made it a perfect location for accessing the North Carolina moonshine market. The county contains many remote mountain hollows where moonshiners can hide their stills. At the same time, its location on the edge of the Piedmont gave Wilkes County moonshiners easy access to growing markets in nearby mill towns and the rapidly expanding urban areas of Winston-Salem, Greensboro, High Point, Statesville, and Charlotte. Indeed, an enterprising whiskey tripper could make two moonshine runs to market per night, especially once the roads improved and automobile technology allowed them to turn their ordinary-looking cars into high-speed liquor haulers.

Surprisingly, North Carolina's other reputed "moonshine capital of the world" was not in the mountains but in Buffalo City, in the swamps of Dare County, nineteen miles west of Manteo. Today the ruins of Buffalo City are in the Alligator National Wildlife Refuge. Indeed, the swamps of northeastern North Carolina probably became the most booming area in the state for moonshine production during national Prohibition. Geography and economics played huge roles in this boom. The swamps had long provided convenient hiding places for stills, but the market in the region was relatively small and transportation difficult. Improvements made to the rivers and channels, the coming of railroads, and the highway improvements that came with the Good Roads Movement improved transportation in the region tremendously. As a result, hauling illegal liquor to Norfolk, Virginia, became much quicker and more feasible. From Norfolk, the hugely profitable East Coast market opened up for enterprising moonshiners. National Prohibition also arrived at a time in the region when the logging boom was going bust. By the mid-1920s the juniper, cypress, and longleaf pine that attracted major timber companies had largely been cut over. In addition, the old-growth forests that remained were so remote, the decline in timber prices that began in the same period made it not worth the effort and expense to extract. The timber companies began a rapid exit from the area, leaving loggers without jobs and with few prospects.[15]

When logging began to die in Buffalo City around 1928, the population rapidly declined as most folks went elsewhere to find work. According to local native

The main street of Buffalo City, declared the "moonshine capital of the world" during national Prohibition. (Courtesy of the Outer Banks History Center, State Archives of North Carolina, Manteo, N.C.)

Jess "Gus" Basnight, "The population at Buffalo City dwindled to 75–100 whites and 15–20 blacks." For those who decided to remain, there were few viable alternatives. As Basnight noted, "There were only two ways left of working at Buffalo City—cutting net stakes for pound nets at 15 cents each or making whiskey." For most folks in the area, the much-preferred alternative was making whiskey.[16]

The market that Buffalo City served up the East Coast called for a different type of liquor than the clear corn liquor traditionally produced in North Carolina. Dare County moonshiners adapted their product in order to break into a market dominated by consumers accustomed to legally produced "red liquor." The area became well known for the production of what became known as East Lake rye. Basnight and his dad used a common recipe for making this concoction using "400 gallons of water, 100 pounds of rye, 300 pounds of sugar and 5 pounds of yeast." For some odd reason, they tried to proof the liquor at precisely 107 proof. They also used either hickory chips or burnt sugar to color their liquor to make it appear aged. The rye liquor found an eager market up the coast, as most of the product went to speakeasies where bartenders decanted it into bottles that had initially contained commercially produced rye whiskey and poured it out to customers as the real thing. As Basnight observed, "After a drink or two, people didn't know the difference. It was strong stuff!" Basnight also noted that he and his dad made one special gallon of 120-proof liquor each week "for a customer who everyone said wouldn't need to be embalmed."[17]

Given their location in a swamp, Buffalo City moonshiners found creative ways to transport their product as well. They sealed the jugs holding the liquor with wax, tied them together with rope, and loaded them into boats to transport down Milltail Creek, up the Alligator River, and then into Albemarle Sound. If they encountered law enforcement, they marked their location, threw the jugs overboard, and then came back later to retrieve them with a boat hook.[18] After a successful run, the moonshiners rendezvoused with wholesalers, who picked the moonshine up at some designated point—in the mid-1930s the Chantilly Beach dance club near Elizabeth City—where liquor runners loaded it into trucks or cars and hauled it north to market. To supply the moonshiners with the huge amount of supplies they needed, the tugboat *Hattie Creef* made regular deliveries from Elizabeth City up Milltail Creek. As Basnight recalled, "The Hattie Creef often came in fully loaded with sugar. Tons and tons of it came to Buffalo City." East Lake rye became so popular that Buffalo City resident Julian Haywood's father made a good living just on the marketing end. When Haywood's father got out of prison for making moonshine in the early 1930s, he went to work as an agent for Buffalo City liquor makers. According to Haywood, his dad worked "as the contact person in Raleigh for big congressmen in Washington, D.C. and people in New York who were ordering Buffalo City whiskey. A lot of 'likker' went to Washington and New York because it was top quality stuff."[19]

Although Buffalo City's moonshine empire died out as demand declined with the end of national Prohibition around 1936 and residents abandoned the town, the swamps of northeast North Carolina remained an important source of illegal liquor well into the late twentieth century. Indeed, the Dismal Swamp had almost as strong a reputation for liquor making as Buffalo City did. In 1922, the Elizabeth City *Daily Advance* published a poetic play on words highlighting this reputation:

> In the Dismal Swamp, old Bruin
> Watches moonshine mashes stewin'
> Peeping through the bushes, doin'
> Nothing else but view the brewin'.[20]

Alvin Sawyer, one of North Carolina's most famous moonshiners, got his start making East Lake rye near Buffalo City after he figured out he could earn much more money making illegal liquor than working for one dollar a day in the timber business. After the Buffalo City liquor scene dried up, he moved his operations to Pasquotank County in the middle of the Dismal Swamp, where he plied his trade and used his knowledge of the swamps to outwit law enforcement until he finally retired from the illegal liquor business in 1990 at the age of seventy-nine.[21]

While boats played an important role in transporting liquor in the swamps, by and large North Carolina's moonshine industry became almost totally de-

Legendary Dismal Swamp moonshiner Alvin Sawyer. Once he became a moonshine celebrity in the area, he made and sold miniature stills. (Courtesy of the Outer Banks History Center, State Archives of North Carolina, Manteo, N.C.)

Alvin Sawyer N.C. Moonshine Hall of Famer

The standard stereotypical moonshiner image displays a mountaineer firing up a still in a remote, rhododendron-shrouded "holler." It should, however, include an eastern North Carolinian toiling away at a massive 1,000-gallon-plus still on a hillock in the midst of a swamp, hauling liquor in a boat instead of a souped-up automobile. Indeed, while there are no reliable statistics on this other than arrest and still bust data from law enforcement agencies, there was probably as much illegal liquor produced in the swamps of the far eastern part of the state as in the mountains of the west. Swamps have always been places where activities on the edge of legality and propriety took place, and they provided plenty of places to hide stills and lots of good water, if you knew how to find it.

Pasquotank County had its own "moonshine king" in Alvin Bruce Sawyer, who made illegal liquor in the Dismal Swamp outside Elizabeth City from the 1930s to the 1990s. Born in 1918, Sawyer lived almost all his life within "spittin' distance" of the Dismal. He quit school at fourteen and went to work at a sawmill in East Lake making one dollar a day. Moonshine operations thrived near timber camps during this period. These camps contained young, single men looking for ways to have a good time, despite national and then local prohibition, and ease the pain incurred from their strenuous labor. They also had money from their weekly wages to spend. Young Sawyer soon realized that he could make a lot more money working in the illegal liquor business and selling it in the timber camps than cutting timber himself. At fifteen he went to work for a moonshiner to learn the trade. As he later recalled, "Everybody that was able to made whiskey up in East Lake." Interestingly, but not that uncommon, Sawyer was pretty much a teetotaler himself and claimed that he "never drank whiskey in my life," although he did admit to tasting it to test its proof. Sawyer followed the mantra of many successful moonshiners, who understood that "liquor is made for sellin', not for drinkin'."

Despite the fact that he entered the business just as it started to decline in the swamps with the repeal of national Prohibition (much of the liquor made in eastern North Carolina went to markets in the Northeast), the moonshine bug had infected Sawyer and he ended up making the illegal liquor business his career. When asked years later why he stayed in the business so long, he replied in a fashion common to many Moonshine Hall of Famers: "It's something that gets in your blood like gambling or dope or whatever." Sawyer not only had a passion for his business but became widely known for the high quality of his East Lake rye. While most moonshiners of his era stuck to a recipe heavy on sugar and cornmeal, he made his mash using equal parts cornmeal and rye meal, with rye flour thrown in as well. Soon, Sawyer's business netted him up to seventy-five dollars a day. As one reporter put it, "Not bad money in a 50-cent-a-day economy." Along the way he also learned to weld, a handy skill for a moonshiner and a way to earn some income when the heat from law enforcement got too intense.

For Alvin Sawyer, the Dismal Swamp was, like the briar patch for Br'er Rabbit, his natural habitat. He generally located his stills—some of them up to 2,000 gallons in capacity—on islands in the swamp and hauled supplies in, and finished product out, in boats. He knew the region's swamps like he knew the back of his own hand, which made it difficult for law enforcement to ever catch him, even when he got into his sixties and seventies. "They couldn't catch me in that swamp. . . . You got to know how to run in that swamp. You got to know where to step at. You got to jump right in mud and water."

Trippers distributed Sawyer's moonshine all along the East Coast, as far away as Connecticut. He generally sold his liquor "to just a few big customers" who transported it to market, but on occasion he hauled it himself, although he preferred to do it unobtrusively in a pickup truck with a camper. He hid the liquor under plywood with a mattress on top. Sawyer's distribution network reveals an aspect of the moonshine business that's rarely discussed but revelatory as to why moonshining continued for so long even as local prohibition declined in the region. He sold most of his liquor to bars in places where alcohol was perfectly legal. The bar owners purchased Sawyer's East Lake rye for about half the price of legal, federally taxed liquor. Bartenders then, in Sawyer's words, would "mix moonshine with a little bit of distilled whiskey, just to give it some color. And then he'd serve it right over the bar. Ain't nobody can notice it no way. Everybody was crazy over that whiskey." Sawyer's quality moonshine helped with the subterfuge, and the owners dramatically boosted their profits by charging the regular price for bonded liquor.

Being in the moonshine business in a big-time way for so long obviously drew attention from both federal and local law enforcement. Authorities busted Sawyer numerous times, convicted him at least five times, and sent him to prison at least three times (for relatively short terms). Like many of his fellow moonshiners, however, he generally had good relationships with the law. For one thing, officers loved his liquor and rarely destroyed it, preferring to haul it back to their offices as "evidence" that soon disappeared. As Sawyer recalled to Sheila Turnage, a reporter for *State* magazine, "To me, the law was a good friend. They all loved my whiskey." Late in life, Sawyer became close friends with Bennie Halstead, a retired federal agent and special deputy for the Pasquotank County Sheriff's Department. When Halstead asked him why he harbored no ill will toward him, Sawyer replied, "My job was to make whiskey, and your job was to catch me. I ain't got a thing in this world against you." The moonshiner also made weekly payments to local law enforcement to ensure that even if they busted his stills, they did not damage them so much that the skilled welder could not easily repair them. "You could pay the sheriff, and they just knocked it [the still] a little bit. . . . They didn't tear it up much."

After getting busted in January 1987 with a 2,000-gallon still, Sawyer announced to the court and the press that, at the age of sixty-nine, he was retiring after more than fifty years in the illegal liquor business. After serving a four-month stint in prison, he even started a small retirement business, banking on his regional celebrity, making small copper stills complete with a brochure containing his moonshine recipe and "greetings from 'The Moonshine King of Eastern North Carolina.'" Alas, his retirement did not take, and not being one to work for Walmart as a greeter—

although he would have been a good one—Sawyer fired up his still once again. When state agents showed up at his door in the predawn hours in February 1990, the bleary-eyed, pajama-clad, seventy-two-year-old moonshiner staggered to the door of his trailer. As agents placed him under arrest, Sawyer asked pitifully if he could just go back into his house to "put on his britches" before being hauled off to jail. Too late the officers realized their prisoner was much spryer than they imagined, and Sawyer took off out the back door and headed for the swamp. They never caught him. The savvy Sawyer then lay low for a few months until "an understanding judge took the bench," turned himself in, and received a thirty-day jail sentence instead of the ten-year sentence that he could have received as a "habitual felon."

Sawyer apparently really did retire after this incident and enjoyed his later years as a statewide celebrity, as newspaper and magazine reporters beat a steady path to his door to hear his homespun stories about his life as a moonshiner. He spent his later years in a retirement home just down the hall from his buddy Bennie Halstead and passed away in 2003.

pendent on the automobile during the 1920s and 1930s. During this period, cars became surprisingly accessible in the region, especially as more and more Ford Model Ts and other cheap cars found their way to the used market or to junkyards. Catawba County residents Alex Mull and Gordon Boger reminisced about those days: "When the Ford Motor Company ceased manufacturing the Model T there were literally thousands still operating. Back then, kids in high school would chip in to buy a Model T for about $50. They would strip it down. . . . A kid with just a little mechanical ability could keep one running with a couple of tin cans, some baling wire, a pair of pliers, and a screwdriver."[22] Junior Johnson, one of the greatest mechanical minds in NASCAR history, has his own Model T memories. "Most of the time us kids, if somebody had a old T-Model or A-Model that they had kindly junked. We would pool our money and buy it and fix it up and ride and mess around on the farm with it. There was all the time something happening to it."[23] Folks in North Carolina generally referred to these modified Model Ts as "skeeters," and they soon became a staple in hauling liquor to market. In 1920, Elkin police "captured a 'Ford skeeter' here yesterday in which was nicely packed fifteen gallons of 'moonshine' liquor. The car was in charge of two 18-year old boys and they had boldly driven thru the Main Street in Elkin in open daylight."[24]

In 1932, Henry Ford produced his last great invention, the first low-priced automobile with an eight-cylinder engine. The so-called flathead Ford V-8 soon took on legendary status as the preferred liquor-hauling automobile for moonshiners and escape vehicle for other criminals. Texas outlaw Clyde Barrow wrote to Ford in 1933 praising him for the car's speed and durability. "I have driven Fords exclusively when I could get away with one.... The Ford has got ever other car skinned and even if my business hasn't been strictly legal it don't hurt anything to tell you what a fine car you got in the V-8."[25] Young men throughout the region quickly learned to bore the engine out, put in new rings, and make the car even faster. "The Ford automobile," stock car racing promoter Humpy Wheeler argued, "in its natural state with the flat-head V-8 became a race car in just a few days with the right hands working on it, and it was durable and fast."[26]

North Carolina's moonshiners soon became adept at modifying the flathead Fords—the inside "hulled out" to hold up to twenty-two six-gallon cases of whiskey—so that they could outrun law enforcement. By the late 1930s, moonshiners also imported so-called hot rod equipment from California such as Edelbrock "slingshot" manifolds and Stromberg carburetors. Creative mechanics could boost a car's power by adding three or four carburetors and adding superchargers, which boosted power as much as fifty horsepower, or by putting in a higher-powered Cadillac ambulance engine. Moonshiners also became skilled at making the car handle better, even when loaded down with whiskey, by using stiffer shocks, overinflated tires, and stronger wheels.[27] Liquor haulers modified the chassis by adding additional springs from Model Ts mounted onto the axles. This additional support made it so a fully loaded car "would sink no more than an inch," thereby avoiding tipping off law enforcement with the telltale signs of a liquor car, which was typically a low-riding Ford V-8.[28] Souped-up, "high-tailed" Ford V-8s became ubiquitous throughout moonshine country by the late 1930s. Vance Packard observed in the late 1940s one "trademark of Wilkes County": "One odd thing you do see everywhere you look is high-powered cars equipped with twin exhausts and with the rear ends remarkably high in the air."[29]

While a lot of the devices allegedly used by moonshiners to help them evade law enforcement are the product of some film or television producer's vivid imagination, liquor runners did actually develop some specialized equipment to help them escape. In 1934, officers hauled Fate Swicegood of Davidson County before a magistrate "to answer for a charge of possessing an automobile with a 'smoke screen' attachment."[30]

The moonshiners enjoyed a major advantage over law enforcement in that they had more disposable income, and greater necessity, to make their cars ever faster. Junior Johnson asserted, "They [law enforcement] had to use what they could buy from the dealerships. We'd take the money that [we] could make in the moonshine business and fix our cars to where we didn't lose the car and didn't lose the moonshine and didn't get caught either."[31] Skilled professional mechanics could make a very good living working on cars for liquor haulers.

The 1940 flathead Ford is the classic "tripper" car. It can be easily modified to make it a high-performance vehicle and holds up to twenty-two cases of moonshine. (Library of Congress)

William Thompson and Buddy Shuman gained notoriety, and lots of cash, in the Charlotte area for their abilities building powerful engines for moonshine trippers.[32]

Outrunning the law took more than a fast car, however; it required a strong dose of audacity as well as driving skill. North Carolina trippers employed a variety of moves to evade law enforcement. They developed the power slide, a method of maintaining speed on the turns on dirt roads by causing the rear wheels to slide while turning the front wheels opposite the turn, accelerating the entire time. The "bootleg turn" also became a favorite tactic for evading the law. Driving at full speed, the pursued moonshiner would either throw "the gear into second, making a sharp turn and letting the car swing around by itself" or "put the car into a skid, pulling on the emergency brake lightly, turning the steering wheel sharply to the left, and then accelerating madly." If executed properly, the driver would quickly be headed in the opposite direction past his startled and angry pursuers. The move took tremendous daring, for an improperly executed bootleg turn could easily land the car on its roof and into law enforcement's hands.[33]

Not all North Carolina liquor haulers went for fast, hopped-up hot rods, however, but used more discreet methods of delivering the product. As Wilkes

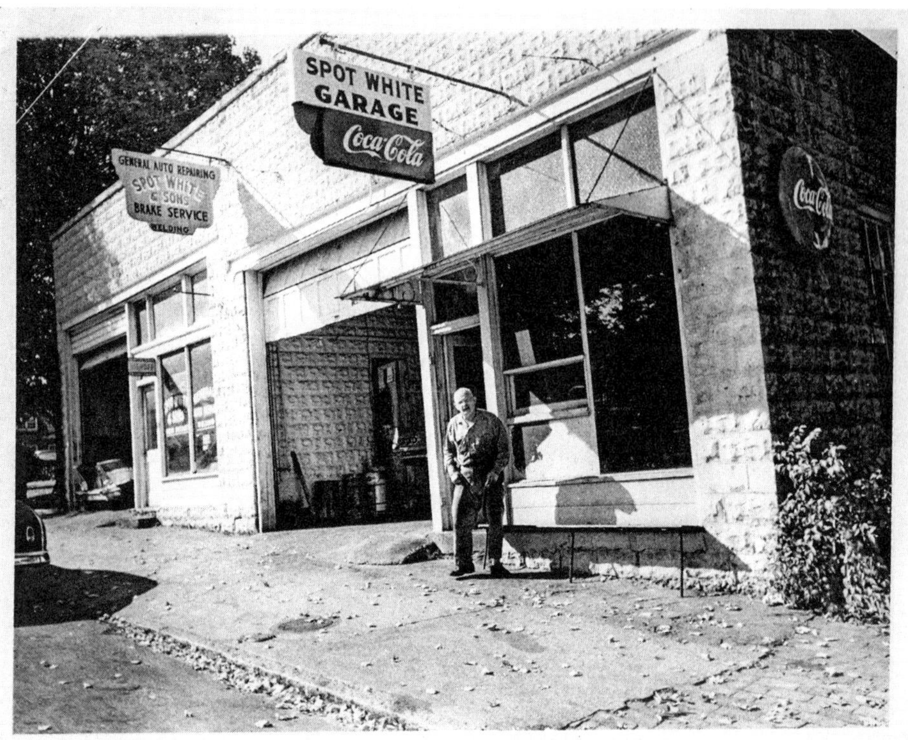

Spot White's garage in Asheville. White, like many skilled mechanics in North Carolina, allegedly helped moonshiners hop up their high-powered automobiles. (Courtesy of North Carolina Room, Pack Memorial Library, Asheville, N.C.)

County's Millard Ashley observed, "I really didn't care about fast cars. I had some of them. I'd rather use a truck. Those cars are hard to keep running." When he did use an automobile, he preferred unobtrusive "old junker cars. I didn't really care for the fast ones." Instead of roaring down the highway in the "dead hour of night," Ashley preferred to blend in with the traffic of people going to work and tried "to go down with the workhands, so they wouldn't notice you." Indeed, the large wholesale operators that arose in the 1920s and 1930s preferred trucks, even large tractor-trailers, for hauling liquor.[34] As for the high-speed chases that became such an important part of moonshine lore, at least in Chatham County, they rarely occurred. As John Vestal observed, "In Chatham, what chasing occurred was almost always on foot." The Mount Vernon Springs moonshiner asserted in an interview with a *News of Chatham* reporter that "he was never chased" and "would have pulled over if an officer had ever signaled him to do so."[35]

Although national Prohibition gave North Carolina liquor a national—or at least an East Coast and upper Midwest—market, and the state's and region's mill towns would always provide a sizeable market, increasing amounts of illegal liquor went into African American communities in the state's growing cities. The 1920s and 1930s saw many African Americans leave rural North Carolina and a life of sharecropping for new opportunities in urban areas. New Deal legislation under the Agricultural Adjustment Act accelerated this process as new regulations limited tobacco production and led eastern North Carolina farmers to take land once farmed by sharecroppers out of production.

North Carolina's liquor kingpins quickly took advantage of this new situation and tailored their efforts to this new urban market. The result was a relatively curious business arrangement that connected demographics in the state that rarely related with one another: rural and urban, white and black. Indeed, this new business model increasingly brought young men driving high-powered automobiles and delivering illegal liquor from virtually all-white counties like Wilkes into urban African American neighborhoods in Winston-Salem, Greensboro, Charlotte, Asheville, Durham, Raleigh, and smaller towns and cities.

The primary retail outlet for this moonshine was the so-called liquor house. Liquor houses had been common in rural African American areas before this period but became even more ubiquitous and important social and cultural institutions in the cities during the 1920s and 1930s. As folklorist Tim Duffy asserted, "They were a mixture of social welfare agency, bar, and clubhouse." For most liquor houses, moonshine was the drink of choice. As Duffy further observed, "Drink houses are the storefront for moonshine.... At the heart of it, these places are for selling moonshine."[36] Of course, there are no sales records for the moonshine business in this period, but a significant portion of the illegal liquor produced during the time probably flowed to and through these liquor houses. Indeed, African Americans like Howard Creech who worked for liquor kingpins like Percy Flowers served as key liaisons to African American–owned liquor houses in the eastern end of the state.[37]

Women such as Ada Thompson often ran these houses and were either married women looking to supplement their income or widowed or divorced women who had few other opportunities, especially if they had small children. As blues historian Ralph Speas noted, "Women operated most of these drink houses." While most liquor houses had a man, usually a big one behind the bar to maintain order "if there was any trouble," women generally cooked and ran the business side of the operation—even dealing with law enforcement. Historian Emily Edwards argued that "women controlled the money."[38] In 1942, a major undercover operation against Wake County liquor houses involving two African American Alcohol Beverage Control (ABC) agents led to the arrest of eighteen individuals. Thirteen of those arrested were women.[39]

Of course, one of the great challenges in running a liquor house was dealing with law enforcement. Generally speaking, these dealings were with local police and sheriff's departments, as most drink houses did not deal in a level of federal tax evasion that would attract the notice of Treasury Department agents. As for local law enforcement, Winston-Salem guitar shop owner Michael Bennett, who grew up playing in liquor houses, noted, "There was a funny sort of bond between the law and the juke joints." Talven Thompson recalled warnings his mother, Ada, received from local police when they were going to conduct a raid: "There has been many times when the police, especially around election time—that's when they would always raid the places. But the policemen ... would call her and say Ada, we'll be coming out later today so get things in order."[40] Bennett recalled one Burke County liquor house that served as a conduit between law enforcement and moonshiners who supplied the sheriff with a supply of "campaign liquor" to dole out during election time. Even when liquor houses got raided, or "popped" in liquor house parlance, this rarely deterred the owners for long. The Boars Head in Burke County, Bennett noted, "got raided all the time. Law would shut the place down and in a few weeks it'd be back open."[41]

National Prohibition came to an end on 5 December 1933 when, ironically, Mormon-heavy Utah voted to ratify the Twenty-First Amendment to the U.S. Constitution, the only amendment to repeal a previous amendment. But while national Prohibition's end dramatically reduced moonshine sales from North Carolina to other states, it did not end Tar Heel prohibition. Indeed, in 1933, North Carolina voters rejected by over 170,000 votes the idea of even calling a convention to consider ratifying the Twenty-First Amendment. When the amendment went into effect, the 1923 Turlington Act, which had conformed North Carolina law to federal Prohibition laws, remained in effect, and so the state remained officially dry.[42] *News and Observer* editorialist Frank Smethhurst noted the irony and the benefits to North Carolina's illegal liquor producers: "As I understand it, this means that we elected [U.S. senator] Bob Reynolds to put a tax on everybody's liquor in the United States except our own in order that we, astute mortals that we are, might not only enjoy our own contraband cheaply but might promote our own domestic industry with a tax exemption subsidy."[43]

It took a few years for the North Carolina General Assembly to come to grips with the new situation. Concerns grew in municipal areas and in counties near the Virginia and South Carolina lines as North Carolinians streamed across state lines to legally buy liquor in neighboring states. Both local and state government officials realized that this traffic cost them millions in potential tax revenue, for which they were desperate at the height of the Great Depression. In 1935, the General Assembly yielded to pressure and passed a number of individual bills allowing counties and municipalities who petitioned them to allow liquor sales in dispensaries run by local ABC boards. The first ABC store in North Carolina opened in Wilson on 2 July 1935 and reportedly had to turn away 100 people lined up at its door at the end of the business day. Concerned that this local system would be subject to corruption, the General Assembly passed the Alcohol Beverage Control Act in 1937, setting up the State Board of Control to oversee the local boards. The act created a "monopoly system," where all liquor retailed in the state must be sold through an ABC store. The act also created a local-option system, where counties or municipalities who wanted ABC stores were required to have majority approval from local voters. Places that did not gain such voter approval were still subject to prohibition under the Turlington Act and still are to this day.[44]

Despite the passage of the Alcohol Beverage Control Act, prohibition in North Carolina was still a force to be reckoned with, even as the number of ABC stores in the state grew slowly well into the 1960s. Of course, prohibition forces had powerful allies in the moonshining and bootlegging kingpins in their counties who, desiring to prevent legal competition, threw their support behind efforts to keep their counties and towns dry. Indeed, while profits for moonshiners would never again be as high as they were during national Prohibition, plenty of business remained out there for them. While moonshine hotbeds like Buffalo City that were primarily dependent on markets in now-wet states dried up, most moonshiners in the state adjusted to the new realities and focused on the large number of customers still available in the state. As an editor at the Burlington *Daily Times-News* put it in a 1934 editorial, even with national Prohibition's end, North Carolina remained "a dry corn likker drinking commonwealth."[45]

10

PROHIBITION, MOONSHINE, AND NORTH CAROLINA CULTURE

During the period of national Prohibition and in the late 1930s, moonshine became even more deeply enmeshed in North Carolina's cultural identity and shaped many important cultural expressions. Indeed, moonshine and the moonshine business shaped everything from the pastimes and sports pursued by the state's residents, music written and produced in the state, souvenirs produced for the state's growing number of tourist attractions, and even more elite productions.

In rural parts of the state, moonshine was closely tied to a number of popular pastimes, especially cockfighting and night hunting with dogs. Cockfighting was (and is) a rough blood sport with wagering at its core and has generally featured heavy drinking at its events. Of course, this was a natural market for moonshiners, and many frequented cockfights to sell liquor. Illegal liquor makers also commonly owned fighting cocks themselves and, having more disposable income than most, particularly the kingpins, often had topflight flocks. Lum Parham of Gaston County was particularly well known in the early years of the twentieth century for staging major cockfighting competitions just over the state line in York County, South Carolina. These "mains," as participants called them, attracted large crowds of spectators and competitors. After a raid on one such event, the *Charlotte Observer* referred to Parham as "a citizen who has long sustained an unsavory reputation in his neighborhood as a vendor of moonshine licker, a promoter of cocking mains and an undesirable citizen generally."[1]

The most notable of North Carolina's cockfighting liquor kingpins was Percy Flowers. As his son Perry Sullivan noted, "Percy was well known for his fast Reds and powerful, hard-hitting Greys fighting cocks. Over the years he had perfected the bloodline for stamina and strength." Flowers even employed an African American man named Eddie, who trained his birds and kept them in top shape. Indeed, Flowers became almost as famous for his fighting cocks as he did for his moonshine and traveled all over the Carolinas and Virginia to pit them against the best in the region.[2]

Moonshine also had a special connection to night hunting with dogs in North Carolina. Using dogs to chase raccoons, foxes, or even opossums at night had long been a popular pastime in the state's rural areas. When making liquor became illegal, however, night hunters had to be careful that they and their dogs did not run up on moonshine operations. It helped to know your hunting grounds and to know who produced moonshine in the area and where. As such, the moonshiners themselves often had a clear field to hunt. In addition, night hunting was associated with drinking and therefore a natural for moonshine producers. Many still operators also often had close relationships with dogs and kept hounds at their stills to warn them if someone approached. Junior Johnson and his family were noted coon hunters in Wilkes County and used money earned from their moonshine business to purchase and breed prize packs. Later in life, Johnson recalled the pleasures of coon hunting: "Winning a NASCAR is very satisfying, but I believe the most enjoyable thing I've known is having my dogs yapping and crawling all over me after they've treed a 'coon."[3]

Fox hunting was another popular night hunting pastime for many moonshiners. Fox hunting in North Carolina—at least outside of elite havens like Tryon, Southern Pines, or the Biltmore Estate—didn't involve fancy red coats and thoroughbred horses jumping hedges. While the dogs were similar, the pastime was very different, with men releasing the dogs and often sitting around a campfire, drinking liquor, and listening to the resultant "fox race," where the dogs chased a fox across the countryside. Fox hunters prided themselves on being able to recognize Old Jenny, Caesar, or Belle by each dog's distinctive bay. In fact, in later years some fox hunters took to using tape recorders so they could re-listen to crucial parts of the race at their leisure.[4] Accustomed to being out and about at night, moonshiners took to fox hunting and, as in the cockfighting business, used their excess income to breed champion dogs. Percy Flowers excelled at breeding topflight dogs as he did with his fighting cocks, probably even more so. As his son Perry noted, "Besides cockfighting, Percy lived for foxhound racing." The *Tarheel* quoted Flowers himself in a newspaper article on his dog-breeding prowess: "I guess I've thrown away more good money trying to breed hounds than any man alive." Flowers not only took his dogs out for fox races in surrounding farmland but also took them to show and compete in regional and national field trial competitions. His hounds won national championships in 1946 and 1948 and in the late 1960s captured first, third, and fifth place at the

Hunters head out for a "fox race" with their hounds in eastern North Carolina as the sun sets. (Courtesy of North Carolina Room, Pack Memorial Library, Asheville, N.C.)

prestigious U.S. Open. At its peak, Flowers's kennel held over 200 dogs. Fellow hunters prized his dogs, which sold for top dollar and are still seen in the bloodlines of champion fox dogs today.[5]

Even if moonshiners were not really fox hunting, keeping a few of their hunting hounds around gave them an excuse for being out in the woods in the middle of the night. In 1922, the Voss *Pilot* reported, "The latest fad is fox hunting with the making of moonshine as a side line. Tuesday afternoon the Sheriff of Hoke county, with his deputies, captured a copper still and two men who claimed to have come from Chatham to Hoke county to fox hunt. The operators were preparing to fire up when the officers arrived on the scene."[6]

At the same time that national Prohibition came along, the tourism business, especially for middle- and working-class individuals, began to boom in western North Carolina. Attractions such as the Great Smoky Mountains National Park, the Blue Ridge Parkway, the Cherokee Indian Reservation, Chimney Rock, Lake Lure, Mount Mitchell State Park, Blowing Rock, and Grandfather Mountain began to attract automobile tourists in droves. Many of those sites, most notably Chimney Rock and Linville Caverns, set up stills at their attractions. The tourism boom created a rising demand for souvenirs, and shops featuring

Moonshiner's Cave at Chimney Rock. (Courtesy of D. H. Ramsey Library Special Collections, University of North Carolina Asheville)

Moonshine still displayed for tourists in Linville Caverns.
(Courtesy of North Carolina Room, Pack Memorial Library, Asheville, N.C.)

such items popped up at the attractions and alongside mountain roads, often featuring a "pet" bear in a cage. North Carolina entrepreneurs soon stepped in to meet the demand, and the top-selling souvenirs often related to moonshine.

Wood-carver Carl Freeman of Bat Cave developed a large business making souvenirs out of rhododendron starting in 1919 and trademarking them with his "The Woodpecker" signature. Freeman marked his pieces with the names of popular tourist attractions and sold them to gift shops in those areas. While tourists bought his souvenir letter openers and toothpick holders, his moonshine-related items sold best. As the *Asheville Citizen-Times* reported in a 1971 article on Freeman, "Whenever you run across a miniature moonshine still or a moonshine jug fashioned from native rhododendron, the odds are a thousand to one that it came from 'The Woodpecker.'" He even sold some of his moonshine-related souvenirs to the (ostensibly) teetotal Baptists at the Ridgecrest Baptist Assembly near Black Mountain. Freeman just took the mash barrels that were a part of his standard still souvenirs, marked them with the conference center's name, and sold them as "pencil holders."[7]

Given its roots in the rural south and in Piedmont mill villages where moonshine was so pervasive, so-called hillbilly music also had strong connections to the moonshine business in North Carolina. The earliest such recorded music

Moonshine-related wood carvings by Bat Cave's Woodpecker sold to tourists from the 1920s to the 1970s in western North Carolina. He even sold moonshine-barrel pencil holders to the Baptists at the nearby Ridgecrest Baptist Assembly. (Photo by Gene Hyde, from the author's personal collection)

came out of Georgia in the 1920s, and the genre's pioneers often took on moonshiner personas. "Fiddlin'" John Carson, the first major recording star of hillbilly music, marketed himself, in historian Patrick Huber's words, as a "whiskey-bent and hell-bound hillbilly fiddler." He once told a reporter, "The only things I does really well is moonshining and fiddling, and since the 'revenoors' caught me moonshinin' twicet, the old lady 'lows I better quit for good." Carson even gave his daughter Rosa, who often accompanied him on guitar, the stage name Moonshine Kate. Gid Tanner, another pioneering Georgia fiddler and recording artist, also played on the moonshine image and regularly performed with his band, the Skillet Lickers. The group recorded a series of wildly popular skits entitled *A Corn Liquor Still in Georgia*. Recordings and later radio performances by Carson, Tanner, and other early hillbilly music stars were popular on farms and in the cotton mill villages in North Carolina and helped spark a number of homegrown contributions to the genre.[8]

Probably the most important North Carolina contribution to early hillbilly music was banjo impresario Charlie Poole, who had his own deep connections to moonshine and the moonshine business. In his book *Linthead Stomp*, Patrick Huber asserted, "Poole's banjo style on his prewar commercial recordings provided the instrumental foundations for modern bluegrass banjo and thus dramatically altered the historical trajectory of postwar country music." Poole also pioneered the persona, and lifestyle, embraced by many later coun-

Moonshine and Tourism

While tourists were not generally welcome at a moonshine still, beginning in the early years of the twentieth century seeing a "real still" and purchasing moonshine-related souvenirs became standard fixtures of the visitor experience in western North Carolina. Years of stereotyping mountaineers by the press, local color writers, and silent-movie makers made seeing a still an almost obligatory experience for the growing numbers of tourists who came to the region. To oblige the tourists' curiosity, many hotels and tourist attractions set up displays of stills and moonshine paraphernalia. The first hotel to put a still on display was probably Asheville's Battery Park Hotel, which had a moonshine still in its lobby as early as 1901. The hotel's manager also gave out small bottles of alleged "mountain dew" to the hotel's guests. Not long after it opened its doors, the Grove Park Inn followed suit with its own still. Probably sometime in the 1920s, Chimney Rock installed a still in a cave in the rock, named it Moonshiner's Cave, and claimed that it once (and it well may have) held an operating still. Linville Caverns later followed suit and installed a still of its own.

As tourism traffic grew as automobiles became more common and roads improved in the 1920s, "tourist traps" featuring both stills and moonshine-related souvenirs proliferated in the region. In 1919, Carl Freeman from Bat Cave began making miniature stills branded with the names of notable western North Carolina tourist attractions such as Chimney Rock, Grandfather Mountain, and the Great Smoky Mountains. Folk artists such as Wayne Martin in Swannanoa included moonshine stills, along with figures of stereotypical mountain folk, in the wood carvings they sold. In the post–World War II era, souvenir stoneware moonshine jugs became popular items sold at tourist attractions even outside the mountains, including at the battleship USS *North Carolina* site and at Carowinds.

Postcards were another aspect of the tourist industry that played on moonshine stereotypes. Most postcard companies in western North Carolina had several moonshine-related cards in their stock. Indeed, one of the best-known moonshine images ever produced comes from a postcard made by the Asheville Postcard Company. The title of the card is "A Typical Moonshine Still in the Heart of the Mountains," although the company adapted the card's title to various markets around the southern Appalachian region. Well-known Japanese photographer George Masa took the photograph used on the card, which features two men tending a copper still. In the staged photo, ironically, one of the men is Bascom Lamar Lunsford, the well-known folklorist who founded Asheville's Mountain Dance and Folk Festival and composed the classic moonshine song "Good Old Mountain Dew."

Displays of moonshine stills at tourist sites saw a revival of sorts in the 1970s. As the *Asheville Citizen-Times* reported in 1971, the National Park Service, as part of its "continuing effort to enlarge and improve upon the interpretation of early mountain culture," set up an operating still at its Pioneer Farmstead, just inside the border of the Great Smoky Mountains National Park near Cherokee. In order to ensure that no one consumed the moonshine, the Park Service treated it with Bitrex, "a compound twenty times more bitter than strychnine." Operating stills also became part of the growing number of "heritage" events cropping up in western North Carolina in the 1970s and 1980s. Jim Tom Hedrick conducted moonshine-making demonstrations at the Great Smoky Mountains Heritage Festival in Robbinsville. Popcorn Sutton did the same type of demonstrations at Mountain Heritage Days at Western Carolina University, at least until university officials caught him trying to take some of the product (not treated with Bitrex) home. Carowinds even got in on the act when it opened its Thunder Road roller coaster in 1976. Park staff placed one still near the entrance to the ride and another larger one near its exit.

try artists like Hank Williams Sr. (and Jr.), George Jones, and Keith Whitley, of "whiskey-soaked rogues and ne'er-do-wells who embraced a wandering, hand-to-mouth existence free from the responsibilities of married life and steady employment."[9]

Born in the mill village of Millboro in Randolph County, Poole spent much of his life wandering from mill village to mill village in south-central Virginia and north-central North Carolina. In some ways, he owed his professional success to a stint in the moonshine-making business. In 1918, Poole and fiddle player Posey Rorer, a mainstay in Poole's band, the North Carolina Ramblers, followed in the footsteps of many young North Carolina men and made moonshine to give themselves a grubstake to start out in life. The two young men partnered with an experienced illegal distiller near Rorer's home in Franklin County, Virginia, to make several runs of blockade liquor. The enterprise proved very successful, though short-lived, and the two walked away with $1,100 each in profit. Perhaps as important, they spent a lot of time at the still waiting for the liquor to distill and used that time to practice together, developing a style that allowed them to avoid life as moonshiners or mill hands and make their living as musicians. In addition, Poole used part of his moonshine money to purchase a "top-of-the-line" Orpheum No. 3 Special banjo for $132, which he later used on all his early recordings.[10]

Even after he became a successful recording artist, Poole was "always attracted to the seamier side" and regularly "performed in roadhouses, at moonshiners' stills, and even in brothels, all venues at which he could satisfy his thirst for corn whiskey." His biggest hits, like "Don't Let Your Deal Go Down Blues," "Ramblin' Blues," and "He Rambled," reflected his love of moonshine. Perhaps the words of his most popular song, "If the River Was Whiskey," best reflect Poole's major goal in life:

*Charlie Poole and the North Carolina Ramblers (*from left, *Poole, Posey Rorer, and Norman Woodlief). Poole and fiddle player Posey Rorer helped finance their early careers by making moonshine. (Courtesy of State Archives of North Carolina, Raleigh, N.C.)*

If the river was whiskey, and I was a duck,
I'd dive to the bottom and I'd never come up.
Oh, tell me how long have I got to wait?
Oh, can't I get you now, must I hesitate?
If the river was whiskey and the branch was the wine,
You could see me bathing just any old time.[11]

Tragically, and like many other artists who followed in his footsteps, Poole's hard-drinking lifestyle led to a heart attack and an early death at age thirty-nine. Unlike the most successful moonshiners, Poole drank too much of his own product, and that purchased from others, and never learned one of the keys to their success, that "liquor is for selling, not for drinking."

The greatest contribution of a moonshine-related song to the hillbilly, country, and bluegrass genres also came from a North Carolinian, Buncombe County's Bascom Lamar Lunsford, and his iconic song "Good Old Mountain Dew." The roots of the song, and its equally iconic tagline, most likely come from the theme song of the Biltmore Forest School, "Still on the Hill." Lunsford built on the tagline of "Still on the Hill" and based the verses to "Good Old

Mountain Dew" on a court case he witnessed in Madison County, where he sometimes practiced law. The first verse of Lunsford's version goes as follows:

On my first day in court I wish to report,
Now witness my story so true.
When the state closed its case a young man raised his face
And began all these facts to review.
Yes, they call it that old Mountain Dew.
Said those who refuse it are few.
While I know I've done wrong, the temptation is strong
When they call for that Old Mountain Dew.[12]

The verses go on with a deacon, a doctor, and a conductor all trying to buy the accused's liquor. The last verse ends with the moonshiner's lawyer opening "the lid on the can" and the judge letting the man go for court costs because he "acted the man when you took that stand, to swear what is so true [that 'those who refuse it are few']." Lunsford had some commercial success with the song when he recorded it in 1928 on Brunswick Records.

However, the song took off in the hands of Scotty Wiseman in the 1930s. Lunsford sold Wiseman the rights to the song for twenty-five dollars in 1938 when they both attended the National Folk Festival in Chicago and Lunsford needed money for a bus ticket home. Wiseman changed the lyrics to the modern version most folks now know and played it at a more upbeat tempo, and the popularity of the tune skyrocketed. He and his wife, LuLu Belle, had great success with the tune over the years, and musicians as diverse as Grandpa Jones, Glen Campbell, Willie Nelson, Stringbean, Trini Lopez, Doc Watson, and even "alternative rock" band Ween have recorded the song since. Most folks who know the song probably learned it as Boy Scouts or at a summer camp where it remains a staple.[13]

North Carolina's liquor houses also served as important cultural incubators. Patrons came not only for the cheap liquor but for food, companionship, handouts, loans, and the music and dancing many offered. Some liquor houses also provided opportunities to frequent prostitutes, play cards—sometimes for high stakes—or play the "numbers," an illegal lottery. Blues musician Lorenzo "Logie" Meacham observed, "The old-fashioned liquor houses had lots of gambling going on."[14] The sizes, sites, and amenities of liquor houses varied widely across North Carolina. Ada Thompson ran a small-scale operation in Asheville's East End area and generally stuck to liquor and food for her patrons. Her son Talven did report that at one point the family ran a numbers game called the "butter and egg" out of the house. The winning numbers came from the going prices those products brought farmers, which local radio personality Farmer

Bascom Lamar Lunsford, who wrote the iconic moonshine song "Good Old Mountain Dew," performing at Grandfather Mountain's Singing on the Mountain. (Photo by Hugh Morton, courtesy of the North Carolina Collection, UNC Libraries, UNC–Chapel Hill)

Russ announced on his radio show.[15] Meacham recalled one of the nicer liquor houses on Cherry Street in Winston-Salem: "It had nice new café tables. They sold food. The sisters were coming in setting things up and they had the traditional stuff in liquor houses. Jars of pickled pigs feet, pickled eggs, Penrose sausages, and crackers."[16]

Bootleggers located liquor houses in private homes, garages, or even tobacco barns. Meacham recalled Frank's Place—also known as the Bucket of Blood—in Winston-Salem: "Frank ran the Bucket out of a garage.... He'd move the cars out and he'd put the sawdust down. He'd set the pickled eggs and pickled pigs feet out and turn the music on the jukebox. We called it a piccolo."[17] Guitarist Max Drake recalled a drink house near Reidsville where a relative of his "converted a tobacco barn into a little juke joint. Bars like that were all over the place. These country people had to party someplace."[18] A number of the individuals interviewed by Emily Edwards recalled weekend crowds of 150 or more, especially when bands played live music. Places with music often did not open until midnight, and the party lasted until dawn. The music that grew out of North Carolina liquor houses formed the foundation for the Piedmont blues, and playing in liquor houses helped launch the careers of such blues legends as Blind Boy Fuller,

Richard Trice, Floyd Council, James "Guitar Slim" Stephens, Robert Lewis "Guitar Gabriel" Jones, "Sweet Daddy" Ray Burnett, and George Washington.

The liquor house experience also varied from a quiet home setting like Ada Thompson's place, where one could sip liquor and enjoy a meal, to the notorious "bucket of blood" variety like Frank's Place, where almost anything could, and did, happen. Edwards defines a "bucket of blood" as "a type of drink house known to be so dangerous that when the owner mopped the place the next morning, the dirty water in the bucket might also be bloody. The bucket of blood was the most violent of the drink houses, where patrons often released pent-up frustration with brutality."[19] Meacham recalled his experiences at Frank's: "On any given night, it could turn into a fight pretty quick.... The Bucket was all fights and knife fights."[20]

Legally operated commercial entertainment venues, often referred to as "juke joints," also played an important role in the distribution of moonshine, especially in African American communities. One such place was Roseland Gardens in the small western North Carolina town of Black Mountain. Built by local African American entrepreneur Horace Rutherford in 1918, the Roseland served as a center of the local black community until it closed in early 1976. The place was only open in summer and attracted not only the local African American community but the black "help" that summer vacationers and visitors to the local religious retreat centers at Ridgecrest, Montreat, and Blue Ridge brought with them. The Roseland's primary attractions were the twice-a-week dances accompanied by either music from a jukebox or the occasional live band. Local legend has it that the song "Black Mountain Blues," written by J. C. Johnson and popularized by Bessie Smith, was based on the Roseland. Rutherford provided a snack bar with "those big jars of pig feet and crackers and all kinds of snacks," according to his granddaughter Katherine Debrow, as well as a wooded area near the creek where local church groups held picnics.[21]

In addition to the dancing, the thing that made the Roseland, according to the *Asheville Citizen-Times*, "the largest private recreation center for colored people in Western North Carolina," was the availability of alcohol. As the mountains around Black Mountain were full of moonshine stills at the time, availability was not a problem. Rutherford also had the advantage of a lifelong friendship with sheriff Laurence Brown, also of Black Mountain, which made the place relatively immune from raiding. If local law enforcement did raid the Roseland, Rutherford surely had plenty of advance warning so he could clear the premises of any illegal alcohol. Rutherford regularly carried a pair of .45 revolvers to control what he called the "riffraff" who wanted to cause trouble. As Debrow recalled, "He was quite handy in getting rid of the guys.... Little pistol whipping I think they used to call it." If things got totally out of hand, Ruther-

Ada Thompson N.C. Moonshine Hall of Famer

What little we know about Ada Thompson we know from an interview with her son Talven "Sugarboy" Thompson, conducted by Andrea Clark in 2008 for her Twilight of a Neighborhood project on the historically black, but rapidly gentrifying, East End neighborhood of Asheville. Ada Thompson grew up in Spartanburg, South Carolina, and migrated to Asheville with her husband seeking work during the Great Depression. She lived in Asheville until she died in 1997. Like many African American women of her generation, Thompson spent most of her working career in the home of a local doctor doing domestic work and childcare. Also like many African American women in North Carolina, she supplemented her income by operating an illegal liquor house, or drink house.

Ada Thompson's career as the proprietor of a liquor house began quite accidentally, when the Thompson family moved into a house on Weaver Street in Asheville. Unbeknownst to Thompson, the previous occupant of the house had operated it as a drink house, a discovery she made when people kept showing up at the back door looking for a drink. As Talven recalled, his mother "had never been a part of anything like that," was a pillar of the Nazareth Baptist Church and an officer in the Progressive Club, and did not even drink. She did see an economic opportunity, however, and launched her career by going to the local liquor store and buying some cheap booze to dispense; according to her son, "that was the beginning."

Thompson saw no conflict between her religious practices and her newfound side job and evidently neither did her pastor or members of her church. Indeed, like many rural white churches, churches in poor black communities did not draw a strict line on liquor, particularly if one was selling it out of economic necessity. There also seems to have been a laxer attitude in many African American churches about what happened on Saturday nights, among both the laity and the clergy, in relation to alcohol. As Talven joked, "We would have preachers to come here on the way to church and we would say they're having communion before they got to church." Like Percy Flowers's, Thompson's generosity to the church itself and to her community solidified her reputation in the church.

Thompson's reputation as a great cook greatly boosted her business, "because mama always had dinner, she always cooked dinners and fed people from this house." Her reputation for good food even extended into the white community. Local radio personality Farmer Russ (Russ Offhaus), by far the most popular morning DJ in all of western North Carolina, told his listeners, "If you want a good meal you go to Ada Thompson's." He often followed that comment up a little while later with "Oh no, here comes my breakfast now," as Thompson would reward him for his advertisement. Most drink houses did not serve full meals like Thompson's did, but many served food, sometimes to-go specialties like fried chicken, fried fish, or chitlin sandwiches. Many simply put out popular cheap accompaniments to moonshine like pickled pigs' feet, pickled eggs, Penrose sausages, and crackers.

Women like Ada Thompson helped make liquor houses key institutions in many poor African American communities. Even after prohibition ended, here was a place where the liquor was cheap, the food fed your body and soul, and the music and dancing lifted your spirit.

In the summers, Black Mountain's Roseland Gardens offered its African American patrons music, dancing, food, and moonshine from the 1920s to the 1970s. (Courtesy Don Talley)

ford also had a direct line to Sheriff Brown, who often showed up personally to haul off troublemakers.[22]

Moonshine also had an effect not only on such "low-down" cultural expressions as hunting, tacky souvenirs for tourists, hillbilly music, and liquor houses but on more "highbrow" enterprises as well. The nationwide folklore movement was influential in North Carolina's intellectual circles, particularly surrounding the "rural life" movement at the Institute for Research in Social Science at the University of North Carolina at Chapel Hill (UNC) and professors Howard Odum, Rupert Vance, and Guy and Guion Johnson. This movement also influenced the work of the drama department at UNC, particularly the work of Paul Greene. As such, moonshine often crept up in artistic expressions produced in North Carolina during this period.

Moonshine themes became popular during the Prohibition era in dramatic productions made in the state. In 1920, UNC's famous Carolina Playmakers created a statewide sensation when they staged a play written by student Hubert C. Heffner of Catawba County entitled *Dod Gast Ye Both!* The one-act comedy, supposedly based on real-life Catawba Countians, featured the moonshining Setzer family and their escapades with "revenoor" Laurence Abner. The big news from the production, however, was that the set included a real-life operating moon-

Detail photo of the concession stand at Roseland Gardens showing moon shapes. Some locals say this indicates that this was where you could get moonshine. (Courtesy Don Talley)

shine still. Heffner decided early on that he needed one to make the production "authentic." He thought he had procured one from the Buncombe County Sheriff's Department, but "trouble arose about having it shipped to Chapel Hill. The railroad was a little suspicious and did not know whether it ought to be done." Fortunately, the local sheriff of Orange County came to the rescue and lent the Playmakers a confiscated still "under a strict promise of good behavior." Dr. A. S. Wheeler of UNC's chemistry department "knew all about how to set a still on its feet, and he was responsible for arranging the various parts in such a natural manner that Orange county citizens at the play blinked their eyes more than once when the curtains were pulled back and there she stood in all her glory."[23] The play was so popular that the Playmakers took the production on the road to Greensboro to wide popular acclaim.[24] Ironically, *Dod Gast Ye Both!* helped springboard Heffner's career. He later became one of the most important figures in American academic drama circles as a distinguished professor at the University of Wisconsin and Indiana University and as the author of *Modern Theater Practice*, a standard textbook in the field.[25]

In 1922, the Burlington Little Theater produced a play entitled *Moonshine*, written by Arthur Hopkins, "as part of its Folklore program." The *Daily Times-News* described the basic plot to its readers: "'Moonshine is a one-act mountaineer drama play with two characters, a moonshiner and a revenue officer. It is a thrilling, subtle and ingenious drama in the moonshine district of the North Carolina mountains. A revenue officer introduces himself into the very midst of a very dangerous band of moonshiners and beats them at their own game."[26]

Moonshine themes even crept into the classical music scene in North Carolina. In the 1920s, Lamar Stringfield, a flautist, Pulitzer Prize–winning composer, conductor (most notably of the Radio City Music Hall orchestra), and a founder of the North Carolina Symphony, became fascinated with folklore work. The collection of folk songs gathered by Buncombe County's Bascom Lamar Lunsford, the composer of "Good Old Mountain Dew," especially fascinated him. Stringfield went on to compose a series of orchestral suites based on themes related to the western North Carolina mountains. One of his more famous compositions was *Moods of a Moonshiner*, a string quartet with three movements, "At a Still," "On a Cliff," and "A Moonshiner Laughs."[27]

While editors often featured cutesy moonshine-related poems during this period in North Carolina newspapers and advertisements, the theme also made its way into the work of highly respected poets. After spending time in Henderson County and the Tryon writer's colony in Polk County in the early 1920s, *Porgy* author DuBose Heyward wrote several poems reflective of mountain life. One of the best known was "The Mountain Woman," a poem chronicling the fortitude of mountain women facing a challenging existence. Particularly poignant is the section telling of the mountain woman's stoicism when her son is killed in a shootout at a moonshine still:

And when the sheriff shot her eldest son
Beside his still, so well she knew her part,
She gave no healing tears to ease her heart;
But took the blow upstanding, with her eyes
As drear and bitter as the winter skies.
Seeing her then, I thought that she had won.[28]

Most notably, Rebecca Cushman, who had a strong association with the Chapel Hill folklorists, included a lengthy poem on legendary moonshiner Quill Rose in her collection *Swing Your Mountain Gal*, published by Houghton Mifflin in 1934 (see Aquilla "Quill" Rose sidebar, p. 124).[29] While more educated individuals wrote and performed these poems, plays, and orchestral compositions, the views of moonshiners in these works were generally not any more sophisticated than in works produced in more lowbrow entertainment venues. Indeed, the elite works often overromanticized the moonshiner and only reinforced the traditional stereotypes of North Carolina blockaders.

By far the most important cultural contribution of North Carolina moonshiners was their key role in southern stock car racing's birth and early development. Liquor haulers played a number of important roles in the early days of the sport. The stories recounting star drivers hauling liquor one night and winning a stock car race at a red clay fairgrounds track the next are basically true. But the illegal liquor business's role went much deeper in the sport; it also provided the sport with skilled mechanics, who made their living on liquor cars, and liquor kingpins, who provided top-notch cars, financed races, and after World War II, provided the best racetracks. As Junior Johnson observed, "There was a lot of bootlegging people involved in racing when it got off the ground. And if anything boosted it and made it successful I would think you have to give the bootlegging people a big, big part of the credit for it."[30]

In North Carolina, stock car racing had its roots in the high-speed driving experience liquor haulers gained by speeding down dirt roads and highways hauling liquor to market and, on occasion, trying to outrun law enforcement. The skills these drivers gained, especially in handling a car at high speed on dirt roads, translated well into racing on a dirt racetrack. As Junior Johnson observed, by the time he reached an actual racetrack, he already had valuable and applicable experience behind the wheel: "It was a kind of a help to me that I had been in the moonshine business, cause I had a head start on my career. I was as good a driver as I was ever going to be."[31]

For most moonshiners, who were already interested in fast cars and were generally competitive individuals to start with, racing each other and finding out who had the fastest car was natural. While there is no real evidence of the makeshift cow pasture races of NASCAR mythology, there is plenty of evidence of bootleggers racing on streets and highways. Young liquor runners cruised the streets of North Carolina's small towns, and even the cities, in the evenings, talking up their cars and showing them off. Talk soon turned to challenge, competitors and spectators made their bets, and contestants headed off to some local stretch of highway late at night to have it out. "They would go out there on the highway," NASCAR legend Richard Petty reminisced, "lined up side by side, somebody waved a handkerchief or an oily rag or something, and it was Katie-bar-the-door!" And Richard Petty should know, not only from his own experience but because his father, Lee, also a NASCAR Hall of Famer, not only hauled liquor but was renowned in Randolph and surrounding counties for his prowess as a street racer well before he ever saw a racetrack. Indeed, the elder Petty became so successful that he often had to paint his car a different color "just so the other cats would race him."[32]

The moonshiners were not the only ones doing this, and a culture developed in the 1930s among young men all over the state that revolved around fast cars and street races. However, competitions among bootleggers were especially intense in communities where moonshining predominated. Participants publicized many of these late-night races, and they attracted hundreds of people and thousands of dollars in side bets. Max Welbourn remembered the excitement when "the first good highway was built from Yadkinville to Wilkesboro [U.S. Route 421]." The bootleggers raced from Brooks's store in Yadkin County to Seagrave's store in Wilkes. "It was a regular Friday or Saturday night event . . . and they'd be two and three cars at a time and they'd race from one end to the other."[33] This activity took on special meaning in a region that offered few entertainment options for young people, especially in the working class.

By the late 1930s, news of the annual stock car races in Daytona Beach and the regular races at Lakewood Speedway in Atlanta—and particularly the fact that a bunch of north Georgia liquor runners won most of these races—attracted the attention of North Carolina moonshiners. In the late 1930s, Arvel "Red" Sluder of Asheville became the first North Carolina bootlegger to make the trek south for the Daytona races. Soon North Carolina bootleggers like Buddy Shuman began heading south to test themselves against the likes of liquor-hauling, and now race car–driving, legends like Roy Hall, Lloyd Seay, Smoky Purser, Gober Sosebee, and the Flying Flock Brothers, Fonty and Bob.[34]

By the late 1930s, organized stock car racing spread into North Carolina. Promoters had the advantage of having lots of available liquor cars and liquor-hauling drivers to keep the racing exciting. In addition, many liquor haulers attracted to racing were already folk heroes to many children and teens in the region, which provided a ready-made fan base for the sport. Donald Johnson of Yadkin County remembered listening to souped-up bootlegger cars as a child as they roared down the highway. "I just thought it wadn't nothing like those bootleggers.... They were folk heroes."[35] Promoters also discovered that the red clay soil of the Piedmont made for great stock car racing, especially on the fairgrounds tracks built initially for horse racing. North Carolina driver Neil "Soapy" Castles asserted, "Everybody ran dirt tracks and your dirt tracks were horse tracks, mostly at your fairgrounds, with long straightaways and short corners, narrow. People started running these old Fords and found they could get around these horse tracks pretty good."[36] "Red clay ... is the greatest natural racing surface in the world," racing promoter Humpy Wheeler observed. "If it is prepared properly, it is a beautiful thing to behold." Stock cars on an appropriately watered-down red clay track created quite a spectacle for the entertainment-starved Piedmont working class. Indeed, the sight of stock cars power sliding through the turns, beating and banging on one another, attracted North Carolina fans by the thousands to the races.[37]

In 1939, the fairgrounds track in Salisbury became the first in the state to host a stock car race. Promoted by South Carolina bootlegger Joe Littlejohn, Salisbury remained a major stop for stockers throughout the prewar period.[38] Greensboro came on board with a stock race, promoted by Bruce Thompson, at the Greensboro Fairgrounds in 1940, reportedly the first race run under lights in the south. Regular races were held there throughout the prewar period.[39] Charlotte joined the club in 1941 with a Ralph Hankinson–promoted event billed as stock car racing's "world's championship," held at the Southern States Fairgrounds. The race drew more than 10,000 fans, quickly making the Queen City a major player in the sport.[40]

High Point became a premier venue for North Carolina stock car racing in 1941 when it drew large crowds to its new one-mile, banked, red clay track. The High Point Speedway, one of the first tracks built in the Piedmont since the

Bill Blair was a moonshiner, pioneering stock car racer, and track owner in North Carolina's Piedmont Triad. (Courtesy of William Blair Jr.)

1920s strictly for auto racing, had seating for 10,000 spectators. On its treated racing surface, stock cars attained lap speeds of almost eighty miles per hour, almost unheard of at the time. The speedway hosted three stock car races in 1941, including one billed as a "national championship race" in August.[41] While auto racing was sidelined from 1942 until August of 1945 due to World War II, North Carolina's moonshiners helped lay a firm foundation for the sport that supported an impressively large building by the 1950s.

If the years between 1920 and 1945 proved anything with regard to moonshine's history in North Carolina, it was that Prohibition was the best thing that ever happened to the illegal liquor business. The national, statewide, and local bans on liquor boosted both demand and prices and created huge incentives for moonshiners to modernize their operations and make production faster and more efficient. At the same time, quality declined and the likelihood that illegal liquor contained dangerous substances increased. Despite this, however, the moonshine business thrived, even as World War II loomed, and stood poised to continue to play an outsized role in North Carolina's economic and cultural life as the state entered postwar boom times, especially as most counties and municipalities in the state remained legally dry.

11

1941 TO 1970—THE HEYDAY OF THE MOONSHINE SYNDICATE

While North Carolina entered an era of unprecedented economic growth and modernization during World War II and in the postwar years, the moonshine business, a vestige of its past, adapted and entered one of its more profitable eras in the 1940s, 1950s, and into the 1960s. While the war proved challenging to moonshiners, they adapted to rationing, labor shortages, and condemnation for what some deemed "unpatriotic behavior." By the later years of the war, those involved in North Carolina's illegal liquor business made profits as large as in the days of national Prohibition. The postwar years proved extremely profitable as well, as the economy boomed and Prohibition remained firmly in place in most parts of the state. While the majority of the people involved in the business were still farmers supplementing their income, more and more of the business became concentrated in the hands of liquor kingpins. They often cooperated with other such operatives, who provided finance capital, stills and supplies, and bail money and lawyers if moonshiners were caught by law enforcement and who handled most of the transportation and distribution. Indeed, the postwar era became the heyday of the moonshine syndicate in North Carolina and helped the state retain its status as the number one moonshine state in the nation.

As World War II began, it looked as if North Carolina's moonshiners had met their match. The business seemed destined for extinction, and early in the war, reports circulated that moonshining had declined dramatically. Ed Patton, head of the North Carolina office for the federal Alcohol Tax Unit, asserted in 1941 that "it is quieter in the mountain area than a long time." Patton attributed the decline in moonshining to the high prices of sugar and grain due to wartime rationing.[1] Rationing also affected liquor runners' ability to secure gas, tires, and spare parts for their cars and trucks. Others noted the "manpower shortage" due to the draft and the comparatively high wages paid in defense industries. In 1943, the *News and Observer* noted, "But now, the blockaders lament, they're lucky if they have enough men around the distillery when they get ready to run off a few boxes of mash. There is no one to spare as a watcher."[2] Moonshiners also ran the risk of appearing unpatriotic at a time of extreme national emergency. In 1942, North Carolina's Alcohol Beverage Control (ABC) system began a campaign to characterize moonshiners as hampering the war effort. Officials argued that illegal liquor producers' tax evasion "deprived the government of desperately needed funds and their consumption of sugar and other commodities deprived the troops of needed supplies."[3] In Wilson County, local officials made a great show of donating confiscated stills to "the copper salvage drive."[4]

As the war progressed, however, North Carolina moonshiners showed the creativity and entrepreneurial drive that had sustained the business and made illegal liquor such an important part of the state's economy and culture for almost eighty years. The huge demand and resultant high prices for moonshine created powerful incentives and led moonshiners to find ways around wartime limitations. Wartime rationing also made liquor scarce in the few places in North Carolina where it was legally available and further boosted demand. The influx of hundreds of thousands of young men, eager for a drink, who were deployed to the state's many military bases created a huge new market. In addition, the stresses of wartime on the home front made many fathers, mothers, wives, and husbands of those in harm's way in need of a stiff drink. The *Burlington Times News* reported in 1943, "The economic law of supply and demand is skyrocketing the price of moonshine, and the few blockaders still in the business don't have to worry about OPA [Office of Price Administration] price controls. For years before the war the price of moonshine varied narrowly between $8 and $11 per five-gallon can at the 'still site.' Now, according to reliable sources ... the same grade of whiskey is bringing $25 per can—if it can be found." In 1944, the *Statesville Daily Record* asserted, "Reminiscent of prohibition days are scenes in the mountain regions where moonshiners are busy again. Quality is terrible, but prices are scandalously high because of the whiskey shortage." The *Record* reported the average local price of illegal liquor at $12.50 per gallon, enough to offset higher costs for supplies and labor and make profits even higher than during the heyday of national Prohibition.[5]

Moonshiners found several ways to deal with wartime conditions. Since copper was "all but impossible to obtain," the use of car and truck radiators for condensers became more common. For the stills themselves, moonshiners made use of whatever materials were available. As the *Daily Record* noted, "the cooking is done largely in old oil drums, sometimes with two or three welded together into a single vessel, and in wooden tanks with sheet metal bottoms to face the flames."[6] Early in the war, distillers substituted molasses or even Karo syrup for sugar, which was rationed. Some producers even went back to the old recipes, using only cornmeal and corn malt.[7] Late in the war the federal government loosened sugar allotments "for industrial purposes," although it was still subject to rationing.[8] A "thriving black market" ensued, facilitated by an equally booming market for counterfeit ration coupons used to purchase the sugar.[9]

These adaptations kept the state in the top ranks of moonshine producers. In 1945, state senator Charles Rouse pointed out to his colleagues that North Carolina was "second in the nation in the operation of illicit distilleries, despite the fact that there are 75 dry counties [out of 100] in the state."[10] While the methods used by most wartime moonshiners ensured that the quality of most of this liquor was terrible, customers still lapped it up. Due to the success of their liquor making, as the war wound down, North Carolina blockaders were flush with cash. John M. Greer, who operated a still in a cavern near the resort community of Little Switzerland in McDowell County during the war, used his cash to build the Skyline Village Inn over the mouth of the cave. The inn served as a convenient front for his operations, providing a way to launder cash into banks and serving as a legitimate income source on its own.[11] Indeed, cash earned from illegal liquor businesses financed many legitimate, and important, enterprises in North Carolina's booming postwar economy.

After the war the moonshine business expanded even faster. The *Statesville Daily Record* reported in 1948 that officials estimated that, just in the previous year, the number of illegal stills in the United States had increased by 50 percent. "The bottled-in-the-barn business is booming. Moonshining is mushrooming. And bootlegging is back."[12] North Carolina regularly stayed at or near the top "in number of stills seized, amount of whiskey captured, number of arrests and amount of mash destroyed" in records published by the Alcohol and Tobacco Tax Unit (ATTU). In 1958 the *News and Observer* declared, "North Carolina still has more backwoods liquor stills than any other southern state." The paper also reported that in the fiscal year ending 30 June 1958, agents destroyed 2,459 stills, confiscated 44,203 gallons of moonshine, and poured out over 1.5 million gallons of mash. As further evidence of the state's moonshine bona fides, the state had more ATTU agents assigned to it than any other state.[13]

The *Gaston Gazette* claimed in 1955 that "more moonshine liquor is probably manufactured between Gastonia and the Tennessee line than in any other comparable area of the United States."[14] But western North Carolina did not have a monopoly by any means on the state's illegal liquor trade. In 1953, Robeson County sheriff M. G. McLeod reported that authorities had destroyed 2,266 stills in the county in the previous three years, an average of "more than two stills a day."[15] In an editorial entitled "CONTINUOUS PROBLEM," a *Robesonian* editor expressed the frustration of law enforcement over the staying power of the business despite all of these busts: "Looks like it would discourage moonshiners plumb out of business, but it doesn't. As quickly as one still is knocked down, another pops up somewhere else."[16] The *Daily Record* attributed the increase in moonshining to the "high taxes on legal liquor" and to the decreases in the cost of key supplies for making illegal liquor, particularly sugar, corn, and copper tubing.[17]

One important factor the paper did not mention was the key role that dry forces continued to play in North Carolina politics. While they fought a rear-guard action and it was obvious to most observers that keeping the state dry was another southern "lost cause," the prohibitionists were not going down quietly or giving up territory easily. Indeed, well into the 1950s, a rite of passage for individuals running for the Democratic Party nomination for governor was to pledge their support for the return of statewide prohibition and promise that they would demand that the legislature call for a statewide referendum on alcohol. While there was no chance the legislature would approve such a referendum, and most governors, and candidates, only paid the issue lip service, it remained a necessary political act and indicates the issue's staying power. As the *Gaston Gazette* noted in 1955, "Every gubernatorial aspirant since the repeal of Prohibition in 1933 has promised the voters of North Carolina that he would ask for such an election, but none of them has ever accomplished it—or even tried very hard." While the effort to return to statewide prohibition was symbolic at best, dry forces had the most success at keeping their counties from approving local referenda to bring legal liquor into the county, at least temporarily.[18]

In this effort, the drys had important and well-funded allies in the local moonshiners, who opposed seeing an ABC store on the town square as vehemently as the staunchest Baptist teetotaler. When Wilkes County had a vote on the issue, a Charlotte television station interviewed Odell Jolson, a "long-time merchant ... with diversified business interests" in the community. What the station did not report was that Jolson's primary "business interest" was the sale of illegal, but legally produced, "red liquor." When the reporter asked, "What is your opinion of the ABC vote situation here?" Jolson sanctimoniously responded: "Horrible, horrible! It would be a most terrible influence on our young people and I'm strongly against it."[19] Dry forces could always count on significant "moral" and financial support from the county's moonshiners and bootleggers any time a referendum to allow ABC stores came up. Indeed, the counties that were the state's most prolific producers of illegal alcohol became some of the last in the state to become wet. One of those counties, Graham, remains the state's only dry county to this day.

While the continuing existence of dry counties and dry municipalities ensured a healthy demand for illegal liquor in North Carolina, increases in the federal excise tax on liquor kept demand high even in counties that had voted for ABC stores, especially among the state's poorest citizens. While the tax in 1939 was four dollars per gallon, by the late 1940s it had climbed to nine dollars plus a state tax of $1.43. The Distilled Spirits Institute decried the tax increase and blamed it for the increasing demand for "the unsafe but tax-free moonshine product," which had climbed to pre–World War II levels.[20] By the late 1950s, the federal tax had climbed to $10.50 per gallon. In 1958, an editorial in the *Asheville Citizen-Times* asserted that the taxes on liquor "have priced liquor out of reach to many. That doesn't stop drinking; it makes these people ready customers for the bootleggers."[21] The *News and Observer* noted in 1959 that due to taxes, "legal liquor is being made so expensive that moonshine is becoming more than ever the poor man's drink."[22]

Some people speculated that increases in prices at the state-monopolized ABC stores also increased demand for moonshine. After a major bust in Burke County in 1954, the Morganton *News-Herald* mused about a recent 5 percent increase in liquor prices in legal stores: "Perhaps very little of the Burke County product goes into North Carolina's ABC areas, but we keep wondering whether the price increase won't turn out to be a 'shot in the arm' for the one industry the Chamber of Commerce is not interested in expanding and about which the citizens feel a bit ashamed."[23]

The decline in costs for materials needed to make liquor, which came with the end of wartime rationing and the postwar economic boom, also boosted profits for those in the illegal liquor business. The Burlington *Daily Times-News* asserted in 1949 that "apparently the war-time pinch on metal material is being relieved in the moonshine industry," when it reported on a raid that yielded not only a moonshine still but thirty pounds of copper.[24] The most important cost saving, however, came from the dramatic decline in the cost of sugar, generally the moonshiner's greatest expense.

As always, broader economic conditions continued to play a role in the moonshining business, and resorting to making a run or two of illegal liquor remained an important insurance policy against hard times for many farmers. While postwar North Carolina offered a variety of new economic opportunities with the expansion of industry in the state, the post–New Deal agricultural rules created new uncertainties for farmers. In 1958, the state's newspapers reported that acreage quota cuts by the U.S. Department of Agriculture caused some farmers to pull their stills out of hiding and get back into the moonshine business. William Richardson, the head of the ATTU office in Dunn, asserted, "We hear a lot of violators say they turn to bootlegging when they can't make a living on the cotton or tobacco acreage."[25] Of course, those farmers who traditionally supplemented their income meeting seasonal liquor demand continued to do so as well. Richardson also noted, "The traffic goes up about this

Folk art moonshine still crafted by master wood-carver Wayne Martin of Swannanoa. (Photo by Gene Hyde, courtesy of D. H. Ramsey Library Special Collections, University of North Carolina Asheville)

time of year when Thanksgiving and Christmas party-goers are in the market for spirits."[26]

The presence of large numbers of dry counties, high liquor taxes, lower costs, and uncertain economic conditions on the state's farms helped maintain North Carolina's status as one of the top moonshine states. In 1957, the *Daily Tar Heel* commented on the state's reputation in light of the filming of the Hollywood picture *Thunder Road* in and around Asheville: "Meanwhile our antiquated North Carolina laws remain on the books and drunks keep on drinking and abstainers keep on abstaining. But we can claim with prideful supremacy over our neighbor states: we're the top state in the nation when it comes to moonshine production, and they even come here to make movies about us."[27] In 1961, the *Daily Times-News* described North Carolina football hero Charlie "Choo-Choo" Justice as quintessentially and genuinely "home grown as tobacco from Rocky Mount, towels from Kannapolis, furniture from High Point, and moonshine from Wilkes County."[28] When the navy requested that the city of Asheville send some special items related to the area for the christening of the USS *Asheville* in Tacoma, Washington, in 1965, the city sent, among other display items, a jug marked "Mountain Dew" and "a wood-carved replica of a mountain moonshine still."[29]

North Carolina even exported moonshiners to other states during this period, with major busts of imported stills and arrests of North Carolinians

Moonshine Humor

From the 1890s through the mid-twentieth century, North Carolinians loved moonshine humor. Folks seemed especially fond of funny moonshine-related poems and ditties. The *Asheville Citizen* printed a humorous obituary poem in 1897:

> He left ten children and a wife
> When death, the tyrant, sought him:
> Made moonshine liquor all his life
> And the government never caught him!

A long poem printed on a postcard from the 1920s extolled the wonders of Asheville. One stanza claimed:

> Streets here are cleanest
> Realtors are the keenest
> And moonshine is the meanest,
> In Asheville.

The *Statesville Daily Record* printed its humorous version of the North Carolina state toast in 1940:

> Here's to North Carolina
> The land of the long leaf pine
> Where the liquor they drink is all
> moonshine,
> Where the roads are all crooked,
> And the trains are all late,
> Here's to North Carolina,
> To hell with the whole darned state.

North Carolinians also enjoyed poems poking fun at revenue agents. Bascom Lamar Lunsford shared one involving Daniel Kanipe, a McDowell County revenue agent alleged to be the only survivor of Custer's Last Stand, who apparently took great pleasure in sampling the products he seized:

> The revenue, the revenue,
> Kanipe and old Sams,
> They'll cut down your mash tub,
> And they'll drink up your drams.

The Burlington *Daily Times-News* reported that some poetic moonshiners left an offering on the windshield of deputy W. L. Wheeles's car after he cut down their 1,000-gallon still:

> W. L. Wheeles is a red-headed man.
> He catch your liquor if he can.
> He slips through the woods with the
> ease of a cat.
> He can smell mash if it is buried in a vat.
> If he goes to heaven and has his will,
> He will catch St. Peter at a moonshine
> still.

Humorous stories and anecdotes related to moonshine were also popular. A Yadkin County resident wrote to the Statesville *Landmark* in 1889 describing the small town of Hamptonville where he lived: "Our town now consists of three large stores, one furniture factory, one blacksmith shop, one physician, one preacher, one lawyer, three good musicians and plenty of good blockade whiskey, which of course keeps everything lively." In 1908, the *Wilmington Messenger* poked fun at prohibition not long before North Carolinians voted the state dry. At a church service, a "temperance advocate" waved his arms and shouted, "Praise to glory the south is going dry! It will bring sunshine into southern homes." A "little man" sitting on the end of the pew responded, "Yes, and moonshine brother!" The *Daily Times-News* in 1940 related an oft-told North Carolina remedy for a cold: "Hang one's hat on the bed post, go to bed and drink moonshine whiskey until two hats are seen."

North Carolinians told and retold

moonshine stories and kept them circulating for years. One such story involved an encounter between an intoxicated "old moonshine loving mountaineer," a huge rattlesnake, and the old adage about moonshine being an effective snakebite cure. On spying the man, the snake "whirled into a coil, reared its head high into the air, and made its rattles sing." The old man looked the snake in the eye and shouted, "Go ahead and bite me, you dirty son of Satan! I was never better fixed for it my whole life." Another popular story involved a "backwoodsman" who came to town with a jug of moonshine and his shotgun. The man offered a townsman a drink from his jug, but he refused, saying he didn't drink. The moonshiner persisted and when the man continued to turn down the offer, he raised his shotgun and said, "Now you'll take a drink or I'll blow you to bits." The townsman took a drink, and after "seven coughs and six strangles" sputtered, "That sure is wicked liquor." The "backwoodsman" then responded, "Yea, I know it. Now hold the gun on me while I take a drink."

Politicians loved moonshine jokes as well. In *Tarheel Laughter*, Richard Walser shares a story attributed to legendary U.S. senator Sam Ervin, whose Burke County home was an equally legendary haven for moonshiners. Ervin told the story of a "constituent" who shared some moonshine with one of his friends. The constituent then asked his friend how he liked it. The friend responded, "Well, it was just right." When the constituent asked what that meant, his friend replied, "I mean that if it had been any better you wouldn't have given it to me. And if it had been any worse, I couldn't have drunk it."

running them occurring in Mississippi, South Carolina, and Illinois. Journalist Vance Packard's exposé of the "millions in moonshine" made in Wilkes County led to a crackdown by federal, state, and local officials, and as a result, in 1952 two Wilkes County moonshiners took their operations to Harrisburg, Pennsylvania.[30] Officers busted an operation in a swamp near Columbia, Mississippi, worth an estimated $55,000 in 1962, run by five men from Lenoir.[31] Authorities arrested two men from Lenoir and one from Wilkes County in 1963 for possessing a still in Clover, South Carolina, valued at $20,000 that could purportedly produce $1 million worth of liquor in three months.[32]

In the postwar era, moonshiners demonstrated once again their ability to adapt and modernize their operations. They proved endlessly creative in finding new ways to produce, distribute, and market their products and became especially adept at organizing their business in a more efficient, modern manner. In 1947, the prosecution of Lumberton taxi driver K. C. Morgan demonstrated a widely known "secret" that taxi drivers often served as key middlemen for bootleggers. Authorities charged Morgan for taking a client to a bootlegger where he purchased two half-gallon jugs of illegal liquor. While Morgan claimed he had no idea that his rider had purchased moonshine, local solicitor Murchison

Biggs asserted that "taxi drivers were frequently found to be 'at the bottom' of the bootleg liquor violations."[33] Indeed, most folks knew that the easiest way to find illegal liquor, especially when one was visiting a new town, was to ask a hotel bellhop or taxi driver, who would gladly take you there. Gastonia police discovered one of the most novel methods of distributing illegal liquor when they busted Paul Johnson, "an ice cream pushcart man," in 1949. Along with his ice cream, Johnson had "25 drink-size bottles ... filled with two ounces of white liquor." After his arrest, the ice-cream vendor commented to the arresting officers, "I should have listened to my wife."[34] Officers also arrested folks hiding eighteen gallons of liquor in a picnic basket and sixty gallons under clothes in the back seat of a "gaily decorated automobile" sporting a "Just Married" sign.[35]

The most notable changes in the moonshine business during this period were the increased commonality of large, elaborate stills located in unlikely locations and the ever-increasing involvement of illegal liquor syndicates doing a high-volume business. Many of the largest busts in the 1950s and 1960s came not in mountain coves, hidden hollows, or swamps but in tobacco barns, dairy barns, chicken houses, attics, and basements, often in fairly populated areas. Increasingly, moonshiners, especially the large-volume dealers, went to great trouble and expense to conceal their stills. Agent Garland Bunting told author Alec Wilkinson about one still he busted that was "set up in the living room of a ranch house." The operator "laid down plywood on the floors and as high as the windows" in the house's five bedrooms and turned them into fermentation vats. To make the house appear as if it were a normal residence for a suburban family, the moonshiner "parked a boat in the front yard and tied up a pony and put up a swing set and paid a woman to sit on the swings all day with her little girl." Bunting's associate in the Rocky Mount Alcohol Tax Unit (ATU) office, Michael Zetts, recalled busting steamer still operations "big as a damn old lumber yard" when he first arrived in the area and local moonshiners "importing sugar by the boxcar." Bunting credited his foes with having a great deal of creative intelligence: "Your mind can't concoct nothing that they haven't already thought of to use."[36]

Moonshiners constructed many of the largest and most elaborate stills underground and added automated equipment to make their operations more efficient. Sheriff's deputies Claude Cardwell and Clyde Mikael destroyed a 900-gallon still with fifty large mash boxes near Lenoir in 1956. ATTU officials called it "the fanciest and most smoothly hidden outfit they ever witnessed." The underground operation had "a secret electric trigger door and a modern ventilation system."[37] In 1960, officials discovered another huge underground still in the Lenoir area worth an estimated $50,000. The entrance to a 100-foot-long tunnel containing the still and mash boxes was a "secret door in a concrete block wall—operated electrically by pulling a certain nail." The operation had automated ventilation, water supply, and waste disposal systems as well as a "200-foot-long escape tunnel leading to a clump of bushes and the countryside."[38] That same year agents discovered another underground still, built beneath a pigpen on a farm near North Wilkesboro. The *Statesville Record and Landmark* called it the "last word in do-it-yourself liquor-making." The highly mechanized plant had electric lighting and ventilation, an "oil-fired boiler with automatic controls," and electric pumps for waste disposal. The pumps also transferred distilled liquor through buried pipes into vats hidden in the basement of a chicken house near the road. The still did such huge volume that the operators even modified a gas station pump to use for filling containers with moonshine.[39] As ABC official L. G. Russell put it, "Some of these guys could be rocket scientists."[40]

In 1968, ATTU agents discovered what probably remains the largest illegal distillery ever uncovered in North Carolina history, in southern Cabarrus County. The still, located under a "rundown barn" on a farm belonging to Willis Efird, contained a tunnel "12 feet wide and 130 feet long" lined with twelve 1,000-gallon-capacity mash tanks. The tunnel also had a conveyer belt to transport jars of liquor to the tunnel entrance for loading, an automated ventilation system, and even a small machine shop for repairs. The Kannapolis *Daily Independent* asserted that the "operation had to be the work of an engineering genius ... certainly not work of an amateur." When the agents raided the still they found "7000 gallons of fermented mash, 723 gallons of white liquor and a quantity of fruit jars," plus stacks of sugar and other supplies. Officials believed operators had been running the still for several years and probably netted up to $1 million in tax-free revenue per year.[41]

The size and sophistication of these stills indicates the increasingly common presence of organized syndicates in the moonshine business. As early as 1949, Governor Kerr Scott recognized this phenomenon and launched a campaign to crack down on the state's moonshine business. He announced, "I think the illegal liquor traffic in North Carolina has grown so big and arrogant that all of us concerned with the welfare of the state must pull together to stamp out this evil or else curb it so drastically that the profit element as weighed against the dangers involved will not be sufficient to attract criminals into the liquor traffic."[42] We do not have a great deal of information on these groups, except the occasional high-profile arrests and trials. It appears as if most were relatively loosely knit groups who cooperated voluntarily to purchase and distribute supplies to distillers and provide transport and wholesaling services to get the finished product to market. On occasion these "big-time bootleggers" had their own stills, but most of the time they purchased the product from a network of independent producers. While there was occasional violence, most often retaliation against informants, one should not confuse these folks with the Mafia. Most of these individuals were respectable and even prominent folks in their communities and often had diversified interests in legitimate businesses, through which they laundered the proceeds of their criminal activities. The *Robesonian* cited federal district judge Edwin Stanley as claiming in 1964 that "many of the big operators try to buy respectability 'with tax free money' by contributing generously to churches and other worthy organizations."[43] The *News and Observer* noted, "The industry's profits have made many a bootlegger a prosperous and influential citizen, influential in his local government, influential in politics and even in his church."[44] The "big operators" were also careful to personally stay away from stills and were rarely caught. Commenting on a 1955 term in court in Montgomery County, one attorney observed that those actually caught for moonshining or transporting illegal liquor were "small 'taters'" and the "'big boys' behind the liquor syndicate . . . are relatively safe."[45] Judge Stanley asserted in 1964 that "big operators profit while underlings take all the risks."[46]

Authorities did have some success in infiltrating some of these operations with informants, and accounts of several large busts provide some insight into their operations. In 1957, a county and state law enforcement operation arrested twenty-two people in the Piedmont Triad area, including a Randolph County special deputy charged with accepting protection money. The alleged leader of the syndicate was William Beard, a thirty-year-old Archdale resident who "masterminded the manufacture of white liquor in Montgomery County and distribution of the whiskey in Guilford, Davidson and Randolph counties." Authorities charged Nathan Andrews of High Point for helping finance the operation with money from his inheritance. In addition, authorities seized "two trucks and five automobiles" used to transport the liquor.[47] Two months later, agents made an even larger bust of eighty-one individuals accused of running an illegal liquor syndicate based in Stanly, Mecklenburg, and Union Counties in an undercover operation which also netted thirty-nine cars, "some of them with special engines." The group served as a conduit between Wilkes County producers and the huge Charlotte market, primarily in African American liquor houses. Authorities estimated the group transported illegal liquor worth "as high as $18 million a year."[48] In 1959, the *News and Observer* speculated on the existence of a "Wilkes-Franklin-Johnston County Whisky Axis . . . an organization cooperating among its membership in lending money, exchanging personnel, hiring lawyers and in moving commodities needed in whiskey making."[49] While rare, there are some accounts of African American syndicates. Alcohol, Tobacco, and Firearms agent Joe Carter recalled one group in the lower Cape Fear region headed by three African American investors who became so successful in their business that they made the Bureau of Alcohol, Tobacco, and Firearm's "major violator list" (similar to the FBI's Most Wanted List).[50] African American New Bern bootlegger Henry Singleton purchased "a shiny, streamlined bus" to haul liquor in—that is until ATU agents stopped the bus, carrying "16 Negro men, women and children," and discovered sixty gallons of moonshine in the luggage compartment.[51] Throughout the 1950s and 1960s a number of huge busts yielded thousands of gallons of moonshine. In 1964, Judge Stanley asserted that "bootlegging is a $200 million business in North Carolina."[52]

The rise of the big-time bootlegger attracted national press interest. In particular, three high-profile cases brought the North Carolina moonshine business widespread attention and opened a window onto its secretive operations. The cases involved high-profile federal and state undercover investigations and the work of nationally known investigative reporters working for major magazines, and they turned the national spotlight on the depth, sophistication, and widespread nature of the state's moonshine business.

The first of these high-profile cases came from an exposé of the Wilkes County moonshine business and its "big-time producers" by investigative reporter Vance Packard. Entitled "Millions in Moonshine," the article ran in the September 1950 issue of the *American Magazine*. Perhaps most revelatory in Packard's article was his contention that Wilkes County's "moonshine barons . . . carry on a vast conspiracy—with the cooperation of thousands of people in the county—to outsmart the 'feds.'" Packard noted, "Moonshining in Wilkes County is big business, requiring vast amounts of raw materials. Federal agents recently tailed a trailer truck carrying 25,000 pounds of sugar from Atlanta, Ga., into Wilkes County."[53]

The journalist noted several reasons why the moonshine business was so difficult to control in the county. The fact that so many of the county's businesses profited from the moonshine industry dampened even the most respectable citizen's desire to stamp it out. Packard observed, "Most of the 'nice businesses' in the county profit in one way or another from the moonshine industry. Hardware merchants buy half-gallon fruit jars by the carload. Those jars are the standard moonshine container. Several filling stations stay open all night and get the business of moonshine-laden cars racing down to Winston-Salem. Even grocers, of course, sell plenty of victuals to the prosperous moonshiners." Businesspeople who did not benefit directly from moonshining feared that taking a stand against it would damage their businesses. One such business owner told Packard that revenue agent friends had invited him to go on raids with them. When Packard asked if he had joined them, the man replied, "No, sir! The boys in the woods would think I had led those revenuers to their stills. It would ruin my business."[54]

Indeed, the greatest problem in controlling the moonshine business in the area, Packard averred, was "the conspiracy of silence which protects moonshining in Wilkes County." This "conspiracy" involved both those directly involved in illegal operations and those that just had information about them. The "big boys" rewarded lower-level operatives, still hands and trippers, for their silence. When law enforcement arrested them, "bond for them is promptly—and mysteriously—posted for them. Talented lawyers, of which Wilkes County has plenty, always turn up so that the boys be put on probation, when their trial comes up. The real owners of most raided stills remain behind a screen of tight-lipped silence." Getting information from others who might know about the financial wheeling and dealing of the "big boys" was also a "maddeningly difficult thing to do." And Packard asserted, "Virtually no one in the county will sign an affidavit."[55]

The big-time moonshine operators of Wilkes County also carefully avoided prosecution for tax evasion or other financial crimes. ATU agent Bob Miller told Packard of one of the county's "big-wheel" moonshiners who was "worth several hundred thousand dollars" and had little real or personal property in his own name: "You can bet that man hasn't got a stick of store wood [*sic*; Miller probably said 'stove wood'] in his own name."[56]

Of course, the article horrified political and business leaders in Wilkes County. The Wilkes County Chamber of Commerce held a meeting after its publication and issued a 1,500-word statement to the *American Magazine* that "loudly protested that the magazine has overplayed the role of moonshine in the county." They also asked the editor to "send another writer to the county to do an article on the other industries there."[57] To be sure, Vance Packard was no longer welcome in Wilkes County. For those a little further removed, however, the article was both enlightening and a source of humor, at both Wilkes County's and Vance Packard's expense. Not long after the article came out, the *Statesville Daily Record* printed the lyrics to a humorous song written by W. R. Johnston and J. R. Delaney and sung to the tune of "Clementine":

On a mountain, in Wilkes County
Squeezing juice from out a still
Dwelt a shiner, a moonshiner
On a high and lonely hill.

[Chorus] Mr. Packard, Mr. Packard,
Come you back to Caroline
Write a story, any story
That will libel friends of mine.

Well this shiner, this moonshiner
Read a story, Oh so fine
Found it mentioned all his brothers
But his name got not one line.

Stood a woman, mountain woman
Ploughing barefoot in the fields
Has a brand new high-tail auto
Can't afford a pair of heels.

Oh, my moonshine, Oh my moonshine
Never leave this promised land
ABC stores can't replace you
For you are a special brand.[58]

A second notorious series of events that opened a window on the operations of syndicates in the state involved the illegal liquor empire of brothers Ralph "Puff" and Grafton "Tuff" Burgess of Alexander County. The Burgesses grew up in the moonshine business, as their father, Clarence Burgess, supplemented his farm income by making illegal liquor. The boys followed in his footsteps but left farm life early on and focused all their energies on moonshine, making considerable profits during the war years. In the booming economy of the post–World War II era, the Burgess brothers also moved into the distribution side of the business. While they always dealt in moonshine, operated stills, and imported tons of sugar into the region for themselves and other moonshiners, they made most of their income importing and selling legally produced red liquor in North Carolina's dry counties. Indeed, by the late 1940s they had become key figures in a huge interstate network involving legal liquor distributors in New Orleans, Baltimore, Washington, D.C., and Cairo, Illinois, and headquartered at a restaurant/nightclub they owned called the Silver Moon. Located on N.C. 16 near the Catawba County line, the Moon, as its patrons generally called it, was a favorite hangout for moonshiners, liquor haulers, and the local stock car–racing crowd. At the Silver Moon, patrons could eat one of the finest steak dinners in the area and—if they knew the right people—could head upstairs to partake of some local moonshine or the Burgess brothers' finest imported red liquor and try their luck at a slot machine or the poker tables.[59]

Between 1951 and 1955, the ATTU focused its efforts on shutting down the Burgess brothers' and their confederates' operations. Agents documented huge red liquor shipments from New Orleans and Washington, D.C., in tractor-trailers, "a minimum of 400 cases" per week according to press reports, and tons of sugar for making moonshine hauled in from Atlanta.[60] The investigation, which included a subpoena of phone records, also revealed a network of illegal liquor retailers across the state, with confirmed confederates in Gastonia, Rockingham, Statesville, Shelby, and Lenoir. Agents also revealed that Ralph Burgess—in movie-script fashion—operated under a variety of aliases, including Fred Robert Dishman. He even had a driver's license under the name.

Investigators also discovered false invoices and signs for the Burgesses' tractor-trailer fleet for a fictitious front company, the Barlow Chemical Company.[61]

The government got its big break in the case when Kenneth Hoglen turned state's evidence and agreed to testify against the syndicate. Hoglen had driven a tractor-trailer making red liquor and sugar runs for the syndicate. In 1954 he ran afoul of his bosses when $18,000 went missing on a trip to purchase liquor in Washington. In one of the few documented cases that fits the classic movie model of the operations of a moonshine syndicate, Ralph Burgess and Wayne Watson, another syndicate kingpin, along with three others, took Hoglen to an isolated cabin on the nearby Catawba River. Watson and the others hung Hoglen by his wrists and proceeded to nearly beat him to death with their fists, pistols, and sticks. Burgess did not personally take part in the beatings but was there for much of the ordeal. Unfortunately for the Burgesses, the beating only served to convince Hoglen to get his revenge, which he did by testifying in both state and federal cases.[62]

Hoglen's testimony, plus other evidence uncovered in raids on the Silver Moon and other Burgess properties in 1954, led to numerous indictments. State authorities charged Ralph Burgess and four others for kidnapping and assault with a deadly weapon for his participation in Hoglen's beating. A federal grand jury indicted Puff and Tuff in March 1956, along with twenty-nine other defendants, for being part of "a three million dollar a year bootlegging ring."[63]

Ralph's trial on state charges for kidnapping and assault came up first in July 1956. The case attracted so much attention that the judge imported a jury from Davidson County—two counties away—to attempt to find one impartial enough (and neither related to nor intimidated by the five defendants) for a fair trial. The five-day trial featuring Hoglen's testimony packed the house at the Alexander County Courthouse, which included a sizeable contingent of State Bureau of Investigation agents and highway patrolmen. Indeed, Burgess's lawyer tried to get the judge to declare a mistrial because he claimed the presence of so many law enforcement officials unduly influenced the jury. The jury convicted all five for assault but acquitted them on the kidnapping charges. Despite the fact he did not participate directly in the beating, Burgess—along with Watson—received the most severe penalties as the ringleader, a two-year sentence "on the roads" and a $5,000 fine. Hoglen also sued Burgess and Watson for damages in civil court.[64]

At the federal trial a year later that involved both Burgesses, Hoglen testified to witnessing payoffs to Mississippi law enforcement officials and false invoices issued by suppliers—including a New Orleans city assessor who ran his liquor business out of city hall. He shared story after story about tractor-trailer loads of illegal liquor and sugar hauled into the region and about his brutal beating.

Both Burgesses pleaded guilty to conspiracy to defraud the federal government, although Grafton only admitted to charges involving activities in 1951. The trial attracted a huge contingent of media to the federal courthouse in Statesville. Charlotte television station WBTV even aired a program entitled *The Big Story*, featuring the exploits of the Burgess brothers and the attractions of the Silver Moon. The defendants agreed to a trial without a jury, and the judge sentenced Ralph to two years in federal prison (to be served after he completed his assault sentence) and another $5,000 fine. Grafton got off with a suspended sentence and $5,000 fine.[65]

The third window on the operations of big-time moonshiners in North Carolina came in 1958 when the *Saturday Evening Post* ran a three-page spread profiling Johnston County illegal liquor kingpin Percy Flowers, complete with photographs of wife Delma and daughter Rebecca. Titled "King of the Moonshiners" and written by John Kobler, the article highlighted Flowers's unique gifts when it came to creating a massive moonshine empire and evading law enforcement. Kobler attributed "Flowers's phenomenal run of good fortune" to his "rare combination of organizational, fiscal and social talents." While Flowers generally left the work of making and transporting liquor to others, he inspired an incredible degree of loyalty among the men, primarily African Americans, like Howard Creech, Abner Bule, and Sylvester Dixon, who made and handled the product. As Kobler observed, he "moves them to risk their own skins in his behalf." These men knew that if law enforcement arrested them, Flowers would bail them out, send one of his high-dollar Raleigh lawyers to defend them, and take care of their families if incarcerated. They also knew Flowers's reputation for a long memory and knew he would make sure that anyone who proved disloyal suffered severe consequences. Individuals on Flowers's bad side saw themselves threatened, attacked, and beaten, even shot at—by Flowers himself on several occasions. Kobler asserted that Flowers "rules his domain with a baronial hand."[66]

Despite the violent undercurrent to all of Flowers's interactions, according to Kobler and many observers, "Percy's most valuable asset was . . . the high esteem of countless fellow citizens." Flowers could count on a steady stream of Johnston County's most well-respected citizens to serve as character witnesses, and he could always rely on the support of the poor of the county who might serve on a jury and practically worshipped him as a modern-day Robin Hood. Indeed, prosecutors in Johnston County knew that no "jury of his peers" in that county would ever convict him. Kobler even quoted Rev. A. D. Parrish of the White Oak Baptist Church, where Flowers's wife, Delma, taught Sunday School, as asserting: "Both Mr. and Mrs. Flowers have helped more people than any couple I know of. Mrs. Flowers is a perfect lady. I've frequently visited in the store. It's operated with thorough decency." Flowers's largess also extended

Johnston County moonshine kingpin Percy Flowers in front of his country store. (Courtesy of Perry Sullivan and the Johnston County Heritage Center, Smithfield, N.C.)

to the state and local Democratic Party, and he developed close relationships with many powerful politicians. He was fox-hunting buddies with Charles M. Johnson, a former state treasurer, who told Kobler, "He's easy to get along with, most agreeable. I never went on a trip with a better-behaved man."[67] When Flowers could not sway folks with his charm or cow them with his threats, he bribed them. Authorities charged Flowers in 1961 with paying $100 a month in protection money to ATTU agent James Haithcock. And Charles Beasley, who testified against Flowers in a 1961 case, claimed Flowers told him, "If you get straightened out with those folks you won't have any trouble."[68]

Flowers also recognized talent and was not averse to adapting to the times. Kobler observed that Flowers had "combed the moonshine belt for specialists in the different phases of the business—the construction of stills, the distilling itself, transport and distribution."[69] Among his best finds were Obie Parker and his son Henry, master distillers and skilled still builders from Wilkes County. Indeed, after the unwanted attention that Vance Packard brought to Wilkes, a

Percy Flowers N.C. Moonshine Hall of Famer

Johnston County has two famous born-and-raised celebrities. Hollywood actress Ava Gardner came from Smithfield, went to Hollywood in her late teens in 1941, and became one of the most acclaimed actresses of her era, starring in such classic films as *Showboat*, *The Barefoot Contessa*, *The Snows of Kilimanjaro*, *On the Beach*, and *The Night of the Iguana*. She received a nomination for the Academy Award for Best Actress in 1953 for her role in *Mogambo*. But ask a longtime resident of Johnston County, particularly one over fifty, and chances are they know as much, or more, about the county's other iconic figure, Joshua Percy Flowers. Indeed, they probably knew "Mr. Percy" personally, and he might even have aided them at some point by one of his many acts of philanthropy in the county, in his community of Wilders Township, or at the White Oak Baptist Church.

Many residents of Johnston County speak fondly and lovingly of Flowers's kindness, affability, and philanthropy. However, the source of his wealth and huge property holdings, prize-winning packs of foxhounds and gamecocks, fleets of Cadillacs, and fame outside Johnston County generally goes unmentioned. But folks outside the county knew Percy Flowers as perhaps the most successful moonshiner in the state's history. He was successful not only in making a fortune producing and selling illegal liquor but also, especially given his high profile, in evading law enforcement. He served only two short terms in federal penitentiary despite being indicted at least a dozen times in the federal courts and probably twenty or more times on local and state charges. Flowers became so well known that in 1958 the *Saturday Evening Post* ran a full-spread, lavishly illustrated feature on him titled "King of the Moonshiners." Given his more than sixty years as a moonshiner, and his ongoing legacy in Johnston County as part of the Flowers Plantation real estate empire owned and operated by his daughter Rebecca, he probably deserves the title of king more than even Lewis Redmond.

Born in 1903, Flowers never lived far from the hardscrabble tobacco farm in Wilders Township where he grew up. He dropped out of school after the seventh grade but tired of the abuse his father inflicted on him and left home at age sixteen. He soon fell in with a local African American moonshiner by the name of Lester and discovered his life's calling. Flowers's experience learning his craft from a skilled African American liquor craftsman was extremely common in eastern North Carolina, where many African Americans had deep involvement in the liquor-making business, going back to the days of slavery. It is a story like those told by many white North Carolina bluegrass musicians and barbeque pit masters who learned their craft from relatively unknown and unrecognized African Americans.

Flowers was such a natural moonshiner, particularly on the organizational and business end, that he soon bought all of Lester's equipment and hired the older man to make the moonshine while he focused on marketing and selling it. Flowers entered the moonshine business at the perfect time as demand skyrocketed due to the passage of the Eighteenth Amendment and national Prohibition. By the early 1930s Flowers's business had taken off. He later told many people that he "made more money in the

1930s" than in any other period in his life. Flowers and his brother bought a tavern—the first of many investments in legitimate businesses, in order to move cash through the legal economy—which became the center of his illegal empire. The tavern was also the place where a young African American man by the name of Howard Creech (also a member of this Hall of Fame) began working for Flowers.

In the late 1930s, Flowers began buying up Johnston County farmland and eventually owned over 4,000 acres. This land proved convenient for his business empire, as it gave him income from tenants who farmed the land and provided convenient hiding places for stills, also generally operated by tenants. During this period Flowers also sold his tavern and built a country store across the highway from his home at the intersection of North Carolina Highway 42 and Buffalo Road. The Percy Flowers Store remained Flowers's operational center until his death, except for the times federal or state authorities padlocked it during investigations.

From the 1930s to the 1960s, Flowers built a moonshine empire based on an interesting combination of old-south paternalism and new-south business entrepreneurship. He fostered relationships with tenants and community members, giving generously to needy individuals, the local Baptist church, and the community. He also punished those who crossed him and, like a feudal baron, ruled his lands with a mixture of love and fear. Flowers was, however, very modern in his business tactics, welcomed innovation, and changed with the times. Both approaches served him well in both making an incredible amount of money—the *Saturday Evening Post* quoted federal agents claiming Flowers made over $1 million a year—and staying out of prison.

While adventures in federal and local courts in the 1950s entailing dozens of indictments ended with better-than-expected results, Flowers pulled back on his moonshine activities in the 1960s. He always maintained some involvement in the business, and federal authorities indicted him and hauled him into federal court on at least two more occasions. He had enough to keep him busy with his legitimate farm and store operations and his pursuit of breeding champion foxhounds and gamecocks. He spent increasing amounts of time watching and hearing his prize hounds in fox races out in the countryside or betting on his gamecocks in fights to the death in some secluded barn at an illegal cockpit.

Flowers also had what might be considered an interesting family life, one that made *Saturday Evening Post* reporter John Kobler's use of "baronial" especially appropriate. Flowers fathered two children with his wife, Delma, Percy Jr. and Rebecca. Percy Jr. was the light of his father's life, and Flowers kept him away from his business and provided every possible advantage. In 1952, while a law student at the University of North Carolina, Percy Jr. died in a solo crash in his private plane. Rebecca went on to inherit the Flowers lands, turning them into a highly successful real estate empire of bedroom communities for nearby Raleigh, known as Flowers Plantation. What many people did not know was that Flowers had established a second family right in the midst of his home community. Indeed, he fathered two children—Perry and Tammy Sullivan—with Bea Sullivan, the wife of his store clerk Willis "Curry" Sullivan. This fact was an open secret shared by most people in the community—including Delma and Curry, who continued to work in the store until Flowers's death. Although he doted on them almost as much as on his other children, Flowers never legally acknowledged them and they have not pursued DNA testing to prove their parentage. When Flowers died, they lost pretty much everything when the store closed, Curry lost his job, they lost their Flowers-owned home, and they were forced to move away. Perry and Tammy found a level of success in life, and Perry chronicled his unusual upbringing and Percy Flowers's amazing career in a 2013 memoir entitled *Lost Flowers*.

Percy Flowers represents an important transition in the moonshine business. His involvement was not so much about defying federal authority and exercising his right to make a little liquor or, at least once he got his start, about economic survival. Indeed, as smart, savvy, and ambitious as Flowers was, it is hard to imagine that he would not have made his fortune in another line of work. His success in the moonshine business and his ability to avoid prison are indicative of the huge profits available to a fortunate few during the era of statewide, national, and local prohibition. It is also an example showing that crime can pay. Indeed, Flowers Plantation is not the only successful business enterprise in North Carolina with a foundation built on the illegal liquor business.

number of its bigger operators relocated their stills to places where they could make liquor with less intense scrutiny. Flowers set the two up on a 180-acre farm, where they fabricated their own 1,000-gallon Wilkes-type steamer still and began building huge stills for other Flowers "whiskey men."[70] Flowers also financed and developed still sites in other counties in the eastern part of the state, especially when things got too hot in Johnston County. In 1965, federal prosecutors indicted him for his involvement in large distilling operations in Brunswick and Martin Counties, both over 100 miles away from his base of operations.[71]

While Flowers proved especially cagey in managing and hiding the millions of dollars in cash that came through his hands, federal authorities launched an all-out onslaught on him in the 1950s. In 1951, the IRS audited his income taxes for the previous seven years when Flowers reported an income of $4,544.44. The agency estimated that this was only one-fortieth of his true income. It took them until 1957 to build a case, but when they brought the tax evasion case to trial, the jury hung and the judge—who asserted the case was too complicated for the jury to understand—declared a mistrial. Later in 1951, federal officials indicted Flowers on illegal liquor charges along with fifteen codefendants, including Obie and Henry Parker and several other Flowers tenants. Once again, the jury hung and Flowers walked free. In the days after the trial, Percy ran afoul of local law enforcement when he shot at one of his former tenants, James

Revenue agents pose in front of a massive haul of illegal liquor in Johnston County in 1951. The bust led to one of many federal indictments for Percy Flowers. (Courtesy of State Archives of North Carolina, Raleigh, N.C.)

Seawell, in a dispute over tobacco allotments. The local court eventually dismissed the charges in that case as well.[72]

The feds finally convicted Flowers for contempt of court when he threatened an African American undercover ATTU agent who had testified in the conspiracy trial during a court recess and in front of numerous witnesses. Flowers allegedly told the agent, "You black s.o.b., if I ever catch you down here again, I'll fix you." Flowers received an eighteen-month sentence in the Atlanta Federal Penitentiary, later reduced to a year. The *Raleigh Times* declared Flowers the "victor" in all these cases despite his contempt conviction and sentencing, as he only received "a very small fraction of the prison time which the law sought to pin on him." Indeed, Flowers's escape with only a short term in federal prison was close to miraculous, as he could have very well been sentenced to spend the rest of his life in prison if he had been convicted on any of the major charges.[73]

One aspect of the big-time moonshine business that remains relatively hidden and secret is the question of what these people did with the mountains of cash obtained in their "business." Like all participants in criminal activity, moonshiners, particularly large operators, had to find ways to move their ill-

The Percy Flowers Store, the center of Flowers's moonshining operations. Owning the store allowed him to make large purchases of sugar and canning jars and launder cash earned from his illegal activities. (Courtesy of Perry Sullivan and the Johnston County Heritage Center, Smithfield, N.C.)

gotten gains into the legal economy. In addition, having lots of cash around invited thieves, as many moonshiners discovered, including a group of moonshiners at a high-stakes poker game in Wilkes County in 1946. Two masked men armed with submachine guns broke into the home of Jim Foster—later the site of the office and ticket booth at the North Wilkesboro Speedway—and stole $11,000 from the four poker players and $17,000 from the owner's safe. The fateful poker game is also an indication of the type of money Wilkes County moonshiners took in and the risks they incurred by having so much cash around. One must understand that at this time the average annual per capita income in Wilkes County was less than $2,000.[74]

In looking at the biographies of some of the illegal liquor kingpins, some methods of laundering and hiding money become obvious. Both the Burgess brothers and Percy Flowers owned businesses, the Silver Moon and the Percy Flowers Store, respectively, where they could regularly move cash from their illegal operations and falsify their books to make it appear as legitimate revenue from their nightclub or store. Flowers also invested his money in real estate and bought up thousands of acres of farmland in Johnston and surrounding counties, where sharecroppers planted tobacco and corn and made moonshine. Although Flowers ultimately got away with it, IRS investigators did find significant evidence that he hid millions of dollars in ill-gotten revenue. Junior Johnson also used his money from his moonshine interests and his NASCAR winnings to invest in farmland in Wilkes County and jumped into the new business of chicken farming in the early 1960s.[75]

Other methods of moving money into the legitimate economy are less obvious, and little concrete evidence exists of these activities, but investigations like Packard's give some hints. While he did not get into specifics about how cash moved into the legitimate economy, Packard did note that while there was little industry in Wilkes County, it seemed strangely prosperous: "North Wilkesboro, the county's No. 1 metropolis, sits in the middle of some rough country. Its mayor boasts of his 'prosperous, bustling city.' . . . In fact, you see more bustling prosperity, with fewer signs of productive capacity to account for it, than you'll find anywhere in the United States."[76] Indeed, while it would be impossible to prove, many long-established businesses and corporations probably received significant financial support from the state's moonshiners and bootleggers.

The rise of the North Carolina moonshine syndicates put new demands on law enforcement. Always strapped for funding, federal, state, and local officials did their best to keep up with, and crack down on, the ever-evolving, well-financed business.

12

THE ROAD TO *THUNDER ROAD*

The rise of the syndicates required law enforcement to have to adapt and find new methods to try to stop, or at least somewhat control, North Carolina's moonshine business. While they involved only a fraction of investigation and enforcement activities, the automobile chases—as agents tried to apprehend young liquor "trippers" in souped-up automobiles—became fascinating for the general public. These chases also attracted the media's attention, helped boost North Carolina's reputation as the nation's number one moonshine state, and turned the state's dirt byways and paved highways into legendary "thunder roads."

In the postwar era, federal revenue agents adopted new policies for combatting the illegal liquor trade. Robert Martin, a special agent for the Alcohol and Tobacco Tax Unit (ATTU), recalled in an interview in 1968 with the *Statesville Record and Landmark* the variety of new methods agents employed. He included a program to track large "purchases of raw materials such as sugar and containers," an increase in undercover operations, and the creation of a "major violator list," similar to the FBI's Most Wanted List, to identify big-time operators. He also cited an improved public relations campaign designed to warn people of the dangers of illegal liquor and "inform the public about federal operations and how citizens could assist the program."[1] Federal agents also concentrated their efforts on catching the kingpins and did not expend much effort on small operations. As agent Joe Carter put it in his book *Damn the Allegators*, they did not waste their time on so-called kickover stills, small plants "that just might as well be kicked over or destroyed. It was not worth an expensive investigation."[2]

Cooperation between federal, state, and local officials also became more common and helped put moonshiners on the defensive in some parts of North Carolina. A Kannapolis policeman told the local *Daily Independent* that "Cabarrus [County] is get-

Greene County "kickover still" captured in the late 1940s. (Courtesy of State Archives of North Carolina, Raleigh, N.C.)

ting to be a tough place to be a bootlegger." He attributed that fact to "the close companionship of the three units ... in the past couple of years in curtailing many illegal operations."[3] Joe Carter, however, pointed to the limitations of this cooperation, especially on the local level. He asserted that while county sheriffs could give good information, their attitude was that catching moonshiners "and destroying stills is the work of the ATF [Bureau of Alcohol, Tobacco, and Firearms]. I'll have enough to do carrying out my other duties." The politics of sheriffs' situations also played a role. They had to weigh what information to pass along to federal agents. As Carter observed, if the person involved "was a big politician who could screw up the next election, the sheriff had to be cautious.... He did his duty but carefully guarded his actions." If he did not, then "he would not have lasted as the county sheriff." Carter, like most federal agents, was willing to accept the rules of the game and knew that when he did get a tip from the sheriff, it would be a good one. "It proved to be good business for us. His information was accurate and saved us a lot of time."[4]

A major goal for enforcement agencies, particularly on the federal and state levels, was to infiltrate major liquor operations to gain incriminating evidence on their leaders. Garland Bunting, a North Carolina Alcohol Beverage Control (ABC) agent, described his method of operation, which involved considerable acting skills, to writer Alec Wilkinson:

> I'd be assigned to a county that was having liquor problems, and I'd report on the phone to one of the men, and we'd arrange to meet outside the county, so I wouldn't be seen with him by any bootleggers, and he'd tell me where to go, and furnish money to buy the whiskey, and pay my motel and car bill, and give me some directions, and maybe late at night drive me around and point out what homes were selling. Then it was up to me to get in with them. I used to do whatever I had to do to get along. If I had to sing, I sang; had to dance, I danced; had to preach, I preached; had to drink liquor, I pretended to drink liquor.
>
> I'd wear overalls in some sections and drive my old beat-up piece of pickup truck that the average person wouldn't drive. If it was a rural town, I'd make out like a farmer, or a fox hunter, or a coon hunter, whatever was around. If a man was selling from a house, I'd try to meet him first at a store. If it was at a garage, I'd borrow some tools. I never went into a place cold-turkey and said, "Hey, man, where can I buy a drink?" Before I ever made any move I tried to make sure the man was relaxed in his mind and didn't doubt me.[5]

Russell Poole, another undercover ABC agent, echoed Bunting's experience and asserted that this was the "only way to do it, you just had to get in good with them." He recalled how suspects often examined his hands, "to see if you had calluses," looking for signs that he was indeed the working man he claimed to be. "I'd kind of grease 'em up a little bit so they'd look worse."[6]

Indeed, the undercover agent's chief role was to blend in and listen carefully. Bunting often engaged fox hunters or coon hunters returning from their night hunts in casual conversation to see if they mentioned encountering a still. Undercover work also involved a good bit of drinking of illegal alcohol, or at least the appearance thereof. Bunting developed a method where he carried a syringe and a small bottle in his pocket where he could siphon off liquor and pretend he was drinking a lot. He then put on an act like he was getting increasingly drunk: "I put on I was drinking—I growled and shook and made some water come out of my eyes—and by-and-by I played off to be drunk—picked up my talk and got loud."[7] Poole, for whatever reasons, just jumped right in and drank with the bootleggers and claimed it did not affect him. "I had to drink right much of it, to be honest about it. But I'd drink a pint all right, it wasn't any problem." His wife, Dot, however, disagreed and asserted, "I couldn't understand the job Russell went on. He'd come home every night with plenty of money and come home in the morning drunk ... and get paid for it."[8] ATTU agent Carter claimed that the undercover agent "had to live the identical life the moonshiners did. He had to make whiskey, buy it, drink it like a man, and drive hot cars loaded to the gills to the large cities. About the only difference in

Colorful revenue agent Joe Carter, who chased moonshiners from the Coastal Plain to the mountains of Wilkes County. (Courtesy Marcella Hatley)

the undercover agent and the criminal was that the criminal didn't have to take notes to later aid him in filling out all the goddam forms required."[9]

Carter also admitted that he and other agents, in their zeal to make a case, on occasion stretched the law and law enforcement standards, sometimes beyond the breaking point. In case of an "emergency" when he ran up against an illegal operation accidentally, Carter sometimes carried "a stack of blank search warrants for on-the-spot completion and execution." As he put it, "Some of the people being searched never could understand how we were so fast in obtaining the search warrant." If Carter knew the suspect was illiterate, then he produced some legal-looking document in lieu of an actual search warrant. "Some of the documents I remember that worked quite well were an insurance policy, an automobile title and, in one case, a repair invoice for the prowl car from the Chevrolet dealer."[10]

Enforcement officials also began using aircraft much more in trying to spot and destroy illegal liquor operations. Federal agents especially took advantage of this tactic, as they had access to Coast Guard airplanes and helicopters because the guard was under the Treasury Department until 1967. The *Statesville Daily Record* reported in 1948 that "the moonshine business ain't what it used to be before the war" due to the spotter planes. When they spotted stills, observers in the planes used radios to direct agents on the ground to the stills, busting as many as ten in a day.[11] By the 1960s, agents more commonly used helicopters because they could land near the stills and did not have to coordinate with agents on the ground. Joe Carter carried dynamite with him when he was on such helicopter missions so that "when we spotted a moonshine outfit, we simply landed and blew the darn thing to smithereens." In 1964, the *News and Observer* reported, "The helicopter is becoming one of the main tools in still busting." While useful, using aircraft was not foolproof, as they were most effective in winter when the leaf cover was gone and stills were easy to spot. In addition, the noise they made alerted moonshiners, who generally escaped capture. Aerial surveillance is one important reason most big-time operators spent the time and expense to conceal their operations in buildings or underground.[12]

Another important tactic enforcement agencies used was to attempt to cut off moonshiners' supplies of crucial materials. Sugar, the key raw material for making illegal liquor, was the commodity most targeted by agents. During the 1950s the ATTU pushed through regulations requiring sugar wholesalers and retailers to record identification information on anyone purchasing more than twenty-five pounds of sugar.[13] In 1957, the agency even produced a comic book entitled *The True Story of Moonshine*, which it distributed to sugar dealers. The comic informed dealers of the new regulations and warned them, "Don't be a sugar daddy to moonshiners."[14] North Carolina ATTU supervisor Charles S. Nicholson Jr. asserted in 1958 that these regulations would prove so effective that "in less than five years bootleg whiskey 'just won't be a problem any more.'"[15] The ATTU became particularly aggressive enforcing the law in the late 1950s, which led to several arrests. Agents arrested Harold Maxwell Sr. for falsifying his records and selling 15,000 pounds of sugar to a grocery store, which, in turn, sold it to moonshiners.[16] In a major sting operation in Wilkes County, agents arrested grocer Tal Joe Pearson for selling 372,485 pounds of sugar in a seven-month period. Pearson's sentence of eighteen months in prison and a $10,000 fine definitely sent a powerful message to those in the sugar business.[17] One federal agent claimed, "We're hurting them, there's no question about it. We know they're hurting because they're screaming that we're not playing fair."[18]

The sugar crackdown led moonshiners to try some desperate measures. Some imported sugar over long distances and reportedly brought sugar from as far away as Florida, Atlanta, and New Orleans. Some became so desperate for raw materials that they hijacked loads of sugar. In 1957, federal agents reported the hijack of a truckload of 300 100-pound bags of sugar in Virginia. Authorities discovered the truck the next day hidden in a patch of woods in North Carolina, but only eighty bags remained.[19]

In 1959, the federal government further cracked down on suppliers of materials to moonshiners when it passed a reporting law on wholesalers and retailers of "containers that can be used in packaging illicit liquor." The law required suppliers of canning jars, glass jugs, and five-gallon metal containers to record the identity of individuals making large purchases. Moonshiners began using plastic squeeze bottles as a result, leading the *Asheville Citizen-Times* to quip, "The latest fad in bootlegging is 'moonshine by the squirt.'" The move also led to a black market for containers and to hijacking of truckloads of containers.[20]

North Carolina ABC officials even tried to stem demand for moonshine by putting a "legal moonshine" product on ABC stores' shelves in the mid-1950s. Distilled by Brown-Forman of Louisville, Kentucky, White Lightning corn whiskey hit the ABC shelves in 1955. The state monopoly advertised the product as safer, better tasting, and of higher proof than the sugar liquor sold by bootleggers. The price, however, once the federal government collected its $10.50-per-gallon tax, did not remotely approach that of the illegal stuff, which reportedly sold for less per gallon than just the tax. Although the first shipment reportedly sold out in Greensboro in three hours, the product soon disappeared from ABC shelves, as it did not find many buyers once the novelty wore off.[21]

But the aspect of the moonshine industry that attracted the most media attention and helped define a new stereotype for North Carolina moonshiners was the ever-present high-powered automobiles used for hauling liquor that became so common throughout the state. Inside looks at syndicate activity, such as the investigations into Wilkes County moonshine and the Burgess brothers and Percy Flowers cases, almost always involved such cars. Vance Packard noted a common sight in Wilkes County in the early 1950s: "One odd thing you do see everywhere you look is high-powered cars equipped with twin exhausts and with their rear ends remarkably high in the air. These souped-up, high-tailed cars are a trademark of Wilkes County. They have extra leaves in the rear springs, so that they can haul a heavy load of illicit moonshine without having their rear end sagging conspicuously."[22] In the late 1940s and early 1950s, the favored make of automobile for hauling liquor was a late 1930s or early 1940s Ford with a flathead V-8 engine. As Packard observed, a souped-up V-8 Ford "can go like a jackrabbit, and, being short, can spin a complete turn on a gravel road."[23] The Fords could also haul a large load of liquor. When the moonshiners removed the back seat, replaced the bench front seat with a bucket seat, and took out the wall between the trunk and interior, such cars could hold up to twenty-two six-gallon cases of liquor loaded up to window level. Later in the 1950s, trippers moved on to newer, even more powerful cars, favoring the Oldsmobile "Rocket" 88, 1955 and 1956 Chevies, or late 1950s Chrysler 300s. Junior

Johnson claimed that the fastest he ever drove in an automobile was not on the Daytona International Speedway but on a Wilkes County highway in a 1951 Ford with a full load of illegal liquor.[24] Moonshiner Jerry Rushing's all-time favorite car was Traveler, a confiscated liquor car that he bought at a federal auction for $150. According to Rushing, the car "was good for better than 140 miles an hour loaded heavy. It could carry the mail."[25] Agent Joe Carter noted that by the late 1950s, North Carolina moonshiners had "developed machines that could run 150 m.p.h. plus." They used these cars to "transport moonshine into the marketplace—Winston-Salem, Greensboro, Charlotte, Richmond, Philadelphia, even New York City, or any place where it could be promptly exchanged for cash."[26]

Of course, these cars were not the same cars that came off the auto dealer's showroom floor and had significant modifications to their engines and chassis. Packard noted that the tripper cars he saw in Wilkes County often had "three carburetors, two exhaust pipes, supercharger, gear-ratio change, auxiliary fuel pump, over-sized cylinders, aluminum pistons."[27] In an interview with the Smithsonian Institution's Pete Daniel, Junior Johnson mentioned the modifications he made to engines: "You could take the motors and bore the cylinders out and get bigger pistons in them. The crank shaft, you could stroke it and make a longer stroke which would put more horsepower into it. You could get high performance cam shafts to go into them and cylinder heads and manifolds. You wound up with a totally different engine."[28] Moonshiners also modified the chassis using stiffer shocks, overinflated tires, and stronger wheels. They installed additional leaf springs, often from pickup trucks or junked Model Ts, to help the car handle better with the heavy loads they carried.[29]

While some moonshiners, like Junior Johnson, had the mechanical ability to make modifications themselves, their need for speed also created a very profitable opportunity for skilled mechanics. As Packard noted, "Souping up cars for the moonshine trade is a major industry in itself in the county [Wilkes] and keeps many garages busy."[30] With deep pockets and such mechanical skill on their side, the contests between the trippers' hot rods and the revenue agents' government cars were generally one-sided. As Joe Carter quipped, "Imagine the U.S. government providing us with little gas-saving Mickey Mouse cars to chase these speed masters with."[31] Most agents tried to get rid of their government car and get their hands on a confiscated tripper car, and that did help level the playing field a bit. Carter asserted, "I would find a way to total or 'accidentally' burn the government's automotive absurdity assigned to me. Then I would go after one of those sweet bellowing babies that I had just chased so ignominiously. Do it through the laws of seizure, confiscation and forfeiture."[32] Even with their own hot cars, however, law enforcement still had a tough time running down the trippers. As Junior Johnson recalled, "It was kind of an intriguing thing to work on them and make them run. You always wanted the law to run you because you had such an advantage over them."[33]

While the practice has often been exaggerated by Hollywood, moonshiners also added special modifications to aid them in evading law enforcement. Packard noted that many Wilkes County trippers equipped their "high-tailed" automobiles with "multiple rear-vision mirrors and a special switch for snapping off the taillight."[34] Rushing demonstrated his streak of evil genius when, in addition to hopping up the engine and strengthening the suspension, he got his mechanic, Buck, to add a "twenty-gallon oil tank between the trunk and back seat that [at the turn of a switch] would spill oil onto the road when he was being pursued by lawmen." He also had a special toggle switch installed that kept his taillights from coming on when he hit the brakes. He explained the reasoning for this device to a reporter: "A lot of times the law would drive by our tail lights when they'd be chasing us on a mountain road. If the brake lights didn't come on, they wouldn't know we'd slowed down on a curve. I've seen a few of 'em go off the mountain." Tactics like this did not endear him to law enforcement and Traveler had a bullet hole in its trunk lid as a result. Rushing admitted the price of his actions: "I was shot at a few times."[35]

Many trippers also developed advanced driving skills to complement the high-performance cars they piloted and help them evade capture. Joe Carter recalled his experience trying to pursue a skilled tripper in a high-powered liquor hauler, which "proved embarrassing as hell":

> I jumped a new booze buggy one moonlight night.... They played cat and mouse with me for thirty minutes until I was getting the idea that he was not so great and that he just might not escape.
>
> Then he got bored with the game. We hit Highway 321 ... on a long straightaway. Suddenly he appeared to turn on a large rocket. His taillights pulled away from me at an incredible rate. He went down the road about two miles and made one of those "Thunder Road" 180-degree turns and came right back at me—on my side of the road.
>
> Here he came, hell-bustin'! He wanted to play chicken. I played with him. But I was the chicken. I got the hell off the road and banged down a large embankment, having to employ a wrecker to retrieve the disgusting example of automotive crap the government forced me to drive.

Carter succinctly and colorfully summed up his experience that night: "It was like sending a one-legged man to an ass-kicking."[36]

On many occasions moonshiners just employed the fast cars as decoys, sending them up a road to attract the attention of law enforcement. They then used their superior horsepower and driving skill to take the agents on a wild-goose chase, while trucks hauling the liquor quietly moved through the area to market. Agent Michael Zetts told author Alec Wilkinson about the bust of Wilson County liquor kingpin Elmo Tate, during which the agents confiscated such a high-powered car: "They had a liquor car down there, what you call a lead car because it runs fast ahead of the trucks as a decoy, and if you chase it they'll draw you here and there and, finally, when they figure the trucks are safe maybe let you catch it."[37]

Indeed, while the "thunder road" stories of wild automobile chases capture the most attention, trippers transported most of the illegal liquor in trucks or even tractor-trailers. The benefits of hauling in big trucks are obvious, as a 1956 bust near Pine Level of a tractor-trailer carrying 1,440 gallons of moonshine reveals.[38] In 1965, an undercover operation in Wilkes County resulted in the arrest of Frank Hutchinson, a local "cattleman, tobacco farmer, sawmill owner," reportedly "a very wealthy man." Hutchinson reportedly masterminded a transport operation using a Michigan trucking company to haul liquor in tractor-trailers from Wilkes County to the Midwest.[39]

Most car chases ended with the trippers getting away or eventually pulling over, jumping out, and heading for the woods, forfeiting the vehicle and the load of liquor. On occasion, however, things escalated and became dangerous for both trippers and law enforcement. In 1965, deputy Ned Herman of Alexander County engaged a 1957 Chevy in a high-speed chase. Herman glanced down at his speedometer as the pair raced down N.C. 90 toward Statesville and saw that "the needle had passed the last mark, 120 miles an hour, and was buried out of sight." The officer pulled alongside the tripper and attempted to stop him, but the moonshiner ran him off the road and into a ditch. Herman was able to "wrestle" the car out of the ditch and continue the chase, but the tripper got away, even after he blew a tire.[40] Although they were not supposed to use their firearms in such instances, officers did on occasion shoot out the tires of trippers. When trippers hauling 120 gallons of white liquor began throwing jugs of moonshine at pursuing officers in a Buncombe County chase in 1962, agents shot the tires out, forcing them to stop. While officers caught driver David Gillis, his passenger escaped by diving into the French Broad River and swimming away.[41]

The most extreme action taken by law enforcement in car chases was the use of a so-called whammy. A whammy was a flat, one-inch-wide piece of iron with "four-inch, razor-sharp spikes" welded to it, placed across the width of the road. This device could only be used when agents had a road staked out and they could prevent other vehicles from innocently coming along. When a tripper's car hit it, the whammy immediately flattened all four tires. While this generally just left the car paralyzed and led to a foot chase, with the officers hiding alongside the road, it could throw the car into a dangerous spin and result in what Joe Carter termed "an embarrassing fatality rate among shine runners.

Tripper Cars

A big part of the fascination with the drama involving the car chases on North Carolina's "thunder roads" revolves around the automobiles themselves. Indeed, many of the cars have become almost as iconic as the colorful moonshiners themselves. For the most part, trippers wanted a car with a high-powered engine and durable suspension that would hold a lot of liquor. They generally favored cars that did not attract attention, painted a dark color, usually black. The following is a list of favorite liquor cars over the years, with a focus on those with a North Carolina connection.

Ford Model T "skeeter." Although moonshiners have been hauling liquor to market from the earliest days of automobiles in North Carolina, the arrival of the Ford Model T in 1908 revolutionized the illegal liquor industry. Durable, rugged, cheap, and in their Touring version, able to hold twenty or more gallons of liquor, Model Ts hauled huge amounts of liquor to market well into the 1940s. The cars were also easily modified with kits sold by Cragar, Navarro, and Frontenac to make them go faster than the normal forty to forty-five miles per hour to outrun law enforcement. In North Carolina, folks called any sort of modified Model T a "skeeter," and many in the state developed their mechanical skills modifying their liquor-hauling skeeters to be even faster and haul larger loads of moonshine.

1940 Ford flathead V-8 coupe. The Ford flathead V-8 came on the market in 1932, ushered in the era of high-speed car chases, and turned North Carolina highways and backroads into "thunder roads." Like the Model T, the flathead could be easily modified. As NASCAR promoter Humpy Wheeler put it, "The Ford automobile in its natural state with the flat-head V-8 became a race car in just a few days with the right hands working on it and it was durable and fast." Junior Johnson and Willie Clay Call liked to replace the Ford V-8 engine in their liquor cars with one taken from a Cadillac ambulance and further boost the power with a turbocharger. The 1940 coupes with their large trunks became the quintessential liquor-hauling cars and remain an iconic part of North Carolina's moonshining past.

1950 Ford Deluxe. The 1949–51 Fords fit the bill as good liquor cars because they looked like a normal family car, with an appropriately large trunk, but when modified by dropping a supercharged "mill" under the hood, they could easily outrun law enforcement. This car became an iconic tripper car when Robert Mitchum chose to use two of them in *Thunder Road*. The cars used in the movie were alleged to be actual liquor cars borrowed from local trippers. One of those Fords was modified with three Holley two-barrel 2100 model carburetors, giving it a huge amount of power.

Early 1950s Oldsmobile "Rocket" 88. The Rocket 88 was probably the first liquor-hauling car that could be considered stylish, and its use reflected the large profits that the big-time moonshiners made in the 1950s. The car is often considered the first muscle car, and trippers favored it because it combined a relatively lightweight car with a high-powered V-8 engine. At the same time, it was large enough to haul plenty of liquor.

1958 Chrysler 300D. The 300D is a bit of an unusual car for this list, as it was one of Chrysler's "luxury" models and as such drew a good deal of attention on the highway, something a liquor hauler did not want. That said, with a 392-cubic-inch FirePower Hemi engine under the hood, the car could flat-out "carry the mail." The car was so fast it did not matter if it stood out. Indeed, a test driver drove a 300D at over 150 miles per hour on the Bonneville Salt Flats in 1958. There is a North Carolina connection to the 300D, as it was the favorite tripper car for Monroe's Jerry Rushing, who named his car Traveller, after Robert E. Lee's horse.

1961 Chrysler New Yorker. This car is another luxury model that stood out on the highway and was an unlikely car to haul liquor. But this one has a connection to another legendary North Carolina liquor hauler, Wilkes County's Willie Clay Call. A 1961 New Yorker "Golden Lion" edition with "dual cross ram induction" was Call's favorite car. He pretty much invited law enforcement to try to catch him, and his New Yorker even sported an attention-grabbing baby blue paint job. However, the car was so fast—Call claimed he went over 180 miles per hour in the car—and handled so well that law enforcement never caught him on the highway. Agents even gave him a nickname: the Uncatchable.

1966 Dodge Coronet. Another Willie Clay Call favorite, the top-end Coronet featured a 426-cubic-inch Hemi engine. It was a midsized car for its day and was prized by moonshiners for its relatively light weight combined with a high-powered engine yet modest appearance.

1969 Dodge Charger. By the late 1960s, the golden age of moonshiner-revenuer chases on North Carolina's highways was dying out. Although I'm sure that at least a few remaining whiskey trippers in the state hauled moonshine in the car, the 1969 Charger is on the list for one reason: it was Bo Duke's car in *The Dukes of Hazzard*. Although Hazzard County was in Georgia, there is a North Carolina connection, as producers based *Dukes* on the life of Monroe's Jerry Rushing. Indeed, the name General Lee, given to the Duke boys' car, was based on Rushing's prize Chrysler 300D he named Traveller.

Too many times, the cars would turn end-over-end, burst into flames and, on a few such occasions kill the driver." Carter further noted, "This was very bad, it being highly illegal anyway. And it required too many goddam government forms to be filled out." For Carter, it was an "even worse" scenario, as agents also lost a potentially hot "dream car" to take the place of their underpowered government-issued sedan. Because of the dangers and the bad publicity, supervisors eventually banned both using the whammy and shooting out tires.[42]

Just as North Carolina's moonshine kingpins attracted national media attention during the 1950s, the state's car chases and ordinary moonshiners drew the interest of popular culture leaders. North Carolina and moonshine were still inextricably tied to each other in the minds of many Americans. Of course, this was the era when Texan J. P. Richardson located "pappy's still" in the classic country song "White Lightnin'." Tourists also continued to look for moonshine-

Souvenir moonshine jugs sold throughout the state at least until the 1970s. (Courtesy of the Lew Powell Memorabilia Collection, North Carolina Collection, UNC Libraries, UNC–Chapel Hill)

related souvenirs when they traveled in the state. Indeed, almost every major attraction sold stoneware moonshine jugs with the site's name printed on them. Democratic Party officials even had a special batch made up labeled "North Carolina Mountain Dew" to hand out as gifts at the 1964 National Democratic Convention.

Moviemakers especially became fascinated with the state's whiskey trippers and the nation's seemingly insatiable appetite for tales of their exploits. Indeed, the country's fascination with moonshiners even helped return a significant moviemaking industry to the state, similar to that in its heyday in the silent film era. In addition, Hollywood's television industry, with the aid of one of its most famous natives, brought North Carolina's moonshiners to a huge national audience.

The moonshine movie genre, building on car chase romanticism, returned to North Carolina in 1957 with a vengeance with the Robert Mitchum vehicle *Thunder Road*. The movie was a personal project for Mitchum, a major Hollywood star and Academy Award nominee. Mitchum not only played the lead role of moonshiner Lucas Doolin but also produced the movie, reportedly directed most of it, cowrote the screenplay, and cowrote the theme song, "The Whippoorwill." In addition, his son James played a major role as Lucas Doolin's

Robert Mitchum (who played Luke Doolin) and his son James (who played Luke's brother Robin) on the set of Thunder Road *near Asheville. (Courtesy of D. H. Ramsey Library Special Collections, University of North Carolina Asheville)*

younger brother Robin. The film also featured Gene Barry, Jacques Aubuchon, Keely Smith, and Sandra Knight as well as a dozen or so locals who had minor speaking roles plus 100 or so local extras. Legend has it that Elvis Presley agreed to play the role of Robin, but his agent, Col. Tom Parker, wanted far too much money for his services.[43]

Mitchum filmed the movie almost entirely in western North Carolina. He shot scenes in the Reems Creek and Bent Creek areas of Buncombe County, in downtown Asheville (which doubled as Memphis), in the Lake Lure area (near the Esmeralda Inn, the center of the silent film era of moonshine movies), and at Toxaway Falls for a spectacular car crash scene. While the story in the film takes place in Kentucky and Tennessee, Mitchum chose Asheville at least partly because of his friendship with local ATTU agent John Corbin. Supposedly, some extras in the movie were local moonshiners, and rumor had it that the hard-living Mitchum had quite a taste for both white lightning and the moonshiner lifestyle, at least the mythical version.[44]

The story is a pretty classic sort of gangster movie scenario. Lucas is a Korean War veteran scarred by the experience, who longs to leave the mountains but is loyal to his moonshining family who needs his help. The local moonshiners are under pressure both from revenue agents, led by Troy Barrett (Gene Barry), and from Memphis organized-crime kingpin Carl Kogan (Jacques Aubuchon), who wants to control all the mountain moonshine. Numerous car chases, fistfights,

Robert Mitchum and Sandra Knight (who played Roxanna Ledbetter) filming in Luke's tripper car on the Thunder Road *set. (Courtesy of D. H. Ramsey Library Special Collections, University of North Carolina Asheville)*

and shootouts ensue, with a little time off for scenes with Doolin's love interests, Francie (Keely Smith) and Roxanna (Sandra Knight). Spoiler alert: The movie ends with a dramatic car chase with both the gangsters and revenue agents involved, the deployment of a whammy, and a spectacular car crash into an electrical substation. Doolin dies tragically and Barrett makes a final assessment of the situation: "Mountain people, wild-blooded and death foolish. It was Doolin all right. He was a real stampeder."[45]

Thunder Road marked a dramatic departure from the moonshine movies of the silent film era filmed in North Carolina and launched an age where the moonshiner was invariably the hero. Film critics, however, proved less than enthused about the movie. Even the movie reviewer in the *Asheville Citizen-Times* wrote, "The story doesn't hang together well; matter of fact, it makes no sense whatsoever at times. The acting is only so-so.... As an exhibit of film art, about the best one can say is that this is not the worst movie ever made. But it's close."[46]

But for movie viewers in North Carolina and other parts of the Southeast, particularly young, working-class people, *Thunder Road* was a near-perfect film that came out at the perfect time. The movie tapped into the burgeoning youth car culture in the region and its fascination with fast cars, moonshine trippers, and James Dean–type antiheroes. It also struck a chord with the growing numbers of NASCAR fans in the region, although the movie makes

Massive silver cloud still that was used in Thunder Road, *tended by Trevor Bardette (who played Vernon Doolin). Robert Mitchum allegedly used both material and expertise from local moonshiners to make the film. (Courtesy of D. H. Ramsey Library Special Collections, University of North Carolina Asheville)*

no direct reference to auto racing. North Carolina moviegoers flocked to the film, with over 23,000 coming to Asheville's Imperial Theater for its initial run alone.[47] The movie also hit at the peak time for drive-in theaters in the region, which helped turn the movie into a cult classic and drive-in favorite well into the 1960s and beyond. The movie still has a sizeable cult following to this day in North Carolina. Robert Mitchum even recorded a version of the movie's opening music as "The Ballad of Thunder Road" (he did not sing in the movie) that made the Billboard Hot 100 in 1958 and again in 1962. Bluegrass duo Jim & Jesse made the country charts with the tune in 1967. For North Carolinians, *Thunder Road* launched a flood of imitators, most of them low-budget productions for the drive-in theater market, many of these produced in the state and based on the lives of local moonshiners.

North Carolina moonshiners achieved perhaps their greatest pop culture fame during the eight-year run from 1960 to 1968 of the state's native son's *Andy Griffith Show*. Especially in the show's black-and-white years, moonshine and moonshiners had a near constant presence on the screen. Andy Griffith drew heavily on his formative years in Mount Airy for plot lines and characters. To be sure, when Griffith grew up in the 1930s and 1940s, there was plenty of moonshine in Surry County, which adjoins Wilkes and several other notorious moonshine counties in North Carolina and Virginia. Iconic episodes such as

Andy Griffith performing his classic comedy sketch "What It Was, Was Football" at halftime of a UNC vs. North Carolina State University football game. His show largely depicted moonshiners in an accurate manner. (Photo by Hugh Morton, courtesy of the North Carolina Collection, UNC Libraries, UNC–Chapel Hill)

"Christmas Story," "Alcohol and Old Lace," "Aunt Bee the Warden," "Rafe Hollister Sings," and "The Haunted House" all had moonshine as a central theme. Of course even in other episodes, moonshine was never far from the scene when Otis Campbell came around; Briscoe Darling always accompanied his boys' bluegrass band by blowing into a moonshine jug; and one of the Darling boys' favorite tunes was "Dooley," a song about a moonshiner. Deputy Barney Fife also seemed to regularly have accidental encounters with moonshine, where he quickly ended up "gassed."[48]

While some of the depictions of moonshine and moonshining in the show are stereotypical, and of course the situations are all played for laughs, for the most part Andy Griffith gets it right and highlights several important real facts related to North Carolina moonshine. The depiction of single women as moonshiners in "Alcohol and Old Lace" is one of the few depictions in popular culture of such important figures. Andy's treatment of moonshiners is also reflective of the type of tolerance common to local sheriffs in North Carolina, especially when dealing with farmers trying to supplement their income. Much to the consternation of Mayor Stoner, Andy lets Jess Morgan go home to harvest his crops as long as he promises to come back when he is done. The sheriff also tries to re-

The Moonshiners of *The Andy Griffith Show*

It's hard to say why Andy Griffith seemed to have such a fascination with moonshining other than that he grew up in a place, Surry County, and in an era where the practice was so common. Whatever the source of his interest, in the first four seasons of his long-running show approximately 10 percent of the episodes involved moonshine and at least a dozen different characters played the role of the moonshiner. One actor, Jack Prince, actually played three of those roles: Ben Sewell, Luke Reiner, and most famously, the moonshiner with an angel's voice, Rafe Hollister.

A rundown of the moonshiners that appear in the show reveals Griffith's nuanced views on moonshine.

Sam Muggins. Sam is the first moonshiner to appear in the show, in episode 11, "Christmas Story." Local department store owner and Mayberry scrooge Ben Weaver hauls Sam to the jail for making moonshine. The typical amicable relationship between moonshiners and local law enforcement is on display here. Andy first tries to release Sam so he can spend Christmas with his family, but then brings Sam's family, a Christmas tree, his own family, and even Barney dressed as Santa Claus to celebrate the holiday in the jail. In the process, Weaver, like Scrooge, learns the true meaning of Christmas.

Clarabelle and Jennifer Morrison. The Morrison sisters star in episode 17, "Alcohol and Old Lace." This is the one episode where moonshine is the theme of the entire show and, as such, reflects Andy's views on the complicated nature of the illegal liquor business. In the language of the early 1960s, Clarabelle and Jennifer are "old maids," older single women. Like many women in North Carolina without male providers, the women get at least part of their income from making moonshine. However, they call it "elixir," to be used only for (highly dubious) "holiday" celebrations, including National Potato Week. Other accurate aspects of the Morrison sisters' activities include the location of their still in town, in their greenhouse, and their informing on competitor moonshiners who are making liquor for "drinking," not for "celebrating." The final scene reflects another important aspect of the way law enforcement often handled women moonshiners as, after Barney destroys the still, Andy releases the sisters without charges.

Ben Sewell. Ben is one of the moonshiners in "Alcohol and Old Lace." This is the first of three episodes where Jack Prince plays a moonshiner. When Andy and Barney approach him at his still, Ben is surprised that they want to arrest him. He apologizes for shooting at them and says, "I thought you was the law." Indeed, it was a common view that local law enforcement should have no interest in illegal liquor because it was a violation of federal, not local, law.

Rube Sloan. Rube also appears in "Alcohol and Old Lace," as the victim of the Morrison sisters' informing. Andy takes his usual generous stance on Rube's behavior and releases him to appear later in court after Barney destroys his still by taking a "great big axe and Pow, Pow, Pow!"

Luke Reiner. Luke, also played by Jack Prince, appears in episode 20, "The Inspector," as a moonshiner who has "holed up" and is shooting at the world. While state inspector Ralph Case panics and wants to "smoke him out with tear gas," Andy once again demonstrates his tolerance and calmly walks up to the door, grabs Luke's gun, and hauls him off to jail while chewing him out for being inhospitable to strangers.

Jubal Foster. In episode 46, "The Keeper of the Flame," Opie joins a secret club and gets to keep the "sacred candle" the club uses in its ceremonies. The club often sneaks into Jubal's barn for its meetings, and the farmer angrily chases them off and complains to Andy about keeping these "brats" off his land. Jubal has reason to keep the boys out of his barn, as he has a moonshine still hidden there. When a moonshining accident starts a fire and burns the barn down, Jubal blames the boys and demands Andy pay to replace it. While Andy starts to pay Jubal the money, Barney begins sipping from a bucket holding what he thinks is well water, has an immediate "liver reaction," and quickly becomes "gassed." With the evidence in hand, Andy arrests Jubal for moonshining and both help a staggering Barney to the squad car. This ongoing theme in the show, of folks getting drunk on moonshine while drinking what they think is water, is funny but very unrealistic. Anyone who has tasted moonshine knows that when you take a sip, you immediately know it is definitely not water.

Billy, Ike, Junior, and Sherman Gordon. Andy arrests the moonshining Gordon boys in episode 55, "Aunt Bee the Warden." When town drunk Otis Campbell comes into the jail, the brothers threaten him and try to attack him; they believe he informed on them because they raised their prices. Andy takes Otis to his own home to serve his jail term so he won't get beaten up by the Gordons. Aunt Bee puts Otis to work, much to his consternation. Barney tries to rehabilitate the Gordon boys, providing them with a leatherwork kit, a metalwork kit, a woodwork kit, and a Mr. Potato Head kit. Being the creative types that many moonshiners were, the boys use the metalwork kit to make a key and escape.

Jess Morgan. Jess is incarcerated in the Mayberry jail for moonshining in episode 69, "Andy and the New Mayor." Andy butts heads with the new mayor, Roy Stoner, when the sheriff wants to release the moonshiner so Jess can go home and harvest his crops. "Law and order" stickler Stoner, however, insists Jess serve his term in jail. Reflective of an attitude common in North Carolina's small towns, Andy goes ahead and releases Jess on his promise to return after three days.

Rafe Hollister. Jack Prince's third appearance as a moonshiner comes in episode 83, "Rafe Hollister Sings." Like many farmers in North Carolina during the period, Rafe supplements his income with an occasional run of illegal liquor. When Andy asks if he's made any moonshine lately, Rafe responds, "No. At least not so's you'd notice." Also like many of the state's moonshiners, Rafe has hidden talents and wows Mayberry with his singing voice at the town musicale, singing "Look Down That Lonesome Road" and "New River Train," wearing overalls and accompanied by Andy on guitar.

Colonel Harvey. Episode 87, "Aunt Bee's Medicine Man," explores the relationship between alcohol and "medicine" when a depressed Aunt Bee buys two bottles of "Colonel Harvey's Elixir" from a traveling snake oil salesman. The "elixir" brings her out of her funk, and Andy comes home and finds her banging away on the piano and singing "Toot, Toot, Tootsie (Goodbye)." She invites Colonel Harvey to dinner, becomes enamored of him, and invites him to speak to her ladies group the next day. Andy has Barney take a sample of the "elixir" to the "boys at the lab" at Walker's Drugstore, and discovers that Colonel Harvey's Elixir is 85 percent alcohol. Andy finds the colonel at his home in a living room full of "gassed" ladies who have been sampling the alcoholic "elixir."

Big Jack Anderson. Opie loses a baseball in the abandoned Rimshaw house in episode 98, "The Haunted House." When eerie noises in the house scare Opie away, Barney and Gomer go to retrieve the ball and are also scared away by noises and eyes in a portrait that follow them around the room. When Andy later joins them to investigate, a "floating axe" from a murder that supposedly occurred in the house also appears, and Barney and Gomer flee once again. Andy keeps his cool and discovers that the noises, scary portrait, and axe are the handiwork of moonshiner Big Jack Anderson who has a still in the basement. Moonshiners often spread scary stories about "haints," Boojums, and strange occurrences to scare folks away from their still sites.

Mr. Frisbee. In episode 111, "Aunt Bee the Crusader," the county has condemned farmer Frisbee's land to build a new highway. Aunt Bee and a number of her friends who buy butter and eggs from him begin protesting the unfairness of the situation, even going to the extent of physically blocking bulldozers from tearing down Frisbee's house and barn. As the women chant "We will not move," Opie finds that the pet rooster Frisbee has given him has the "blind staggers" and is apparently drunk. Andy investigates the rooster's strange behavior and discovers a hidden distillery operation in a cellar under Frisbee's barn. The teetotal women then turn on the farmer, and Andy observes, as he hauls Frisbee off to jail, that it must be difficult making a living on butter and eggs, showing his understanding of the ways farmers used moonshine to supplement their farm income.

lease Sam Muggins from jail, incarcerated for making a little Christmas 'shine, so he can spend the holiday with his family. While Andy and Barney discovered moonshine stills in mountain hollers in a few episodes, Griffith understood that they could be located in all kinds of places such as greenhouses, barn cellars, or a "haunted" house. Indeed, in the "Haunted House" episode, moonshiner Big Jack Anderson fed rumors about ghosts in the house to the community to mask his operations. All in all, the moonshiners in *The Andy Griffith Show* are sympathetic figures, folks in need who have strayed a bit but who are still good people.[49]

North Carolina moonshine and its colorful moonshiners also came to a national audience in an iconic article in *Esquire* magazine in 1965. In one of the strangest pairings in history, the overall-wearing Junior Johnson encountered international fame when journalist Tom Wolfe traveled in Wilkes County in spats and a seersucker suit. As a result of his visit, Wolfe wrote a breathless piece, one of the classics of the New Journalism style, entitled "The Last American Hero is Junior Johnson. Yes!" Johnson later recalled his encounter with Wolfe: "That Wolfe guy was something else. He showed up down here in Wilkes County talkin' funny, with a New York accent, and wearin' fancy clothes, including spats. Spats! I doubt anybody in Wilkes County ever had seen spats, at least not in recent times. I didn't have much time to spend with him. I didn't figure he'd get much of a story. But somehow he got local people to talk to him and his story turned out to be pretty doggone good and accurate."[50] Wolfe in turn described the Wilkes County driver as "a coon hunter, an ex-whiskey runner, a good old boy who hard-charges stock cars 175 m.p.h. Mother dog! He is the lead-footed chicken farmer, the true vision of the New South."[51]

Like *Thunder Road*, "The Last American Hero" glorified the car chase. In one story Wolfe shared, the author illustrates not only Johnson's bravery but also his native ingenuity and raw intelligence. Wolfe, in his inimitable way, describes a night when federal revenue agents thought they had Johnson trapped with a roadblock: "There's no way out of there, they had the barricades up and they could hear his souped-up car roaring around the bend, and here it comes—but suddenly they can hear a siren and see a red light flashing in the grille, so they think it's another agent, and boy, they run out like ants and pull those barrels and boards and sawhorses out of the way, and then—Ggghhzzzzzzzhhhhh gggggzzzzzzeeeeong!—gawdam! There he goes again, it was him, Junior Johnson!, with a gawdam agent's si-reen and a red light in his grille!"[52]

The success of these pop culture imaginings of North Carolina moonshiners also helped spark a revival of the state's movie industry, which in the 1960s produced a spate of generally forgettable B-grade moonshine movies destined for immediate release at a local drive-in. In 1964, Pat Patterson, who got his start in Hollywood as one of the Little Rascals, filmed *Moonshine Mountain*, a "family comedy about the 'likker' business," in Charlotte and Asheville.[53] Dick Clark, of *American Bandstand* fame, produced and played a supporting role in *Killers Three*, supposedly a combination of *Thunder Road* and *Bonnie and Clyde*, in 1968. Filmed in the community of Ramseur in Randolph County, the movie also featured Merle Haggard as a local sheriff. Haggard sang the movie's theme song as well.[54]

13

NORTH CAROLINA MOONSHINE, NASCAR, AND THE "BOOTLEGGER TRACKS"

While North Carolina moonshiners played a key role in the early days of southern stock car racing, they played an even more important role in the origins and early development of NASCAR, the sport's most important sanctioning body. Stock car racing had already established a foothold in North Carolina before World War II, but the sport's acknowledged centers were Daytona Beach and Atlanta's Lakewood Speedway. That would change rapidly after the war, and by the late 1940s North Carolina became the site of many of NASCAR's most important events and the home of its most important drivers. This shift was almost entirely the result of moonshine's influence on the sport, and the state's illegal liquor kingpins were especially important in forming NASCAR's foundation and helping it become a statewide and regional fixture.

The first major event that helped kick-start the migration of stock car racing's center to North Carolina began only a few weeks after V-J Day in 1945. The federal government had banned auto racing during the war due to gasoline and tire rationing, and racing fans and those directly involved in the sport were eager to start up again. Almost as soon as the ink dried on the Japanese surrender documents, promoters at Lakewood Speedway announced a big race for Labor Day, the traditional day for the nation's biggest stock car race. The event attracted a huge amount of interest from participants and fans, and promoters anticipated a huge field and crowd for the event. The race also drew the interest of the forces of propriety in Atlanta, including *Atlanta Constitution* editor and publisher Ralph McGill and members of the local Baptist and Methodist ministerial alliances. The presence in the race of so many well-known moonshiners, trippers, and bootleggers with long police records concerned McGill and the preachers. They saw Lakewood as complicit in glorifying criminal activity and demanded that authorities ban these liquor-hauling drivers from competing. While they were unsuccessful at keeping the outlaw drivers off the Lakewood track, and the race was won by Roy Hall, one of the most notorious trippers in the country, they were successful in getting a ban passed that kept those involved in illegal liquor out of future races.[1]

With the Lakewood ban in effect, stock car racing's tripper-racer stars had to look to other venues. At this juncture, Bill France, Daytona Beach racer and promoter of the famous beach races held every winter, made one of his most important moves: he transferred his summer operations to North Carolina and began promoting races in the Carolinas and Virginia. France had an advantage over his competitors because he had competed with and knew well the moonshining stars of the sport, and they trusted him. As such, France successfully brought the Atlanta-area stars of stock car racing to his promotions, including Roy Hall (at least until he went to prison for armed robbery); Red Byron; the Mad Flock Brothers, Fonty and Bob; Gober Sosebee; Bill Carden; Ed Samples; and Glen "Legs" Law. In the summer of 1946, France launched his National Championship Stock Car Circuit, moved his base for the summer racing season to Winston-Salem, and had successful races at fairgrounds tracks in Greensboro, Salisbury, and Rocky Mount. By this point, France had added Charlotte-area bootleggers Glenn Dunnaway and Buddy Shuman to his stable of star drivers.[2]

The most important contribution North Carolinians made to the creation of NASCAR, however, came in 1947 when France formed key alliances with some big-time bootleggers who ended up constructing the most important stock car tracks in the nation. These alliances helped form the very foundation of NASCAR and contributed much to its success in the 1940s and 1950s. The movement began in 1946, not surprisingly, in Wilkes County. In that year Enoch Staley, John Masden, and Charlie Combs—all from Wilkes County and heavily involved in the illegal liquor business—heard about the successful stock car races in the region that France was promoting and decided to attend one in Spartanburg, South Carolina. After the race, the three sought out the promoter and talked to him about the possibility of building a track near their home and hosting France-promoted stock car races.[3] While ambitious and creative, France was short on funds and eager to find investors with a love of racing and deep pockets. In the Wilkes County bootleggers, France found what he was looking for. As driver Frank Mundy observed, "The bootleggers were the only ones who had any money, who were able to put up the purses."[4] The three went home and over the course of the next six months began one of the most successful "if you build it, they will come" projects in sports history, grading out a six-tenths-of-a-mile-long track with seating for 7,500.[5]

Both Staley and Combs—the two principals in the operation—had strong connections to Wilkes County's most famous product: moonshine whiskey. Staley, who eventually controlled half of the stock in the business, was the youngest son of Ranse Staley, one of the county's major illegal liquor operators. According to a number of individuals, Enoch Staley continued the family business although he held down other jobs, including one driving a delivery truck for a local dairy. Indeed, one source alleges that he delivered illegal liquor in his milk truck. For the most part, however, he was generally known as someone who worked in the background of the business, primarily in the financial end. According to Yadkinville auto dealer Max Welborn, "He [Staley] was mainly financing." Welborn's friend and fellow auto dealer Donald Johnson agreed, asserting that Staley kept a low profile in his daddy's business and was not directly involved in making moonshine or hauling it: "Enoch would not touch it."[6] "I think my dad became part of Grandpa's operation," admitted Mike Staley, Enoch's son, in an interview with writer Peter Golenbock. "He didn't say much about it."[7] Combs was the black sheep of his family of devout churchgoers and often held jobs in automobile sales, but he was also involved heavily in the illegal alcohol business. Federal prosecutors indicted Combs in 1955 in the Burgess brothers' illegal liquor syndicate case; Combs had a close "business" relationship with Grafton Burgess.[8]

Combs and Staley also fit the model of the typical speedway owners, star driver Jack Smith posited; they were gamblers and "didn't mind taking a chance on [their] money." Indeed, not long before the opening of the North Wilkesboro Speedway, a jury convicted Combs on an illegal gambling charge and sentenced him to one year of hard labor on the roads—although he was later acquitted on appeal—related to an armed robbery of a poker game in a private home.[9] In another high-stakes gamble, Combs and Staley—along with their other partners Austin Ashley, Lawson Curry, and John Masden—wagered that a speedway in rural Wilkes County could be successful. Using money they scraped together from their various "business" enterprises, and lots of sweat equity, the group graded out an oddly configured, sloping speedway, slapped up a board fence, and built bleachers, a concession stand, outhouses, and a ticket booth.[10]

Amazingly the North Wilkesboro track was an immediate and huge success. The owners granted Bill France an exclusive contract to promote the races at the new track and held four stock car racing events in 1947. In a county with only a little more than 40,000 total residents, with the town of North Wilkesboro having only 3,500 residents and located sixty miles away from the closest reasonably sized city—Winston-Salem—the five events (they also hosted an Indianapolis-style "big-car" event) brought in an estimated 70,000 fans. Those successful races placed "the track at the head of the Carolinas speedways" in one short year. As evidence of this success, North Wilkesboro offered the largest purse—$4,350, with $1,400 to the winner—for its penultimate race of the year, the Bill France–promoted Eastern Stock Car Racing Championship. Twelve thousand fans watched Daytona mechanic Marshall Teague race to victory over "Wild" Bill Snowden and Red Byron. Obviously, Staley, Combs, and France had hit on a winning formula of moving the sport of stock car racing into the more rural sections of the Piedmont south and its foothills. Indeed, given the lack of entertainment options, as well as the cultural values of working-class people in the area who did not perceive arrests for moonshining as a stain on one's reputation, North Wilkesboro was an ideal place for a track.[11]

The success of stock car racing in general and of the North Wilkesboro track in particular attracted others with ties to illegal alcohol to the racetrack business and to partnership with Bill France. Later in 1947, bootlegger H. Clay Earles built a track in Martinsville, Virginia, just over the border with North Carolina—the only one of these so-called bootlegger tracks still on the schedule in NASCAR's top series—and partnered with France to promote races there. Other moonshiners heard—probably through an informal network of bootleggers—about the success of North Wilkesboro and Martinsville and decided to try their hand at the racetrack business. Stokesville, North Carolina, bootleggers Harvey and Pat Charles showed up on the doorstep of the farmhouse of C. C. Allison west of Charlotte off Wilkinson Boulevard in 1947. The Charles brothers worked out a deal to partner with Allison to build a three-quarter-mile dirt track on the property, and the first race at the Charlotte Speedway, in July 1948 and promoted by Bill France, drew a huge crowd. In 1948, France also partnered with Staley and Combs to build a one-mile speedway just east of Hillsborough, North Carolina. In the early 1950s, other bootleggers joined the ranks of Staley, Combs, Earles, and the Charles brothers as track builders and owners of the most important tracks in NASCAR. In 1951, Gene Sluder, red liquor kingpin of Buncombe County and the owner of an earth-moving company, built the Asheville-Weaverville Speedway, one of the fastest tracks in the early days of NASCAR.[12]

The racetrack business also proved a perfect fit for the Burgess brothers, Grafton and Ralph, who partnered with Combs to build a facility in 1951 near the booming furniture center of Hickory. Grafton, along with local trucking company owner Marshall McRee, signed on as a partner in the venture, while Ralph, under federal indictment at the time, was a silent investor. The Burgess brothers, given their other "business" interests, loved fast cars and the stock car racing scene, which attracted a lot of folks in their particular line of work. In addition, the brothers' nightclub, the Silver Moon, was a major hangout for drivers, mechanics, car owners, and fans of the sport. The Hickory Speedway soon became an important track on the NASCAR Grand National Circuit and helped launch the careers of such racing legends as Junior Johnson, Ralph Earnhardt (Dale's daddy), Ned Jarrett, Bobby Isaacs, Morgan Shepherd, and

Early race at Tri-City Speedway near High Point. Track builder and moonshiner Bill Blair (no. 2) sits on the outside pole. (Courtesy of William Blair Jr.)

Dale Jarrett.[13] While the illegal activities of the track owners of these major NASCAR tracks are well documented, the state's moonshine kingpins are probably also responsible for the explosion of small dirt tracks throughout North Carolina in the late 1940s and early 1950s.

Due to the lack of available records and detailed testimony, one can only speculate about why so many individuals involved in illegal liquor in North Carolina became involved in the racetrack business in the late 1940s and early 1950s and in the stock car racing that became NASCAR. We can, however, make some educated guesses about why this phenomenon became so common. Some reasons for bootlegger involvement are obvious and are similar to those of the tripper-drivers who so heavily populated the ranks of early stock car races: a love for fast cars and a gambler's instincts. Other possible reasons are purely speculative but, given the nature of these men's business, make sense.

As a business investment, speedway construction had some specific advantages for many bootleggers. As racing promoter Humpy Wheeler observed, constructing a speedway on the red clay of the North Carolina Piedmont did not require a great deal of talent or a huge capital investment—most were probably built for less than $100,000. The ready availability of cheap earth-moving equipment in the postwar era and the cheapness of farmland in the region made it a relatively inexpensive investment.[14] Indeed, several of the bootleg-

Ralph "Puff" and Grafton "Tuff" Burgess

N.C. Moonshine Hall of Famers

Most moonshine movies, like the B-movie classic *Thunder Road*, feature some kind of organized crime syndicate trying to muscle in on local moonshiners. While law enforcement often spoke to the press, especially in the 1950s and 1960s, about big-time crime syndicates operating in North Carolina's illegal liquor business, there is little concrete evidence that organized crime played a huge role in this state. What organization there seemed to be was in the way of informal networks that developed over the years, like Percy Flowers recruiting Wilkes County moonshiners to work for him or Junior Johnson partnering with moonshiners in Cocke County, Tennessee, to import huge amounts of sugar into the region.

The best evidence we do have about organized crime syndicates centers around brothers Ralph and Grafton Burgess of Alexander County. Well known throughout the Piedmont region, the flamboyant Burgess brothers—nicknamed Puff and Tuff—held court at their North Carolina Highway 16 restaurant and club, the Silver Moon, located near the Catawba County line.

Not much is known about their early life, but the Burgesses grew up on a farm not far from Taylorsville. They were both big boys, and their 1940 draft registration cards listed Grafton (b. 1912), the elder by seven years, at a height of five feet, eight inches, and weight of 230 pounds and Ralph (b. 1919) at a height of six feet and weight of 300 pounds. It is not hard to imagine how Ralph got the nickname Puff. The brothers both reported that they were self-employed on their draft cards, and it seems logical that at this point they were already involved with illegal liquor. Their father, Clarence, was alleged to support the family making moonshine, and the brothers apparently learned the family business early on.

After World War II, the brothers moved away from producing moonshine themselves and concentrated on supplying others with sugar, distributing the product, and importing legally produced "red liquor" into North Carolina's dry counties. The Burgesses made millions of dollars during this period and like all participants in illegal activity had to find ways to move their ill-gotten gains into the legal economy. Hauling large amounts of cash to the bank would generate unwanted inquiries from the IRS and state authorities, and you can only bury so much in the backyard. They used their Silver Moon club, the Hickory Speedway, and other legitimate business enterprises they owned to launder the massive amounts of cash their illegal liquor business generated.

During the 1950s, the brothers came under intense scrutiny from the federal government. A number of indictments followed for a variety of illegal liquor charges, tax evasion, and for Ralph, kidnapping and assault with a deadly weapon. Ralph spent almost three years in both state and federal prison and paid fines totaling $10,000. Grafton got off rather lightly and only paid a fine of $5,000. The brothers seem to have lived out the rest of their lives in a relatively quiet fashion, and if they remained in the illegal liquor business, law enforcement never caught them again. It appears they were able to reopen the Silver Moon for at least a little while. Grafton retained his ownership interest in the Hickory Speedway and in 1959 became the track's general manager, a position he held at least into the late 1960s when Ned Jarrett retired from racing and became the track's manager. Tuff also owned a service station in Taylorsville and died in 1973. Little is known about Puff after he served his terms in prison, but he stayed out of the news and died in 1984.

While they lived out their later years relatively quietly, in their heyday the Burgess brothers cut a wide swath (literally), creating a vast empire connecting many worlds of the moonshine, red liquor, and NASCAR universes. While movies and law enforcement often spoke of the vast criminal conspiracies involved in illegal liquor during the 1940s, 1950s, and 1960s, we have solid evidence about only this—at least temporarily—highly lucrative one. While the Silver Moon is long gone, the Burgesses did help NASCAR—now a multibillion-dollar enterprise—get off the ground, and while the Hickory Speedway does not host races in NASCAR's top division any more, it still hosts weekly racing from spring to fall and stands as a testimony to the behind-the-scenes influence of illegal liquor in the sport's beginnings.

gers, like Gene Sluder, had already invested in heavy earth-moving equipment and started legitimate excavation businesses before they became involved in racetracks. Most of the bootleggers provided more in sweat equity—from themselves, family, and friends—to their tracks than they did in cash.

Owning a racetrack also provided another possible advantage for folks involved in the illegal liquor business: the opportunity to launder large amounts of cash. Again, there is no direct evidence that this occurred at these tracks. However, the opportunity racetracks provided to move extra money through a facility where race fans paid huge amounts of cash for tickets and concessions and into a bank is obvious. While Alcohol and Tobacco Tax Unit agents surely kept an eye on such activities, it was easy to inflate attendance numbers—something every promoter did—and no one really knew how many hot dogs vendors sold in the concession stands. While cash moved through such means was subject to some taxes, that cost was probably worth it. Whatever their motivations, Staley, Combs, and company and their North Wilkesboro track started a movement among bootleggers and racetrack owners that formed the very financial foundation on which NASCAR was built.

Bill France's success in North Carolina led him to try to extend his stock car racing promotions to other parts of the country, particularly the Midwest and Northeast. In December 1947, he called a meeting of noted racing promoters at the Streamline Hotel in Daytona Beach. The major outcome of that meeting was the creation of the National Association of Stock Car Auto Racing (NASCAR). While there were few bootleggers in attendance at that meeting, their influence was omnipresent in the sport's top drivers, mechanics, car owners, promoters, and racetrack owners.[15]

In June 1949, France organized the first ever NASCAR "strictly stock" race, which launched NASCAR's top division, the precursor of the current Cup Series. Not surprisingly, France scheduled the race at one of the bootlegger tracks, the Charles brothers' Charlotte Speedway. Also not surprisingly, a North Carolina tripper, Glenn Dunnaway, won the race in a car that hauled liquor that very same week, owned by moonshine kingpin Hubert Westmoreland. Indeed, NASCAR officials disqualified Dunnaway after a postrace inspection revealed illegal modifications to the suspension, "blocks welded to the crossmember ... [and] old buggy springs." Westmoreland later admitted that those modifications were there "so it would hold up on the road because we hauled liquor in it." After Dunnaway's disqualification, NASCAR declared Kansan Jim Roper, who had read about the coming race in a *Smilin' Jack* comic strip, the winner. Although Roper had no known connections to illegal liquor, much of the field did, including North Carolinians Lee Petty—who four times rolled the 1948 Buick Roadmaster he had borrowed from his friend Gilmer Goode—Buck Baker, Bill Blair, and Jimmie Lewallen.[16]

North Carolina moonshiners continued to play a key role in NASCAR's growing popularity in the 1950s. The addition of the Asheville-Weaverville and Hickory tracks to the bootlegger track ranks, as well as the construction of other tracks in the state not obviously connected to illegal liquor, made North Carolina the top venue for NASCAR races during the period. In addition, North Carolinians with deep ties to the moonshine business, such as Petty, Baker, Blair, Lewallen, Dunnaway, Bob Welborn, and Buddy Shuman, became stars in the young series.

North Carolinian moonshiners also made significant contributions to the mechanical side of NASCAR. In 1955, Ford field service manager Bill Benton of Charlotte traveled to Ford headquarters in Dearborn, Michigan, to convince his bosses to enter factory-sponsored cars in NASCAR races, as Chevrolet and Chrysler had already done. Benton took Charlotte-area mechanic, stock car racer, and moonshiner Buddy Shuman with him to explain the technical side of stock car racing to Ford engineers. Shuman strolled into the prime habitat of men in "gray flannel suit[s]" wearing a loud shirt—no suit, no tie—and talked shop with the highly educated engineers in a North Carolina Piedmont twang. Many of the Ford executives wondered what they were getting into. As historian Leo Levine put it, the Ford employees discovered they were "dealing with a totally unfamiliar type of person." They found out how "unfamiliar" Shuman was when the company's Industrial Relations Division (an in-house investigative agency) did a routine background check that revealed a long police record and time spent on a county chain gang for illegal liquor violations. When an

Industrial Relations Division investigator called Ford chief engineer Bill Burnett to tell him about Shuman's record and encouraged him to cut ties with him, Burnett, who recognized Shuman's value and true genius as a mechanic, "cut him off in a hurry." "As far as I know, he's doing a good job for us, we're getting along fine with him, and we don't intend to throw him out."[17] While best known for his exploits as a driver, Junior Johnson also displayed true genius as a mechanic. Once a reporter asked him if he went to Detroit for advice on how to prepare his race cars. Johnson responded in his inimitable droll manner, "No, Detroit comes to us."

Johnson is the most recognizable North Carolinian associated with NASCAR and moonshine. Although often characterized as a pioneer, Johnson actually was one of the last trippers to enter the sport. In 1949, Johnson raced on a stock car track for the first time when he took his brother's car to the local North Wilkesboro Speedway and entered an amateur race primarily featuring local bootleggers. He finished second in the race and immediately caught the racing bug. He made his racing debut in NASCAR in 1953 and in 1955 began competing full-time, winning five races. Johnson continued his success in the 1956 season, but Alcohol and Tobacco Tax Unit agents sidetracked his career in June of that year. While he became a star on the NASCAR circuit, Johnson continued to help out his family in the moonshine business when time allowed. That fateful June morning, his daddy asked him to go out and fire up a still hidden nearby in the woods. Unbeknownst to Junior, federal agents had the still staked out, and when he started firing it up, they moved in to arrest him. Junior took off running but got tangled in a barbed-wire fence, and agent Joe Carter had the bust of his career. As Carter recalled in his memoir *Damn the Allegators*, Johnson "proved very cooperative, if rather silent. He even helped us bust up the still." That bust cost Johnson an eleven-month-and-three-day stint in the Chillicothe, Ohio, federal penitentiary and a season and a half at the prime of his NASCAR career.[18]

In 1956, Johnson returned with a vengeance to the racing scene, winning six races. Fans loved him because he drove like a man possessed. Leading by half a lap late in a race that year at North Wilkesboro, he went into the third turn on the recently paved track too fast, got into the loose asphalt—or "marbles," as racers call it—near the top of the track, and flew over a four-feet-high earthen bank and off the track. For most drivers this would mean a wrecked car and the end of their race, but Johnson "never touched the brakes," headed through the weeds, and sped back over the bank and onto the track, never surrendering his lead. Sportswriter Dick Thompson asserted that the 225-pound Johnson "looks like a wrestler and drives like a maniac."[19] Even though he planned to give the moonshine business up altogether and make his living entirely from racing and other legitimate enterprises, Johnson continued to help out his family, espe-

Junior Johnson in victory lane. Johnson is easily North Carolina's most famous moonshiner. (Courtesy of State Archives of North Carolina, Raleigh, N.C.)

cially after authorities sent his father to prison for three years in 1958. "I could have walked away real quick like, but what would that have meant for my family? . . . How could I just cut off their money?"[20]

In September 1958, authorities arrested Johnson's father as part of a "saturation program," when federal and state agents swept into the county and destroyed sixteen stills, including one on the Johnson property. The agents also raided the home and found illegal liquor on the premises and arrested Johnson, his brothers L. P. and Fred, and their mother, Lora Belle. They later found another still on the property and added that to the list of charges. Loath to lose a star driver at a pivotal time in the sport's history, NASCAR owner "Big" Bill France helped Johnson and his lawyers launch a spirited defense at his trial in May 1959. Johnson's car owner, Paul Spaulding, testified that testing and racing occupied Johnson's time and he was too busy to be involved in the family moonshine operation. NASCAR field manager Johnny Bruner backed up Spaulding's testimony with copies of the NASCAR bulletin, and scorer Joe Epton testified that Johnson was in Raleigh on 2 July 1958, when agents had busted up another still on the Johnson property. L. P. pleaded guilty and the judge sentenced him to two years; a jury convicted Fred, sentenced him to thirty months, and fined

Robert Glenn "Junior" Johnson N.C. Moonshine Hall of Famer

Of course, any self-respecting North Carolina Moonshine Hall of Fame (and Shame) must have at least one person from Wilkes County, unarguably the state's moonshine capital, and a stock car racer. And it is an obvious and natural choice to select the most undeniably famous moonshiner in the state's history, Robert Glenn "Junior" Johnson. In terms of fame, he is hard to top, with several books and countless national magazine articles written about him, near-constant exposure on national television, and one well-known Hollywood feature film (starring Jeff Bridges) and numerous spin-offs that reference his biography. He was one of the first five inductees into the NASCAR Hall of Fame and, like Lewis Redmond, received a presidential pardon (Johnson's was from President Ronald Reagan). Johnson even has an eight-and-a-half-mile stretch of U.S. Route 421 in Wilkes County (a road he drove many times with a load of illegal liquor) named in his honor.

Born in 1931, Junior Johnson has deep roots in both Wilkes County and in the moonshine business. Johnson's father was a big-time moonshine operator for much of his life. Indeed, the moonshine business was the family business. Johnson's brothers L. P. and Fred also had numerous run-ins with the law, and his mother, Lora Belle, was busted on more than one occasion.

Johnson himself began working in the business as a child and started hauling liquor in his early teens. He soon demonstrated a genius for driving a heavily laden liquor car "hell-for-leather" on curvy mountain roads and for modifying ordinary-looking automobiles with massive high-powered engines and reinforced suspensions. Johnson not only had the talent and the obligation to support his family's business but, like many young North Carolinians of his era, flat-out loved the adrenaline rush of almost every aspect of moonshining, especially the chase. While he got caught at the still a few times, Johnson is always quick to point out that law enforcement never caught him on the highway.

In 1949, Johnson began his racing career at an amateur race at the North Wilkesboro Speedway. He raced for seventeen years, winning countless races on local short tracks and fifty races on the NASCAR Grand National Circuit, the sport's top division at the time, including the Daytona 500. He had to take an eleven-month break from racing in 1956–57 when he served time for moonshining in federal prison. His fame became national when Tom Wolfe called him the "last American hero" in a legendary *Esquire* magazine article in 1965. That article became the basis for a major Hollywood movie, *The Last American Hero*, in 1973, which further boosted his notoriety.

Even before he retired as a driver, Johnson used his NASCAR winnings and profits made in moonshine to launch a successful career as a car owner and demonstrated mechanical skills as great as, or even greater than, his driving skills. He was a natural genius as a mechanic, with a particular command and understanding of aerodynamics. While Johnson was an eighth-grade dropout and probably never read a physics textbook, he could probably write one. As a car owner, his teams won six NASCAR Winston Cup Championships (the sport's top level at the time) with drivers Cale Yarborough and Darrell Waltrip.

Johnson also invested his various "earnings" outside of racing and built up quite an empire in chicken houses (Holly Farms Chicken was an early sponsor), beef cattle, meat processing, and in the 2000s, "legal moonshining" in partnership with Piedmont Distillers. Junior Johnson's Midnight Moon is now available in all fifty states.

Junior Johnson epitomizes the classic southern "hell of a fellow" archetype chronicled by journalist W. J. Cash in his classic work, *The Mind of the South*, integral to the beginnings and success of NASCAR. The reckless abandonment he displayed on the highway hauling a load of liquor and on the racetrack beating and banging with his fellow adrenaline junkies, combined with his coolness under extreme pressure, attracted hundreds of thousands of fans to NASCAR. In addition, he firmly cemented the legend of the southern moonshine hauler in the pantheon of American heroes.

him $5,000; and Lora Belle received an eight-month suspended sentence and a $7,500 fine. However, the nine-person jury declared Johnson innocent of all charges. After this incident, he curtailed his moonshine interests, or at least became more circumspect, and continued racing until 1966, when he retired as a driver. He was one of the most successful racers in NASCAR history, winning fifty races, including the Daytona 500, and six championships as a car owner in the sport's top division. NASCAR chose him as one of the first five members of the NASCAR Hall of Fame.[21]

While people with experience in the illegal liquor business appeared on the NASCAR scene occasionally in the 1960s, Junior Johnson represented the end of an era where top drivers' first high-speed driving experiences involved hauling moonshine. Indeed, by the late 1960s, the moonshine business in North Carolina was in the midst of a precipitous decline, reflected in a changed NASCAR. Most of the upcoming generation of the sport's stars—like David Pearson, Bobby Isaacs, Leeroy Yarbrough, and even Dale Earnhardt—began their lives in cotton mill villages, gained racing experience from street racing and at the local short tracks, and had little connection to moonshine. When North Carolina governor Bob Scott claimed that approval of "liquor by the drink" in the state would "put a gradual end to moonshining," racing promoter Joe Littlejohn, a longtime bootlegger, quipped, "Where will our race drivers get their early training?"[22] In addition, several of the bootlegger tracks fell on hard times, and new superspeedways in Charlotte and Rockingham replaced them. Most of the connections to moonshine disappeared as, in many cases, the bootlegger builders got arrested, came upon economic hard times and sold out, or went legitimate full-time. The Charlotte Speedway on Wilkinson Boulevard fell victim to the construction of I-85 in the early 1960s, while Hillsborough closed in 1968 and Asheville-Weaverville was shuttered in 1969. Hickory held on but fell off the schedule for races in NASCAR's top division in 1971, and the Burgesses by then had sold their interest in the track. By that point, the only North Carolina bootlegger track that remained on the schedule was North Wilkesboro, which held on until 1996, still owned by the Staley and Combs families.[23]

14

THE END OF AN ERA

While the North Carolina moonshine business experienced somewhat of a golden age in the 1950s and early 1960s, especially for big-time producers, by the late 1960s the business was in steep decline. Alcohol Beverage Control (ABC) enforcement agent Al Dowtin reported in 1970 to the *Asheville Citizen-Times* that while his western North Carolina division had averaged over 100 stills busted per year in the late 1950s, it only captured twenty-two stills in 1968 and twelve in 1969.[1] By the 1970s the decline in the illegal liquor business led both federal and state agencies to dramatically cut back on their enforcement staffs. In addition, authorities closed down several federal courts in formerly active moonshine counties "because of lack of use."[2]

Observers attributed the decline to a number of factors. Business and industrial growth in the state created new employment opportunities that drew young men away from the business. The post–World War II expansion of the furniture, textile, and tobacco industries opened up thousands of new jobs, many located in rural counties such as Wilkes. In addition, new opportunities for supplementing farm income brought significant legal income to rural residents. In 1965, the *High Point Enterprise* claimed, "In Wilkes, many stills have been replaced by sprawling chicken farms," and observed that "one of the biggest" was owned by Junior Johnson.[3] James Elder, an agent for the Bureau of Alcohol, Tobacco, and Firearms (formerly the Alcohol and Tobacco Tax Unit), noted that the improved employment picture had an especially strong impact on the number of small producers in the business: "When the smaller producer can get a legal job that would pay as much as he could make making moonshine, he'd rather have the job. There are fewer worries."[4] In addition, factory work was generally much easier. As federal agent Sam Cabe observed, "Making liquor is real hard work. I've tried it when I was doing undercover work. Those gallon jugs of likker get awful heavy, carrying 'em up that mountain to the road."[5] A related factor, road improvements in rural areas, made it easier for people to commute to factory jobs; for farmers to get tobacco, chickens, or other products to market; and for law enforcement to access the formerly remote areas where moonshiners often hid their stills. As one rural Wilkes County resident observed, "Makin' liquor was fine until they put good roads up here. Now the law can get at you too easy."[6]

Legal alcohol's increasing availability also helped tamp down demand for the illegal product. By the 1960s and 1970s more and more North Carolina municipalities and counties passed referenda approving ABC stores and allowed legal sales in their areas for the first time in over sixty years. In 1965, despite the combined and determined efforts of Baptists and bootleggers, Wilkesboro and North Wilkesboro approved "state-controlled liquor stores."[7] While illegal producers still had a major price advantage over the tax-paid product, the expansion in employment meant more North Carolinians could afford to purchase the safer, legal, and better-tasting products offered by ABC. In a 1969 editorial on the decline of moonshine, the *Robesonian* averred, "Industrial payrolls also may have enabled some former customers of moonshiners to buy better-quality liquor, thus reducing demand for the local product, which is not noted for quality."[8] One moonshiner interviewed in an Associated Press report, whose name was listed as simply "Sam," even claimed that urban renewal programs in North Carolina's major cities were to blame for a decline in demand for moonshine: "I'll tell you, people are getting rid of the slums, and when you ain't got no slums, you ain't got much of a market for this stuff. A guy moves into one of the low-income homes and the first thing that happens is he starts uptown for the whiskey store to buy something fancy. They think they get too good for the corn."[9]

The increasing prices of sugar and other crucial supplies moonshiners needed also cut into profits and caused many moonshiners to seek legal employment. Sam noted that the cost of setting up a moonshine "rig" in the early 1970s had risen from about $700 to over $1,200. He asserted, "A man just can't afford to build a factory no more." When the price of sugar tripled during the same period, Sam lamented, "I'm ruined. I think this business would break a banker." These costs led Sam to reconsider his chosen line of work and he declared, "I ain't the only one that's going to logging or something like that."[10] The *Gaston Gazette* noted that increased costs had pushed the price of moonshine as high as eight dollars a pint, "not much more than a bottle of cheap, legal liquor costs in a state package store."[11]

More modern and stricter law enforcement also put a dent in enthusiasm for the moonshine business and made the enterprise even more costly. Al Dowtin also credited the decline in moonshine to many of the factors mentioned above, but he asserted in 1970, "I suppose our law enforcement efforts have done more to discourage whisky makers than anything else." He especially attributed improved enforcement to cooperation between federal, state, and local agencies. In addition, new sentencing guidelines and tougher judges produced longer sentences for offenders.[12] The crackdown by law enforcement led Sam to further lament, "The woods is getting smaller.... You spend all that money and work and set up a clean rig, and the next day you show up to start a run and half your stuff has been hauled off by the cops, and the rest beat to pieces. You just want to cry."[13]

One of the more modern tactics used by law enforcement that proved effective was an education and antimoonshine propaganda campaign launched in the early 1960s, which focused on the dangers of consuming illegal alcohol. Enforcement agencies had long warned the public about the lack of sanitation, leaching of dangerous substances into the liquor during distillation, and adulteration that often took place in moonshining operations. In 1946, an Alamance County deputy had noted the "crude 50-gallon oil barrels, grimy with rust and caked with slimy mash" he discovered at a still site. He continued, "I wish very much that every man who has tipped a fruit jar to his lips for a drink of this 'white lightning' could see just how it is made."[14] Such warnings and even chemical analyses of moonshine indicating the presence of poisonous substances, however, seemed to have had little impact on illegal liquor consumers.

The facts that did resonate most with the drinking public, however, were the deaths that sometimes occurred from drinking poisonous moonshine. In 1949, three Sylva men "died in agony" after they consumed liquor "laced ... with paint thinner." According to local officials, the traffic in illegal liquor had dried up as a result, and "locally made white lightning is going begging at 5 cents a pint."[15] The deaths of forty-one individuals in Atlanta in 1952 after they consumed moonshine tainted with wood alcohol also created widespread concern about the safety of illegal liquor in North Carolina.[16] Surry County had a poison moonshine scare in 1958 when liquor adulterated with wood alcohol led to the death of Clinton William White and the hospitalization of three others.[17] While these incidents had an impact, their relatively isolated or distant nature, plus the sad fact that they most often occurred in African American communities, led few illegal liquor drinkers to change their behavior.

That changed in North Carolina in 1960 when Winston-Salem experienced a major wave of moonshine-related deaths. While the scare terrorized many moonshine consumers, it also proved a godsend for enforcement personnel. In January 1960, deaths in the Piedmont Triad area related to moonshine consumption began to mount, with five reported deaths and numerous hospitalizations. By March the number of deaths had risen to eight and by July to twelve, with as many as fifty hospitalized with serious illnesses ranging from sudden blindness to "crippling cramps, nausea, internal hemorrhaging, muscular collapse, paralysis tremors, convulsions, and anemia."[18] ABC officials reported similar illnesses attributed to consumption of contaminated liquor in Thomasville, Charlotte, Greensboro, and as far away as Raleigh.

Testing of moonshine seized in the aftermath of these deaths soon revealed the culprit to be lead salts in high concentrations. Lead salts had always been a problem for moonshiners, as they leached into the product "through lead pipes and other makeshift lead parts of the distillery apparatus, including the solder used to put the still together back in the hollow."[19] Such poisoning, however, was cumulative, generally slow, and had the most effect on alcoholics who consumed large amounts. When they died, folks just simply assumed that they "drank themselves to death." Officials attributed the relatively sudden deaths in the Winston-Salem area to a new innovation imported into the North Carolina moonshine business from Tennessee, the Cosby silver cloud distillery. Silver cloud stills were large affairs, with anywhere from a 400- to 1,000-gallon capacity; distillers fermented the mash in the still itself, as in a groundhog still. Silver clouds got their name from the shiny galvanized sheet metal used to fabricate them, and according to most accounts, they originated in the notorious moonshining hotbed of Cosby in Cocke County, Tennessee. Donald Mason, head of the Greensboro ABC Board, explained that the problem with the silver cloud was that "about 1.6 percent of the zinc used for galvanizing is lead. And the acedic [*sic*] acid of fermentation releases this lead. It combines with the alcohol and water to become a permanent part of it."[20] The fact that the mash fermented in the still only increased the amount of exposure the moonshine had to lead salts. Mason noted, "As the mash ferments in the galvanized tubs, the action of the acid heats the galvanizing and causes it to disperse into the whisky," producing "death-dealing moonshine."[21] While officials initially believed that those poisoned had consumed moonshine imported from Tennessee, they soon discovered a thriving enterprise operated by a "big-time whiskey operator" in Wilkes County turning out "'silver cloud' stills ... in quantity."[22]

The Winston-Salem-area poisonings had a dramatic and immediate impact on illegal liquor sales in North Carolina. ABC officials in Alamance County noted that "moonshine is selling for $16 a case when it usually sells for $40." Donald Mason commented, "We haven't been able to make more than one or two arrests in the past three weeks ... and the reason is the moonshiners and bootleggers are hard put to sell their product."[23] The moonshiners themselves became alarmed at the damage to their sales and reputations the Winston-Salem incidents created. The *High Point Enterprise* reported that some moonshiners had taken matters into their own hands: "The silver cloud was devised by moonshiners as a quick, inexpensive way to make whisky, whisky so deadly however, that some moonshiners will turn in a fellow moonshiner who uses

Agents destroy a silver cloud still. Lead acetate in the metal poisoned many moonshine consumers and led to several deaths in the 1960s. (Courtesy Great Smoky Mountains National Park Archives, National Park Service Collections Preservation Center, Townsend, Tenn.)

such a still as 'bad for business.' Many have destroyed their own silver cloud stills."[24]

The state ABC Board used the tragedy to launch a major publicity campaign warning drinkers of the dangers of moonshine. In June 1960, they distributed 52,000 warning posters with the imprimatur of state health director Dr. J. W. R. Norton, featuring a skull-and-crossbones image and text reading:

> **WARNING**
> DEADLY POISON
> **MOONSHINE LIQUOR**
> **Being Distributed Locally**
> DO NOT DRINK ANY Type of BOOTLEG LIQUOR regardless
> Of source. DEADLY POISONOUS Lead Salts are being

Found in WHITE LIQUOR. This poison can cause **DEATH** or
serious illness as much as a year after drinking.
The next SMALL DRINK May Bring the amount of Lead
Salts in the Body to the concentration point necessary to cause
DEATH![25]

Later, in early 1961, the ABC Board produced cards it issued to hunters and fishermen encouraging them to "help eliminate the poison moonshine deaths in your county" by reporting any still they found in the woods.[26]

In the late 1960s, Alcohol and Tobacco Tax Unit (ATTU) officials launched a campaign in North Carolina patterned after the successful antismoking campaign conducted by the Department of Health, Education, and Welfare. The campaign featured the tagline "Doctors Agree, MOONSHINE KILLS!" The agency produced posters in 1968 with the slogan and put them up in areas reputed to be moonshine hotbeds, and the ATTU even got permission to post them on mail trucks.[27] In 1969, agents distributed hand fans, popular in rural and African American churches, reading:

WARNING!!
MOONSHINE
IS
POISON
Doctors Agree: MOONSHINE KILLS
DON'T YOU BE A VICTIM OF POISONOUS MOONSHINE![28]

In the early 1970s, the agency even produced and distributed cigarette lighters with the slogan and a picture of a "prostrate man with a daisy sprouting from his chest."[29] While it is hard to gauge the effectiveness of the propaganda, ATTU agent Joe Carter believed it had a major impact on driving down demand for moonshine and called it "the most devastating action ever taken against the moonshiners."[30]

Still another factor contributing to the decline in moonshine production was the increasing popularity, and resultant increase in profitability, of "another kind of intoxicant," marijuana. Already on the wrong side of the law, skilled in the arts of concealing their operations, familiar with farming, and having longstanding distribution networks, many longtime moonshiners found the transition to cultivating pot a natural one. In a 1972 editorial, the *Asheville Citizen-Times* pointed out marijuana's advantages to former moonshiners: "The stuff grows wild, naturally, and it can be a lot harder to find than the illegal plumbing of Snuffy Smith's private distillery."[31] In 1976, State Bureau of Investigation agent Greg Radcliff pointed out other reasons moonshiners had moved into the illegal drug business: "Marijuana is easier and brings in more money." In

Hand fan produced by federal agencies in the 1960s warning of the dangers of moonshine. (Photo by Gene Hyde, from the author's personal collection)

addition, Radcliff noted, in the 1970s, sentences for drug violations were lighter than they were for moonshining. Not surprisingly, those areas once known for their moonshine production became known as hotbeds for marijuana. The *High Point Enterprise* quipped, "The good ol' boys who gave Wilkes County in the mountains the reputation as the moonshine capital of North Carolina have gone to pot." Indeed, in 1976, Wilkes led the state in number of pot plants seized.[32]

The move from moonshine to illegal drugs probably had the greatest impact in North Carolina on Robeson County's Lumbee and Tuscarora populations. As county sheriff Hubert Stone noted, "In the 1960s, we destroyed more illegal liquor stills in this county than the whole state put together. Then marijuana came along and liquor dried up. Cocaine, we still have a problem with, especially among the Indians." Robeson County's long dealings with illegal substances and its location along I-95, roughly halfway between Miami and New York, made it an illegal drug hotbed and helped fuel decades of social and political unrest, widespread police corruption, and numerous unsolved murders.[33]

Even as the numbers of actual North Carolina moonshiners declined, depictions of their fictional counterparts, or of real former moonshiners and liquor runners, increased in the 1970s, perhaps due to nostalgia for a dying era where moonshine played such a prominent role. Charlotte filmmaker Charles Elege filmed *Hot Summer in Barefoot County* in the Monroe and Charlotte areas in 1974. The film was unique in that it featured a story about a widow and her three daughters working in the moonshine business. It was also unique in earning an R rating for a skinny-dipping scene.[34]

The notoriety of Tom Wolfe's *Esquire* article and Junior Johnson's fame brought Twentieth Century Fox to North Carolina, leading to the filming of *The Last American Hero* in North Carolina in 1973, the first major Hollywood-produced moonshine movie since *Thunder Road*. Starring Jeff Bridges as Junior Jackson, Valerie Perrine as his love interest, and Gary Busey as Junior's brother Wayne, the movie roughly tracks Junior Johnson's career from illegal liquor runner to stock car racing superstar. Fox shot the film, with a substantial $2.8 million budget, in Catawba and Gaston Counties, with the racing scenes filmed at the Hickory Speedway. Local enthusiasm for the film got Gaston County sheriff Dwight Bean in trouble when he allowed deputy James Warren to participate in a chase scene in his patrol car. While filming the scene, Warren lost control of the car and went off the road, and "the county-owned car was demolished." Warren "suffered two broken ribs" and Sheriff Bean "was unavailable for comment" after the incident.[35] *The Last American Hero* is perhaps best known for its hit theme song, Jim Croce's "I Got a Name."

The most influential moonshine film produced in North Carolina during this period was *The Moonrunners*, a film loosely based on the life and adventures of Union County moonshiner Jerry "Snake" Rushing. In the early 1970s, when Rushing tried to sell a talent agent a semiautobiographical song, the agent encouraged the moonshiner to tape-record some of his stories about making and running illegal liquor. Rushing recorded his memories, and Gy Waldron, an Atlanta television producer, found them so compelling that he shared them with Hollywood B-movie producer Bob Clark, his collaborator on a movie script about moonshining in the south. In 1973, the men hired Rushing as a "technical advisor," and Snake advised the producers, did some stunt driving for the production, and even had a cameo role in the film. *The Moonrunners*, starring Robert Mitchum's son James and narrated by Waylon Jennings as "the Balladeer," premiered in 1974 primarily in drive-in theaters.[36] Ads for the movie in the Carolinas had the words "BASED ON REAL LIFE CAROLINA MOONSHINER JERRY RUSHING OF UNION COUNTY, N.C." at the bottom, acknowledging Rushing's role in the making of the film.[37]

The regional success of *The Moonrunners*, combined with the wild national popularity of the Burt Reynolds movie *Smokey and the Bandit*, sparked Warner Brothers Television's Phil Mandelker's interest. Mandelker encouraged Waldron to adapt his film into a television show. The result was *The Dukes of Hazzard*, which ran on CBS for seven years and whose success far exceeded that of the film that inspired it as well as the expectations of the producers and CBS. Details in *The Dukes of Hazzard* unmistakably identify Rushing as the model for Bo Duke, and facts from his life set up key story lines for the show. Unfortunately for Rushing, although he did have a cameo role as a crooked used car salesman in the series's first season, he received no royalties from the show. In 1979, he sued CBS and the show's producers and received an undisclosed settle-

Jerry Rushing N.C. Moonshine Hall of Famer

In the late 1970s and early 1980s most Americans (and practically all preteen boys) knew and loved Bo Duke, the main character on the CBS sitcom *The Dukes of Hazzard*. Bo was a moonshiner who drove a Hemi-powered Dodge Charger decorated with a Confederate flag and named the General Lee. He regularly outran and outwitted law enforcement—particularly corrupt Hazzard County, Georgia, politician Boss Hogg and sheriff Roscoe P. Coltrane. Bo was an expert with a bow and shared adventures with his brother Luke and his beautiful cousin Daisy. He was a classic "good old boy" who lived an outrageous existence power sliding through life with a twinkle in his eye. American, and international, audiences loved Bo and his exploits and catapulted the series into the Nielsen ratings' top ranks. The show consistently ranked in the top twenty in its first four seasons, topping out during the 1980–81 season with a final ranking of number two, with an average of almost 22 million viewers per episode.

As popular, and as iconic, a figure as Bo Duke was (and is), few people know that the model for the character came from a real-life Union County, North Carolina, moonshiner–liquor hauler par excellence by the name of Jerry Rushing. In his illegal liquor career that spanned from the late 1950s to the mid-1970s, Rushing hauled moonshine along the Carolina backroads and as far away as Florida. As one Associated Press reporter put it, "To Jerry Rushing . . . watching the *Dukes of Hazzard* is like watching his own life on the screen." Indeed, the show's producers obviously borrowed many details and stories from Rushing's life for the show. Rushing had a brother who often ran liquor with him, a beautiful cousin named Dixie who liked to hang around the moonshiners, and an Uncle Dooley who was his mentor in the moonshine business, and he hung out at a beer joint named the Pig Pen run by a man nicknamed Hog Jaw. Most notable, however, is the fact that Rushing named his favorite car—a white 1958 Chrysler 300D—Traveler, after Robert E. Lee's legendary gray horse.

Like many Moonshine Hall of Famers, Rushing grew up in a moonshine-making family and was at least a third-generation moonshiner. He was around moonshine as a young child, watching his daddy, Espy, and granddaddy Atlas work their stills. He made his first liquor run at the age of twelve when his daddy sent him to his Uncle Dooley's for some emergency liquor. By his midteens he had dropped out of school and worked in the illegal liquor business full-time, both making and hauling it.

Rushing—widely known as Snake by this time—embraced the outlaw lifestyle and wore a trademark black Stetson. Folks in Union County knew him for his smooth liquor, his quick temper and quick fists, and his fast cars and skill at outrunning and outwitting law enforcement. Authorities caught him at stills on a couple of occasions, and he served a short term in prison at age seventeen on a charge of larceny and receiving stolen property. But as Rushing proudly noted, authorities never caught him on the highway. He made runs to Wilkes County, Cocke County, or other hotbeds of illegal liquor to buy moonshine—especially when law enforcement became too active in Union County—often hauling it to Florida where it commanded a better price.

Rushing's real claim to fame, however,

came from his celebrity status. Like his Hall of Fame predecessors Amos Owens, Lewis Redmond, and Quill Rose, popular media picked up on Rushing's life story and turned him into a moonshiner celebrity. The classic tripper movie *The Moonrunners* and the character Bo Duke in *The Dukes of Hazard* are both based on Rushing's life.

In the 1970s Rushing became interested in bowhunting (a passion of Bo Duke as well), hunted all over the world, opened the Sherwood Bow Shop in Monroe, and helped found the North Carolina Bow Hunters Association. He became a committed Christian later in life, and his bowhunting friend Michael Barnes worked with the reformed moonshiner to pen a combination Jerry Rushing biography and evangelistic tract entitled *The Real Duke of Hazzard* in 2005. Rushing spent his final years running a hunting preserve in Alexander County not far from the site of the Burgess brothers' Silver Moon nightclub and died in 2016.

While the actual moonshine business was in serious decline by the 1970s, successful films like *Smokey and the Bandit* and television shows like *The Dukes of Hazzard* demonstrated the staying power of the outlaw moonshiner icon, an icon that North Carolina liquor runners like Junior Johnson and Jerry Rushing helped firmly embed in the national consciousness.

ment. In later years he did stunt work and played bit parts in twenty-six different productions, including the movies *Carny*, *The Night the Lights Went Out in Georgia*, and *The Journey of August King*.[38]

By the 1970s, moonshine was seen as a vestige of North Carolina's history, commemorated in nostalgic television shows and movies and bluegrass standards like "Good Old Mountain Dew" and "Rocky Top," and now a subject more suitable for museum exhibits than state's exhibits in courtrooms. Indeed, as evidence of this new, and reduced, status, in 1971 the National Park Service constructed a pioneer stillhouse, complete with furnace and copper still, and started conducting moonshine-making demonstrations at the Pioneer Farmstead site just inside the Great Smoky Mountains National Park near Cherokee. John Parris opened his Roamin' the Mountains column in the *Asheville Citizen-Times* on the demonstrations with a nostalgic explanation of the park service's motivations:

> The old-time blockader, the mountain man of a thousand stories and a thousand legends, has disappeared from the laurel thickets of the Great Smokies where he practiced his ancient craft.
>
> But the folks of the National Park Service have preserved his moonshine still, and now they are operating it so posterity can see what blockading was like when the old-time blockader held sway in the hills.[39]

A North Carolina Moonshine Playlist

Even as moonshining died out in the 1970s and 1980s, moonshine-related tunes remained popular among bluegrass and country music fans. Hee Haw *star Grandpa Jones performed one of the most popular versions of "Good Old Mountain Dew." (Courtesy of the Country Music Hall of Fame, Nashville, Tenn.)*

North Carolina moonshine and its moonshiners have long inspired songs written in and about the state and enjoyed by its people. Given that, here are my suggestions for an appropriate playlist to listen to while sipping North Carolina moonshine, reading this book, or both:

"Good Old Mountain Dew." No moonshine-song playlist would be complete without this song. Its roots in the Biltmore Forest School, original composition by Bascom Lamar Lunsford, and adoption as an anthem by countless North Carolina Boy and Girl Scout troops and summer camps make it a classic Tar Heel song. Grandpa Jones's energetic version sets the standard in my book, but for a North Carolina list, I'd recommend Watauga County legend Doc Watson's rendering.

"White Lightnin'." Another no-brainer. While Texan J. P. Richardson wrote the song and another Texan, George Jones, made it famous, its up-front location in North Carolina and its status as a country music classic put it near the top of my list.

"Rye Whiskey" ("Jack of Diamonds"). While the song has no direct North Carolina connection, other than being sung and performed by countless Tar Heels, its history traces this state's moonshine heritage. Like North Carolina moonshine, the song's roots come from the British Isles. Musicologists generally trace the song to the Scottish family tune "Toddlin Hame." Also like our state's moonshine, the song has strong African American influences, with one famous early recorded version performed by bluesman Blind Lemon Jefferson. For this playlist I'd recommend Graham County native Jim Tom Hedrick's version performed on the *Moonshiners* television show.

"If the River Was Whiskey." While

Charlie Poole and his North Carolina Ramblers did not record a song that directly references moonshine, he wrote drinking songs aplenty. His connections to the moonshine business, as both a distiller and as a drinker, make "If the River Was Whiskey" an appropriate addition to this list. The song begins:

> If the river was whiskey, and I was a duck,
> I'd dive to the bottom and I'd never come up.

Unfortunately, Poole "dove to the bottom" of Whiskey River far too many times and died far too young. Fortunately, he left wonderful music as his legacy.

"Wreck on the Highway." While this Dorsey Dixon classic is a downer, we have to acknowledge moonshine's downside. In the song, Dixon describes a scene enacted many times on North Carolina highways and reflects prohibition's strong roots in the state. Roy Acuff performs the classic version.

"The Ballad of Thunder Road." This song, cowritten by Robert Mitchum and Jack Marshall for the classic movie *Thunder Road*, tells the story of a fateful moonshine run from Harlan, Kentucky, to Knoxville, Tennessee. It does have strong North Carolina bona fides, however, as it mentions Asheville in the lyrics, and Mitchum filmed the movie entirely in Asheville and surrounding counties. Mitchum did not perform the song for the movie, but his version, which made the Billboard Top 100 twice, is the best.

"Good Ol' Boys." Waylon Jennings wrote and performed this theme song for *The Dukes of Hazzard*, which takes place in Georgia. But since producers based the TV show on Monroe native Jerry Rushing's life and exploits, it's a song that should make any North Carolina moonshine song list. Besides, *Dukes* was probably the top-rated show in North Carolina markets in its heyday.

"Rocky Top." Folks generally associate this classic moonshine song with Tennessee, as it identifies the location in the lyrics as Rocky Top, Tennessee. It is also the unofficial fight song for the University of Tennessee and was written by Felice and Boudreaux Bryant in Gatlinburg. That said, North Carolina can make a legitimate claim to the song. Those familiar with the Great Smoky Mountains know that the Bryants misidentified Rocky Top's location, which is actually over the state line, in North Carolina. Of course, it is also a song extremely popular in the state and one requested, often ad nauseam, by bluegrass music concertgoers.

"Play Rocky Top (or I'll Punch Your Lights)." Since "Rocky Top" made the list, we need to include this song written by Bill Hicks of Chapel Hill's Red Clay Ramblers. While the song does not mention moonshine, it reflects the frustration musicians feel when they get constant requests to play the song. It's performed by a quintessentially North Carolina group, and it's lots of fun.

"Carolina Moonshine Man." Not as well known as many songs on the list, but a worthy modern addition written and performed by bluegrass musicians Lou Reid & Carolina. Reid grew up on a tobacco farm in Moore Springs.

The business was not totally dead, however, and occasionally reports surfaced of some local resurgence in the 1980s and 1990s. In 1988, the Associated Press reported that "good old mountain dew is making a comeback in drink houses . . . after several years of decline" in the Winston-Salem area. The report noted that lower sugar prices and a reversal in sentencing guidelines—which made marijuana-production penalties much higher than those for moonshining—led Wilkes and Surry County producers to go back to their old trade.[40] The Associated Press also reported a spike in the Piedmont and eastern North Carolina in 1993 and declared, "Alcohol agents in Wake County have made more arrests and seized more liquor in the past three years than they did in the previous 15."[41] In response to the energy crisis and environmental concerns related to fossil fuels, a move allowing farmers and loggers to produce their own corn-based ethanol to operate their machinery also led some to skirt the law and make and market a drinkable version of their "fuel." In 1994, agents arrested Thomas Henry Dodson, a logger in Transylvania County, for violating the terms of his fuel-alcohol permit when state authorities found eighty-four gallons of moonshine and a sixty-gallon still on his property.[42]

However, these resurgences were brief and localized, and the once-thriving business of making moonshine in North Carolina seemed destined for extinction as the twenty-first century dawned. But John Parris, a longtime observer of North Carolina's moonshine business, and other pundits should have known better than to relegate the moonshiner to "posterity." Indeed, while Parris would not live to see it, moonshine experienced an unlikely renaissance in the twenty-first century.

15

MOONSHINE REVIVAL

Widespread reports of the demise of moonshine in North Carolina were decidedly premature, and an amazing revival began around the turn of the twenty-first century that made moonshine both culturally and economically relevant for the first time in decades. However, moonshine in the twenty-first century took on a decidedly strange and even postmodern spin. A number of factors contributed to this moonshine renaissance. One of those was the arrival of the internet, where one could find a multiplicity of recipes for the illegal product and the supplies and equipment for making it. Suppliers designed most of the contraptions for sale on Craigslist and other sites for use on a kitchen stovetop, although regular stills were and still are available. The latent curiosity people still possessed fed this market and led thousands to try their hand at making liquor. Most failed miserably, produced pretty vile, undrinkable stuff, gave up, and went back to their local Alcohol Beverage Control store. Some found they had a knack for it and started supplying friends and family with "keeper liquor." For the most part, local, state, and federal alcohol enforcement agents have ignored these small-scale operations as long as the distillers don't try to sell their product.

Some of these twenty-first-century moonshiners have attracted the attention of law enforcement, however. One of the most famous busts involved Dean Combs, a former journeyman NASCAR driver from Wilkes County. Dean is the nephew of moonshiner Charlie Combs, a confederate of the Burgess brothers and speedway owner. Curious about his family heritage, Dean Combs invested a considerable amount of time and money into constructing a large stainless-steel still hidden in an outbuilding at a defunct go-kart track he owned near the now-abandoned North Wilkesboro Speedway. Combs told reporters: "It's something I was always interested in. I wanted to see if I could make something drinkable." He evidently had the knack for making good liquor because he was soon producing hundreds of gallons of corn-sugar liquor and even apple brandy, a time-consuming effort. Combs asserted, "There's not been any good apple brandy out here for years. It's better than what you buy at a store."[1]

While Combs claimed the liquor he made "was mostly cold medicine" and that he did not sell it but gave it away to friends and family, the amount he produced attracted the attention of State Alcohol Law Enforcement agents. In March 2009, authorities raided the still and seized 200 gallons of moonshine and 3,000 pounds of sugar. The still was so large and heavy that the agents were at a loss as to how to destroy it. Agents claimed the boiler alone weighed 1,000 pounds. Finally, Combs himself intervened, hooked a chain to his tractor and hauled the still into a nearby field where authorities blew it up as Combs filmed the whole thing on his cell phone. While Combs did not end up serving time, the state fined him and he had to answer lots of questions from the IRS. He wrapped up his experience with reporters and said his main problem was that "I guess I gave someone a quart I shouldn't have."[2]

While many North Carolinians experimented with making moonshine after the turn of the century, it was a pair of real, career moonshiners—Jim Tom Hedrick and Popcorn Sutton—who sparked North Carolina's twenty-first-century renaissance. The pair gave the old business its most postmodern manifestation and took it to levels of popularity it had not seen in many years. Hedrick and Sutton took advantage of the popular image of the moonshiner and sold it back to unsuspecting individuals, generally tourists and media folks. The two had very similar roots, both born and raised in rural mountainous areas of western North Carolina, Hedrick near the Snowbird community in Graham County (one of the most remote areas in the eastern United States) and Sutton in the Hemphill Bald area of Haywood County. Hedrick was born around 1940, while Sutton came into the world in 1946. Hedrick claims to have started out as a moonshiner at the age of fifteen, when "one of the best whisky makers that ever come along learned me how."[3] He later revealed that his teacher was "an old guy by the name of Clyde Barker," who broke at least two federal laws by making moonshine and making it on federal land in the Great Smoky Mountains National Park in the early 1960s. Hedrick hauled in sacks of sugar for Barker and did other physical labor in exchange for a quart of moonshine a day and the knowledge of how to make liquor. His parents did not care for his career choice, and his sister Pat Williams later recalled, "Mom and dad sure didn't approve of that."[4]

Sutton grew up in the mountains above Maggie Valley in Haywood County and came from a long line of moonshiners. He learned the craft in Cocke County, Tennessee, working with some of that county's legendary distillers. After a few years he went back over the Smokies to Maggie Valley and made liquor with his

Popcorn Sutton stands next to his trademark Ford Model A truck with a moonshine still in the back. (Courtesy of Don Dudenbostel)

daddy "in one place for 20 years, never was caught at that location because we was careful as hell."[5]

Sutton got busted three times—for tax evasion, possession and sale of untaxed alcohol, and assault with a deadly weapon—before he became a celebrity, but he received probation on each occasion. For him, arrests came with the territory: "If you're worried about the law you shouldn't be doing this. They gonna catch you sooner or later."[6] Authorities, surprisingly, never seem to have busted Hedrick for making moonshine. "The law tried to catch me," he told an *Asheville Citizen-Times* reporter in 1984. "Never have yet. But they've been pretty close."[7] He has, however, had numerous arrests for drunk driving and claimed in the 1999 documentary *Moonshine* to hold the record in North Carolina for DUI arrests, with twenty-one.[8]

By the 1980s, both had reputations in their communities as moonshiners

Jim Tom Hedrick and Marvin "Popcorn" Sutton

N.C. Moonshine Hall of Famers

Jim Tom Hedrick and Popcorn Sutton are obviously deserving of induction into this Hall of Fame (and Shame), and both make it in based on one previously unmentioned criterion: they both have brands of legal liquor named after them. Two other inductees share this distinction: Lewis Redmond, whose picture graced the bottles of Redmond's Hand Mash in the late 1890s, and Junior Johnson, who partners with Piedmont Distillers to produce Junior Johnson's Midnight Moon.

In November 2010, after Sutton's death, Jamey Grosser publicly launched Popcorn Sutton's Tennessee White Whiskey in front of a crowd of country music royalty in Nashville. Grosser, a former professional motocross racer who purchased Sutton's recipes and studied his techniques, started the "legal moonshine" enterprise in partnership with Hank Williams Jr. and Pam Sutton, Popcorn's widow. The company—which now produces its liquor in Cocke County—advertises that it "make[s] Popcorn Sutton using the same recipe and rebel attitude as our namesake." Sutton's "legal moonshine" is available in much of the nation in liquor stores from Philadelphia to Denver.

Hedrick got his own brand of liquor in 2014, when Sugarlands Distilling Company in Gatlinburg, Tennessee, launched Jim Tom's Unaged Rye Moonshine. Sugarlands advertises Hedrick's liquor as "an earthy balance between spicy rye and toasted grains with hints of black pepper" and claims it "pairs well with black cherry, dark chocolate, licorice, sorghum and cola." I can't imagine a better ad for a liquor named for one of the first postmodern moonshiners.

Indeed, the stories of Hedrick and Sutton well represent this postmodern turn. For both, their significance lies not in the traditional moonshiner skills of making good moonshine or audaciously and effectively evading law enforcement. No, their greatest legacy lay, as it often did for their ancestor moonshiners, in their adaptability and their agency. In this case, that meant each man's ability to respond to the times and play the role of "authentic" moonshiner in the media, to give the American people what they expect. And to smile, wink at the camera, and head off to the bank with the proceeds of his "authenticity" on his moped or in his Ford Model A truck.

and as local characters. In addition to his DUIs, Hedrick was known in Graham County as the survivor of a head-on collision with a station wagon while driving his Harley-Davidson motorcycle over 100 miles per hour on Halloween 1962.[9] He lived simply, making moonshine, dumpster diving, and crafting miniature copper stills, which he sold to tourists. As his sister Pat Williams observed, "He don't care what kind of shack he lives in. He says as long as he has a loaf of bread, and a pound of bologna, and a pound of cheese, he's fine. He don't care which way the wind blows. He's happy. He's happy the way he is."[10] Folks in

Graham County also knew Hedrick as a big talker and storyteller who often regaled spectators who came to watch the demonstrations of corn liquor making he put on for tourists at special heritage events and at local businesses. Hedrick would set up a copper still at events like the Great Smoky Mountains Heritage Festival in Robbinsville. "All this is to show people how it's done and how our folks here in the mountains have made 'cork [probably "corn"—the reporter most likely misunderstood given Hedrick's thick mountain accent] liquor' as long as anybody can remember, and even beyond that."[11]

Sutton developed the same kind of reputation in Maggie Valley and looked and acted the part of the moonshiner for the tourists who came to the area. He generally sported overalls, a flannel shirt, and a well-worn felt fedora and drove around in a Model A truck with a still in the back. Sutton also had a reputation for his salty language and for his series of marriages (he was supposedly married four times and never divorced) and love affairs that produced an estimated twelve children, only one of whom he legally acknowledged. Varying stories circulate involving the source of Popcorn Sutton's name, but all the stories include an uncooperative popcorn machine that took his money but produced no treat. Whether he then shot the machine with a pistol or hammered it with a pool cue has never been affirmatively determined, but whatever happened lived on in the nickname, which Sutton embraced. Like Hedrick, Sutton also conducted demonstrations of moonshine making, most notably at Mountain Heritage Days at nearby Western Carolina University.[12]

Both moonshiners were also surprisingly religious. The *Moonshine* documentary shows Hedrick singing along (and he definitely is no stranger to the words) to the hymns at a Wednesday night prayer meeting in a small Baptist church. It also features "ordained Bible minister" Gilford Williams helping him make liquor and ends with Hedrick playing "What a Friend We Have in Jesus" on a lap organ he found in a dumpster dive.[13] Sutton shared that his grandfather used the proceeds of a liquor run to help build the first Baptist church constructed in Hemphill.[14] When photographer Don Dudenbostel asked him if he could come by on a Sunday for a photo shoot, Sutton responded, "Hell no, goddammit. If it's Sunday I'll be in church."[15]

Until 1999, however, Hedrick's and Sutton's reputations were strictly local and few knew these mountain characters outside the immediate area. That began to change around the turn of the century, and over the next fifteen years, both developed an international reputation, as did their mountain moonshine. The road to fame for Hedrick came when Kelly L. Riley, a student at the Rhode Island School of Design, discovered the moonshiner and came to Graham County in 1999 to film a short documentary. The resulting film, simply entitled *Moonshine*, became a cult classic after Riley screened it at several film festivals and bootleg copies spread rapidly throughout the region. The film features

Hedrick hauling the pieces of a moonshine still out of the woods, assembling it, and making a run of illegal corn liquor. The highlight of the film, however, is Hedrick's ongoing commentary and his observations on moonshine, life, religion, motorcycle crashes, and his many DUI convictions. It also shows his love of music as he belts out snatches of "The Ballad of Thunder Road" and "Cigarettes and Whiskey and Wild, Wild Women" while he makes his moonshine.[16]

About the same time that Riley discovered Hedrick, Sutton decided that he ought to write a book about his life. In collaboration with girlfriend Ernestine Upchurch, who wrote down Sutton's words and translated some of them into comprehensible English, he self-published a book titled *Me and My Likker*. The book—in a sort of postmodern, stream-of-consciousness manner—tells Sutton's life story with frequent asides into whatever caught his attention at the time. He does give a warning up front that "this book is not going to be wrote in chapters or uniform in any way," and he does not lie. In the book, Sutton began to refine the image he carefully crafted over the next nine years as the last of the old-time moonshiners, the practitioner of a dying craft. "I am one of the last true moonshiners left that knows how to make likker the way the old moonshiners did." He also explained why he kept doing it: "Making likker is the hardest work you have ever done. But once you get in to it, it gets in your blood. You won't quit."[17]

Sutton followed up on his book with a decidedly amateur video with the same title. In the video he instructs viewers, using as much profanity as he can possibly squeeze into each sentence, on the nuances, and dangers, of producing moonshine, using a huge 300-gallon stainless-steel gas-fired still.[18] Sutton marketed his book and video—and later souvenir clocks and T-shirts reading "Jesus turned the water into wine. I turned it into liquor.—Popcorn Sutton"—at his Maggie Valley junk shop and in area restaurants, gas stations, and barbershops. Like *Moonshine*, Sutton's book and video soon became underground hits in the region, and his reputation began to spread beyond Haywood County.[19]

In 2002, another documentarian, Neal Hutcheson, discovered Hedrick and Sutton and gave both significant air time in a film entitled *Mountain Talk*. The film was a production of the North Carolina Language and Life Project, an ongoing endeavor started by North Carolina State University English professor Walt Wolfram to document the unique dialects of North Carolina and the United States at large. While the focus of the film was on mountain dialect, and Hedrick's and Sutton's speech provided the film with fascinating footage, both talked a bit about their experience in the moonshine business. In addition, footage of Hedrick cruising around Graham County on his moped (he had evidently, once again, lost his driver's license since the filming of *Moonshine*) and Sutton driving Hutcheson around in his Ford Model A pickup further heightened their images as genuine mountain "characters."[20] However, the most important by-product of the film was the ongoing, long-term collaboration between Hutcheson and Sutton, a collaboration that would bring the Maggie Valley moonshiner to a national audience.

That partnership began when, not long after making *Mountain Talk*, Hutcheson filmed Sutton driving around on dirt mountain roads in his Model A to find an appropriate still site, setting up a small, copper, wood-fired still, and making what Sutton repeatedly told the camera was "the last damn run of likker I'll ever make." It is apparent that in the time between filming *Me and My Likker* and his work with Hutcheson, Sutton had reinvented his image a good deal to better fit his narrative of being the "last true old-time moonshiner" making 'shine the "way the old moonshiners did." His still in his first video was decidedly modern, made of stainless steel and fired by propane gas, not very romantic, even industrial. He operated it in a cinderblock outbuilding on his Maggie Valley property. By the time Hutcheson filmed him, Sutton depicted himself as an old-time, copper-pot craftsman, making liquor the old-fashioned way up in a remote "holler" in the Smokies and hauling it in his antique truck, the last of a dying breed. Of course, the prime feature of the footage was Sutton's ongoing, profane commentary on making and drinking "likker," women, and even the raccoon penis bone that he stuck through his trademark fedora and used to ensure that the condensed moonshine flowed smoothly into a collection container.[21] Like many other southern Appalachian natives, Sutton was very artful in figuring out what image the world wanted and then happily selling it back to them. As his biographer, Tom Jester, put it, "Yes, Popcorn was the embodiment of a colorful stereotype, and he knew how to work it."[22] Sutton's longtime friend Doug O'Neil of the *Newport (Tenn.) Plain Talk* asserted, "He gave the world what they expected of a moonshiner. He dressed the part and he talked the talk."[23]

Hutcheson made a rough cut of the footage he shot, entitled it *This Is the Last Dam Run of Likker I'll Ever Make*, and turned it over to Sutton, who added VHS copies of the film to his collection of products offered at his junk store. It shocked the documentarian when the film became a "bootleg sensation." "It just went everywhere so fast," particularly in the Southeast.[24] Footage from *Last Dam Run* soon began a long and profitable life for both Sutton and Hutcheson. Cable television company CMT used footage from the project for "Moonshine Madness," a 2004 episode of its *Most Shocking* program, which gave Sutton a national audience for the first time.[25]

Yet another postmodern turn in the North Carolina moonshine business came in 2005 with the arrival in the state of so-called legal moonshine. Of course, as many observers have noted, "if it's legal, it ain't moonshine." Reporter Clay Risen even wrote an article in the *Atlantic* in 2011 entitled "The World's Silliest Liquor: Fake Moonshine."[26] Be that as it may, the "legal moonshine" business was a by-product of changes in the laws regarding the manu-

Piedmont Distillers, producer of Midnight Moon, was the first "legal moonshine" distiller in North Carolina. (Courtesy of Piedmont Distillers, Madison, N.C.)

facture of liquor passed in many states, including North Carolina in the 2000s, that allowed small-batch distillers to operate legally and profitably. For many consumers "legal moonshine" provides the opportunity to satisfy their curiosity about the taste of moonshine but also offers the safety of consuming a product subject to state and federal health regulations. In addition, producers soon realized that most folks do not have a palate that appreciates even good corn liquor, so they began dropping the proof and adding flavors such as apple, peach, lemon, strawberry, and dozens of other varieties.

The oldest such distillery in North Carolina is Piedmont Distillers in Madison, a business founded by Joe Michalek, a New York native and former R. J. Reynolds Tobacco Company marketing executive. In 2005 in an old train depot, he started producing a spiced eighty-proof corn liquor product he named Catdaddy. While Michalek had some initial success with his "legal moonshine," his business really took off in 2007 when he partnered with former moonshiner and NASCAR legend Junior Johnson to produce Junior Johnson's Midnight Moon. The product, supposedly following an "old Johnson family recipe," exploded in popularity.[27] Making some "legal moonshine" even more postmodern, and the dirty secret of many such producers, Piedmont began producing less and less of its base liquor and started "sourcing grain-neutral spirits." In other words, Piedmont's products are made using a base of high-proof (generally around 190-proof) ethanol the company imports in bulk from elsewhere, probably the Midwest Corn Belt.[28] Be that as it may, Piedmont built on moonshine's growing popularity—fueled by the likes of Hedrick and Sutton, Johnson's legendary status, and connections to NASCAR—and quickly became a leading producer with nationwide distribution.

Imitators in North Carolina, however, followed slowly, as the regulatory environment was still fairly onerous and start-up costs high. But the business received a considerable boost in the late 2000s as Popcorn Sutton followed up on his local and regional popularity to become a nationally recognized media superstar. As Sutton's fame spread, regional and national media, as well as ordinary people who read about him or saw one of his videos, began to beat a path to his Maggie Valley junk shop's doorstep. He told a reporter from the *Asheville Citizen-Times* in 2005, "Likker put me in the spotlight. My likker has been in every state and to England, Scotland, France, places like that. People bought it here and took it back with them." James Carver's Maggie Valley Restaurant even put up a sign reading, "Maggie Valley, Home of Popcorn Sutton." Carver commented on his friend's influence, "Popcorn is a good ambassador for the valley and promotes tourism. He has friends all over. He talks to people, encourages them to come to Maggie."[29] In 2007, producers from Moore Huntley Productions reached his doorstep and made him a key part of their documentary *Hillbilly: The Real Story*, which aired for several years on the History Channel. While ostensibly starring Billy Ray Cyrus, who served as the narrator for the film, Sutton really stole the show.[30]

By this time, Neal Hutcheson realized what a gold mine he had and recut the footage he had shot back in 2002 into an hour-long documentary entitled *The Last One*. He hit the festival circuit with the film, which quickly gained significant notoriety. The film also aired on PBS stations across the nation, and later on the Documentary Channel, and won a 2009 Southeast Emmy Award for Best Cultural Documentary.[31]

The thing that probably gave moonshine its greatest public relations boost came, ironically, with Popcorn Sutton's suicide in 2009. Just as Sutton reached the height of celebrity, like many a tragic character, hubris brought it all crashing to an end. While tourists bought the occasional Popcorn T-shirt or clock, what everyone really wanted was genuine Popcorn-made moonshine. It turned out that the moonshine Sutton had made for Neal Hutcheson back in 2002 was not "the last damn run of likker" he'd "ever make," and Sutton returned to cranking out the sugar liquor with a 1,000-gallon still on his Parrottsville, Tennessee, farm to supply the demand. He also needed the money to cover his growing medical expenses for multiple ailments, including a recent cancer diagnosis. His friends tried to warn the moonshiner he was flying too close to the sun by trying to be a major media figure while making lots of moonshine, but he ignored their warnings. Mark Ramsey told him, "Old man, you can't be a movie star and make liquor too." Sutton replied, "You can't sell it if nobody knows you got it."[32]

However, Sutton's open defiance of the law drew the attention of federal agents, who launched an undercover operation to catch him. A fire that broke out in an outbuilding on his Parrottsville farm in April 2007 aided their investigation. When the fire department and local law enforcement arrived to put out the blaze, they discovered the remains of a large still and 650 gallons of "untaxed alcohol" in another outbuilding. Local officials charged Sutton with "possession of untaxed liquor in excess of three gallons," but once again, he received a light sentence, two years' probation.[33]

The probation sentence seemed to embolden Sutton, and he resumed his moonshining even as federal authorities began closing in. In February and March 2008, federal undercover agents bought "large amounts of moonshine" from Sutton. He recalled selling the liquor to the agents: "Undercover guy got me, see. He'd made buys off of me before and he got me to where he's wantin' to buy me out, everything I had. I thought that was all right, you know. He's supposed to be a backer, said he'd knowed me for five years. Hell, I've sold likker to everybody in the world. I can't remember who I've sold it to and who I didn't. So he just kept on till he got the goods on me and they come down on me, all in one day."[34]

That day came on 13 March, when twenty-two agents from the Bureau of Alcohol, Tobacco, and Firearms raided Sutton's farm and a storage building in Maggie Valley. They found three 1,000-gallon stills, 850 gallons of moonshine, and "hundreds of gallons of mash and other ingredients used to make liquor." They also discovered firearms and ammunition, which added charges for firearm possession by a convicted felon to the illegal liquor charges. Sutton faced up to twenty-five years in federal penitentiary and some serious fines if convicted on all charges, essentially a life sentence for a sixty-one-year-old chain smoker already in poor health. Special agent Jim Cavanaugh—a principal figure in the (in)famous Branch Davidian compound raid in Waco, Texas, in 1993—defended Sutton's arrest: "Moonshine is romanticized in folklore and the movies. The truth, though, is that moonshine is a dangerous health issue and breeds other crime. The illegal moonshine business is fraud on taxpayers in Tennessee and across the country."[35]

Sutton pleaded guilty to the charges and—despite his request for leniency, a number of petitions calling for his release, and a Facebook campaign entitled "Leave Popcorn Sutton Alone"—the judge sentenced him to eighteen months in a federal penitentiary. At this point, Sutton paid the ultimate penalty for his celebrity. He had sworn publicly that he would not go back to prison and—priding himself on being a man of his word—on 16 March 2009 committed suicide. He sent his wife Pam to the grocery store, ran PVC pipe from the tailpipe into the trunk of his favorite car—a green 1960s Ford Fairlane that he'd paid for with three jugs of moonshine—and cranked the car up. A public funeral held in October brought out a crowd of more than 350 people—including country music star Hank Williams Jr.—and featured an antique hearse pulled by two black Percheron horses, a procession through Parrottsville, and private internment on the family property. News media reported his death nationally, including an obituary in the *Wall Street Journal*.[36]

Sutton's demise, however, did not end his fame and, if anything, heightened it. His legend financially benefitted Neal Hutcheson, the producers of *Hillbilly: The Real Story*, and Sutton's last wife, Pam, to whom he had left 2,000 autographed copies of *Me and My Likker*, which she sold for fifty dollars a copy. Hutcheson recut old footage and added some that he had filmed between 2002 and the time of the moonshiner's death—including scenes of Sutton meeting the "Dancing Outlaw," YouTube star Jesco White—and produced a new film entitled *Popcorn Sutton: A Hell of a Life*.[37]

Most notably, Sutton, or at least footage of Sutton filmed by Hutcheson, became the star of the 2011 first season of a reality show on the Discovery Channel titled *Moonshiners*. The show's first season featured the exploits of two Climax, Virginia, moonshiners, Tim Smith and his comedic-relief sidekick, Steven Ray Tickle (known simply as Tickle). Producers interspersed Sutton clips with "reality" pieces featuring Smith and Tickle. The Sutton segments fit perfectly with the show's premise of depicting "real-life" moonshiners at work plying their craft. And it all fit perfectly with Sutton's postmodern spin on the real-life moonshiner playing one in the popular media while emphasizing the popular stereotypes of moonshiners still prevalent in American society. In fact, Smith and Tickle are almost as adept as Sutton was at selling the stereotype back to the American people. The show quickly became a hit, one of the top-rated cable shows on the air.[38]

Sutton's death and the rise of *Moonshiners* also greatly boosted Jim Tom Hedrick's career. He became a regular on the show in its second season, ostensibly replacing Sutton in the authentic, old-time moonshiner role. In the third and fourth seasons, Discovery even aired special episodes featuring Hedrick. *Moonshiners* producers followed him as he tried to "make it" in the country music business singing such favorites as the classic "Rye Whiskey" and his original tune "Golly That's Good/Moonshine Man," which he made into a popular music video.[39]

The success of Piedmont Distillers and Junior Johnson's Midnight Moon, combined with the popular culture moonshine craze fueled by Sutton, Hedrick, and now *Moonshiners*, also sparked a boom in the North Carolina distillery business that continues to this day. The first "legal moonshiners" to follow in Joe Michalek's footsteps were Keith Nordan and Chris Hollifield of Carolina Distillery, "after about a year of Monday afternoon meetings around a table at a local restaurant." The pair started producing apple brandy in 2009 in an old carriage house in Lenoir. They use apples from the Perry Lowe Orchards in Moravian Falls. While their new 40,000-square-foot distillery, in the basement of an old Rose's department store building on Lenoir's main street, has an industrial look with the 1,000-gallon fermenting barrels and huge copper still, Nordan asserts, "We're traditional, old-school. We're strictly the way they did it a hundred years ago."[40]

On the heels of Carolina Distillery's foray into the market, two very different operations began in Asheville. Troy Ball and her husband, Charlie, a successful real estate developer, moved to Buncombe County from Austin, Texas, in 2004 looking for a place similar to Austin that would provide a healthier environment for their two special-needs sons. They bought an investment property in a rural area thirty minutes north of Asheville and experienced moonshine for the first time when some of their friendly neighbors brought them some. While most of what they received was pretty vile, neighbor Forest Jarrett told Ball about "keeper moonshine," taken from the run's heart, that skilled illegal distillers kept for themselves, family, and close friends. Jarrett brought her some "keeper," and unlike the other stuff she had sampled, Ball found it "very smooth and easy to drink." This sparked an idea in Ball's mind, as she was "interested in finding a business that I could create."[41]

That business became the Asheville Distilling Company, which produces Troy & Sons whiskeys. But before that business could begin, Ball needed to learn something about making liquor. She solicited help from longtime moonshiners whose trust she gained, including one from Alabama, whose recipe she decided to try herself. She and Charlie made a small still using a pressure cooker and started experimenting in 2008. In this experimental phase, the Balls discovered Crooked Creek corn, an heirloom variety grown by John McEntire on his farm near Old Fort. Best known for the grits it produces, Crooked Creek turned out to be a perfect variety for corn liquor. The Balls got a permit from the state to build a still to develop a legal product, started working on their recipes, and set up their operation on McEntire's farm. As Ball recalls, "Those were some of the best days, that year and a half or so that we spent there in Old Fort just experimenting with formulas and recipes and different grain mixtures and different filtration techniques." The Balls also solicited advice from pioneering Asheville beer brewer Oscar Wong of Highland Brewing, who counseled them on navigating the maze of regulations and marketing their product.[42]

With the Asheville real estate market mired in recession, Troy and Charlie

Troy Ball, founder and owner of Asheville Distilling Company, which produces a decidedly "high-class" version of "legal moonshine" with its Troy & Sons products. (Courtesy of Asheville Distilling Company, Asheville, N.C.)

decided in 2010 to take a leap of faith that a moonshine operation using high-quality ingredients, exacting standards, and attractive packaging would be successful, and they made a major investment in a German-made 2,000-liter Kothe distillery and started production. With the blonde, attractive, and charismatic Troy fronting their products and with marketing that emphasized her compelling story as a pioneering female distiller of "legal moonshine," the Troy & Sons products became almost immediate hits. The Balls also found a successful formula marketing their products in elite circles as a cocktail base. Indeed, from her first taste of "keeper moonshine," Ball saw an opportunity: "I just got to thinking, why aren't we drinking American cocktails instead of Russian vodka cocktails? It just seemed like the hole in the doughnut—what was missing from the marketplace. It was also very authentic, an American story. And I thought that was something that would appeal to people." She was right, and soon media outlets like *Southern Living*, *The Today Show*, and even *Moonshiners* came calling and helped the Balls open up markets for their products, from Miami's South Beach to Disney World and Los Angeles.[43]

Cody Bradford of Howling Moon Distillery also started making "legal moonshine" in the Asheville area not long after Asheville Distilling opened, but his story could not be more different from Ball's. While Ball came to moonshine later in life, corn liquor is part of Bradford's DNA, and it is unlikely that marketing his looks is going to sell much moonshine. His roots are in Yancey County, and the liquor-making tradition goes back in his family for generations. Indeed, legendary Yancey County moonshiner-outlaw Hiram Wilson is Bradford's distant cousin. After earning a history degree from the University of North Carolina Asheville in 2005, Bradford worked in retail for several years, living modestly and saving his money. In 2010 he made the move to making moonshine, not with an expensive state-of-the-art German still but with a stainless-steel model he fabricated himself and set up in the basement of a house in a working-class Asheville suburb. As author John Trump put it, "The distillery is unpretentious. Straightforward. If there has ever been a perfect place to make moonshine, this is it."[44] Bradford's main desire from the start was to "do it real," so he avoids fancy column stills and makes moonshine the way his ancestors did. As for his competitors, "I tried some of it because I love moonshine, drank it my whole life, and just wanted to see what it was about in stores, and it was just vodka. That's all it was. I was like, 'Wow, this isn't moonshine.' I tried several of them and they were all the same."[45]

Howling Moon is a business built on family and tradition. Bradford and his brother Austin do all the production, maintenance, and marketing, with occasional help from their dad, Darick, who made some moonshine himself in his day, and longtime friend Chivous Downey. They really do use an old family recipe. Bradford noted, "My dad used the same recipe, and my grandfather

Fourth-generation moonshiner Cody Bradford, founder and owner of Howling Moon Distillery in Woodfin. (Courtesy of Cody Bradford)

and great-uncle used the same recipe, and my great-great-grandfather used the same recipe. I know that for sure." On one of his three stills, he even uses a more-than-100-year-old copper condenser fabricated by his great-grandfather that he found in a family barn. Bradford makes his liquor in traditional stills encased in stone to hold in the heat and even uses the old-fashioned method of preventing steam leaks by using rye paste at critical joints. While his operation is not huge, he stays plenty busy trying to keep up with demand, despite having to market the product as well as make it. Indeed, folks have found their way to his still, including *Moonshiners*; Norman Reedus, star of the *The Walking Dead*, who filmed part of an episode of *Ride with Norman Reedus* there; and even *Monday Night Football*, which did a feature on Howling Moon when the show came to Charlotte for a game. As Bradford observed, "We put out a real product, and we've done really good with it. We've got a lot of recognition. I've got over a thousand gallons' worth of capacity in all my stills, and I can't keep up with North Carolina."[46]

Since 2010, the craft distilling business has taken off in North Carolina, with almost forty distilleries operating by 2018. Not all make moonshine, but this is the favored product at most of these operations. Not surprisingly, distilleries have popped up in places with long traditions of moonshining in the state. In

A North Carolina Moonshine Tour

If after reading this book you're curious about actually seeing the places mentioned, here's a recommended tour that will take you across the state from Manteo to (near) Murphy.

Manteo's a good place to start, as this is the location of the famous Lost Colony, where Europeans first arrived in what would become North Carolina. I don't have any evidence, but I suspect that the colonists brought a still or two with them. Be that as it may, you can visit the site where the Lost Colony drama is performed every summer and where Andy Griffith got his start as a professional actor playing the role of Sir Walter Raleigh. Head west from Manteo on U.S. 64 for twenty-five miles to Buffalo City, now part of the Alligator National Wildlife Refuge. There's not much to see, but you can gain insight into the kinds of places moonshiners plied their craft in North Carolina's Tidewater.

Keep heading west on U.S. 64 to Johnston County and the stomping grounds of the legendary Percy Flowers. Along the way you might drop south and celebrate the intimate connection between moonshine and North Carolina barbeque at B's Barbeque in Greenville or the Skylight Inn in Ayden. Not far off U.S. 64, you'll find the Percy Flowers Store, a great place for a hot dog. This is obviously not the store Flowers knew, but it's on the site of the epicenter of his moonshine empire. Ironically, one end of the building contains an Alcohol Beverage Control store. His home is across the highway. Take N.C. 42 and drive to Clayton. Along the way you'll notice several Flowers Plantation developments, part of the real estate empire built by Rebecca Flowers, Percy's daughter, on the land her father purchased in his moonshining heyday.

From Clayton pick up I-40 East to Benson and the Broadslab Distillery, located on Jeremy Norris's family's farm. Norris, owner and master distiller at Broadslab, traces his roots in the whiskey business back to moonshine's earliest days in Johnston County. Take the tour and sample Norris's products. From Benson take I-95 South to head for Lumbee country in Robeson County. The Museum of the Southeast American Indian at the University of North Carolina at Pembroke is a good place to get an orientation on the Lumbee and learn something about Henry Berry Lowry, Rhoda Lowry, and the Swamp Angels. Backtrack from Pembroke to Lumberton and pick up a Lumbee delicacy, the collard sandwich, at Fuller's Old Fashioned Barbeque.

From Lumbee country, U.S. 74 takes you west to our next stop, Monroe, the hometown of Jerry Rushing. Not much to see here, but stop in at a local diner and ask an older person if they knew Rushing or his family. You might get some interesting stories. It's only a little over thirty minutes from Monroe to downtown Charlotte and the NASCAR Hall of Fame. While NASCAR doesn't talk much about its deep connections to the moonshine business, the museum does include some information on the subject and features a genuine Wilkes-type steamer still. The story goes that the still came to the museum in parts and workers could not figure out how to put it together. A call to Junior Johnson brought the legendary moonshiner and stock car driver down to Charlotte, pipe wrench in hand, and he promptly assembled it.

I-77 takes you north to Surry County

Legendary Wilkes County moonshiner/liquor hauler Willie Clay "The Uncatchable" Call with his son Brian Call, owner of Call Family Distillers in Wilkesboro. (Courtesy of Call Family Distillers)

and Mount Airy. Here you can visit the Andy Griffith Museum and the Mount Airy Museum of Regional History, grab a pork chop sandwich at the Snappy Lunch, and tour the Mayberry Spirits Distillery. From Mount Airy, backtrack south on I-77 to U.S. 421, the Junior Johnson Highway. As you drive west toward Wilkesboro, imagine you're hauling a load of liquor, but watch out for the law! Right before you get to Wilkesboro, take the exit for Old U.S. 421/ Speedway Road and stop by the North Wilkesboro Speedway, the first foundational "bootlegger track" in NASCAR and an amazing "if you build it, they will come" project. The track is padlocked, but walk around the fence and see its unique layout. It's only a ten-minute-or-so drive from the speedway to Call Family Distillers. The Call family has deep roots in the Wilkes County moonshine business, and Willie Clay Call was a legendary liquor tripper and running buddy of Junior Johnson's. Call Family also offers tours and tastings.

From Wilkesboro head south on N.C. 16 for the Hickory Motor Speedway, another NASCAR bootlegger track and one of only two still in operation. Along the way you'll pass through Taylorsville, the Burgess brothers' home and the location of the hunting camp owned by Jerry Rushing in his later years. If you're in Hickory on a Friday evening between late spring and early autumn, take in a race at this speedway built by bootleggers that launched the careers of so many NASCAR stars.

I-40 West leads you to Burke County and the moonshine hotbed in the South Mountains. A detour south on U.S. 64 takes you through the mountains and toward Cherry Mountain in Rutherford County, the home of pioneering moonshiner Amos Owens. The next stop on the tour is

Asheville. Here you can tour the Asheville Distilling Company, home of Troy & Sons whiskeys. The distillery is in the same building as Highland Brewery, the first craft brewery in western North Carolina. You can also do a driving tour of downtown Asheville and surrounding Buncombe County (try Brevard Road on the south side of Asheville and Ox Creek Road in the Reems Creek area) to see if you can spot sights where Robert Mitchum filmed *Thunder Road*.

North Carolina's far western region is rich in moonshine-related sites. From Asheville, take I-40 West to Maggie Valley, the stomping grounds of Popcorn Sutton. Head for a restaurant and ask some locals about their Popcorn memories. Maggie Valley is also the site of one of the newer "legal moonshine" distilleries, Elevated Mountain Distilleries. Follow U.S. 19 west through Cherokee and to Bryson City. Here's where Horace Kephart, author of *Our Southern Highlanders*, spent his last twenty years and where he did most of his writing. Ask for directions to the Bryson City Cemetery and you can find his grave there along with that of Hol Rose, a former moonshiner turned prohibition officer killed in the line of duty. The area around Bryson City is also where federal agents finally caught Lewis Redmond.

Take U.S. 74 and N.C. 28 from Bryson City toward Fontana Dam. An overlook on the right gives you a view of Hazel Creek, Kephart's "back of beyond" where he lived, observed the activities of many local moonshiners, and took the field notes that became *Our Southern Highlanders*. Drive on to Fontana Dam. You can look back over the lake to Eagle Creek, legendary moonshiner Quill Rose's home.

The last stop on the tour is Robbinsville, the county seat of Graham County and the last totally dry county in North Carolina. Not surprisingly, given this fact and its mountainous terrain, the county has long harbored many moonshiners. Indeed, four of the "stars" of Discovery Channel's *Moonshiners* live in Graham County: Jim Tom, Jeff, Lance, and Mark. Walk around the streets of this small town and you might even cap off your tour by sighting a real-life celebrity moonshiner.

2012, Brian Call, the son of Willie Clay Call, legendary moonshiner and running buddy of Junior Johnson, opened up Call Family Distillers in Wilkesboro; not long afterward, George Smith opened Copper Barrel Distillery in North Wilkesboro. Smith's master distiller is Buck Nance, a longtime Wilkes County moonshiner whose father allegedly invented the steamer still, a process Copper Barrel uses. Of course, it was almost inevitable that someone would build on the heritage of *The Andy Griffith Show* and its colorful moonshiners, and in 2015 Vann McCoy opened Mayberry Spirits Distillery in Andy Griffith's hometown of Mount Airy.[47] One would also expect that someone would have capitalized on the moonshine legacy of Percy Flowers and the Johnston County illegal distillers, and farmer Jeremy Norris has. He established his successful operation by building on his family's traditions in the business; his Broadslab Distillery is on his family's farm in Benson, where he pumps the water from an old well. Norris recalled, “I had the name, I had the history, I had the farm, I had the recipe. I got the water. I had everything. I had the know-how. I grew up around it. Everything comes natural.”[48] In yet another postmodern development, Norris does distillery tours, has turned his farm into an “event space,” and has constructed a barnlike building for weddings and other special events. Of course, the historical irony is that a place that once did everything to keep “furriners” away now does everything it can to bring them in.[49] About the only North Carolina moonshine hotspots that do not have legal distilleries so far are the South Mountains, Robeson County, and the Albemarle Sound/Dismal Swamp areas, but they are probably on the way.

Indeed, moonshine (or at least unaged corn liquor) is as alive and well in North Carolina today as it was 100 years ago. To be sure, the now-ubiquitous presence in popular media of images of Jim Tom Hedrick, Popcorn Sutton, and the myriad of other postmodern moonshiners they have inspired belies the predictions of the imminent demise of moonshine and moonshiners that were made around the turn of the century. However, as is generally the case, what has resulted is not a return to some “authentic” moonshine past but something new, very modern, and even postmodern.

EPILOGUE

On a beautiful day in late March 2018, I headed through the stone gate leading into Montreat on the eastern edge of Buncombe County to meet my friend Rex Hoffman for our regular Sunday afternoon hike. Today's hike, however, was a bit different from our usual walks to scenic overlooks or waterfalls or in search of wildflowers. Today we were off on an archeological expedition with longtime Montreat resident Steve Aceto and his family, searching for old moonshine still sites. Steve has roamed these mountains for almost fifty years and his son Ben has accompanied him for at least half that time. They know the area like the backs of their hands, and in their roamings have come across the evidence of several remote, off-trail still sites where locals made moonshine whiskey over the years.

Rex and the Aceto tribe got to the trailhead before me and went on in toward one of the sites. I had to follow directions from Rex over the phone. He instructed me to head up a faint trail running next to a small stream through a rhododendron tunnel. The tunnel ended in a relatively open forest of larger trees, and here Rex told me to make a left turn and head straight up the mountain to the top of the ridge. Fortunately, it was March and the undergrowth was not very thick. I would not want to try this in summer, as it would probably be thick with briars and ticks. Just over the ridge I finally connected with Rex, Steve, and Steve's remarkably adventurous granddaughter Kylie near a rocky outcropping that Steve speculated may have served as a lookout for moonshiners. We headed down into a fold in the mountains where a small stream burbled. After a short climb up the creek bed, we found the rest of the family in a small flat area next to the stream. In the center of that area was a stone circle with a rusted galvanized steel barrel sitting inside.

I immediately recognized that stone circle as the furnace for a moonshine still. We pulled the barrel out and you could see its ingenious design, with a small air duct in front and another that went out the furnace's back and up the hill to a hole to provide cross-ventilation and a chimney for the smoke. On top of that furnace, given its size, the moonshiners would have placed a small forty-to-fifty-gallon pot still, probably made of copper. The illegal distillers would not

Old still site located in the backwoods of Montreat. (Courtesy of Robin T. Parish)

have placed the galvanized steel barrel in the furnace. They probably used it as a mash barrel. We climbed on up the stream bed and saw another similar site not very far away.

After we bushwhacked our way back to the trailhead, Rex, Steve, Ben, and I decided to visit another site and headed up a nearby trail. I thought the first couple of sites were hard to get to, but that trip paled in comparison to the scramble up a sheer mountain slope that faced us. We took a regular marked trail for 100 yards or so and then headed left and straight up the mountain, our noses seemingly almost touching the slope in front of us. We definitely were not following any trail and pulled ourselves up the mountain as best we could. Steve had not been to this site in a while, so he was trying to recollect as best he could how to get there. We finally arrived at a large rock outcropping that he recognized, skirted it, and then crossed the top and headed up a small rivulet of water. We came to a flat spot similar to the ones we had encountered earlier, and there were a still furnace's ruins, not as well preserved as the first one we saw. A spring flowed from the mountain about twenty yards above the furnace, and someone had carved out a bowl in the rock at its base to serve as a collection basin.

This place was nearly an ideal place to site a moonshine still. It would be nearly impossible for revenue agents or sheriff's deputies to sneak up on the moonshiners here, given the steepness of the terrain below and a rocky outcropping that protected the site from above. Most important, the spring that provided a dependable water supply flowed back underground just past the furnace site and did not reemerge until well down the mountain. Since law enforcement generally followed streams to find still sites, this area would appear to be a dry wash, and as such unlikely to contain a still site and not worth the considerable effort it would take to bushwhack in to look for one. Indeed, about the only way a revenue agent would have come across an operating still here was to have someone inform on the owners and lead the agents to the site. I gained new respect for the ingenuity of moonshiners and stood amazed that whoever operated here could have brought a still, jars, cornmeal, sugar, and other supplies in and hauled full containers out. I was even more impressed when we made our way back down the mountain, scratched and bleeding from the briars, rhododendron thickets, and rocks we encountered, although those are scars I now proudly bear. These guys (and perhaps gals) had to be tough.

That Sunday bushwhack led me to reflect on what I have learned in more than five years researching moonshine and moonshiners in North Carolina and to speculate about the stories these old still furnaces might tell. I first wondered who these people were who built these furnaces and made illegal liquor on the steep slopes of Montreat. The size of these sites and the size of the furnaces indicate that, like most moonshiners in North Carolina, they were small-timers. They made moonshine to supplement their farm income or their income from a manufacturing job, in this case probably making blankets at the nearby Beacon Manufacturing Company in Swannanoa. Steve also told me that some of the Montreat moonshiners worked occasionally in Gastonia cotton mills and returned to moonshining when they were laid off. There are also old stories in the community that some of these moonshiners were locals, either employed by the Montreat Conference Center or by Montreat-Anderson College. They probably operated only in late fall or early spring, when they could more easily access these remote sites. After they had made several runs, they would have taken the still and coil back out and either hidden them carefully in some rhododendron thicket or secreted them in a barn, pulled them out again when the need for some extra cash arose, and headed back up the mountain.

My visit also prompted me to wonder why they would pick Montreat as a site for their activities. Like many moonshiners, the Montreat variety preferred to put their stills on someone else's property. Since 1897, Presbyterians, under various manifestations, have owned this 4,500-acre watershed as a summer retreat center, now known as the Mountain Retreat Association. While there were and still are homes in its lower reaches, most of the property is too steep for development and the Mountain Retreat Association has designated it as wilderness. In addition to the remote nature of much of Montreat, these moonshiners also benefitted from the fact that until the late twentieth century few people lived year-round in Montreat. It was only in summer, the least favorable

Author at Montreat still site. (Courtesy of Robin T. Parish)

time to make moonshine, that conference goers and most of the homeowners came to the area. Locating in Montreat also made it difficult for law enforcement to know, when they did run across a still, who was making the liquor. So while the moonshiners might lose a still, they would not lose their freedom or get hit with a sizeable fine.

The location also made it unlikely that locals would inform on the moonshiners even if they ran across a still. Again, most people who had homes here came only in summer, and there was evidently a "don't ask, don't tell" kind of policy for administration at the conference center and college. Indeed, they were smart enough to know that retaliation could be severe and that mysterious forest fires could proliferate if they started campaigning against the moonshiners in their midst. In addition, Presbyterians generally had a more "biblical" view of alcohol than Baptists or Methodists. Local lore has it that a maintenance worker at the college once set up a still on the back of the 200-acre property of Montreat's most famous resident, evangelist Billy Graham. When college officials learned about it, they quietly told the man to take his still off the property and said nothing else.

The Montreat moonshiners had another advantage for a good chunk of the twentieth century, as they operated in the backyard of sheriff Laurence Brown, head of the Buncombe County Democratic Party machine, who lived in Black Mountain. While it might appear to some as a disadvantage, most of these moonshiners probably knew Brown personally or were relatives. They could probably depend on a heads-up before the sheriff's department launched a raid into the area or if the local law knew a federal action was coming. If sheriff's deputies did bust them, they could generally depend on leniency and at most a modest fine.

Of course, making illegal liquor is one thing and getting the moonshine to market and selling it are another, so I was also led to speculate about the Montreat moonshiners' market. I imagine that at least some of them sold their product to local African American entrepreneur Horace Rutherford, who in turn sold it discreetly at his Roseland juke joint just outside the Montreat gate. They also probably sold to proprietors of area liquor houses, like Ada Thompson in nearby Asheville. Particularly once national Prohibition came along, they probably sold to some local liquor kingpin, perhaps to Gene Sluder who also ran the Asheville-Weaverville Speedway, one of NASCAR's foundational tracks.

Reflecting on these moonshiners in my own backyard also caused me to reflect on backyards all across North Carolina and, indeed, all across the south. Truth be told, without a great deal of research and effort, all residents of the state, and region, no matter where they live, could conduct their own explorations into the connections of their place and the moonshine business. If they do so, they will probably come up with just as rich a base of archeological evidence and vivid stories, real and imagined, detailing local moonshiners' exploits. Indeed, you do not have to scratch far below the surface in this state, or be from Wilkes County, to find an old still site; a home that once served as a liquor house; people whose kin made, transported, or sold illegal liquor; or people whose kin aided and abetted the business.

And moonshine is still very much with us in North Carolina in the twenty-first century. Turn on cable TV and you will find a reality show featuring a North Carolina moonshiner on there somewhere. Talk to some local hipsters in Asheville, Chapel Hill, Charlotte, Raleigh, or Durham and you might be surprised to learn they are making a little 'shine on a stovetop still purchased on Craigslist. Or ask around and you might find someone like Dean Combs, who has a regular still going on his property, who might sell, or give, you a jar. Or if you prefer a safer route where the moonshine is FDA approved, seek out one of North Carolina's legal stills, although the state's prohibition past still casts a large shadow, as state law currently limits their ability to offer samples or sell their product at their distilleries. But go anyway, take the distillery tour, and meet and hear the stories of North Carolina's postmodern moonshiners like Troy Ball, Cody Bradford, Brian Call, Buck Nance, Vann McCoy, or Jeremy Norris.

And if you do get a chance to sample some North Carolina moonshine—ironically, and in a decidedly postmodern twist, generally served in a disposable Communion cup—do the appropriate thing and lift that cup in honor of this state's rich moonshine heritage. As you toast that memory, remember the likes of Amos Owens, Lewis Redmond, Rhoda Lowry, Quill Rose, Betty Sims, Percy Flowers, Ada Thompson, Howard Creech, Junior Johnson, Alvin Sawyer, Jerry Rushing, Popcorn Sutton, and the hundreds of thousands of men and women who made the illegal liquor business such an integral part of North Carolina life for so long. And after a few toasts, you might feel compelled to honor our state's moonshiners further by singing the chorus of that wonderful song birthed in North Carolina by the boys of the Biltmore Forest School and Bascom Lamar Lunsford, "Good Old Mountain Dew":

They call it that good ole mountain dew
And them that refuse it are few
I'll shut up my mug, if you fill up my jug
With that good ole mountain dew.

Cheers!

ACKNOWLEDGMENTS

A book on the history of moonshine is not something you necessarily expect from a guy raised in the home of a teetotal Southern Baptist pastor. Given that fact, I could not have completed such a project without the support of lots of folks.

I am especially indebted to the fine staff at the North Carolina Collection at the University of North Carolina at Chapel Hill who supported my early research with an Archie K. Davis Fellowship. One important event in the course of conducting research occurred on a visit to the collection, when curator Bob Anthony took me aside to a nearby computer and introduced me to Newspapers.com. That resource changed the project's whole direction and focus and allowed me to find out many things about moonshine in North Carolina—especially the deep involvement of women, African Americans, and Native Americans—that would have been difficult to learn otherwise.

I am also grateful to work at an institution like the University of North Carolina Asheville. I am blessed to serve in the most functional department in academia and cannot thank department chair Tracey Rizzo and department members Sarah Judson, Grant Hardy, Ellen Pearson, Alvis Dunn, Eric Roubinek, Bill Spellman, Darin Waters, and even Samer Traboulsi enough for their support and encouragement. Our department got even better this past fall when we hired our former student Ashley McGhee as departmental assistant. Ashley has proved herself as outstanding in this capacity as she was as a student. Her assistance in finding sources, contacting the rights holders, and securing images for this book has been invaluable. In addition, the university's grant of the NEH Distinguished Professorship in the Humanities in 2015 was key in giving me the time to conduct the research and write this book.

The University of North Carolina Press supported my work with an advance contract far too many years ago. I had such a positive experience with the press when it published my book *Real NASCAR* back in 2010 that it was a virtual no-brainer to go with the press again on this project. I have thoroughly enjoyed working with its talented staff in editing, design, and marketing. I especially appreciate the patience demonstrated by my editor, Mark Simpson-Vos, over the years. Mark is one of the true "good guys" in this business, and his professionalism, guidance, and friendship in shepherding this project through to the end were invaluable.

A number of good friends also aided me along the way. Cody Bradford, Howling

Moon Distillery founder and owner and my former student, turned the tables and educated me about the moonshine business past and present. Cody taught me all I know about making moonshine, and his love and appreciation for the deep traditions of this business constantly inspire me. Fellow historian Bruce Stewart has been extremely generous in sharing his expertise on North Carolina and moonshine. Hiking buddies Rex Hoffman and Steve and Ben Aceto took me off-trail in Montreat to several old still sites. Cuts, scratches, and sore muscles aside, these trips helped me understand a great deal about the challenges faced by mountain moonshiners. Robin Parish and Gene Hyde graciously shared their photography skills, and Robin even hauled her equipment into the Montreat backcountry to conduct a photo shoot at an old still site.

Finally, I am truly blessed to have the support of a loving family. Although my teetotaler mom, Archie, has never quite understood my interest in moonshine, she remains my biggest fan. The love of my children—Anna Clare, Taylor, Sully, and Coulter—sustains me in so many ways. While my wife, Lydia, thinks I have far too much fun with my "work," her unfailing love, encouragement, and patience with my eccentricities have sustained me through the long process of producing this book.

NOTES

Abbreviations

AC	*Asheville Citizen*
ACT	*Asheville Citizen-Times*
ADG	*Asheville Daily Gazette*
AGN	*Asheville Gazette-News*
BDTN	*Daily Times-News* (Burlington)
BR	*Biblical Recorder*
CDT	*Concord Daily Tribune*
CN	*Charlotte News*
CO	*Charlotte Observer*
CR	*Chatham Record* (Pittsboro)
DR	*Davie Record* (Mocksville)
FAM	*Farmer and Mechanic* (Raleigh)
GDN	*Daily News* (Greensboro)
GG	*Gaston Gazette*
GP	*Greensboro Patriot*
HPE	*High Point Enterprise*
KDFP	*Daily Free Press* (Kinston)
KDI	*Daily Independent* (Kannapolis)
MNH	*News-Herald* (Morganton)
NBWJ	*New Berne Weekly Journal*
NC	*North Carolinian* (Raleigh)
NOC	*News of Chatham*
NSSN	*National Speed Sport News*
NYT	*New York Times*
RMP	*Morning Post* (Raleigh)
N&O	*News and Observer* (Raleigh)
SDR	*Statesville Daily Record*
SEP	*Salisbury Evening Post*
SRL	*Statesville Record and Landmark*
TP	*Tobacco Plant* (Durham)
WJP	*Wilkes Journal-Patriot*
WM	*Wilmington Messenger*
WMS	*Wilmington Morning Star*
WSJ	*Winston-Salem Journal*
WSTCDS	*Twin-City Daily Sentinel* (Winston-Salem)

Introduction

1. Jones, George, "White Lightning," video, 2:30, posted 4 June, 2009, https://www.youtube.com/watch?v=WE5pM1HXxlI.

2. *N&O*, 2 May 1909.

Chapter 1

1. Joseph Earl Dabney, *Mountain Spirits* (Asheville, N.C.: Bright Mountain Books, 1984), 33.

2. Alex Gabbard, *Return to Thunder Road: The Story behind the Legend* (Lenoir City, Tenn.: Gabbard Publications, 1992), 191.

3. Dabney, *Spirits*, 43.

4. W. J. Rorabaugh, *The Alcoholic Republic: An American Tradition* (New York: Oxford University Press, 1981), 69.

5. Dabney, *Spirits*, 73.

6. Dabney, 73.

7. Eliot Wigginton, ed., *The Foxfire Book: Hog Dressing; Log Cabin Building; Mountain Crafts and Foods; Planting by the Signs; Snake Lore, Hunting Tales, Faith Healing; Moonshining; and Other Affairs of Plain Living* (New York: Doubleday, 1972), 336.

8. Bruce Stewart, *Moonshiners and Prohibitionists: The Battle over Alcohol in Southern Appalachia* (Lexington: University Press of Kentucky, 2011), 15–16.

9. Stewart, 15–16.

10. Dabney, *Spirits*, 10.

11. Dabney, 10.

12. Dabney, 51–53.

13. Rorabaugh, *Alcoholic*, 8.

14. *GP*, 12 June 1895.

15. Brantley York, *The Autobiography of Brantley York* (Durham, N.C.: Seeman Printery, 1910), https://docsouth.unc.edu/nc/york/york.html.

16. *TP*, 6 July 1889.

17. Stewart, *Moonshiners and Prohibitionists*, 27–28.

18. Stewart, 28.

19. *North Carolina Chronicle* (Murfreesboro), 26 May 1827.

20. *Raleigh Minerva*, 18 June 1819.

21. Stewart, *Moonshiners and Prohibitionists*, 29.

22. Horace Kephart, *Our Southern High-*

landers (Knoxville: University of Tennessee Press, 1976), 121.

23. *Western Carolinian* (Salisbury), 14 August 1821.

24. Dabney, *Spirits*, 50.

25. Rorabaugh, *Alcoholic*, 74.

26. *Carolina Watchman* (Salisbury), 29 October 1836.

27. Dabney, *Spirits*, 50.

28. Natasha Geiling, “Long before Jack Daniels, George Washington Was a Whiskey Tycoon,” *Smithsonian*, 12 May 2014, www.smithsonianmag.com/history/george-washington-whiskey-businessman-180951364/; and Allison Aubrey, “Drinking Whiskey in the Spirit of George Washington,” *NPR*, 22 October 2011, https://www.npr.org/sections/thesalt/2011/10/22/141589394/drinking-whiskey-in-the-spirit-of-george-washington.

29. Sarah Meacham, *Every Home a Distillery: Alcohol, Gender, and Technology in the Colonial Chesapeake* (Baltimore: Johns Hopkins University Press, 2009), 48–49.

30. Frederick H. Smith, *The Archaeology of Alcohol and Drinking* (Gainesville: University Press of Florida, 2008), 93–94.

31. Clay Risen, “Jack Daniel’s Embraces a Hidden Ingredient: Help from a Slave,” *NYT*, 26 June 2016.

32. *Newbern Sentinel*, 2 January 1819.

33. “Murphey, Archibald DeBow,” Documenting the American South, accessed 15 March 2016, http://docsouth.unc.edu/global/getBio.html?type=bio&id=pn0001250&name=Murphey,%20Archibald%20DeBow.

34. Malinda Maynor Lowery, *The Lumbee Indians: An American Struggle* (Chapel Hill: University of North Carolina Press, 2018), 65–66.

35. Lowery, 65–66.

36. Wigginton, *Foxfire*, 314.

37. Wilbur Miller, *Revenuers and Moonshiners: Enforcing Federal Liquor Law in the Mountain South, 1865–1900* (Chapel Hill: University of North Carolina Press,1991), 19.

38. Rorabaugh, *Alcoholic*, 76.

39. *1840 Census: Compendium of the Enumeration of the Inhabitants and Statistics of the United States* (Washington, D.C.: Printed by Thomas Allen, 1841), 186; and *Raleigh Register*, 28 May 1841.

40. *Carolina Watchman* (Salisbury), 29 October 1836.

41. *Fayetteville Weekly Observer*, 20 March 1839.

42. *ACT*, 12 December 1982.

43. Financial ledgers, William Holland Thomas Papers, Financial and Business Papers, David M. Rubenstein Rare Book and Manuscript Library, Duke University, Durham, N.C.

44. *BR*, 16 December 1835.

45. Reprinted in daily *CO*, 5 September 1878.

46. Dabney, *Spirits*, 74.

47. Stewart, *Moonshiners and Prohibitionists*, 29–30.

Chapter 2

1. Bruce Stewart, *Moonshiners and Prohibitionists: The Battle over Alcohol in Southern Appalachia* (Lexington: University Press of Kentucky, 2011), 64–73.

2. Wilbur Miller, *Revenuers and Moonshiners: Enforcing Federal Liquor Law in the Mountain South, 1865–1900* (Chapel Hill: University of North Carolina Press, 1991), 61–68.

3. *Southern Home* (Charlotte), 9 September 1878.

4. *CO*, 4 February 1894.

5. Miller, *Revenuers*, 99.

6. *WMS*, 13 February 1883.

7. *Rutherford Star*, 7 November 1868.

8. M. L. White, *A History of the Life of Amos Owens, the Noted Blockader, of Cherry Mountain, N.C.* (Shelby, N.C.: Cleveland Star Job Print, 1901), 19.

9. Reprinted in *GP*, 8 November 1870.

10. Miller, *Revenuers*, 53.

11. White, *Amos Owens*, 21–24; and *WMS*, 23 September 1871.

12. Daniel J. Whitener, *Prohibition in North Carolina* (Chapel Hill: University of North Carolina Press, 1945), 79.

13. *Charlotte Democrat*, 10 December 1896.

14. Stewart, *Moonshiners and Prohibitionists*, 88.

15. Miller, *Revenuers*, 97–126.

16. Stewart, *Moonshiners and Prohibitionists*, 132.

17. The best source on Lewis Redmond is Bruce Stewart, *King of the Moonshiners: Lewis R. Redmond in Fact and Fiction* (Knoxville: University of Tennessee Press, 2009).

18. *CO*, 16 April 1881.

19. *CO*, 28 August 1881.

20. *FAM*, 25 March 1885; and White, *Amos Owens*, 25–27.

21. *CO*, 1 June 1880.

22. Stewart, *Moonshiners and Prohibitionists*, 132.

23. Stewart, 136.

24. Miller, *Revenuers*, 139.

25. Miller, 134.

26. *CR*, 23 December 1880.

27. Stewart, *Moonshiners and Prohibitionists*, 134–35.

28. *TP*, 6 July 1889.

29. *ADG*, 29 March and 11 August 1899.

30. Miller, *Revenuers*, 144.

31. *Union Republican* (Winston-Salem), 25 August 1887.

32. Stewart, *Moonshiners and Prohibitionists*, 149–62.

33. Reprinted in *CR*, 3 June 1897.

34. *N&O*, 14 September 1895.

35. Reprinted in *Morganton Herald*, 17 January 1895.

36. Reprinted in *Raleigh News*, 11 June 1879.

37. *Washington Progress*, 15 April 1890.

38. Wilbur Ziegler and Ben Grosscup, *The Heart of the Alleghanies* (Raleigh: A. Williams, 1883), 141.

39. Reprinted in *CR*, 3 June 1897.

40. *NC*, 30 May 1896.

41. *RMP*, 23 May 1899.

42. *NC*, 30 May 1896.

43. *Carthage Blade*, 30 March 1897.

44. *Raleigh News*, 13 June 1897.

45. Allen Cook, *Moonshine, Murder & Mountaineers: The Wildest County in America* (Spruce Pine, N.C.: Chestnut Ridge, 2014).

46. *NYT*, 5 January 1893.

47. Among the dozens of papers quoting the commissioner were the *Scranton Republican*, 6 January 1893; *Pharos-Tribune* (Logansport, Ind.), 6 January 1893; and *Rock Island Argus*, 6 January 1893.

48. Cook, *Moonshine*.

49. *Solomon Valley Democrat*, 25 January 1900.

50. *CO*, 1 June 1895.

51. *CO*, 1 January 1898.

52. *N&O*, 29 May 1895.

53. *N&O*, 29 May 1895.

54. *N&O*, 31 May 1895.

Chapter 3

1. *CO*, 5 June 1895.

2. Reprinted in *CO*, 18 December 1884.

3. *Messenger and Intelligencer (Wadesboro)*, 8 September 1898.

4. *CO*, 22 December 1896.

5. Reprinted in *Rutherford Tribune*, 22 August 1901.

6. Horace Kephart, *Our Southern Highlanders* (Knoxville: University of Tennessee Press, 1976), 130.

7. Kephart, 130.

8. Joseph Earl Dabney, *Mountain Spirits* (Asheville, N.C.: Bright Mountain Books, 1984), 173.

9. Kephart, *Highlanders*, 136–37.

10. Dabney, *Spirits*, 99.

11. *N&O*, 6 December 1894.

12. *RMP*, 9 April 1899.

13. *WM*, 2 November 1889.

14. *BDTN*, 28 January 1954.

15. *ADG*, 12 April 1901.

16. *AC*, 23 March 1898.

17. *BR*, 4 September 1901.

18. Dabney, *Spirits*, 131.

19. *CO*, 7 January 1880.

20. The first mention of the State of Wilkes that I have found is in *Western Sentinel* (Winston-Salem), 26 January 1893.

21. *Blue Ridge Blade* (Morganton), 8 May 1880.

22. *Lenoir Topic*, 19 February 1880.

23. *Marion Record*, 18 May 1894.

24. *BR*, 15 February 1899; and *AC*, 15 September 1897 and 14 September 1899.

25. *CO*, 25 November 1883.

26. *WMS*, 16 August 1889.

27. *N&O*, 7 May 1895.

28. *WMS*, 26 March 1895.

29. *RMP*, 8 January 1899.

30. *TP*, 6 July 1889.

31. *Greensboro Telegram*, 27 January 1898.

32. *WM*, 3 March 1896.

33. *NBWJ*, 9 May 1895.

34. *WM*, 22 August 1891.

35. *CO*, 24 August 1897; and *WMS*, 13 December 1899.

36. *Fayetteville Observer*, 13 January 1897.

37. *CO*, 1 June 1895.

38. *CO*, 1 June 1895.

39. *WMS*, 3 December 1897; and Malinda Maynor Lowery, *The Lumbee Indians: An American Struggle* (Chapel Hill: University of North Carolina Press, 2018), 95.

40. *ADG*, 11 August 1899.

41. *RMP*, 9 December 1897.

42. *Raleigh Observer*, 27 November 1878.

43. *Morganton Herald*, 19 December 1889.

44. *RMP*, 9 April 1899.

45. *SRL*, 11 December 1890.

46. *AC*, 31 March 1898.

47. *N&O*, 26 April 1895.

48. Lowery, *Lumbee*, 65–66, 95.

49. *NC*, 30 May 1895.

50. *AC*, 31 August 1894 and 28 June 1895.

Chapter 4

1. The term "alcoholic republic" comes from Malinda Maynor Lowery, *The Lumbee Indians: An American Struggle* (Chapel Hill: University of North Carolina Press, 2018).

2. *Friend of Temperance*, 31 July 1872.

3. *CO*, 11 September 1903.

4. *CO*, 4 February 1894.

5. *AC*, 14 September 1918.

6. *Dispatch* (Lexington), 19 June 1918.

7. Popcorn Sutton, *Me and My Likker: The True Story of a Mountain Moonshiner* (self-pub., 2000), 17.

8. *N&O*, 6 August 1897.

9. *N&O*, 6 August 1897.

10. Bruce Stewart, *Moonshiners and Prohibitionists: The Battle over Alcohol in Southern Appalachia* (Lexington: University Press of Kentucky, 2011), 210.

11. Reprinted in *GP*, 12 June 1895.

12. *N&O*, 25 June 1899.

13. *WM*, 3 August 1899.

14. *RMP*, 9 July 1899.

15. Daniel J. Whitener, *Prohibition in North Carolina* (Chapel Hill: University of North Carolina Press, 1945), 59.

16. *Charlotte Democrat*, 3 October 1879.

17. Whitener, *Prohibition*, 59.

18. Whitener, 61–63.

19. *FAM*, 20 January 1881.

20. *Henderson Gold Leaf*, 21 January 1909.

21. Whitener, *Prohibition*, 69–70.

22. Stewart, *Moonshiners and Prohibitionists*, 199.

23. Whitener, *Prohibition*, 107–8.

24. Whitener, 108.

25. Stewart, *Moonshiners and Prohibitionists*, 205–7.

26. *State Chronicle*, 25 May 1890.

27. Whitener, *Prohibition*, 108–9.

28. Whitener, 133–34.

29. Stewart, *Moonshiners and Prohibitionists*, 209.

30. Whitener, *Prohibition*, 155–56.

31. Whitener, 156.

32. Reprinted in *Oregon Daily Journal*, 29 September 1907.

33. Whitener, *Prohibition*, 57.

34. *CO*, 4 August 1881.

35. Whitener, *Prohibition*, 133–35.

36. Whitener, 138.

37. Whitener, 151.

38. *N&O*, 24 February 1907.

39. Whitener, *Prohibition*, 163–64.

40. Stewart, *Moonshiners and Prohibitionists*, 212.

41. *N&O*, 27 December 1908.

42. *CDT*, 10 May 1909.

43. *Statesville Sentinel*, 2 May 1910.

Chapter 5

1. *Roanoke News*, 6 December 1906.

2. *CN*, 7 November 1906.

3. *KDFP*, 26 July 1904.

4. *CO*, 19 December 1919.

5. *WSTCDS*, 28 November 1910.

6. *ACT*, 30 March 1916.

7. *GDN*, 16 July 1915.

8. *CO*, 6 February 1916.

9. *N&O*, 13 November 1904.

10. *ACT*, 17 October 1916.

11. *GDN*, 13 March 1915.

12. *NBWJ*, 1 August 1899; and *Western Vindicator* (Rutherfordton), 9 February 1899.

13. Charles Thompson, *The Spirits of Just Men* (Champaign-Urbana: University of Illinois Press, 2011), 169.

14. *CO*, 14 July 1909.

15. *WMS*, 13 September 1910.

16. Horace Kephart, *Our Southern Highlanders* (Knoxville: University of Tennessee Press, 1976), 137.

17. Reprinted in *Lincoln County News*, 4 May 1916.

18. Eliot Wigginton, ed., *The Foxfire Book: Hog Dressing; Log Cabin Building; Mountain Crafts and Foods; Planting by the Signs; Snake Lore, Hunting Tales, Faith Healing; Moonshining; and Other Affairs of Plain Living* (New York: Doubleday, 1972), 342.

19. *CO*, 13 December 1917.

20. *CO*, 25 March 1917.

21. *Everything*, 10 November 1917.

22. *Union Republican* (Winston-Salem), 16 January 1919.

23. *Gastonia Daily Gazette*, 1 October 1919.

24. *CN*, 17 December 1919.

25. *ACT*, 16 August 1919.

26. *GDN*, 1 May 1919.

27. Kephart, *Highlanders*, 190.

28. *HPE*, 24 January 1918.

29. *ACT*, 6 June 1901.

30. *Western Sentinel* (Winston-Salem), 28 March 1911.

31. *Webster's Weekly* (Reidsville), 25 July 1913.

32. *CDT*, 31 August 1911.

33. *NBWJ*, 27 July 1915.

34. *GG*, 18 December 1903.

35. *CDT*, 14 September 1920.

36. *RMP*, 9 September 1905.

37. *Watauga Democrat*, 20 February 1919.

38. *AC*, 15 March 1908.

39. Kephart, *Highlanders*, 118–19.

40. *Daily Industrial News* (Greensboro), 21 March 1907.

41. *Concord Times*, 21 January 1909.

42. *ACT*, 17 August 1917.

43. *SEP*, 24 January 1918.

44. *CO*, 13 January 1918.

45. *CO*, 29 January 1918.

46. *GDN*, 10 October 1918.

47. *N&O*, 29 December 1917.

48. *GDN*, 26 January 1919.

49. *N&O*, 13 August 1917.

50. *CN*, 30 August 1918.

51. *N&O*, 12 October 1918.

52. *N&O*, 26 January 1918.

53. *CO*, 21 March 1918.

54. Reprinted in *CO*, 22 June 1918.

55. *SEP*, 21 May 1919.

Chapter 6

1. Charles Thompson, *The Spirits of Just Men* (Champaign-Urbana: University of Illinois Press, 2011), xxix.

2. *ACT*, 17 October 1916.

3. *GDN*, 10 December 1915.

4. John Finger, *Eastern Band of the Cherokees: 1819–1900* (Knoxville: University of Tennessee Press, 1984).

5. *ACT*, 19 September 1901.

6. *GDN*, 14 April 1919.

7. Malinda Maynor Lowery, *The Lumbee Indians: An American Struggle* (Chapel Hill: University of North Carolina Press, 2018), 104–5.

8. Mr. Singleton, interview by Guy Johnson, 12 August 1948, transcript, Folder 1231, Guy Benton Johnson Papers, Southern Historical Collection, Louis Round Wilson Special Collections Library, University of North Carolina at Chapel Hill, https://finding-aids.lib.unc.edu/03826/#folder_1231#1.

9. Lowery, *Lumbee*, 105.

10. *CO*, 9 December 1906.

11. *ACT*, 3 July 1919.

12. *Public Ledger* (Oxford), 3 November 1905.

13. *WSJ*, 7 September 1913.

14. *KDFP*, 11 August 1916.

15. *N&O*, 23 February 1913.

16. *ACT*, 7 May 1921.

17. *WSJ*, 22 September 1907.

18. *Dispatch* (Lexington), 17 February and 7 March 1921.

19. Reprinted in *Dispatch* (Lexington), 24 February 1921.

20. *ADG*, 26 February 1902.

21. *FAM*, 10 March 1903.

22. *N&O*, 15 May 1909.

23. Reprinted in *CDT*, 15 May 1909.

24. *ACT*, 9 August 1957.

25. *CO*, 6, 17 May, and 12 December 1906.

26. *ACT*, 28 August 1918.

27. *N&O*, 26 October 1904.

28. *Daily Industrial News* (Greensboro), 22 November 1905.

29. *KDFP*, 27 March 1919.

30. *N&O*, 2 May 1920.

31. Mary Sloop, *Miracle in the Hills* (New York: McGraw-Hill, 1953), 110.

32. *Courier* (Asheboro), 11 May 1922.

33. *Mount Airy News*, 18 February 1909.

34. *Raleigh Times*, 6 September 1906.

35. *GDN*, 24 April 1912.

36. *WMS*, 4 September 1915.

37. *Daily Economist* (Elizabeth City), 2 June 1906.

38. *CO*, 15 June 1917.

39. *GG*, 16 June 1905.

40. *N&O*, 29 December 1918.

Chapter 7

1. *CR*, 7 February 1907.

2. *WMS*, 6 September 1915.

3. *Randolph Bulletin*, 19 May 1915.

4. *ACT*, 29 November 1904.

5. *N&O*, 20 May 1905.

6. *Raleigh Times*, 17 October 1906.

7. *Statesville Sentinel*, 2 May 1910.

8. Original article in *Sylvan Valley News*, reprinted in *Watauga Democrat*, 9 September 1915.

9. *ACT*, 18 April 1919.

10. *CO*, 11 November 1908.

11. *AGN*, 15 November 1915.

12. *WMS*, 10 March 1910.

13. *ACT*, 25 April 1909.

14. *CO*, 2 June 1911.

15. *Mount Airy News*, 22 June 1911.

16. *ACT*, 1 August 1909.

17. *CO*, 6 February 1916.

18. Horace Kephart, *Our Southern Highlanders* (Knoxville: University of Tennessee Press, 1976), 239–40.

19. *Wilmington Dispatch*, 30 March 1916.

20. *SEP*, 5 September 1912.

21. *RMP*, 22 June 1904.

22. *N&O*, 13 July 1905.

23. Quoted in *ACT*, 12 September 1919.

24. *CO*, 20 June 1907.

25. *GDN*, 28 December 1907.

26. *AGN*, 13 May 1911.

27. *CO*, 15 August 1911.

28. *NBWJ*, 22 December 1905.

29. *GDN*, 28 December 1907.

30. *CO*, 20 January 1907.

31. *ADG*, 23 December 1902.

32. *N&O*, 22 December 1904.

33. *CO*, 2 August 1904.

34. *SRL*, 27 July 1906.

35. *CO*, 20 January 1907.

36. *GDN*, 4 April 1908.

37. *SRL*, 17 May 1926.

38. *GDN*, 5 November 1916.

39. *AGN*, 26 August 1915.

40. *HPE*, 6 February 1917.

41. *CO*, 6 January 1908.

42. *King's Weekly*, 26 March 1901.

43. *CO*, 11 August 1904.

44. *Public Ledger* (Oxford), 18 August 1904.

45. *WSJ*, 9 February 1919.

46. *SRL*, 11 September 1903.

47. *HPE*, 1 December 1915.

48. *N&O*, 16 October 1903.

49. *HPE*, 1 December 1915.

50. *N&O*, 13 February 1902.

51. *GDN*, 11 February 1919.

52. *ACT*, 23 May 1901.

53. *ACT*, 11 June 1902.

54. *ACT*, 14 January 1917.

55. *N&O*, 16 February 1917.

56. William McCall, *Cherokees and Pioneers* (Asheville, N.C.: Stephens, 1952), 101.

57. Cratis Williams, "Metaphor in Mountain Speech," *Mountain Life and Work* 38, no. 4 (Winter 1962): 9–12.

58. *CN*, 10 January 1908.

59. *Free Press* (Southern Pines), 19 June 1903.

60. *CO*, 11 May 1919.

61. *CO*, 9 July 1905.

62. *MNH*, 11 September 1913.

63. Plot synopsis, "Moonshine Maid and the

Man," IMDb, accessed 22 April 2017, https://www.imdb.com/title/tt0826118/.

64. *ACT*, 31 December 1915.

65. *ACT*, 21 April 1916.

66. *French Broad Hustler*, 16 May 1918.

67. *CO*, 24 February 1917; and *CN*, 13 February 1921.

68. *ACT*, 17 October 1916; and lyrics published in John Guthrie, ed., *The Forest Ranger*, (Boston: Gorham, 1919), 104.

69. Obituary in *American Forestry* 21, no. 275 (November 1916): 686.

Chapter 8

1. Reprinted in *DR*, 12 May 1920.

2. *GDN*, 17 January 1920.

3. Horace Kephart, *Our Southern Highlanders* (Knoxville: University of Tennessee Press, 1976), 188.

4. Charles Thompson, *The Spirits of Just Men* (Champaign-Urbana: University of Illinois Press, 2011), 167.

5. *WSTCDS*, 14 March 1921.

6. *CN*, 9 January 1921.

7. *BDTN*, 13 January 1934.

8. *WSTCDS*, 1 November 1921.

9. *CO*, 21 April 1921.

10. *WSJ*, 17 January 1921.

11. *BDTN*, 6 December 1933.

12. *WSJ*, 17 June 1920.

13. Joseph Earl Dabney, *Mountain Spirits* (Asheville, N.C.: Bright Mountain Books, 1984), 158.

14. *BDTN*, 4 October 1940.

15. *SRL*, 25 July 1935.

16. Reprinted in *DR*, 12 May 1920.

17. Reprinted in *DR*, 12 May 1920.

18. Alec Wilkinson, *Moonshine: A Life in Pursuit of White Liquor* (New York: Knopf, 1985), 25.

19. *SDR*, 27 July 1935.

20. *Stanly News-Herald*, 13 May 1921.

21. *SEP*, 7 March 1922.

22. Wilkinson, *Moonshine*, 25.

23. Wilkinson, 26–27.

24. *MNH*, 22 September 1921.

25. *CO*, 14 October 1922.

26. *CDT*, 12 January 1923.

27. *ACT*, 14 February 1971.

28. Talven Thompson, interview by Andrea Clark, 25 September 2008, copy of transcript in possession of author.

29. *GDN*, 16 December 1921.

30. *CO*, 2 June 1922.

31. *Fayetteville Observer*, 6 January 1921.

32. *N&O*, 29 September 1919.

33. *Sun Journal* (New Bern), 31 May 1920.

34. *WSTCDS*, 14 January 1920.

35. *GDN*, 15 February 1920.

36. Garland Bunting, interview by Lawrence Early, 2 August 1988, copy of transcript in possession of the author.

37. Charles Thompson, *Just Men*, 118–19.

38. *WSTCDS*, 5 July 1922.

39. Kephart, *Highlanders*, 191–201.

40. *Burlington Daily Times*, 8 May 1930.

41. *GDN*, 17 December 1938.

42. *SDR*, 23 December 1940.

43. *NOC*, 7 March 1991.

44. *NOC*, 7 March 1991.

45. *GDN*, 17 January 1920.

46. *CN*, 17 January 1922.

47. *BDTN*, 2 August 1935.

48. *SRL*, 16 December 1935.

49. *GG*, 6 May 1921.

50. Kephart, *Highlanders*, 189.

51. *Stanly News-Herald*, 3 May 1921.

52. Kephart, *Highlanders*, 238–64.

53. *Monroe Journal*, 17 May 1921.

54. *WSTCDS*, 14 March 1921.

55. *ACT*, 24 July 1983.

Chapter 9

1. *DR*, 12 May 1920.

2. *GDN*, 16 December 1921.

3. Vance Packard, "Millions in Moonshine," *American Magazine*, September 1950, 103.

4. *NOC*, 7 March 1991.

5. *NOC*, 7 March 1991.

6. Perry Sullivan, *Lost Flowers: True Stories of the Moonshine King, Percy Flowers* (self-pub., CreateSpace, 2013).

7. *WMS*, 14 May 1921.

8. *Alamance Gleaner*, 1 November 1923.

9. John Kobler, "King of the Moonshiners," *Saturday Evening Post*, 2 August 1958, 17, 60, 62.

10. Kobler, 17, 60, 62.

11. Packard, "Millions," 102.

12. Bill Yanacsek, *North Carolina Moonshiners* (Charlotte, N.C.: Carolina Racing, ca. 2000), vhs.

13. Tom Higgins and Steve Waid, *Junior Johnson: Brave in Life* (Phoenix: David Bull, 1999), 19–21.

14. 1960 NASCAR grand national champion Rex White told me this story.

15. Suzanne Tate, *Logs & Moonshine: Tales of Buffalo City, N.C.* (Nags Head, N.C.: Nags Head Art, 2000), 8–9.

16. Tate, 8–9.

17. Tate, 8–9.

18. Tate, 20.

19. Tate, 6–8, 15.

20. *Daily Advance* (Elizabeth City), 22 April 1922.

21. Sheila Turnage, "The Moonshine King," *State*, July 1993.

22. Alexander Mull and Gordon Boger, *Recollections of the Catawba Valley* (Boone, N.C.: Appalachian Consortium Press, 1983), 116.

23. Junior Johnson, interview by Pete Daniel, 21 July 2001, transcript, Documenting the American South, http://docsouth.unc.edu/sohp/C-0053/menu.html.

24. *WSTCDS*, 20 August 1920.

25. James Flink, *The Automobile Age* (Cambridge, Mass.: MIT Press, 1988), 230–31.

26. Alec Wilkinson, *Moonshine: A Life in Pursuit of White Liquor* (New York: Knopf, 1985), 54.

27. Junior Johnson, interview by Pete Daniel, 21 July 2001, video and transcript, James G. Kenan Research Center, Atlanta History Center.

28. Joseph Earl Dabney, *Mountain Spirits* (Asheville, N.C.: Bright Mountain Books, 1984), 111.

29. Packard, "Millions," 47.

30. *SRL*, 28 June 1934.

31. Johnson interview.

32. Wilkinson, *Moonshine*, 83.

33. Dabney, *Spirits*, 155.

34. Millard Ashley, interview by Pete Daniel, 21 July 2001, video and transcript, James G. Kenan Research Center, Atlanta History Center.

35. *NOC*, 7 March 1991.

36. Emily Edwards, *Bars, Blues, and Booze: Stories from the Drink House* (Jackson: University Press of Mississippi, 2016), 14.

37. Sullivan, *Lost Flowers*, 196–99.

38. Edwards, *Bars, Blues*, 17.

39. *N&O*, 17 December 1942.

40. Talven Thompson, interview by Andrea Clark, 25 September 2008, copy of transcript in possession of the author.

41. Edwards, *Bars, Blues*, 19.

42. *Star-News* (Wilmington), 6 March 2010.

43. *N&O*, 17 July 1934.

44. *Star-News* (Wilmington), 14 September 2015.

45. *BDTN*, 16 July 1934.

Chapter 10

1. *CO*, 4 March 1910.

2. Perry Sullivan, *Lost Flowers: True Stories of the Moonshine King, Percy Flowers* (self-pub., CreateSpace, 2013), 77–78.

3. Tom Higgins and Steve Waid, *Junior Johnson: Brave in Life* (Phoenix: David Bull, 1999), 146.

4. Much of my knowledge of this type of fox hunting comes from my late uncle Emmett Smith of Prentiss, Mississippi, who did, indeed, tape-record fox races.

5. Sullivan, *Lost Flowers*, 93–99.

6. *Pilot* (Voss), 3 March 1922.

7. *ACT*, 28 February 1971. My Southern Baptist–pastor, teetotal dad had a Ridgecrest souvenir Woodpecker liquor barrel/pencil holder on his desk for years.

8. Patrick Huber, *Linthead Stomp: The Creation of Country Music in the Piedmont South* (Chapel Hill: University of North Carolina Press, 2008), 67–72.

9. Huber, 108.

10. Huber, 119.

11. Huber, 138, 149.

12. A recording of Lunsford performing his version of "Good Old Mountain Dew" can be found at Lunsford, Bascom Lamar, "Mountain Dew," video, 0:32, posted 2 May 2009, https://www.youtube.com/watch?v=DkoIKMcFAX8.

13. Loyal Jones, *Minstrel of the Appalachians: The Story of Bascom Lamar Luns-*

ford (Lexington: University Press of Kentucky, 2002), 15.

14. Emily Edwards, *Bars, Blues, and Booze: Stories from the Drink House* (Jackson: University Press of Mississippi, 2016), 24.

15. Talven Thompson, interview by Andrea Clark, 25 September 2008, copy of transcript in possession of the author.

16. Edwards, *Bars, Blues*, 23.

17. Edwards, 25.

18. Edwards, 32.

19. Edwards, 15.

20. Edwards, 25.

21. Anne Chesky Smith, "Finding Freedom at Roseland Gardens," *Black Mountain News*, 1 June 2016.

22. Smith, "Finding Freedom."

23. *GDN*, 3 May 1920.

24. *Daily Tar Heel* (Chapel Hill), 15 May 1920.

25. Guide to Hubert Heffner Papers, Indiana University Archives, accessed 23 March 2017, http://webapp1.dlib.indiana.edu/findingaids/view?brand=general&docId=InU-Ar-VAA6210&doc.view=print.

26. *BDTN*, 10 March 1922.

27. Jones, *Minstrel*, 47; and *BDTN*, 12 March 1940.

28. DuBose Heyward, *A Dubose Heyward Reader*, ed. James Hutchinson (Athens: University of Georgia Press, 2003), 101.

29. Rebecca Cushman, *Swing Your Mountain Gal: Sketches of Life in the Southern Highlands* (Boston: Houghton Mifflin, 1934), 30.

30. David Padrush, *Rumrunners, Moonshiners, and Bootleggers* (New York: Big Rock/Pinball Productions, 2002), video.

31. Junior Johnson, interview by Pete Daniel, 21 July 2001, video and transcript, James G. Kenan Research Center, Atlanta History Center.

32. Richard Petty, *King Richard I: The Autobiography of America's Greatest Auto Racer*, with William Neely (New York: Paperjacks, 1987), 43.

33. Max Welbourn and Donald Johnson, interview by Suzanne Wise, 10 August 2005, video, Stock Car Racing Collection, Belk Library, Appalachian State University, Boone, N.C.

34. Daniel S. Pierce, *Real NASCAR: White Lightning, Red Clay, and Big Bill France* (Chapel Hill: University of North Carolina Press, 2010), 49–52.

35. Welbourn and Johnson interview.

36. Sylvia Wilkinson, *Dirt Tracks to Glory: The Early Days of Stock Car Racing as Told by the Participants* (Chapel Hill, N.C.: Algonquin Books, 1983), 60.

37. Wilkinson, 54.

38. *CO*, 26 June 1939.

39. *GDN*, 7 September 1940.

40. *CO*, 4 July 1941.

41. *HPE*, 3 October 1940, 12 May, 30 June, and 1 September 1941.

Chapter 11

1. *HPE*, 16 August 1941.

2. *N&O*, 16 April 1943.

3. *HPE*, 17 March 1942.

4. *HPE*, 21 June 1942.

5. *SDR*, 11 July 1944.

6. *SDR*, 11 July 1944.

7. *BDTN*, 19 April 1943.

8. *SDR*, 11 July 1944.

9. *SRL*, 19 February 1945.

10. *N&O*, 28 February 1945.

11. *ACT*, 13 December 2005.

12. *SDR*, 22 December 1948.

13. *N&O*, 20 July 1958.

14. *GG*, 5 January 1955.

15. *Robesonian*, 9 December 1953.

16. *Robesonian*, 8 October 1953.

17. *SDR*, 22 December 1948.

18. *GG*, 5 January 1955.

19. Joseph Carter, *Damn the Allegators* (Albemarle, N.C.: Joe E. Carter, 2000), 28.

20. *GG*, 8 August 1949.

21. *ACT*, 9 December 1958.

22. *N&O*, 22 November 1959.

23. *MNH*, 13 September 1954.

24. *BDTN*, 7 January 1949.

25. *SRL*, 28 November 1958.

26. *SRL*, 28 November 1958.

27. *Daily Tar Heel* (Chapel Hill), 18 December 1957.

28. *BDTN*, 26 May 1961.

29. *ACT*, 1 May 1965.

30. *SDR*, 2 June 1952.

31. *ACT*, 20 March 1962.

32. *SRL*, 19 April 1963.

33. *Robesonian*, 18 February 1947.

34. *GG*, 8 August 1949.

35. *ACT*, 14 July 1953; and *GG*, 30 January 1957.

36. Alec Wilkinson, *Moonshine: A Life in Pursuit of White Liquor* (New York: Knopf, 1985), 46, 114.

37. *SRL*, 4 April 1956.

38. *ACT*, 16 November 1960.

39. *SRL*, 6 December 1960.

40. *ACT*, 28 December 1984.

41. *KDI*, 17 March 1968.

42. *ACT*, 13 October 1949.

43. *Robesonian*, 6 November 1964.

44. *N&O*, 22 November 1959.

45. *KDI*, 23 October 1955.

46. *Robesonian*, 6 November 1964.

47. *SRL*, 8 February 1957.

48. *N&O*, 30 April 1957.

49. *N&O*, 22 November 1959.

50. Carter, *Allegators*, 44–45.

51. *SDR*, 9 March 1953.

52. *Robesonian*, 6 November 1964.

53. Vance Packard, "Millions in Moonshine," *American Magazine*, September 1950, 47, 104.

54. Packard, 104–5.

55. Packard, 104.

56. Packard, 104.

57. *BDTN*, 5 September 1950.

58. *SDR*, 9 October 1950.

59. W. D. Washburn, *Hickory Motor Speedway: The World's Most Famous Short Track* (Hickory, N.C.: Tarheel Press, 2003), 13–38; and searches on Ancestry.com for Ralph and Grafton Burgess.

60. *ACT*, 28 August 1954.

61. *SRL*, 22 March 1956 and 21 March 1957.

62. *SRL*, 21 March 1957; and *BDTN*, 23 March 1957.

63. *SRL*, 22 March 1956.

64. *SRL*, 21 July 1956.

65. *SRL*, 21 and 22 March 1957.

66. John Kobler, "King of the Moonshiners," *Saturday Evening Post*, 2 August 1958, 17, 60, 62.

67. Kobler, 17, 60, 62.

68. *N&O*, 10 April 1961.

69. *N&O*, 10 April 1961.

70. *SRL*, 30 January 1958.

71. *KDI*, 17 August 1965.

72. Kobler, "King," 62; and *Robesonian*, 19 February 1958.

73. *ACT*, 19 February 1958; and Kobler, "King," 62.

74. *WJP*, 10 March 1947.

75. Kobler, "King," 62; and Washburn, *Hickory Motor Speedway*, 13–38.

76. Packard, "Millions," 47.

Chapter 12

1. *SRL*, 1 May 1968.

2. Joseph Carter, *Damn the Allegators* (Albemarle, N.C.: Joe E. Carter, 2000), 52.

3. *KDI*, 21 April 1965.

4. Carter, *Allegators*, 26–27.

5. Alec Wilkinson, *Moonshine: A Life in Pursuit of White Liquor* (New York: Knopf, 1985), 31.

6. *NOC*, 14 March 1991.

7. Wilkinson, *Moonshine*, 30.

8. *NOC*, 14 March 1991.

9. Carter, *Allegators*, 39.

10. Carter, 3.

11. *SDR*, 22 December 1948.

12. *N&O*, 3 March 1964.

13. *ACT*, 16 November 1957.

14. *ACT*, 15 May 1957.

15. *ACT*, 18 January 1958.

16. *ACT*, 7 June 1958.

17. *ACT*, 22 June 1958.

18. *ACT*, 11 September 1957.

19. *ACT*, 11 September 1957.

20. *ACT*, 9 February 1961.

21. *KDI*, 12 and 14 July 1955.

22. Vance Packard, "Millions in Moonshine," *American Magazine*, September 1950, 47.

23. Packard, 104.

24. Junior Johnson, interview by Pete Daniel, 21 July 2001, video and transcript, James G. Kenan Research Center, Atlanta History Center.

25. *Courier-Journal* (Louisville, Ky.), 20 May 1983.

26. Carter, *Allegators*, 31.

27. Packard, "Millions," 104.

28. Johnson interview.

29. Joseph Earl Dabney, *Mountain Spirits*

(Asheville, N.C.: Bright Mountain Books, 1984), 33.

30. Packard, "Millions," 104.

31. Carter, *Allegators*, 31–32.

32. Carter, 31–32.

33. Johnson interview.

34. Packard, "Millions," 104.

35. *Courier-Journal* (Louisville, Ky.), 20 May 1983.

36. Carter, *Allegators*, 31–32.

37. Wilkinson, *Moonshine*, 49–50.

38. *Robesonian*, 7 September 1956.

39. *KDI*, 28 March 1965.

40. *SRL*, 6 November 1965.

41. *ACT*, 18 May 1962.

42. Carter, *Allegators*, 32.

43. "Thunder Road," IMDb, 16 April 2016, https://www.imdb.com/title/tt0052293/.

44. *ACT*, 10 July 1957.

45. *Thunder Road*, directed by Arthur Ripley (D.R.M. Productions, 1958).

46. *ACT*, 8 May 1958.

47. *ACT*, 25 May 1958.

48. Ken Beck, *The Andy Griffith Show Book* (New York: St. Martin's, 1985), 149–71.

49. Beck, 149–71.

50. Tom Higgins and Steve Waid, *Junior Johnson: Brave in Life* (Phoenix: David Bull, 1999), 62.

51. Tom Wolfe, "The Last American Hero Is Junior Johnson. Yes!," *Esquire*, March 1965, 73.

52. Wolfe, 73.

53. *BDTN*, 12 November 1964.

54. *ACT*, 3 May 1968.

Chapter 13

1. *Atlanta Constitution*, 31 August, 2, 3, 4, 5, 8, 11, 16, and 21 September 1945.

2. Daniel S. Pierce, *Real NASCAR: White Lightning, Red Clay, and Big Bill France* (Chapel Hill: University of North Carolina Press, 2010), 76–80.

3. *WJP*, 10 March, 14 April, and 11 September 1947.

4. Peter Golenbock, *NASCAR Confidential: Stories of Men and Women Who Made Stock Car Racing Great* (St. Paul, Minn.: Motorbooks International, 2004), 31.

5. *WJP*, 14 April 1947.

6. Max Welbourn and Donald Johnson, interview by Suzanne Wise, 10 August 2005, video, Stock Car Racing Collection, Belk Library, Appalachian State University, Boone, N.C.

7. Golenbock, *NASCAR Confidential*, 46.

8. Welbourn and Johnson interview.

9. *WJP*, 10 March 1947.

10. *WJP*, 14 April 1947.

11. *NSSN*, 3 September 1947.

12. Pierce, *NASCAR*, 84–88.

13. W. D. Washburn, *Hickory Motor Speedway: The World's Most Famous Short Track* (Hickory, N.C.: Tarheel Press, 2003), 13–19.

14. Howard "Humpy" Wheeler, interview by Pete Daniel, 28 August 2000, transcript, James G. Kenan Research Center, Atlanta History Center.

15. *NSSN*, 3 December 1947.

16. Gary McCredie, "The First NASCAR Race," *American Racing Classics*, April 1992, 118–27.

17. Leo Levine, *Ford: The Dust and the Glory; A Racing History* (Warrendale, Pa.: Society of Automotive Engineers, 2000), 212.

18. Joseph Carter, *Damn the Allegators* (Albemarle, N.C.: Joe E. Carter, 2000); and Tom Higgins and Steve Waid, *Junior Johnson: Brave in Life* (Phoenix: David Bull, 1999), 31–37.

19. *NSSN*, 6 October 1965.

20. Higgins and Waid, *Junior Johnson*, 40–44.

21. Higgins and Waid, 40–44.

22. *NSSN*, 30 June 1971.

23. Pierce, *NASCAR*, 281.

Chapter 14

1. *ACT*, 8 November 1970.

2. *Robesonian*, 11 July 1976.

3. *HPE*, 21 November 1965.

4. *GG*, 15 August 1974.

5. *SRL*, 7 June 1976.

6. *HPE*, 21 November 1965.

7. *HPE*, 21 November 1965.

8. *Robesonian*, 8 December 1969.

9. *ACT*, 21 November 1974.

10. *ACT*, 21 November 1974.

11. *GG*, 15 August 1974.

12. *ACT*, 8 November 1970.

13. *ACT*, 21 November 1974.

14. *BDTN*, 18 April 1946.

15. *GG*, 13 January 1949.

16. *SDR*, 21 May 1952.

17. *BDTN*, 9 April 1958.

18. *BDTN*, 15 March 1960; *SRL*, 28 March 1960; and *ACT*, 19 July 1960.

19. *SRL*, 28 March 1960.

20. *HPE*, 30 July 1961.

21. *HPE*, 19 June 1960.

22. *SRL*, 4 June 1960.

23. *SRL*, 8 July 1960.

24. *HPE*, 30 July 1961.

25. *HPE*, 19 June 1960.

26. *SRL*, 9 February 1961.

27. *ACT*, 20 March 1968.

28. *HPE*, 9 August 1969.

29. *HPE*, 24 March 1971.

30. Joseph Carter, *Damn the Allegators* (Albemarle, N.C.: Joe E. Carter, 2000), 120.

31. *ACT*, 4 July 1972.

32. *HPE*, 1 September 1976.

33. Malinda Maynor Lowery, *The Lumbee Indians: An American Struggle* (Chapel Hill: University of North Carolina Press, 2018), 168–73.

34. *SRL*, 4 April 1974.

35. *SRL*, 7 October 1972; and *ACT*, 1 November 1972.

36. Jerry Rushing, *The Real Duke of Hazzard: The Jerry Rushing Story*, with Michael Barnes (Lake Mary, Fla.: Creation House, 2005) 235–37; and "Moonrunners," IMDb, 17 May 2017, https://www.imdb.com/title/tt0071854/.

37. *SRL*, 6 November 1974.

38. Rushing, *Real Duke*, 4–7.

39. *ACT*, 29 August 1971.

40. *ACT*, 28 December 1988.

41. *ACT*, 22 August 1993.

42. *ACT*, 26 March 1994.

Chapter 15

1. *WSJ*, 5 March 2009.

2. *WSJ*, 5 March 2009.

3. John Parris, "Whiskey Maker Displays Ancient Craft at Festival," *ACT*, 1 July 1984.

4. *Moonshine*, directed by Kelly Riley (Highproof Films, 1999), DVD, 22 min.

5. Popcorn Sutton, *Me and My Likker: The True Story of a Mountain Moonshiner* (self-pub., 2000), 1–5.

6. Tom Wilson Jester, *Popcorn Sutton: The Making and Marketing of a Hillbilly Hero* (self-pub., 2011), 41.

7. *ACT*, 1 July 1984.

8. *Moonshine.*

9. *Moonshine.* You can see Hedrick tell the story on YouTube; see "Jim Tom Hedrick (Moonshiners) tells about crashing his Harley Davidson," video, 4:35, posted 18 February 2010, www.youtube.com/watch?v=uyJz7zpWCqA.

10. *Moonshine.*

11. *ACT*, 1 July 1984.

12. Jester, *Popcorn Sutton*, 4–5, 61.

13. *Moonshine.*

14. *The Last One*, directed by Neal Hutcheson (Raleigh, N.C.: Sucker Punch Pictures, 2009), DVD, 58 min.

15. Jester, *Popcorn Sutton*, 8.

16. *Moonshine.*

17. Sutton, *Me and My Likker*, 2, 19.

18. *Me and My Likker*, directed by Popcorn Sutton (self-produced video, 2000), vhs.

19. Jester, *Popcorn Sutton*, 38–39.

20. *Mountain Talk*, directed by Neal Hutcheson (Raleigh, N.C.: Language and Life Project, 2002), DVD, 57 min., https://languageandlife.org/documentaries/mountain-talk/.

21. *This Is the Last Dam Run of Likker I'll Ever Make*, directed by Neal Hutcheson, (Raleigh, N.C.: Sucker Punch Pictures, 2003), video, 1:45 min.

22. Jester, *Popcorn Sutton*, 65.

23. Campbell Robertson, "Yesterday's Moonshiner, Today's Microdistiller," *NYT*, 20 February 2012.

24. *N&O*, 20 November 2014.

25. *CMT Most Shocking*, season 1, episode 12, "Moonshine Madness," directed by Eamon Harrington (Malibu, Calif.: Planet Grande Pictures, 2004).

26. Clay Risen, "The World's Silliest Liquor: Fake Moonshine," *Atlantic*, 23 August 2011.

27. "Legacy," Midnight Moon Moonshine, 14 June 2018, http://www.juniorsmidnightmoon.com/legacy/; and John Trump, *Still and Barrel: Craft Spirits in the Old North State* (Durham, N.C.: John F. Blair, 2017), 118–19.

28. Trump, *Still and Barrel*, 119.

29. *ACT* (Haywood County Edition), 13 October 2005.

30. *Hillbilly: The Real Story*, directed by David Huntley (Knoxville, Tenn.: Moore Huntley Productions, 2008), aired 26 April 2008, on the History Channel.

31. *Last One.*

32. Robertson, "Yesterday's Moonshiner."

33. *Greenville Sun*, 15 March 2008.

34. Jester, *Popcorn Sutton*, 49.

35. *ACT*, 18 March 2008.

36. Stephen Miller, "Legendary Tennessee Moonshiner Plied His Trade to the End," *Wall Street Journal*, 21 March 2009.

37. *Popcorn Sutton: A Hell of a Life*, directed by Neal Hutcheson (Raleigh, N.C.: Sucker Punch Pictures, 2009), DVD, 87 min.

38. *Moonshiners*, Discovery, 19 June 2018, https://www.discovery.com/tv-shows/moonshiners/.

39. *Moonshiners.*

40. Trump, *Still & Barrel*, 51–53.

41. Trump, *Still & Barrel*, 23–28; and Troy Ball, "Making Moonshine Saved My Family from Financial Ruin," *Country Living*, February 16, 2017.

42. Trump, *Still & Barrel*, 24.

43. Trump, 24.

44. Trump, 36.

45. Trump, 34–37.

46. Trump, 34–37.

47. Trump, 94–108.

48. Trump, 166–72.

49. Jeremy Markovich, "The 'Shine That Saved the Family Farm," *Our State*, 4 April 2018, https://www.ourstate.com/the-shine-that-saved-the-family-farm/.

A NOTE ON SOURCES

Researching the history of illegal activity presents a number of challenges. Given the business's criminal nature, moonshiners did not leave behind many business records. In addition, moonshiners were generally not the type to write memoirs, and many individuals who worked in the blockade business never publicly admitted their participation. That said, there is a rich source base that I drew on for this work that can benefit those wishing to do research on their own or wishing to check my facts. One purpose in writing this book was to give a general overview of the subject and point out areas that other researchers can fruitfully explore.

Primary Sources

A quick look at the endnotes in this book reveals that I relied heavily on newspaper accounts. Of course, the papers regularly covered moonshiner arrests and prosecutions. By the late nineteenth century, the public developed a seemingly insatiable appetite for stories, jokes, poems, and songs about blockaders and their business. Newspapers understood this and eagerly filled the demand. Fortunately for me, about five years ago North Carolina Collection curator Bob Anthony introduced me to digital newspaper collections available through the North Carolina Digital Project, the Library of Congress's Chronicling America, and for this project, Newspapers.com. The ability to search hundreds of newspapers from the 1700s to the present day, particularly those in North Carolina, enabled me to better understand moonshine's rich and complex history in the state. Most important, these databases allowed me to do something in a couple of years that would have taken decades before these searchable databases came along.

Not surprisingly, archival records on moonshine are pretty rare. The best sources of archival material come from law enforcement and court records. The National Archives at Atlanta contains the best collection of such records, those of the federal courts in the southeast region, including North Carolina. Another good archival source is the Alcohol Beverage Control (ABC) Commission records held at the North Carolina State Archives. Local law enforcement and court records are generally less easily accessed and often sparse, incomplete, and not cataloged. There are some oral histories related to North Carolina moonshine in archives, most notably ones conducted by Smithsonian Institute historian Pete Daniel held in the Southern Oral History Collection, in Appalachian State University's Special Collections, and a few I conducted, held in UNC Asheville's Special Collections.

While there are not many available, memoirs related to the North Carolina moonshine business are very informative. Popcorn Sutton's *Me and My Likker* is a lively, stream-of-consciousness account of his early career. Treasury agent Joe Carter's memoir *Damn the Allegators* is almost as entertaining as Sutton's and provides great insight into the way federal law enforcement worked in the state in the 1950s and 1960s. The most poignant moonshine-related memoir is *Lost Flowers*, written by Percy Flowers's son Perry Sullivan. Sullivan's memoir gives us a window into the life and operations of one of North Carolina's most legendary moonshine kingpins.

Secondary Sources

There are dozens of books, hundreds of articles in magazines, and numerous documentaries on moonshine's history. The best general sources are Joseph Dabney's *Mountain Spirits* and the chapter on moonshine in the first *Foxfire* book. Wilbur Miller's *Revenuers and Moonshiners* and Bruce Stewart's *Moonshiners and Prohibitionists* are two of the few academic works on the subject; they give excellent insights into the origins of the business and have a great deal of North Carolina–specific material. *The Spirits of Just Men* by Charles Thompson is another excellent academic work and is one of the finest written on the subject of moonshine. A recent work, *North Carolina: An Illicit History*, provides a solid overview of moonshine in the state, mainly in the twentieth century, and has lots of good photos.

Biographical works on North Carolina moonshiners and law enforcement agents also provide important information. Alec Wilkinson's *Moonshine: A Life in Pursuit of White Liquor* chronicles the life and exploits of North Carolina ABC agent Garland Bunting. Bruce Stewart recounts Lewis Redmond's life and legend in *King of the Moonshiners*. Junior Johnson has been profiled countless times, but the two best sources on his life are Tom Higgins and Steve Waid's *Junior Johnson: Brave in Life* and the classic *Esquire* magazine article "The Greatest American Hero is Junior Johnson. Yes!" written by Tom Wolfe. We learn a great deal about Percy Flowers in the *Saturday Evening Post* article written by John Kobler from August 1958 entitled "King of the Moonshiners." The *State* (now *Our State*) profiled Alvin Sawyer in an article entitled "The Moonshine King," written by Sheila Turnage in 1990. Tom Jester gives his firsthand account of his experiences with Popcorn Sutton in *Popcorn Sutton: The Making and Marketing of a Hillbilly Hero*, a book illustrated with wonderful photos by Don Dudenbostel.

Moonshine-related documentaries can provide important information, but most aim more for entertainment than in-depth exploration. Neal Hutcheson's documentaries combine entertainment with solid coverage of Popcorn Sutton's life and legend. If you can find it, Sutton's homemade production, *Me and My Likker*, is a fascinating look at the Maggie Valley moonshiner. While short, Kelly Riley's *Moonshine* gives a solid profile of Jim Tom Hedrick. Researchers should be careful using Discovery's *Moonshiners* show. The show's "stars" do generally know moonshine, but researchers need to understand that the action is staged.

Books on related topics or partially about moonshine help flesh out the picture of North Carolina moonshine. Horace Kephart's classic work *Our Southern Highlanders* contains several informative chapters on moonshine based on his experiences in the far western part of the state in the early twentieth century. The most important work on antebellum liquor production in America is W. J. Rorabaugh's *Alcoholic Republic*. While it was first published in 1945, Daniel Whitener's book *Prohibition in North Carolina* is still the best work on that subject. Malinda Lowery's *Lumbee Indians: An American Struggle* provides excellent insights into the role of illegal alcohol production among the Lumbee. One of the few sources on women in moonshine, a subject in great need of further exploration, is a chapter in Elizabeth Engelhardt's *Mess of Greens*. Despite their deep involvement in the business, there are very few sources on African Americans (slaves and freedmen) and distilling (legal and illegal). A few articles in the *New York Times* by Clay Risen provide a good overview of the state of research on slave distilling. For information on Buffalo City and its role as an alleged "moonshine capital," see Suzanne Tate's *Logs and Moonshine*. Emily Edwards's book *Bars, Booze, and Blues: Stories from the Drink House* takes the reader into the world of the liquor house and explores its role in the moonshine business. There are lots of books on the NASCAR-moonshine connection, but the best are Sylvia Wilkinson's *Dirt Tracks to Glory*, Neal Thompson's *Driving with the Devil*, and my *Real NASCAR*. For information on the modern "legal moonshine" industry, see John Trump's *Still and Barrel*.

INDEX

MIX
Paper from
responsible sources
FSC® C008955
FSC
www.fsc.org